INTERNATIONAL
COMMUNICATION

INTERNATIONAL COMMUNICATION

Continuity and Change

DAYA KISHAN THUSSU
Goldsmiths College,
University of London

A member of the Hodder Headline Group
LONDON

Co-published in the United States of America by
Oxford University Press Inc., New York

First published in Great Britain in 2000
This impression reprinted in 2002 by
Arnold, a member of the Hodder Headline Group,
338 Euston Road, London NW1 3BH

http://www.arnoldpublishers.com

Co-published in the United States of America by
Oxford University Press Inc.,
198 Madison Avenue, New York, NY 10016

The advice and information in this book are believed to be true and accurate
at the date of going to press, but neither the author nor the publisher can
accept any legal responsibility or liability for any errors or omissions.

British Library Cataloguing in Publication Data
A catalogue record for this book is available from the British Library

Library of Congress Cataloging-in-Publication Data
A catalog record for this book is available from the Library of Congress

ISBN 0 340 74130 9 (hb)
ISBN 0 340 74131 7 (pb)

3 4 5 6 7 8 9 10

Production editor: James Rabson
Production Controller: Bryan Eccleshall
Cover Design: Terry Griffiths

Typeset in 10/12 Sabon by Saxon Graphics Ltd, Derby
Printed and bound in India by Replika Press Pvt Ltd., 100% EOU,
Delhi-110 040

What do you think about this book? Or any other Arnold title?
Please send your comments to feedback.arnold@hodder.co.uk

Dedicated to my mother Shrimati Sona Thussu, for her boundless love and care, and to the memory of my father Pandit Shambhu Nath Thussu, who taught me how to be critical.

Contents

Introduction

The world is on the threshold of a new industrial revolution. A revolution which promises to be at least as significant as that which has brought most of the growth of the world's economy in the past two centuries. A revolution which promises to have just as far reaching an impact on a wide variety of aspects of life, and a revolution with global reach. Telecommunications are at the epicentre of this revolution.

(ITU, 1999a: 5)

As the new millennium dawned, global television tracked the rise of the sun across the world, with images broadcast live via 300 satellite channels to audiences in each of the world's 24 time zones. At the beginning of the twenty-first century, millions of people can communicate with each other in real time, across national boundaries and time zones, through voice, text and pictures, and, increasingly, a combination of all three. In a digitally linked globe, the flow of data across borders has grown exponentially, boosting international commerce, more and more of which is being conducted through new technologies.

Defined as 'communication that occurs across international borders' (Fortner, 1993: 6) the analysis of international communication has been traditionally concerned with government-to-government information exchanges, in which a few powerful states dictated the communication agenda (Fischer and Merrill, 1976; Frederick, 1992; Fortner, 1993; Hamelink, 1994; Mattelart, 1994; Mowlana, 1996 , 1997). Advances in communication and information technologies in the late twentieth century have greatly enhanced the scope of international communication – going beyond government-to-government and including business-to-business and people-to-people interactions at a global level and at speeds unimaginable even a decade ago.

Apart from nation–states, many non-state international actors are increasingly shaping international communication. The growing global importance of international non-governmental bodies – Public Interest Organizations (PINGOs), such as Amnesty International, Greenpeace and the International Olympic Committee; Business Interest Organizations (BINGOs), such as GE, News Corporation and AT&T, and

Intergovernmental Organizations (IGOs), such as the European Union, NATO, ASEAN – is indicative of this trend (Hamelink, 1994).

In the contemporary world, international communication 'encompasses political, economic, social, cultural and military concerns' (Fortner, 1993: 1), and, as it becomes more widespread and multi-layered, the need to study it has acquired an added urgency. Intellectual and research interest in international aspects of communication, culture and media has grown as a result of the globalization of media and cultural industries. Communication studies itself has broadened to include cultural and media studies, and is increasingly being taught in a comparative and international framework. However, international communication is not yet considered a separate academic discipline, since its concerns overlap with other subject areas (Stevenson, 1992). In some institutions, mainly in universities in the United States, it has been taught within international relations or political science departments, while in Europe and the rest of the world, international communication has yet to find a firm mooring, the proliferation of new courses in global, intercultural and international communication notwithstanding.

The US-based Iranian scholar Hamid Mowlana identifies four key inter-related approaches to international communication: idealistic-humanistic, proselytization, economic and the political (Mowlana, 1997: 6–7). Examples of the first would be the work of British communication scholar Colin Cherry, who has argued that communication can promote global harmony (Cherry, 1978). The economic and strategic implications of international communication have been explored by Armand Mattelart (Mattelart, 1994), while Cees Hamelink has examined politics of world communication (Hamelink, 1994).

The emphasis of this book is on the economic and political dimensions of international communication and their relationship with technological and cultural processes. It aims to provide a critical overview of the profound changes in international media and communication at the threshold of the new millennium, at a time when the political, economic and technological contexts in which media and communication operate are becoming increasingly global. Intercultural communication, which examines the interpersonal contact of peoples of different cultural backgrounds, is outside the remit of this volume, which also does not aim to cover other more personal forms of international communication, such as travel and tourism, educational and cultural exchanges.

From the beginnings of human society, communication has taken place over distance and time – from cave paintings in Australia to the mobile Internet – through contact between different cultures via travel and trade, as well as war and colonialism. Such interactions have resulted in the transporting and implanting of ideas, religious beliefs, languages and economic and political systems, from one part of the world to another, by a variety of means that have evolved over millennia – from the oral, to being mediated by written language, sound or image (Schramm, 1988). The word 'communicate' has its roots in the Latin word *communicare*, 'to share'. International communication, then, is about sharing knowledge, ideas and beliefs among the various peoples of the world, and therefore it can be a contributing factor in resolving global conflict and promoting mutual understanding among nations. However, more often channels of international communication have been used not for such lofty ideals but to promote the economic and political interests of the world's powerful nations, who control the means of global communication.

The expansion of international communication should be seen within the overall context of the growth of capitalism in the nineteenth century. The availability of fast and reliable information was crucial for the expansion of European capital, and, 'in a global system, physical markets have to be replaced by notional markets in which prices and values are assessed through the distribution of regular, reliable information'. Thus the information network 'was both the cause and the result of capitalism' (Smith, 1980: 74). If Britain dominated international communication during the nineteenth and the first half of the twentieth century – primarily through its control of the world's telegraph and cable networks – the United States emerged as an information superpower after the Second World War. In 1944, the US business magazine *Fortune* published an article on 'World Communications', which warned that the future growth of the USA depended on the efficiency of US-owned communications systems, just as Britain's had done in the past: 'Great Britain provides an unparalleled example of what a communications system meant to a great nation standing athwart the globe' (cited in Chanan, 1985: 121).

One key use of international communication has been for public diplomacy, with the aim of influencing the policies of other nations by appeals to its citizens through means of public communication (Fortner, 1993). During the Cold War years, the propaganda of ideological confrontation dominated the use of international communication channels. Ignoring the complexity of media systems, this bipolar view of the world opposed the 'free' US system at the desirable end of a continuum and totalitarian systems at the other, an approach which was 'a strong ideological weapon in the spread of American media enterprises overseas' (Wells, 1996: 2).

With the dismantling of the Soviet Union and the retreat of socialism, as well as the marginalization of the global South in international decision-making processes, the West, led by the USA, emerged as the key agenda-setter in the arena of international communication, as in other forms of global interactions. In the post-Cold War world, so much had changed that, by 2000, a US-led consortium was planning to lease the ailing Russian space station *Mir* as an international space destination and even as a set for Hollywood films (Whittell, 2000).

The move towards the worldwide privatization of former state-run broadcasting and telecommunication networks, championed by such international organizations as the World Trade Organization and the World

Bank, has transformed the landscape of international communication. As UNESCO's *World Communication Report* observes:

> The world of communications is gradually changing from an economy of scarcity and government-structured controls to a free economy oriented towards abundant supply and diversity. This change quickens the pace of the elimination of monopolies in the delivery and distribution of information, in both telecommunications and the audiovisual field.
>
> (UNESCO, 1997: 11)

In a market-driven media and communication environment, the public-service role of the mass media has been undermined. Although some national broadcasters continue to receive high audience shares – varying from India's Doordarshan's 80 per cent and the BBC's nearly 35 per cent – in more commercialized television environments such as Brazil, Rede Brasil, the only public-service channel, had an audience of just 4 per cent (UNESCO, 1997). As mass media, especially television, gain more leverage over setting the international agenda (Shaw, 1996), concerns about the growing concentration of media power and its impact on international communication are also increasing.

Although the Internet has received greater attention in recent public debates on international communication, television, being much more widely accessible, is perhaps more influential in setting the global communication agenda. In an era of multi-channel digital broadcasting, the quantity of mainly Western images has multiplied manyfold and with that their power to promote 'virtual wars' or a consumerist way of life. Television images can transcend linguistic barriers and affect national media cultures in a way that other text- or voice-based media cannot. According to the *1999–2000 Satellite Industry Guide*, co-published by the Satellite Industry Association, direct-to-home television was one of the fastest growing segments, accounting for $20 billion and growing at 30 per cent annually (*Satnews*, 1999c).

Though other major economic blocs, such as the European Union and Japan, and some developing countries, notably India, Brazil and China, have gained from opening up the field of global communication, the biggest beneficiary of a liberalized international communication system is the United States, the world's information superpower with the most extensive network of communications satellites, the largest exporter of cultural products and a global leader in electronic commerce.

The USA, and the transnational corporations based there, have a major stake in creating and maintaining an international communication system that favours the free market. It can employ its public diplomacy through extensive control of the world's communication hard and software to promote a vision of a 'borderless' world (for capital but not people). As one commentator put it, the USA dominates (the) global traffic in information and ideas. American music, American movies, American television, and American software are so dominant, so sought after, and so visible that they are now available literally everywhere on the Earth. They influence the tastes, lives, and aspirations of virtually every nation.

(Rothkopf, 1997: 43).

The 'emerging infosphere – and its potential as a giant organic culture processor, democratic empowerer, universal connector, and ultimate communicator,' is seen as crucial for US public diplomacy (ibid.: 52).

In the post-Soviet world, there appears to be a consensus emerging among US policy-makers that in order to retain US hegemony the preferred option is the deployment of its 'soft power' – its domination of global communication and mediated culture – rather than the force employed by the European empires during the colonial era (Nye, 1990). As Joseph Nye, a former US Assistant Secretary of Defense and William Owens, a former Vice Chairman of the Joint Chiefs of Staff argue: 'Information is the new coin of the international realm, and the United States is better positioned than any other country to multiply the potency of its hard and soft power resources through information' (Nye and Owens, 1996: 20).

Promotion of democracy and human rights and a 'free flow of capital' worldwide are the proclaimed aims of US public diplomacy. US foreign policy 'must project an imperial dimension,' counsels a commentator:

The US role should resemble that of nineteenth-century Great Britain, the global leader of that era. US influence would reflect the appeal of American culture, the strength of the American economy, and the attractiveness of the norms being promoted. Coercion and the use of force would normally be a secondary option.

(Haass, 1999: 41)

However, this rhetoric of democracy, prosperity and human rights sits awkwardly with the unmistakable trend towards corporatization and concentration of global information and communication networks among a few, mainly Western, megacorporations, making them what US media critic Ben Bagdikian has called a 'private ministry of information' (Bagdikian, 1997). Cross-border mergers in the media and telecommunication industries – most notably the merger of America On-line with Time Warner, and the $190 billion British Vodafone takeover of German mobile telephone company Mannesmann – in the first few months of the new millennium – have further concentrated media and telecommunication power among a few conglomerates.

Extolling the virtues of such mergers for consumers, *Time* magazine wrote that the AOL-Time Warner deal had the potential for consumers to offer 'whatever they want – books, movies, magazines, music – wherever they want it, whatever way they choose, whether on a TV, a PC, a cell phone or any of the myriad wireless devices that are hurtling toward the market-place' (Okrent, 2000: 47). However, concerns have also been raised about the adverse effects of such corporatization of international information and entertainment networks on the diversity and plurality of global media cultures, by undermining cultural sovereignty and accentuating the already deep divisions in terms of information resources between and among nations. Crucially, it could also increase the economic and technological dependence of the information-poor South on the information-rich North.

An analysis of the evolution of international communication reveals a dominance and dependency syndrome – the dominance of a few countries by virtue of their control of both the software and hardware of global communication and the dependence of many nations upon them. To understand contemporary international communication one must look at the historical continuities which have given a headstart to some countries and created information poverty among many others. From nineteenth-century imperialism to the 'electronic empires' of the twenty-first century, the big powers have dominated global political, military and economic systems as well as information and communication networks. Though technologies employed for transmission of messages across national borders have changed – from telegraph, telephone, radio, television, to the mobile Internet – the main actors in international communication have remained the same, despite the emergence of some regional players representing different 'geo-linguistic' groups. The dynamic between continuity and change is then the central theme of this volume.

A recurring issue in the book is the political and economic implications of such supremacy for Southern countries dependent on information and communication channels which remain largely within the control of a few countries and the corporations based there. Admittedly, the South is far from being a homogeneous entity, with varying degrees of media and communication resources, yet the developing countries share a fundamental disadvantage in their inability to influence the global communication agenda, which continues to be set and implemented by the world's most powerful nations.

The book is divided into seven chapters, with a series of case studies to exemplify the main concepts and arguments. Chapter 1 provides a historical context for the study of international communication, examining how communication had an international dimension for centuries before the modern colonial empires emerged. Its role in the expansion of European capitalism across the world is illustrated by a case study of the rise of the British news agency Reuters, whose fortunes paralleled the growth of the British Empire. In the second section, the chapter examines how mass media, especially radio, was used by both blocs during the ideological confrontation of the Cold War. Covert international communication is analysed by focusing on *Radio Free Europe* and *Radio Liberty*, two prime examples of US secret propaganda during the years of East–West ideological battles regularly fought over the airwaves. The third section of the chapter examines the relationship between international communication and development, with a critique of Southern demands for a New World Information and Communication Order (NWICO) which dominated the debate during the 1970s and 1980s and was also affected by the bipolar view of international relations. The case study of India's Satellite Instructional Television Experiment (SITE) programme assesses a pioneering attempt to use television for education and development.

Following on from the historical context, Chapter 2 aims to provide a theoretical overview of competing theories that inform the study of international communication, from Marxist to culturalist and postmodernist analyses of the subject. The chapter introduces a range of theoretical perspectives on international communication over the past century, setting out the arguments of the main theorists and their approaches to its study. The perspectives discussed range from traditional Marxist analysis to dependency theory and neo-Marxism, modernization theory and its critics, theories of globalization and of the information society, as well as cultural studies approaches.

Chapter 3 maps out the expansion of transnational media and telecommunications corporations in the post-Cold War era of free-market capitalism. These are analysed within the macro-economic context of liberalization, deregulation and privatization and the policies of multilateral institutions such as the World Trade Organization (WTO) and the International Telecommunication Union (ITU). The chapter examines the ideological policy shifts in international institutions – from a state-regulated to a market-led environment – along with the convergence of the telecommunications, computers and media industries, lying behind the transnationalization and global expansion of mainly Western media and communication corporations.

It then explores the unprecedented growth of the global satellite industry – which provides the hardware for international communication – as a result of the liberalization of the international agreements on satellite broadcasting and telecommunication, focusing on the changing nature of the international satellite consortium, Intelsat, which is in the process of transforming itself from an intergovernmental to a private corporation. In the third section, the chapter discusses why transnational corporations have benefited most from the liberalization and privatization of international communication, taking Rupert Murdoch's News Corporation, the most global of media companies, as a case study.

In Chapter 4 the focus is on the global media market, which has evolved partly as a result of the deregulation and liberalization of the international communication sector in the 1990s, and partly as consequence of the rapid expansion of new communication technologies, notably satellite and cable. It surveys the key players in the global media and cultural industries: advertising, film, music, publishing, television and newsagencies. The chapter includes up-to-date information about the world's most powerful media and communication companies and discusses their strategies in a range of media sectors, demonstrating corporate synergies and the links between production, distribution and marketing of their products in a global marketplace. The chapter addresses questions about the implications of the concentration of ownership of the world's media and cultural industries among a few vertically integrated, global conglomerates. Two case studies – Disney's Entertainment and Sports Network (ESPN), and Cable News Network (CNN), part of AOL-Time Warner, the world's biggest media and entertainment company – contextualize the discussion about the globalization of media markets.

Having established the general pattern of ownership which shows the overwhelming US dominance of the international flow of information and entertainment, Chapter 5 examines the effects of the largely one-way flow of international communication in different socio-cultural contexts, looking particularly at exports of US films and television across the world. The predominance of US media products, especially Hollywood films, is discussed in relation to the European Union and its concerns about threat to its cultural sovereignty. The chapter then examines questions of homogenization and resistance to the English language programmes which promote a Western consumerist lifestyle. It explores how mass media interact with and influence consciousness and media cultures and cultural identities and discusses these within the framework of the debates on media and cultural imperialism.

The internationalization of the mainly US-based children's TV channels and Music Television (MTV) are discussed as two examples of how consumerist culture is being promoted through the powerful medium of television. In the final section the chapter examines the process of cultural adaptation, arguing that the homogenization of global cultural products has been counterbalanced by heterogeneous tendencies leading to a hybrid form of global–local interaction. The issue of hybridity – how global genres are adapted to suit national cultural codes – is analysed through the case study of Zee TV, India's biggest private multimedia network.

The focus of Chapter 6 is on contra-flow in international media products. Through a series of case studies, the chapter investigates the role of regional actors and the growing reverse flow in media products, which demonstrates how the transnationalization of media organizations has profoundly altered the market in global communications. Such regional players as the pan-Arabic channel Middle East Broadcasting Centre and China's Phoenix television channel, based in Hong Kong, are discussed as powerful regional actors with well-defined geo-lingusitic media and cultural constituencies. The chapter also examines the trend towards the movement of cultural products from global South to the media-rich North. Brazil's *TV Globo*, one of the world's biggest exporters of television programmes, and India's film industry, the world's largest producer of feature films, are analysed as two prime examples to underline the complexity of international cultural transactions.

The final chapter identifies and analyses some of the key issues in an age of computer-mediated international communication. It examines the impact on contemporary media culture of changes in technology, especially the unprecedented growth of the Internet. Microsoft Corporation, the world's biggest computer software maker, is discussed as a case study of the forces that are leading the new information revolution and also acting as tax inspectors on the new global knowledge industry. The chapter also explores how information and communication technologies such as satellites can be used for both entertainment and surveillance.

The liberating and empowering potential of new information and communication technologies is contrasted with the crucial issue of access to them. Examples of alternative communications in an international context are discussed to contextualize the potential of new technologies such as the Internet to empower citizens, while maintaining the refrain that a vast majority of the world's population is excluded from the global information revolution and not benefiting from electronic commerce. It also argues for the need to broaden the analysis of international communication, incorporating a variety of approaches, to provide a framework within which this increasingly complex subject can be analysed.

The book includes maps, diagrams and charts to provide the reader with easily digestible statistical information and references and to combine a clear exposition of both the empirical and the theoretical terrain, with examples from a wide range of international media, including television, film, advertising, news media and publishing. A glossary and a detailed chronology, as well as a comprehensive bibliography are also appended to make the volume useful for students and researchers alike. Given its international scope and multiperspectival approach, it is hoped that this book will act as a guide to understanding institutions, technologies, production and consumption of global media and communication.

In writing a book of this nature, one accumulates many intellectual and other debts. First and foremost, I am indebted to all the scholars in the field of international communication and other professionals, especially those from trade and business publications, from whose work this volume has benefited enormously. I also want to record my gratitude to the geniuses behind the World Wide Web, giving researchers access to a first-rate international library in one's own home, and on which I have drawn extensively for the book.

Colleagues at Coventry University, where I worked for most of the period this book was in gestation, deserve heartfelt thanks, not least for covering for me while I was on study leave during the autumn of 1999. I also drew sustenance from the generosity of new colleagues at University of North London, whose good-naturedness and understanding were very important in the crucial final weeks of finishing the manuscript. I have been fortunate to work with Lesley Riddle of Arnold, benefiting from her kind support and professionalism and with Susan Dunsmore, to whose eagle eye for detail in the editing process I am very grateful.

Finally, a special thanks to my wife Elizabeth who was involved in the project from its very inception. I have no hesitation in admitting that any weaknesses of the book are mine, but its strengths reflect her excellent editorial input. Our children – Shivani, 8 and Rohan, 5 – displayed exemplary behaviour and extraordinary patience during the writing of the book, sometimes under trying conditions. As a reward, they have been promised a trip to Disneyland. Having been glued to my computer in a tiny study for the best part of a year, scrolling through hundreds of websites and poring over thousands of pages of reports, books, journals, newspapers and magazines, even I could do with some Disney magic.

1

The historical context of international communication

The study of contemporary international communication can be illuminated by an understanding of the elements of continuity and change in its development. The nexus of economic, military and political power has always depended on efficient systems of communication, from flags, beacon fires and runners, to ships and telegraph wires, and now satellites. The evolution of telegraphic communication and empire in the nineteenth century exemplifies these interrelationships, which continued throughout the twentieth century, even after the end of empire. During the two World Wars and the Cold War, the power and significance of the new media – radio and then television – for international communication were demonstrated by their use for international propaganda as well as recognizing their potential for socio-economic development.

Communication and empire

Communication has always been critical to the establishment and maintenance of power over distance. From the Persian, Greek and Roman empires to the British, efficient networks of communication were essential for the imposition of imperial authority, as well as for the international trade and commerce on which they were based. Indeed, the extent of empire could be used as an 'indication of the efficiency of communication' (Innis, [1950] 1972: 9). Communications networks and technologies were key to the mechanics of distributed government, military campaigns and trade.

The Greek historian, Diodorus Cronus (4th century BC) recounts how the Persian king, Darius I (522–486 BC), who extended the Persian Empire from the Danube to the Indus, could send news from the capital to the provinces by means of a line of shouting men positioned on heights. This kind of transmission was 30 times faster than using runners. In *De Bello Gallico*,

Julius Caesar (100–44 BC) reports that the Gauls, using the human voice, could call all their warriors to war in just three days. Using fire at night and smoke or mirrors during the day is mentioned in ancient texts, from the Old Testament to Homer.

While many rulers, including the Greek polis, used inscription for public information, writing became a more flexible and efficient means of conveying information over long distances: 'Rome, Persia and the Great Khan of China all utilised writing in systems of information-gathering and dispersal, creating wide-ranging official postal and dispatch systems' (Lewis, 1996: 152). It is said that the *Acta Diurna*, founded by Julius Caesar and one of the forerunners of modern news media, was distributed across most of the Roman Empire: 'as communication became more efficient, the possibility of control from the centre became greater' (Lewis, 1996: 156).

The Indian Emperor Ashoka's edicts, inscribed on rock in the third century BC, are found across South Asia, from Afghanistan to Sri Lanka and writ writers had a prominent place in the royal household. During the Mughal period in Indian history, the *waqi'a-nawis* (newswriters) were employed by the kings to appraise them of the progress in the empire. Both horsemen and despatch runners transmitted news and reports. In China, the T'ang Dynasty (618–907) created a formal hand-written publication, the *ti pao* or 'official newspaper' which disseminated information to the elite and in the Ching Period (1644–1911) private news bureaux sprang up which composed and circulated official news in the printed form known as the *Ch'ing pao* (Smith, 1979).

In addition to official systems of communication, there have also always been informal networks of travellers and traders. The technologies of international communication and globalization may be contemporary phenomena but trade and cultural interchanges have existed for more than two millennia between the Graeco-Roman world with Arabia, India and China. Indian merchandise was exported to the Persian Gulf and then overland, through Mesopotamia, to the Mediterranean coast, and from there onwards to Western Europe. An extensive trans-Asian trade flourished in ancient times, linking China with India and the Arabic lands. Later, the Silk Route through central Asia linked China, India and Persia with Europe. Information and ideas were communicated across continents, as shown by the spread of Buddhism, Christianity and Islam.

The medium of communication developed from the clay tablet of Mesopotamia, the papyrus roll in ancient Egypt and in ancient Greece, to parchment codex in the Roman empire. By the eighth century, paper introduced from China began to replace parchment in the Islamic world and spread to medieval Europe. Also from China, printing slowly diffused to Europe, aided by the Moors' occupation of Spain, but it was not until the fifteenth century, with the movable type printing press developed by Johann Gutenberg, a goldsmith in Mainz in Germany, that the means of communication were transformed.

By the beginning of the sixteenth century, the printing presses were turning out thousands of copies of books in all the major European languages. For the first time the Scriptures were available in a language other than Latin, undermining the authority of priests, scribes and political and cultural elites. As a consequence, 'the unified Latin culture of Europe was finally dissolved by the rise of the vernacular languages which was consolidated by the printing press' (Febvre and Martin, 1990: 332). Coupled with vernacular translations of the Bible by John Wycliffe in England and Martin Luther in Germany, the printing revolution helped to lay the basis for the Reformation and the foundations of nation–state and of modern capitalism (Tawney, 1937; Eisenstein, 1979).

The new languages, especially Portuguese, Spanish, English and French, became the main vehicle of communication for the European colonial powers in many parts of the world. This transplantation of communication systems around the globe resulted in the undermining of local languages and cultures of the conquered territories. The Portuguese Empire was one of the first to grasp the importance of the medium for colonial consolidation, with the kings of Portugal sending books in the cargoes of ships carrying explorers. They opened printing presses in the territories they occupied – the first printing press was opened in Goa in 1557 and in Macao in 1588. Other European powers also used the new technology and the printed book played an important role in the colonization of Asia. European languages – especially Portuguese, Spanish, English and French – became the main vehicle of communication for the colonial powers in many parts of the world. This transplantation of communication systems around the globe created a new hierarchy of language and culture in the conquered territories (Smith, 1980).

The Industrial Revolution in Western Europe, founded on the profits of the growing international commerce encouraged by colonization, gave a huge stimulus to the internationalization of communication. Britain's domination of the sea routes of international commerce was to a large extent due to the pre-eminence of its navy and merchant fleet, a result of pioneering work in the mapping out of naval charts by the great eighteenth-century explorers, such as James Cook, enabled also by the determination of longitude based on the Greenwich Meridian. Technological advances such the development of the iron ship, the steam engine and the electric telegraph all helped to keep Britain ahead of its rivals.

The growth of international trade and investment required a constant source of reliable data about international trade and economic affairs, while the Empire required a constant supply of information essential for maintaining political alliances and military security. Waves of emigration as a result of industrialization and empire helped to create a popular demand for news from relatives at home and abroad, and a general climate of international awareness (Smith, 1980).

The postal reform in England in 1840, initiated by the well-known author, Anthony Trollope as Post-Master General, with the adoption of a single-rate, one penny postage stamp (the Penny Black), irrespective of distance, revolutionized postal systems. This was followed by the establishment of the Universal Postal Union in 1875 in Berne, under the Universal Postal Convention of 1874, created to harmonize international postal rates and to recognize the principle of respect for the secrecy of correspondence. With the innovations in transport of railways and steamships, international links were being established that accelerated the growth of European trade and consolidated colonial empires.

The growth of the telegraph

The second half of the nineteenth century saw an expanding system of imperial communications made possible by the electric telegraph. Invented by Samuel Morse in 1837, the telegraph enabled the rapid transmission of information, as well as ensuring secrecy and code protection. The business community was first to make use of this new technology. The speed and reliability of telegraphy were seen to offer opportunities for profit and international expansion (Headrick, 1991).

The rapid development of the telegraph was a crucial feature in the unification of the British Empire. With the first commercial telegraph link set up in Britain in 1838, by 1851 a public telegraph service, including a telegraphic money order system, had been introduced. By the end of the century, as a result of the cable connections, the telegraph allowed the Colonial Office and the India Office to communicate directly with the Empire within minutes when, previously, it had taken months for post to come via sea. By providing spot prices for commodities like cotton, the telegraph enabled British merchants, exporting cotton from India or Egypt to England, to easily beat their competitors (Read, 1992).

The new technology also had significant military implications. The overhead telegraph, installed in Algeria in 1842, proved a decisive aid to the French during the occupation and colonization of Algeria (Mattelart, 1994). During the Crimean War (1854–56), the rival imperial powers, Britain and France, trying to prevent Russian westward expansion that threatened overland routes to their colonial territories in Asia, exchanged military intelligence through an underwater cable in the Black Sea laid by the British during the conflict. (The Crimean conflict was notable for the pioneer war reports of Irishman William Howard Russell in *The Times* of London, who was to become the first 'big name' in international journalism.)

Similarly, during the Civil War in the US (1861–65) over 24 000 kilometres of cable was laid to send more than 6.5 million telegrams. The American Civil War was not only one of the earliest conflicts to be extensively reported, but also the first example both of co-operative news gathering among the American and European journalists, and of the use of photo-journalism.

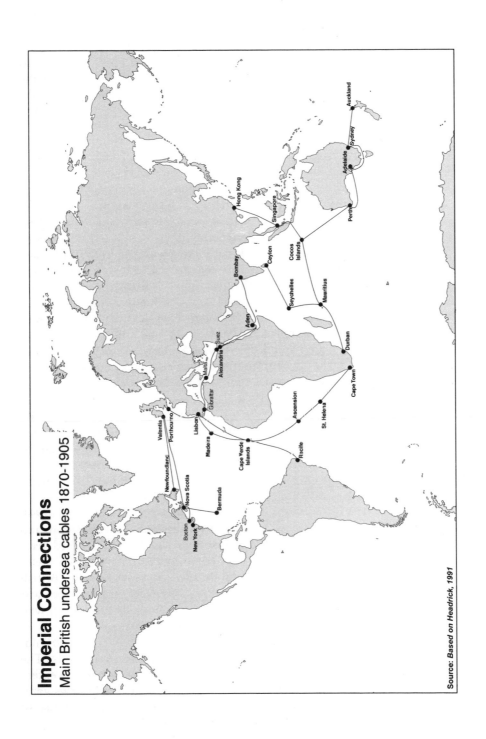

Imperial Connections
Main British undersea cables 1870-1905

Auckland
Sydney
Adelaide
Perth
Hong Kong
Singapore
Cocos Islands
Bombay
Ceylon
Seychelles
Mauritius
Aden
Suez
Alexandria
Malta
Durban
Gibraltar
Ascension
Cape Town
St. Helena
Lisbon
Madeira
Valentia
Porthcurno
Cape Verde Islands
Recife
Newfoundland
Nova Scotia
Bermuda
Boston
New York

Source: *Based on Headrick, 1991*

The first underwater telegraphic cable which linked Britain and France became operational in 1851 and the first transatlantic cable, connecting Britain and the USA, in 1866. Between 1851 and 1868, underwater networks were laid down across the North Atlantic, the Mediterranean, the Indian Ocean, and the Persian Gulf. During the 1860s and 1870s, London was linked up by cable to the key areas of the Empire (*see* map, p.15). The first line between Europe and India via Turkey was opened in 1865. Two other cables to India – one overland across Russia and the other undersea via Alexandria and Aden were both started in 1870. India was linked to Hong Kong in 1871 and to Australia in 1872 and Shanghai and Tokyo were linked by 1873 (Read, 1992). By the 1870s, telegraph lines were operating within most countries in Asia and an international communication network, dominated by Britain, was beginning to emerge. The expansion of cable was marked by the rivalry between British and French Empires, which intensified after 1869, with the opening of the Suez Canal.

The decade from 1870 to 1880 saw the successive inaugurations of communications links between the English coast and the Dutch East Indies (Batavia), the Caribbean network, the line from the British West Indies to Australia and China, the networks in the China and Japanese seas, the cable from Suez to Aden, communication between Aden and British India, the New Zealand cables, communication between the east and south coasts of Africa, and the cable from Hong Kong to Manila (Read, 1992).

In South America, the south transatlantic cable, opened in 1874, linked Lisbon with Recife, Brazil, via the Cape Verde Islands and Madeira. Two years later, a network was established along the coast of Chile. The British cable of 1874 was joined in 1879 by a new French cable across the North Atlantic, with a spur to Brazil, and by a new German cable from Emden to the Azores to Morovia on the African coast, and from there to Recife. By 1881, a network along the pacific coast from Mexico to Peru was in operation. In the 1880s, France established a series of links along the coast of Indochina and Africa, with networks in Senegal (Desmond, 1978).

The British-sponsored Indo-European landline telegraph between India and the Prussian North Sea coast had gone into operation in 1865. The cable had been extended from British shores to Alexandria by 1869, to Bombay in 1870, and other cables had been extended from Madras to Ceylon and from Singapore to Australia and New Zealand by 1873, and also to Hong Kong, Shanghai and the Japanese coast. Connections were made in China in 1896 with a spur of the Great Northern Telegraph Company Danish-owned line across Siberia to Russia and other points in Europe. This made a Tokyo–Shanghai–St Petersburg–London communications link possible (Desmond, 1978).

Undersea cables required huge capital investment, which was met by colonial authorities and by banks, businessmen and the fast-growing newspaper industry, and the cable networks were largely in the hands of the private sector. Of the total cable distance of 104 000 miles, not more than 10 per cent was administered by governments. To regulate the growing internationalization of information, the International Telegraph Union was founded in 1865 with 22 members, all Europeans, except Persia, representing, 'the first international institution of the modern era and the first organisation for the international regulation of a technical network' (Mattelart, 1994: 9).

According to the International Telegraph Union, the number of telegraphic transmissions in the world shot from 29 million in 1868 to 329 million in 1900 (Mattelart, 1994).

> For the first time in history, colonial metropolis acquired the means to communicate almost instantly with their remotest colonies ... The world was more deeply transformed in the nineteenth century than in any previous millennium, and among the transformations few had results as dazzling as the network of communication and transportation that arose to link Europe with the rest of the world.
>
> (Headrick, 1981: 129–30)

Military operations – such as the Japanese–Russian war of 1904–5, were both assisted and reported by the first transpacific cable which had been completed in 1902, joint property of the governments of Australia, New Zealand, Britain and Canada. It ran from Vancouver to Sydney and Brisbane, by way of Fanning Island, Suva, and Norfolk Island, with a spur from Norfolk Island to Auckland. A connection already existed, established in 1873, linking Tokyo and London, with spurs to Shanghai, Hong Kong, Singapore, Colombo, Calcutta, Bombay, and Alexandria, and with cable and telegraphic spurs by way of Singapore and Batavia to Darwin, Sydney and Auckland, where ties were made to the new transpacific cable to Vancouver.

A second transpacific cable was completed in 1903 by US interests, providing a link between San Francisco and Manila, through Honolulu, to Midway Island and Guam, and from there to the Asian mainland and Japan by existing British cables. All of these landing points were controlled by the United States: the Hawaiin Islands had been a US territory since 1900 and Midway was claimed by it in 1867, while Guam and the Philippines had become US colonies as a result of the 1898 Spanish-American War (Desmond, 1978). Control over cables as well as sea routes was also of enormous strategic importance in an age of imperial rivalry (Kennedy, 1971). The cables were, in the words of Headrick, 'an essential part of the new imperialism' (1981: 163).

The outcomes of the two imperial wars – the Spanish-American War (1898) and the Boer War (1899–1902) – strengthened the European and US positions in the world and led to a rapid expansion in world trade that demanded immediate and vastly improved communications links, as well as more advanced naval capabilities. The new technology of 'wireless' telegraphy (also called radiotelegraphy) promised to meet these needs.

In 1901 Guglielmo Marconi harnessed the new discovery of electromagnetism to make the first wireless transatlantic telegraph transmission, with support from naval armament companies and newspaper groups. The British Empire had a great technological advantage since the Marconi Wireless Telegraph Company of Great Britain dominated global telegraph traffic and had a virtual monopoly on international telegraph exchanges, as it refused to communicate with any other system other than its own. The operators of a Marconi apparatus were prohibited from responding to radio signals emanating from a non-Marconi transmitter, a policy that had the effect of blocking the exchange of critically important information relating to the safe passage of ships. However, at the Berlin Conference on Wireless Telegraphy in 1906 the first multilateral agreements on radiotelegraphy were signed and the International Radiotelegraph Union was born. By 1907 Marconi's monopoly was being challenged by other European countries as well as the United States.

The dominance of British cable companies, which lasted until the end of the First World War, was based on direct control through ownership, and indirect control by means of diplomatic censorship, which Britain exercised over the messages travelling through its cables. Britain had a critical advantage in its control of the copper and gutta-percha markets – the raw materials for the manufacture of cable – since the world rates of these were fixed in London and British mining companies owned copper deposits and mines in Chile, the world's biggest producer (Read, 1992).

Colonial governments supported the cable companies, either scientifically by research on maps and navigation, or financially by subsidies. In 1904, 22 of the 25 companies that managed international networks were affiliates of British firms; Britain deployed 25 ships totalling 70 000 tons, while the six vessels of the French cable-fleet amounted to only 7 000 tons. As a result, British supremacy over the undersea networks was overwhelming: in 1910, the Empire controlled about half the world total, or 260 000 kilometres. France, which in contrast to the USA and UK, opted for the state administration of cable, controlled no more than 44 000 kilometres (Headrick, 1991; Mattelart, 1994). As Table 1.1 demonstrates, the Anglo-American domination of international communication hardware was well established by the late nineteenth century, with the two countries owning nearly 75 per cent of the world's cables.

Much of the global cabling was done by private companies, with Britain's Eastern Telegraph Company and the US-based Western Union Telegraph Company dominating the cable industry. By 1923, private companies had nearly 75 per cent of the global cabling share, with British accounting for nearly 43 per cent, followed by the American companies which owned 23 per cent (Headrick, 1991). Within a quarter of a century, the world's cable networks had more than doubled in length.

As British companies were losing their share of global cable, the Americans increased their control on international communication channels

Table 1.1 Cabling the world

| | 1892 | | 1923 | |
	length (km)	global share (%)	length (km)	global share (%)
British Empire	163 619	66.3	297 802	50.5
United States	38 986	15.8	142 621	24.2
French Empire	21 859	8.9	64 933	11
Denmark	13 201	5.3	15 590	2.6
Others	9 206	3.7	68 282	11.7
All cables combined	246 871	100	589 228	100

Source: Based on data from Headrick (1991)

by leasing cables from British firms. US companies challenged Britain's supremacy in the field of international cables and telegraph traffic, which, they claimed, gave unfair advantage to British trade. The American view was that the pre-war cable system had 'been built in order to connect the old world commercial centres with world business' and that now was the time to develop 'a new system with the United States as a centre' (cited in Luther, 1988: 20).

The cables were the arteries of an international network of information, of intelligence services and of propaganda. Their importance can be gauged from the fact that the day after the First World War broke out, the British cut both German transatlantic cables. After the war, the debates over who should control the cables, which had been taken over early in the war, one by the British and another by the French, dominated discussions at the 1919 peace talks at Versailles and reflected the rivalry between the British cable companies and the growing US radio interests for ownership and control of global communications networks. The USA proposed that the cables be held jointly under international control or trusteeship and that a world congress be convened to consider international aspects of telegraph, cable and radio communication (Luther, 1988).

Unlike cables, the Americans dominated the new technology of telephones. Following the patenting of the telephone by the Bell Telephone Company, established by the inventor of telephony Alexander Graham Bell in 1877, telephone production increased in the US. In 1885, American Telephone and Telegraph (AT&T), later to become the head office of Bell Systems, was founded and for the next 80 years it succeeded in keeping a near-monopoly over US telecommunications networks.

The first international telephone calls were made between Paris and Brussels in 1887. At the end of the nineteenth century, the USA had the largest number of telephones, due largely to the fact that they were manufactured there. International Western Electric, subsidiary of Western Electric, itself owned by AT&T, was the first multinational network of production and sales, setting up branches in most European countries including

Britain, Spain, France and Italy as well as in Japan, China and Australia (Mattelart, 1994). However, the area covered by telephones was very limited – telephone networks acquired a global dimension only in 1956 when the first telephone cable was laid under the Atlantic.

The era of news agencies

The newspaper industry played a significant role in the development of international telegraph networks, to be able to exploit the rapid increase in demand for news, especially the financial information required to conduct international commerce. The establishment of the news agency was the most important development in the newspaper industry of the nineteenth century, altering the process of news dissemination, nationally and internationally. The increasing demand among business clients for commercial information – on businesses, stocks, currencies, commodities, harvests – ensured that news agencies grew in power and reach.

The French Havas Agency (ancestor of AFP) was founded in 1835, the German agency Wolff in 1849 and the British Reuters in 1851. The US agency, Associated Press (AP) was established in 1848, but only the three European agencies began as international ones; not until the turn of the century did an American agency move in this direction. From the start, Reuters made commercial and financial information its speciality, while Havas was to combine information and advertising.

These three European news agencies, Havas, Wolff and Reuters, all of which were subsidized by their respective governments, controlled information markets in Europe and were looking beyond the continent to expand their operations. In 1870 they signed a treaty to divide up the world market between the three of them. The resulting association of agencies (ultimately to include about 30 members), became known variously as the League of Allied Agencies (les Agences Alliées), as the World League of Press Associations, as the National Agencies Alliances, and as the Grand Alliance of Agencies. More commonly, it was referred to simply as the 'Ring Combination' (Desmond, 1978). In the view of some it was a 'cartel', and its influence on world opinion was used by governments to suit their own purposes (Boyd-Barrett, 1980; Mattelart, 1994).

The basic contract, drawn up in 1870, set 'reserved territories' for the three agencies. Each agency made its own separate contracts with national agencies or other subscribers within its own territory. Provision was made for a few 'shared' territories, in which two, sometimes all three agencies had equal rights. In practice, Reuters, whose idea it was, tended to dominate the Ring Combination. Its influence was greatest because its reserved territories were larger or of greater news importance than most others. It also had more staff and stringers throughout the world and thus contributed more original news to the pool. British control of cable lines made London itself an unrivalled centre for world news, further enhanced by Britain's wide-ranging commercial, financial and imperial activities (Read, 1992).

In 1890, Wolff, Reuters and Havas signed a new treaty for a further ten years. Havas emerged stronger than ever – it gained South America as an exclusive territory, and also Indo-China. But Havas yielded its position in Egypt, which became exclusive Reuters territory but continued to share Belgium and Central America with Reuters. 'The major European agencies were based in imperial capitals. Their expansion outside Europe was intimately associated with the territorial colonialism of the late nineteenth century' (Boyd-Barrett, 1980: 23).

After the First World War, although Wolff ceased to be a world agency, the cartel continued to dominate international news distribution. The first challenge to their monopoly came from AP when it started supplying news to Latin America. With the international news cartel broken by the 1930s, AP and other US agencies such as United Press (UP), founded in 1907, (which later became United Press International (UPI) in 1958 after merger with Hearst's International News Service), began to encroach on their terrain. AP began to expand internationally, paralleling political changes in Europe with the weakening of the European empires after the First World War.

The rise of Reuters

Communication was central to the expansion and consolidation of modern European empires, the largest and the most powerful being the British Empire, which at its height, 1880–1914, dominated a quarter of humanity. The fortunes of Reuters, the most famous international news agency, can be seen to run in parallel with the growth of the British Empire.

The expansion of trade and investment during the nineteenth century had led to a huge growth in the demand for news and contributed to the commercialization of news and information services. Reuters astutely exploited this demand, helped by the new communication technologies, especially the telegraph. For British and other European investors Reuters telegrams were essential reading for the latest news from various corners of the British Empire. By 1861 these were being published from more than a hundred datelines, including from the major colonies – India, Australia, New Zealand, and South Africa.

By the 1870s, Reuters had offices in all the major strategic points of the empire – Calcutta, Bombay and Point de Galle on the southern tip of Sri Lanka, the end of the cable connection with London, from where Reuters supervised its services to Southeast Asia, China, Japan and Australia. In 1871, Shanghai became the headquarters of the growing Reuters presence in East Asia, and after the beginning of commercial mining of gold in southern Africa in the late nineteenth century, Cape Town became another nodal point in Reuters' global network. By 1914, Reuters news service had three main channels covering the empire: London to Bombay; London to Hong Kong via the Mediterranean to Cairo, Aden, Ceylon and Singapore, and another to Cape Town, Durban, Mombasa, Zanzibar, the Seychelles, and Mauritius (Read, 1992).

The expansion of European capitalism had created a pressing need for improved commercial intelligence and with the development of communication, the value of world trade itself grew more than 25-fold between 1800 and 1913. This relationship between capital and communication was an aspect of what has been called 'the Reuters Factor', which 'functions like a multiplier that turns an increase in the supply of information into an increase in business' (Chanan, 1985: 113).

Reuters also enjoyed very close relationships with the British foreign and colonial administrations. During the second half of the nineteenth century the agency increasingly functioned, in the words of its official historian 'as an institution of the British Empire' (Read, 1992: 40). As Britain's most important colony, India played a 'central part in the Reuter empire within the British Empire', constituting a major market for commercial news (Read, 1992: 60). Reuters' revenues from India more than trebled from 1898 (£11 500) to 1918 (£35 200) (ibid. 83).

Though it claimed to be an independent news agency, Reuters was for the most part the unofficial voice of the Empire, giving prominence to British views. This subservience to imperial authority was most prominent during imperial wars such as the Boer War (1899–1902), during which agency reports supported the British cause and the British troops. In the same way Reuters news from India was mostly related to economic and political developments in the Empire and largely ignored the anti-colonial movement.

Defending the Empire came naturally to Reuters: in 1910 Reuters started an imperial news service and a year later, the agency made a secret arrangement with the British Government under which it offered to circulate on its wires official speeches to every corner of the Empire, in return for an annual fee of £500 from the Colonial Office. During the First World War, Reuters launched a wartime news service by arrangement with the Foreign Office, which by 1917 was circulating about one million words per month throughout the Empire.

Reuters' Managing Director during the war years, George Jones, was also in charge of cable and wireless propaganda for the British Department of Information. Though this service was separate from the main Reuters wire service, whose support for the war was more subtle, it rallied opinion within the Empire and influenced the attitudes of the neutral countries. As one British official wrote in 1917, 'At Reuters the work done is that of an independent news agency of an objective character, with propaganda secretly infused' (quoted in Read, 1992: 127–8).

Though this service was discontinued after the end of the war, Reuters entered into another agreement with the Foreign Office under which the agency would circulate specific messages on its international wires, to be paid for by the government. This agreement remained in force until the Second World War. However, apart from support from the government the major reason for the continued success of Reuters was the fact that it 'sold useful information enabling businesses to trade profitably' (Lawrenson and Barber, 1985: 179).

The wider availability of wireless technology after the First World War enabled Reuters in 1920 to launch a trade service, which became a crucial component of the economic life of the Empire. New technology made it easier to send and receive more international industrial and financial information at a faster speed. As the globe was being connected through trans-oceanic trade, such information – for example, New York prices for Indian cotton – had a high premium for traders who were depending on the accuracy of Reuters commodity prices and stock market news from around the world.

Reuters' domination of international information was helped by its being a member of the cartel and it remained the world news leader between 1870 to 1914. But the weakening of the British Empire and the ascendancy of the USA forced Reuters to compete with the American news agencies, especially Associated Press, with which it signed, in 1942, a wartime news-sharing agreement, effectively creating a new cartel for news. In the post-war period, Reuters continued to focus on commercial information, realizing that in order to succeed in a free trade environment, it had to work towards integration of commodity, currency, equity and financial markets, 'around the clock and around the world' (Tunstall and Palmer, 1991: 46).

By 1999, Reuters was one of the world's biggest multimedia corporations dealing 'in the business of information', supplying global financial markets and the news media with a range of information and news products, including 'real-time financial data, collective investment data, numerical, textual, historical and graphical databases plus news, graphics, news video, and news pictures'. In the past five years to 1998, financial information products revenue accounted for 64 per cent of the total while media products revenue accounted for less than 7 per cent of the total revenue (Reuters Annual Report, 1999).

By the end of the twentieth century, what had been started in 1851 by entrepreneur Julius Reuter, whom Karl Marx called 'a grammatically illiterate Jew' (quoted in Read, 1992: 26), had become the world's largest provider of financial data, besides being the largest news and television agency with nearly 2 000 journalists in 183 bureaux, serving 157 countries. Its news was gathered and edited for both business and media clients in 23 languages, more than 3 million words were published each day. With 1998 revenue of £3 032 million, Reuters was one of the world's largest media and information corporations, with regional headquarters in London, New York, Geneva and Hong Kong, and offices in 217 cities (Reuters Annual Report, 1999).

One major growth area for the agency which started sending news and commercial information via pigeon in its early years, is the Internet, given the steady growth in on-line trading. By 1999, it was providing news and information to over 225 Internet sites reaching an estimated 12 million viewers per month. It was planning a global news service on the Internet and had created Reuters Ventures to co-ordinate its on-line operations which include a joint venture with Dow Jones to provide a business database (Barrie and Martinson, 1999).

The advent of popular media

The expansion of printing presses and the internationalization of news agencies were contributing factors in the growth of a worldwide newspaper industry. *The Times of India* was founded in 1838 while Southeast Asia's premier newspaper *The Straits Times* was started as a daily newspaper from Singapore in 1858. Advances in printing technology meant that newspapers in non-European languages could also be printed and distributed. By 1870 more than 140 newspapers were being printed in Indian languages; in Cairo *Al-Ahram,* the newspaper which has defined Arab journalism for more than a century, was established in 1875, while in 1890, Japan's most respected newspaper *Asahi Shimbun* (Morning Sun) was founded. In Europe, the growth of popular press was unprecedented in the 1890s – France's *Le Petit Parisien* had a circulation of 1 million in 1890, while in Britain, the *Daily Mail*, launched in 1896, which redefined boundaries of journalism, was doing roaring business.

Newspapers were used by leaders to articulate nascent nationalism in many Asian countries. The Chinese nationalist leader Sun Yat Sen founded *Chung-kuo Jih-pao* (Chinese daily paper) in 1899 while in India Mahatma Gandhi used *Young India*, later named *Harijan* to propagate an anti-colonial agenda.

However, it was the USA which had the biggest international impact on media cultures symbolized by William Randolph Hearst, one of the world's first media moguls. His *New York Journal* heralded the penny press in the USA, while the International News Service, which sold articles, crossword puzzles and comic strips to newspapers, created the world's first syndicate service. It was succeeded in 1915 by the King Feature Syndicate, whose comic strips were used by newspapers all over the world, for most of the twentieth century.

The internationalization of a nascent mass culture, however, began with the film industry. Following the first screening in Paris and Berlin in 1895, films were being seen a year later from Bombay to Buenos Aires. By the First World War, the European market was dominated by the firm Pathé, founded in 1907 in France, whose distribution bureaux were located in seven European countries as well as in Turkey, the USA and Brazil. The development of independent studios between 1909 and 1913 led to the growth of the Hollywood film industry which was to dominate global film production (Mattelart, 1994).

In the realm of popular music, the dog and trumpet logo of 'His Master's Voice' (HMV) label of the Gramophone Company, became a global image. Within a few years of the founding of the company, in 1897, its recording engineers were at work in the Balkans, the Middle East, Africa, India, Iran and China. By 1906, 60 per cent of the company's profits were earned from overseas sales (Pandit, 1996: 57). After its merger with the US giant Columbia Gramophone Company in 1931 it formed EMI (Electric and Musical Industries), beginning a process of Anglo-American domination of the international recording industry that has lasted throughout the twentieth century.

By the end of the nineteenth century, US-based advertising companies were already looking beyond the domestic market. J. Walter Thompson, for example, established 'sales bureau' in London in 1899. The USA, where advertising was given its modern form, was an early convert to the power of advertising, making it the world's most consumerist society. The spending on advertising in the USA increased from $0.45 billion at the start of the century to $212 billion by its end (*see* Figure 1.1).

In the twentieth century, advertising became increasingly important in international communication. From the 1901 advertisement for the record label His Master's Voice to the famous 1929 line 'The pause that refreshes', to De Beers' hugely popular campaign 'A diamond is forever' put out in 1948, advertisers have aimed at international audiences. This trend became even stronger with the growth of radio and television, with messages such as Pepsi-Cola's 1964 'The Pepsi generation'; Coca-Cola's 1970 rebuke 'It's the real thing'; Nike's 1988 slogan 'Just do it' and Coca-Cola's 1993 one-word advice, 'Always', being consumed across the world.

The American cowboy and masculine trademark of The Marlboro Man, introduced in 1955 and identified with Philip Morris's Marlboro cigarettes, became a worldwide advertising presence, making Marlboro the best-selling cigarette in the world. Though tobacco advertisements were banned on the USA television in 1971 and since then health groups have fought against promoting smoking through advertisement in the USA and other Western countries, The Marlboro Man was nominated as the icon of the twentieth century by the US trade journal *Advertising Age International*.

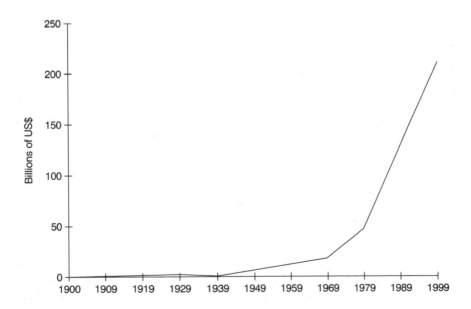

Figure 1.1 A century of advertising: US advertising spend, 1900–99

Radio and international communication

As with other new technologies, Western countries were the first to grasp the strategic implications of radio communication after the first radio transmissions of the human voice in 1902. Unlike cable, radio equipment was comparatively cheap and could be sold on a mass scale. There was also a growing awareness among American businesses that radio, if properly developed and controlled, might be used to undercut the huge advantages of British-dominated international cable links (Luther, 1988). They realized that, while undersea cables and their landing terminals could be vulnerable, and their location required bilateral negotiations between nations, radio waves could travel anywhere, unrestrained by politics or geography.

At the 1906 international radiotelegraph conference in Berlin, 28 states debated radio equipment standards and procedures to minimize interference. The great naval powers, who were also the major users of radio (Britain, Germany, France, the USA and Russia), had imposed a regime of radio frequency allocation, allowing priority to the country that first notified the International Radiotelegraph Union of its intention to use a specific radio frequency (Mattelart, 1994).

As worldwide radio broadcasting grew, stations that transmitted across national borders had, in accordance with an agreement signed in London in 1912, to register their use of a particular wavelength with the international secretariat of the International Radiotelegraph Union. But there was no mechanism for either assigning or withholding slots; it was a system of first come, first served. Thus the companies or states with the necessary capital and technology prevailed in taking control of the limited spectrum space, to the disadvantage of smaller and less developed countries (Hamelink, 1994).

Two distinct types of national radio broadcasting emerged: in the USA, the Radio Act of 1927 enshrined its established status as a commercial enterprise, funded by advertising, while the British Broadcasting Corporation (BBC), founded in 1927, as a non-profit, public broadcasting monopoly, provided a model for several other European and Commonwealth countries (McChesney, 1993).

As the strongest voice in the World Radio Conference in Washington in 1927, private companies helped to write an agreement that allowed them to continue developing their use of the spectrum, without regard to possible signal interference for other countries. By being embodied in an international treaty, these provisions took on the character of 'international law', including the principle of allocating specific wavelengths for particular purposes (Luther, 1988). A major consequence of this conference was to reinforce US and European domination of the international radio spectrum. However, it was the Soviet Union which became the first nation to exploit this new medium for international broadcasting.

The battle of the airwaves

The strategic significance of international communication grew with the expansion of the new medium. Ever since the advent of radio, its use for propaganda was an integral part of its development, with its power to influence values, beliefs and attitudes (Taylor, 1995). During the First World War, the power of radio was quickly recognized as vital both to the management of public opinion at home and propaganda abroad, directed at allies and enemies alike. As noted by a distinguished scholar of propaganda: 'During the war period it came to be recognised that the mobilisation of men and means was not sufficient; there must be mobilisation of opinion. Power over opinion, as over life and property, passed into official hands' (Lasswell, 1927: 14).

The Russian communists were one of the earliest political groups to realize the ideological and strategic importance of broadcasting, and the first public broadcast to be recorded in the history of wireless propaganda was by the Council of the People's Commissar's of Lenin's historic message on 30 October 1917: 'The All-Russian Congress of Soviets has formed a new Soviet Government. The Government of Kerensky has been overthrown and arrested. Kerensky himself has fled. All official institutions are in the hands of the Soviet Government' (quoted in Hale, 1975: 16).

The Soviet Union was one of the first countries to take advantage of a medium which could reach across continents and national boundaries to an international audience. The world's first short-wave radio broadcasts were sent out from Moscow in 1925. Within five years, the All-Union Radio was regularly broadcasting communist propaganda in German, French, Dutch and English.

By the time the Nazis came to power in Germany in 1933, radio broadcasting had become an extension of international diplomacy. The head of Hitler's Propaganda Ministry, Josef Goebbels, believed in the power of radio broadcasting as a tool of propaganda. 'Real broadcasting is true propaganda. Propaganda means fighting on all battlefields of the spirit, generating, multiplying, destroying, exterminating, building and undoing. Our propaganda is determined by what we call German race, blood and nation' (quoted in Hale, 1975: 2).

In 1935, Nazi Germany turned its attention to disseminating worldwide the racist and anti-Semitic ideology of the Third Reich. The Nazi *Reichsender* broadcasts were targeted at Germans living abroad, as far afield as South America and Australia. These short-wave transmissions were rebroadcast by Argentina, home to many Germans. Later the Nazis expanded their international broadcasting to include several languages, including Afrikaans, Arabic and Hindustani and, by 1945, German radio was broadcasting in more than 50 languages.

In Fascist Italy, under Benito Mussolini, a Ministry of Print and Propaganda was created to promote Fascist ideals and win public opinion for colonial campaigns such as the invasion of Abyssinia (Ethiopia) in 1935, and support for Francisco Franco's Fascists during the Spanish Civil War (1936–39). Mussolini also distributed radio sets to Arabs, tuned to one station alone – *Radio Bari* in southern Italy. This propaganda prompted the British Foreign Office to create a monitoring unit of the BBC to listen in to international broadcasts and later to start an Arabic language service to the region.

The Second World War saw an explosion in international broadcasting as a propaganda tool on both sides. Japanese wartime propaganda included short-wave transmissions from *Nippon Hoso Kyokai* (NHK) the Japan Broadcasting Corporation, to South-east and East Asia and also to the West coast of the United States, which had a large Japanese-American population. In addition, NHK also transmitted high-quality propaganda programmes such as *Zero Hour* aimed at US troops in the Pacific islands (Wood, 1992).

Although the BBC, apart from the Empire Service (the precursor of the BBC World Service), was not directly controlled by the British Government, its claim to independence during the war, was 'little more than a self-adulatory part of the British myth' (Curran and Seaton, 1996: 147). John Reith, its first Director General and the spirit behind the BBC, was for a time the Minister of Information in 1940 and resented being referred to as 'Dr Goebbels' opposite number' (Hickman, 1995: 29).

The Empire Service had been established in 1932 with the aim of connecting the scattered parts of the British Empire. Funded by the Foreign Office, it tended to reflect the government's public diplomacy. At the beginning of the Second World War, the BBC was broadcasting in seven foreign languages apart from English – Afrikaans, Arabic, French, German, Italian, Portuguese and Spanish (Walker, 1992: 36). By the end of the war it was broadcasting in 39 languages.

The French General De Gaulle used the BBC's French service, during the war years, to send messages to the resistance movement in occupied France and for a time between October 1942 and May 1943, the BBC broadcast a weekly 15-minute newsletter to Russia with the co-operation of the Russian news agency TASS (*Telegrafnoe agentstvo Sovetskogo Soiuza*). It also broadcast *The Shadow of the Swastika*, the first of a series of dramas about the Nazi Party. The BBC helped the US Army to create the American Forces Network, which broadcast recordings of American shows for US forces in Britain, Middle East and Africa. More importantly, given Britain's proximity to the war theatre, the BBC played a key role in the propaganda offensive and often it was more effective than American propaganda which, as British media historian Asa Briggs comments was 'both distant and yet too brash, too unsophisticated and yet too contrived to challenge the propaganda forces already at work on the continent' (1970: 412).

Until the Second World War radio in the USA was known more for its commercial potential as a vehicle for advertisements rather than a government propaganda tool, but after 1942, the year the Voice of America (VOA) was founded, the US Government made effective use of radio to promote its political interests – a process which reached its high point during the decades of Cold War.

The Cold War – from communist propaganda to capitalist persuasion

The victorious allies of the Second World War – the Soviet Union and the West led by the United States – soon fell out as differences emerged about the post-war order in Europe and the rest of the world. The clash was, in essence, about two contrasting views of organizing society: the Soviet view, inspired by Marxism–Leninism, and the capitalist individualism championed by the USA. The defeat of Nazism and militarism of Japan was accompanied by the US-proclaimed victory of democracy and the creation of the United Nations system. Though the 1947 General Assembly Resolution 110 (II) condemned 'all forms of propaganda which are designed or likely to provoke or encourage any threat to the peace, breach of the peace, or act of aggression', both camps indulged in regular propaganda as the battle lines of the Cold War were being drawn (quoted in Taylor, 1997).

Soviet broadcast propaganda

In the same year, the Soviet Union revived the Comintern (Communist International) as Cominform (Communist Information Bureau), to organize a worldwide propaganda campaign orchestrated by the Administration of Agitation and Propaganda of the Communist Party Central Committee (AGITPROP). Communist propaganda, a central component of post-war Soviet diplomacy, was primarily aimed at the Eastern bloc, and, increasingly, to what came to be known as the Third World.

During the Cold War years, TASS remained a major source of news among the media in eastern bloc countries. The news agency which began as the St Petersburg Telegraph Agency (SPTA) in 1904, underwent a number of name changes before becoming Telegraph Agency of the Soviet Union (TASS) in 1925. In 1914, it was renamed the Petrograd Telegraph Agency (PTA) and in 1917, the Bolsheviks made the PTA the central news agency; a year later the PTA and the Press Bureau, also under the Council of People's Commissars, were united to form the Russian Telegraph Agency (ROSTA).

Soviet propaganda – in heavy polemical Marxist terms about the ideological clash between communism and imperialism – was couched in the language of the class struggle between the capitalist bourgeoisie and the global proletariat, ideas which fell on receptive ears in countries colonized by European powers.

However, one of the first major propaganda battles the Soviet Union waged was in 1948 against a fellow socialist country – Yugoslavia, where Marshal Tito's efforts to chart a foreign policy independent of dictates from Soviet leader, Joseph Stalin, resulted in a massive propaganda effort to overthrow the leadership in Belgrade. Another test of Soviet propaganda in Eastern Europe came with the crisis in Hungary in 1956, where it had to fight hostile Western propaganda and protect a client regime. Similarly, during the invasion of Czechoslovakia by Warsaw Pact countries under Moscow's orders, Russian broadcasts to Czechoslovakia jumped from 17 hours per week just before the August 1968 invasion to 168 at the height of the crisis, falling back to 84 by September (Hale, 1975: 24).

By the late 1960s, Moscow Radio was the world's largest single international broadcaster – between 1969 to 1972 it broadcast more programme hours than the United States. In addition, it used more languages – 84 – than any other international broadcaster, partly because the Soviet Union itself was a multilingual country. Between 1950 and 1973 external broadcasting from the Soviet Union grew from 533 hours to around 1950 hours per week. This is comparable with the whole of US external broadcasting – the world's largest – including the official Voice of America (VOA) and the clandestine Radio Liberty (RL) and Radio Free Europe (RFE) – at 497 hours per week in 1950 and 2 060 in 1973 (Hale, 1975: 174).

Soviet broadcast policies were aimed at countering Western propaganda and promoting Moscow's line on international affairs among the world's communist parties, which became increasingly important in Soviet thinking after the Sino-Soviet split of 1968. The Sino-Soviet split – more influenced by geo-strategic than ideological differences – led to mutual propaganda battles between the communist giants, with Radio Moscow increasing its Chinese language broadcasts from 77 hours a week in 1967 to 200 hours in 1972, while China, which by early 1970s had become the world's third largest international broadcaster, also increased its broadcasts criticising Soviet 'revisionism'.

While Soviet broadcasts – known more for their party line than professional journalism – had little impact in the West, in contrast to the popularity of Western broadcasts in the Eastern bloc, they nevertheless set the news agendas in Eastern Europe. The Soviet presence was also evident in the way the news media were organized in many communist countries and among socialist nations of the South.

However, Radio Moscow was no match for Western broadcasters in terms of the power of its transmitters and the availability of broadcasting outlets outside the communist world. Apart from broadcasters in Eastern Europe, Soviet broadcasts had only one other outlet – Radio Habana in Cuba, which was suspended after the ending of the Cold War. With their worldwide network of relay stations, the Western powers had a distinct advantage and were able to beam propaganda with little interference (Nelson, 1997). Since there was scant interest among Western populations for Russian international broadcasts, Western governments did not have to worry about jamming them. In contrast, the authorities in Moscow tried to interfere with Western broadcasts, seeing them as a network of 'radio saboteurs' subverting the achievements of socialism.

US broadcast propaganda

Although the Voice of America had been a part of US diplomacy during the Second World War, with the advent of the Cold War, propaganda became a crucial component of US foreign broadcasting (Sorensen, 1968; Lisann, 1975; Rawnsley, 1996). The key instruments of US international broadcasting – The Voice of America, Radio Liberty and Radio Free Europe, and the American Forces Network – were all state-funded. The VOA was the official mouthpiece of the US Government, the largest single element in the US Information Agency (USIA) and ultimately answerable to the US State Department. Unlike the BBC World Service, it depended on official comment as it only used VOA staff for commentaries, thereby restricting the range of opinions expressed by its programmes and thus straining its credibility as an international broadcaster.

An early indication of the increasing use of radio for propaganda was evident in the way VOA was used to promote US President Harry Truman's 'Campaign for Truth' against communism, following the outbreak in 1950 of the Korean War. The campaign was aimed at legitimizing US involvement in the Korean War, which claimed more than a million lives and became the first test of superpower rivalry in the developing world, a pattern repeated in several other Cold War-related conflicts in Africa, Asia and Latin America.

A year later, in 1951, Truman set up a Psychological Strategy Board, responsible to the National Security Council, to advise on international anti-communist propaganda. In 1953, his successor President Dwight Eisenhower appointed a personal adviser on 'psychological warfare' – resulting in an increased stridency in the anti-communist rhetoric emanating from VOA.

In the United States, propaganda was part of what John Martin, a former researcher for the USIA, called 'facilitative communication' which he defined as 'activity that is designed to keep lines open and to maintain them against the day when they will be needed for propaganda purposes' (Martin, 1976: 263). This included press releases, seminars, conferences, and exhibitions, as well as books, films, educational and cultural exchange programmes and scholarships for technical and scientific research.

VOA operated a global network of relay stations to propagate the ideal of 'the American way of life' to international listeners. The nodal points in this worldwide network linked to the control centre in Washington, included Bangkok for Southeast Asia; Poro and Tinang in the Philippines for China and Southeast Asia; Colombo for South Asia; Tangier in Morocco, for North Africa; Rhodes in Greece, for the Middle East; Selebi-Phikwe in Botswana, for southern Africa; Monrovia in Liberia for Sub-Saharan Africa; Munich for Eastern Europe and the former Soviet Union, Woofferton in England (leased from the BBC) for the former Soviet Union; Greenville in the USA for Latin America; and Punta Gorda in Belize for Central America (*see* map).

The transmitters were chosen for their strategic locations, close to the target zone to ensure a stronger and more stable signal and to overcome possible jamming. In many instances the locations of transmitters remained a secret as did the broadcasting of subversive and misleading information to confuse the West's Cold War adversaries.

Covert communication – Radio Free Europe and Radio Liberty

Among the explicitly propagandist radio stations that thrived during the Cold War were Radio Free Europe (RFE) and Radio Liberty (RL), operating from West Germany. While the Voice of America was the legitimate broadcasting arm of the United States Information Agency, the Munich-based RFE and RL were covert organizations carrying out a propaganda war against communism in Europe. They were part of what is now called 'psychological warfare' in which the 'campaign for truth' became the 'crusade for freedom'.

Free Europe Inc. was established in 1949 as a non-profit-making, private corporation to broadcast news and current affairs programmes to Eastern European countries behind the Iron Curtain. Radio Liberation (the name Radio Liberty was adopted in 1963) was created two years later along the same lines to broadcast to the Soviet Union (Mickelson, 1983).

Both were covertly funded by the US Government, mainly through the Central Intelligence Agency until 1971, when funding and administrative responsibilities were transferred to a presidentially appointed Board for International Broadcasting (BIB). The two corporations were merged into RFE/RL in 1975. In 1994, its duties were transferred to the Broadcasting Board of Governors (BBG), which oversaw all non-military US international broadcasting.

Regular broadcasts of RFE began in 1951 and though RL was also established in 1951, it did not begin broadcasting until 1953. Both stations broadcast from studios in Munich: RFE using transmitters in Germany and Portugal for its programmes in Polish, Czech, Slovak, Romanian, Hungarian and Bulgarian; RL from transmitters in Germany, Spain and Taiwan for its programmes in Russian (over half the output) and 17 other languages spoken in the Soviet Union. Fighting communism was the *raison d'être* of these radio stations and therefore programmes were deliberately provocative to the

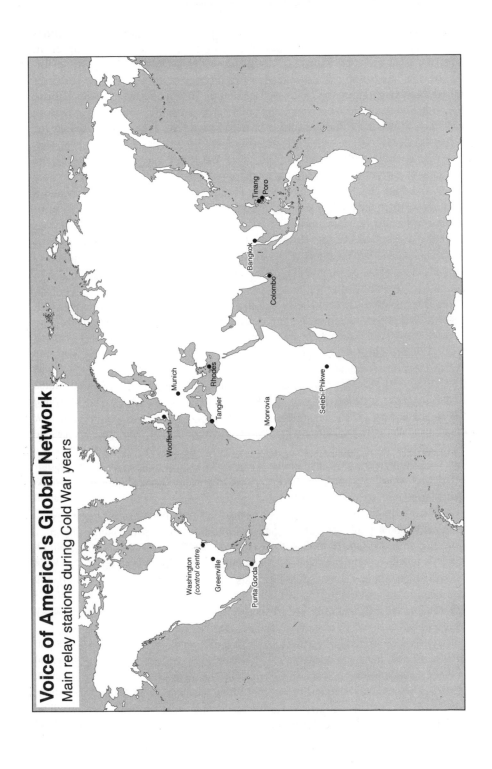

Voice of America's Global Network
Main relay stations during Cold War years

Tinang
Poro
Bangkok
Colombo
Munich
Rhodes
Tangier
Selebi-Phikwe
Monrovia
Woofferton
Washington (control centre)
Greenville
Punta Gorda

communist governments, broadcasting *émigré* petitions and extracts from banned books, including works by anti-establishment writers like Alexander Solzhenitsyn and scientists such as Andrei Sakharov.

The often crude and insensitive propaganda broadcast led to accusations from the Soviet Union of stirring up the 1956 revolt in Hungary. During the crisis, RFE encouraged the Hungarian people to rebel against the communist authorities, even misleading them with the promises of the imminent arrival of a 'UN Delegation' – a euphemism for US military intervention – which never materialized while the Soviet tanks crushed the uprising.

RFE and RL claimed to provide an alternative 'Home Service', intended to challenge the state or party monopoly over the media in the communist countries. The Soviet Union and other members of the Warsaw Pact regularly jammed RFE/RL's signals, denouncing them as a network of 'radio saboteurs,' and an integral part of US 'electronic imperialism' (Kashlev, 1984).

Under US President Ronald Reagan's administration US public diplomacy became more strident and radio stations were directed to undertake a 'vigorous advocacy' of American foreign policy (Tuch, 1990). The Polish service of RFE played a key role in its support for Solidarity, the first 'independent' trade union in a communist country. During the industrial unrest of 1980s, two-thirds of the Polish adult population tuned in and this level of penetration of Western radio was 'a major factor in the Soviet's decision not to intervene militarily in the country as they had in Czechoslovakia in 1968' (Lord, 1998: 62). In 1981, the Munich headquarters of RFE/RL were bombed, allegedly by Soviet secret services (ibid.).

In 1988, Soviet leader Mikhail Gorbachev ended the jamming, allowing RFE/RL signals to reach a broader audience. RFE/RL's contribution to the end of communism in this region is now widely acknowledged (McNamara, 1992; Sosin, 1999). As one broadcaster wrote: 'well before the Iron Curtain rusted – let alone was dismantled – its metal had been perforated by the sounds on the airwaves' (Partos, 1993: 91). Even the Russian President Boris Yeltsin personally intervened to help create an RFE/RL bureau in Moscow after the failed August 1991 coup. After many years in Munich, RFE/RL's headquarters moved to Prague in 1995.

It was only in the 1990s, after the end of the Cold War, that these covert organizations came under public scrutiny, especially with the memoirs of George Urban, a former Director of Radio Free Europe (Critchlow, 1995; Urban, 1997). Because of RFE/RL's role in fighting communism, many thought that the radios had fulfilled their mission and might be disbanded. But officials across the region stressed the continuing need for precisely the kind of broadcasts RFE/RL had brought to this region. Nevertheless, RFE/RL did cut back in some areas even as it expanded in others. It closed its Polish Service, while its Czechoslovak Service was substantially reduced and joined with Czech Public Radio to establish a new public affairs radio programme. In 1994, RFE/RL began broadcasts to the former Yugoslavia, and in 1998, it launched its Persian Language Service and Radio Free Iraq. Such out-of-area activities were not new for these radios – during the years of Soviet invasion of Afghanistan, RFE/RL established a bureau in Peshawar in Pakistan for propaganda purposes and in 1984 a new service Radio Free Afghanistan was created within RL, broadcasting in two major languages of Afghanistan – Dari and Pashto (Lord, 1998: 64).

In 1999, RFE/RL was reaching 20 million listeners, broadcasting for more than 700 hours a week, in 25 languages, to countries stretching from Poland to the Pacific and from the Arctic to the Persian Gulf and 'providing an alternative "home service" to countries where the media are struggling amid chaotic economic conditions to achieve genuine financial and editorial independence' (website). RFE/RL maintains 22 bureaux across the region and has broadcasting links with more than 1000 free-lancers and stringers. It uses short-wave broadcasts to reach its listeners, but increasingly it is utilizing AM/FM stations through more than 90 affiliate partners and more than 220 transmission sites located in all its broadcast countries except Belarus, Iran, Iraq, Tajikistan and Turkmenistan. In addition, RFE/RL maintains an active presence on the Internet, claiming that more than 5 million people visit its website every month.

Apart from Radio Free Europe and Radio Liberty, the United States supported other clandestine radio stations such as Radio Free Russia which aimed to use the Christian message to subvert atheistic states. It started operations in 1950 from South Korea and Taiwan as well as from West Germany. Run by the militantly anti-communist Popular Labour Union (NTS), this station also carried religious propaganda in Russian and in the Baltic languages, produced by a parallel organization, Radio Omega.

In addition to political propaganda, religious radio stations also contributed to the ideological battles against 'Godless communism'. One key player was Trans World Radio, which started transmitting the gospel message from Tangier in Morocco in 1954 and has since evolved into one of the world's largest radio networks, broadcasting in 75 languages. It now has an international network of transmitters located in every continent – Monte Carlo and Cyprus for Europe, the former Soviet Union and the Middle East, Swaziland for Africa; Sri Lanka for Asia, Guam for the Pacific region and Montevideo in Uruguay for Latin America (Wood, 1992: 216).

The BBC

In contrast to US state propaganda, the BBC's External Services prided themselves on presenting a mature, balanced view, winning by argument, rather than hammering home a point, in the best tradition of British under-statement. This proclaimed policy of 'balance' gave the BBC more international credibility than any other broadcasting organization in the world. The BBC's dependence on the British Government was evident, since its budget was controlled by the Treasury through grant-in-aid from the Foreign and Colonial Office (now called the Foreign and Commonwealth Office), which could also decide which languages were used for programmes and for how long they were broadcast to each audience. For example, during the Berlin blockade of 1948–49 almost the entire output of the BBC external services was directed to Eastern bloc countries. In addition, the government exerted indirect influence on the BBC since the relay stations and overseas transmitters were negotiated through or owned by the Diplomatic Wireless Service.

What distinguished the BBC was its capacity to criticize its own government, however indirectly.

The 'special relationship' that characterized US/UK ties during the Cold War years also was in evidence in the realm of international broadcasting. With the establishment of its Russian language unit in 1946, the BBC World Service played a key part in the Cold War through its strategically located global network of relay stations. These included: stations in the Ascension Island and in Antigua (where it shared transmitters and relay station with the German radio station Deutsche Welle to cover the Western hemisphere); a multi-frequency broadcasting centre in Cyprus (for the Middle East, Europe and northern Africa); at Masirah, leased from Oman (for the Gulf region); in Seychelles (for east Africa); in Kranji in Singapore (for Southeast Asia); and in Hong Kong (for east Asia, especially China).

Other Western stations such as Deutsche Welle and Radio France International (RFI) also contributed to the war of words. RFI, particularly strong in the former colonies of France, had two main relay stations – at Moyabi in Gabon and in Montsinery in French Guiana. In addition, it leased transmitting facilities from commercial *Radio Monte Carlo* in Cyprus to broadcast to the Middle East. Unlike Britain, France did not play such an important role in the Cold War broadcasting battles – RFI was not jammed by the Soviet authorities. Concerned with maintaining its independent foreign policy and with a cultural focus, French international broadcasting concentrated on promoting its culture and commerce in its former colonies in Africa, the Middle East, the Caribbean and parts of the Pacific, not least to boost the export of French broadcasting equipment (Wood, 1992: 199).

Cold War propaganda in the Third World

Another major battle for the hearts and minds of people during the Cold War was fought in the Third World, where countries were emerging from centuries of subjugation under European colonial powers. The Soviet Union had recognized that, since the nature of the anti-colonial movements in Asia and Africa was largely anti-Western, the political situation was ripe for promoting communism. The West, on the other hand, was interested in continuing to control raw materials and develop potential markets for Western products. Radio was seen as a crucial medium, given the low levels of literacy among most of the population of the developing countries. In addition, the nascent media in the newly independent countries in Asia and Africa were almost always state-controlled and thus less able to compete with foreign media, with their higher credibility and technological superiority.

The Middle East was a particular target for Western broadcasters, given its geo-strategic importance as the source of the world's largest supply of oil.

It is no coincidence that the Arabic Service, created in 1938, was the first foreign-language section of the BBC's Empire Service, to be followed by the Persian service in 1940. The French, British and American broadcasters dominated the airwaves in the Arab world, while the Arabic service of Kol Israel (the Voice of Israel) also played a key propaganda role in the Middle East. Western support for the conservative Arab countries and the feudal order they perpetuated was also reflected in the treatment of Arab radical nationalism in Western broadcasting.

The British Government used a Cyprus-based British commercial broadcaster Sharq-al Adna to broadcast 'Voice of Britain' anti-Egyptian propaganda, however, 'with little effect' (Walker, 1992: 75). To counter this, Egyptian President Gamaal Nasser used the radio to promote the idea of pan-Arabism. The Cairo-based 'Voice of the Arabs,' was an international service, which in the 1950s and 1960s became the 'pulpit of revolution', notably in the leftist revolution in Iraq in 1958.

Pan-Arab sentiment also helped the Palestinian 'liberation radios' which regularly and often clandestinely broadcast from PLO offices in Cairo, Beirut, Algiers, Baghdad and Tripoli, moving position to avoid Israeli attacks. These radios played an important role in keeping the Palestinian struggle alive. In Algeria the Voice of Algeria, the radio station of the Front National de Libération (FNL) played an important role in the national war of liberation against the French colonial authorities. In the words of Frantz Fanon, the radio 'created out of nothing, brought the nation to life and endowed every citizen with a new status, *telling him so explicitly*' (Fanon, 1970: 80, italics in the original).

In Asia, in addition to direct broadcasts from the USA, VOA operated from Japan, Thailand (where the Voice of Free Asia was part of VOA) and Sri Lanka. Following the Chinese revolution in 1949, US priority was to stop the expansion of communism into other parts of Asia. In 1951, the CIA funded the Manila-based Radio Free Asia, notable for its anti-communist stridency. It was later replaced by Radio of Free Asia which continued until 1966 (Taylor, 1997: 43).

During the Vietnam War, US propaganda reached new heights (Chandler, 1981; Hallin, 1986). The Joint US Public Office became the delegated authority for all propaganda activities, the chief aims of which were to undermine the support for communists and to keep the support of the South Vietnamese. These messages were conveyed mainly through dropping leaflets and broadcasting from low flying aircraft. It is estimated that during the seven years it operated in Vietnam, the USIA, supported by the armed forces, dropped nearly 50 billion leaflets – nearly '1,500 for every person in both parts of the country' (Chandler, 1981: 3). Radio played a crucial role in the psychological warfare. The CIA also ran Voice of the Patriotic Militiamen's Front in South Vietnam and two anti-Sukarno operations in Indonesia – Voice of Free Indonesia and Radio Sulawesi.

In Latin America, an area that the USA has traditionally regarded as its sphere of influence, US media propaganda has been intense, especially since the communist revolution in Cuba in 1959 led by Fidel Castro. During the 1962 Cuban missile crisis, President John Kennedy launched a virulent anti-Castro propaganda campaign with his *Alianza para el Progreso* programme, in what was, in the words of the former Director of VOA, George Allen, one of 'the largest concentrations of propaganda effort unleashed against an individual since Stalin tried to purge Tito in 1948' (quoted in Hale, 1975: 101). Unable to dislodge Castro from power and concerned that his success might promote anti-US sentiments in other parts of Latin America, the US Government resorted to using propaganda, notably with the introduction in 1983 of Radio Marti and later, in 1990, of TV Marti, which Cuba considered an hostile act, violating its sovereignty (Alexandre, 1993).

Given its limited geo-strategic importance in international relations Africa remained a low priority area for Cold War propaganda. However, as large areas of the continent were parts of the British Empire, the BBC had been broadcasting to Africa since 1940. In later years, the main broadcasting languages were English, French, Hausa, Portuguese and Swahili.

In the 1970s, VOA broadcast to Africa in English, French and Swahili, primarily to what were known locally as 'wa-benzi' (Mercedes-Benz owners, the African elite). Though Radio Moscow broadcast in several African languages – usually a translation of anti-imperialist material – its effectiveness was limited given the lack of communication infrastructure in many African countries. The Soviet Union invested in transmitters and training courses in the Cameroon while the Chinese supported broadcasting in Zambia and Tanzania. Under the socialist government of President Julius Nyerere, Radio Tanzania became the nerve centre of liberation movements in southern Africa and played an important role in the anti-apartheid struggle. However, socialist radio stations were no match for the powerful transmitters of Western broadcasters, such as those for BBC from Ascension Island and for VOA from Monrovia.

Broadcast propaganda was also used in areas where the Cold War was often very hot, such as Angola, where US and South Africa-backed UNITA (National Union for the Total Independence of Angola) rebels used their own radio station – The Voice of the Resistance of the Black Cockerel – which began broadcasting from South Africa in 1979 and was installed in Angola under the CIA's covert aid programme (Windrich, 1992).

Although developing countries were initially receptive to the Soviet message of freedom from colonialism, in the 1950s and 1960s, the economic power of the West and the dependency on colonial ties, coupled with the increasing influence of modernizing elites, meant that attraction for communism was waning. As major developing countries, such as India, Indonesia and Egypt, opted for Non-Alignment – a movement founded in 1961 among developing countries which claimed to eschew Cold War bloc politics, joining neither Western nor Eastern alliance – a new perspective on international communication began to emerge. Looking beyond the Cold War bipolarity, the Non-Aligned countries demanded that international communication issues be seen in terms of North–South rather than East–West categories.

International communication and development

For nearly half a century, the Cold War divided the world into hostile East–West blocs. This had significant implications for the development of Third World countries, most of whom wanted to avoid bloc politics and concentrate on the economic emancipation of their populations. The phrase 'Third World' itself was a product of the Cold War, said to have been coined by French economic historian Alfred Sauvy in 1952, when the world was divided between the capitalist First World, led by the United States and the communist Second World with its centre in Moscow. The 'Third World' was the mass of countries remaining outside these two blocs[1] (Brandt Commission, 1981; South Commission, 1990). National liberation movements in Asia, Africa and Latin America had altered the political map of the world. The vast territory occupied in 1945 by European colonial powers extended over 36 million sq. km; by 1960 as a result of decolonization the area under colonial occupation had shrunk to 13 million sq. km. For the newly independent ex-colonial states, international communication opened up opportunities for development.

The Non-Aligned Movement, through the Group of 77, established in 1964, began to demand greater economic justice in such UN forums as UNCTAD and in 1974, the UN General Assembly formally approved their demand for the creation of a New International Economic Order (NIEO), a democratic interdependent economic order, based on equality and sovereignty, including the right to 'pursue progressive social transformation that enables the full participation of the population in the development process' (Hamelink, 1979: 145). While this remained largely an ideal, it provided a new framework to redefine international relations, for the first time after the Second World War, not in terms of East–West categories but by the North–South divide. At the same time, it was argued that the new economic order had to be linked to a New World Information and Communication Order (NWICO).

The general improvement in superpower relations in the age of détente, as marked by the 1975 Helsinki Conference on Security and Co-operation in Europe (CSCE), encouraged the Non-Aligned countries to demand these changes in global economic and informational systems. The conference recognized the need for 'freer and wider dissemination of information of all kinds' (Nordenstreng, 1986). As Chilean scholar Juan Somavia, writing in the mid-1970s, observed:

It is becoming increasingly clear that the transnational communications system has developed with the support and at the service of the transnational power structure. It is an integral part of the system which affords the control of that key instrument of contemporary society: information. It is the vehicle for transmitting values and lifestyles to Third World countries which stimulate the type of consumption and the type of society necessary to the transnational system as a whole.

(Somavia, 1976: 16–17)

Apart from highlighting the structural inequalities in international communication, there were also efforts made among many developing countries, often with financial or technical support from the West, to use communication technologies for development. This could take different forms – from promoting literacy and information about healthcare to spreading consumerism. One area which received particular attention from policy-makers was satellite television, which given its reach, was considered a powerful medium that could be harnessed for educational purposes, and in the long run, to help change social and cultural attitudes of 'traditional' people and 'modernize' societies.

Satellite Instructional Television Experiment (SITE)

The use of modern technologies for development purposes was pioneered by the Indian Government when in 1975 it launched the Satellite Instructional Television Experiment (SITE). The programme, supported by UNESCO, aimed to use satellite technology to assist development by transmitting daily programmes on health, agriculture and education to rural communities.

India's Department of Atomic Energy negotiated a deal with the US National Aeronautics and Space Administration (NASA) which loaned India one of its satellites, Applications Technology Satellite-6 (ATS-6), for a year to make these broadcasts in exchange for sharing the knowledge from the project.

The SITE programmes lasted from 1 August 1975 to 31 July 1976, and the estimated cost to India of the world's largest techno-social experiment was about $6.6 million. The government chose 2 400 villages, selected from 20 districts of some of the poorest regions of six contiguous provinces – Orissa and Bihar in the east, Madhya Pradesh in central India, Rajasthan in the west and two southern states, Andhra Pradesh and Karnataka. Most of these villages had little existing communication infrastructure (Agrawal, 1978).

In each village a direct-reception system (DRS) television, a 25-inch, black-and-white set, was installed in a public place for community viewing. Signals were beamed from Ahmedabad and Delhi earth stations to ATS-6, which had a capacity of two audio and one video transmission signals. The use of direct reception systems eliminated the need for costly microwave relay towers. In addition, conventional television sets in 2500 villages and towns received the programmes through terrestrial transmitters.

Members of government institutions, such as the Indian Space Research Organisation (ISRO), teamed up with other experts from the areas of health, education, agriculture and development and the Satellite Television Wing of All India Radio, to produce the daily four-hour programming at three base production units located in Delhi, Cuttack and Hyderabad. The science-education programmes for schools were produced by Space Applications Centre's Ahmedabad and Bombay studios. Several international experts, including Wilbur Schramm, were also involved in the project.

Programmes were broadcast mornings and evening in four languages – Hindi, Kannada, Oriya and Telugu. A 30-minute national programme in Hindi (partly live) was broadcast from Delhi for all villages, while the remaining three-and-a-half hours were broadcast in region-specific languages. More than 80 per cent of the reception systems were functioning at any given time in the villages. The availability of visuals and sound generated much interest among the viewers, with a large numbers watching the first programmes but gradually audience size stabilized to about 100 for the evening broadcast.

Inspired by the dominant paradigm of modernization theories of communication for development (Lerner 1958; Schramm, 1964, see Chapter 2, pp 56–60) the project was aimed to bring about behavioural changes among the rural communities and help them reject traditional social attitudes, which were seen as antithetical to the goals of modernization but it also reflected current domestic political concerns. Among the primary objectives was to use television for population control – 'family planning' was a major priority for the then government of Prime Minister Indira Gandhi.

Modernizing agricultural practices by using high-yielding seeds and pesticides and fertilisers – all part of the ongoing 'Green Revolution' – was another key plank of the programme. Attempts to improve school education, contribute to teacher training and improve health and hygiene were other main objectives of SITE. It is, however, ironical that this innovative project was in operation at a time Gandhi had imposed an Emergency, muzzling the press and arresting opposition leaders.

Of the four hours of programming, one and half hours were targeted at children aged between 5 and 12 years of age, to be watched in schools as supplements to the regular school curriculum. The objective was to make learning more interesting through audio-visual teaching tools, hitherto unknown in most villages, and to reduce the drop-out rate, as well as to improve the children's' basic skills and instil in them a sense of hygiene (Agrawal, 1978).

Another major objective of the SITE programmes was the development of agriculture, a key sector in a predominantly rural country. The aim was to disseminate relevant information, give demonstrations and provide advice on such matters as improved farming methods, pest control, crops management and poultry and animal husbandry. The programmes were also supposed to provide information about the district-level government organizations responsible for the supply of seeds, fertilizers and agricultural implements. In addition, programmes also advised on crop marketing and commodity prices, agricultural credit schemes and had regular reports on weather forecasts. The agricultural programming constituted 30 minutes each day, for each linguistic group.

The third priority area was healthcare and birth control. Advice was given on nutrition and hygiene, as well as on pregnancy and post-natal care, a vital topic, given that thousands of women died in childbirth in India every year, especially in rural areas.

The programmes were more varied and imaginatively made than the standard fare on Indian television, and many organizations were involved in their preparation. Some programmes used techniques borrowed from traditional folk theatre to make their message accessible to the rural audience, while children's programming used puppets (Gupta, 1998).

Despite such worthy objectives, the results were not very encouraging. A major two-volume report by ISRO evaluating the impact of the programmes recorded only 'modest gains' in the sphere of education, while there was no evidence that the introduction of television in the classrooms had affected drop-out rates. SITE villages showed only a 2–4 per cent higher adoption of birth control, although a year is not long enough to judge any tangible change in traditional attitudes towards 'family planning'. Also, given the community viewing patterns where gender mixing was unavoidable, women in the age of 15–24 were discouraged from watching.

There was also little evidence that television viewing had made any significant increase in farmers' knowledge about agricultural practices or a change in attitude towards crop patterns. Anthropological findings, however, indicated that there were subtle social and cultural changes, based on gender, caste and class in the rural setting (Agrawal, 1977).

The advice on crop patterns, the use of pesticides and high-yield seeds, was mostly of use to rich farmers with the money to buy new seeds and other agricultural implements. In a country where land distribution is highly skewed in favour of rich farmers, such advice was of little consequence to the poor majority, whose condition could hardly be improved without wider structural changes in the social system. In such desperately poor rural communities, where the majority of inhabitants are landless farmers, school enrolment and drop-out rates, and awareness about health and hygiene, depend primarily on economic factors. Even today, in rural India, many children have to work on the farms, rather than attend school, to supplement their families' meagre incomes.

The government's view was that television would be a key instrument to disseminate development-oriented information and generate public participation and support for social and economic modernization. However, SITE showed that TV played only a limited role in changing behaviour among the audience and instead resulted in indifference towards the medium as well as the message itself. In the absence of relevant and effective complementary support in the lives of the viewers, innovative communication and the use of satellite technology were merely information inputs which in rural India remained little more than a high-sounding idea. Despite its top-down approach to communication and the dissemination of information, the tendency to privilege rural elites and insensitivity to the needs of the rural poor, SITE did create awareness about social problems and brought the experience of audio-visual media to rural communities.

The experiment came to an end when NASA withdrew its satellite, reflecting the dependence of the South on Northern technology. However, this spurred the Indian government to sanction the development of an indigenous satellite technology, with India becoming one of the first Southern countries to invest heavily in satellite communication. India's first communication satellite, Indian National Satellite (INSAT-1A), was launched in 1982, providing Doordarshan with transponders for networking. The more advanced INSAT satellites increased the capacity to transmit satellite-based programmes for school children across the country, though their viewership remained very low.

With the gradual commercialization of television in India in the 1980s and 1990s, development-oriented programming became a low priority area, even for state-run broadcasters. For private television companies, both domestic and international, driven by advertising demand, the rural poor are not demographically desirable viewers, and health, education and rural development do not make profitable television. By 2000, India had one of the most sophisticated satellite networks in the developing world but it was being used more to promote entertainment, of a hybrid variety, than to address the development agenda. Yet SITE was one of the most important examples of using modern technologies for developmental purposes.

The ISRO estimates that India would require more than 130 satellite transponders by 2002 to meet increasing demand and has asked the private sector to participate in satellite manufacturing. With the launch of the Insat-3B satellite, providing extended C-band transmission and mobile satellite services and also to have Ku-band transmission for the first time, India was technologically equipped to make use of satellite technology for education. Given the potential consumers in rural India – more than 60 per cent of India's one billion people live in the countryside – it is possible that private TV companies and the advertisers which sponsor their programmes may find after all that there is an economic logic for transmitting educational television to rural areas – perhaps in partnership with state broadcasters.

The demand for a New World Information and Communication Order

The international information system, the NWICO protagonists argued, perpetuated and strengthened inequality in development, with serious implications for the countries of the South, which were heavily dependent on the North for both software and hardware in the information sector. It was argued by Third World leaders that through their control of major international information channels, the Western media gave an exploitative and distorted view of their countries to the rest of the world.

The existing order, they contended, had, because of its structural logic, created a model of dependence, with negative effects on the polity, economy and society of developing countries. Their demands were articulated by Tunisian Information Minister Mustapha Masmoudi, who was later a member of the MacBride Commission. The chief complaints from the long litany of the Third World demands were as follows:

- owing to the socio-technological imbalance there was a one-way flow of information from the 'centre' to the 'periphery,' which created a wide gap between the 'haves' and the 'have nots;'
- the information rich were in a position to dictate terms to the information poor, thus creating a structure of dependency with widespread economic, political and social ramifications for the poor societies;
- this vertical flow (as opposed to a desirable horizontal flow of global information) was dominated by the Western-based transnational corporations;
- information was treated by the transnational media as a 'commodity' and subjected to the rules of the market;
- the entire information and communication order was a part of and in turn propped up international inequality that created and sustained mechanisms of neo-colonialism.

(Masmoudi, 1979: 172–173)

Masmoudi argued that there existed a 'flagrant quantitative imbalance between North and South created by the volume of news and information emanating from the developed world and intended for the developing countries and the volume of the flow in the opposite direction'.

He contended that gross inequalities also existed between developed and developing countries in the distribution of the radio-frequency spectrum as well as in the traffic of television programmes. He saw

a de facto hegemony and a will to dominate – evident in the marked indifference of the media in the developed countries, particularly in the West, to the problems, concerns and aspirations of the developing countries. Current events in the developing countries are reported to the world via the transnational media; at the same time, these countries are kept 'informed' of what is happening abroad through the same channels.

According to Masmoudi, 'by transmitting to developing countries only news processed by them, that is, news which they have filtered, cut, and distorted, the transnational media impose their own way of seeing the world upon the developing countries' (1979: 172–173).

These structural problems were also echoed by other scholars who viewed the Western-dominated, international information system, with its origins in the international news media network, as geared to Western economic and political interests and projecting their version of reality through these global networks to the rest of the world (Harris, 1981: 357–8).

The demands and proposals for NWICO emerged from a series of meetings of the Non-Aligned Movement, most notably Algiers in 1973 and Tunis in 1976 (Oledzki, 1981). A landmark was reached with the Mass Media Declaration by UNESCO General Conference in 1978, which recognized the role the mass media played in development, and in December of that year, the 33rd session of the United Nations General Assembly adopted a resolution on the New World Information and Communication Order (NWICO).

As a result, in 1979 the International Commission for the Study of Communication Problems, was set up. The MacBride Commission, as it was popularly known, submitted its final report to UNESCO in 1980, a document which, for the first time, brought information- and communication-related issues on the global agenda.

The MacBride Commission

The International Commission for the Study of Communication Problems that was established under the chairmanship of Sean MacBride by UNESCO occupies a prominent place in the debate regarding the establishment of a NWICO. The Commission report, commonly known as the MacBride Report, gave intellectual justification for evolving a new global communication order. For this reason the NWICO protagonists considered it to be a seminal document. The Commission was created in 1977 as a direct response to Resolution 100 of the 19th General Session of UNESCO held in Nairobi in 1976. The Commission took two years after going through one hundred working papers especially commissioned for it, to bring out one interim and a final report in 1980.

The Commission had the following 16 members: Sean MacBride, chairman (Ireland), Elie Abel (USA), Hubert Beuve-Mery (France), Elebe Ma Ekonzo (Zaire), Gabriel Garcia Marquez (Columbia), Mochtar Lubis (Indonesia), Mustapha Masmoudi (Tunisia), Betty Zimmerman (Canada), Michio Nagai (Japan), Fred Isaac Akporuaro Omu (Nigeria), Bogdan Osolnik (Yugoslavia), Gamal el Oteifi (Egypt), Johannes Pietar Pronk (the Netherlands), Juan Somavia (Chile), Boobli George Verghese (India), and Leonid Zamatin (USSR) (Zamatin was replaced by Sergei Losev during the study).

The Commission was established to study four main aspects of global communication: the current state of world communication; the problems surrounding a free and balanced flow of information and how the needs of the developing countries link with the flow; how, in light of the NIEO, a NWICO could be created, and how the media could become the vehicle for educating public opinion about world problems.

The interim report generated a good deal of controversy as it tended to legitimize the movement towards the establishment of a NWICO. It levelled charges against the Western wire services for their inadequate coverage of the Third World. The 100 background papers that the Commission prepared generated international interest in NWICO and helped provide insights into the various dimensions of the problems of global information system. This enriched the debate and raised its standard from mere rhetoric to more sophisticated criticism of international inequity in media relations.

Among its 82 recommendations that covered the entire gamut of global communication issues, the most innovative were those dealing with democratization of communication (MacBride Report, 1980: 191–233). The Commission agreed that democratization was impeded by undemocratic political systems, bureaucratic administrative systems, technologies controlled or understood only by a few, the exclusion of disadvantaged groups, and illiteracy and semi-literacy. To break through these barriers, the Commission recommended many steps, including:

> participation in media management by representatives of the public and various citizens groups, horizontal communication, counter-information and three forms of alternative communication: radical opposition, community or local media movements and trade unions or other social groups with their particular communication networks.

Following the UNESCO definition of 'a free flow and a wider and more balanced dissemination of information', the MacBride Report related freedom of the press to freedom of expression, to the rights to communicate and receive information, rights of reply and correction, and the civil political economic–social–cultural rights set forth in the UN's 1966 covenants. The MacBride Report pointed out that the freedom for the 'strong' and the 'haves' had had undesirable consequences for the 'weak' and the 'have nots'. It called for abolition of 'censorship or arbitrary control of information' asking for 'self-censorship by communicators themselves'. The report was critical of the constraints imposed by commercialization, pressures from advertisers and concentration of media ownership. It related the growth of transnational corporations to 'one way flow', 'market dominance' and 'vertical flow'.

It pointed out that some of the strongest transnational corporations, while vociferous for freedom for themselves, were reluctant to open up flows to share scientific and technological information. The Commission charged that under the guise of the free flow of information, some governments and transnational media had 'on occasion tried to undermine internal stability in other countries, violating their sovereignty and disturbed national development'.

The MacBride Report, which was hailed as 'the first international document that provides a really global view on the world's communication problems', received a mixed response. The protagonists of NWICO generally welcomed the report while the West criticized it. The World Press Freedom Committee (WPFC), consisting of journalistic organizations, including the International Federation of Journalists, AP, UPI and the American Newspaper Publishers Association (ANPA), was critical of what it considered to be the report's bias against private ownership of media and communication facilities and the 'problems created in a society by advertising' (Singh and Gross, 1981).

Following the submission of the report of the MacBride Commission, at the 21st General Conference Session of UNESCO held in Belgrade in 1980, a resolution for the attainment of a NWICO was passed, thereby formally approving the demand. The resolution proposed:

(i)   elimination of the imbalance and inequalities which characterise the present situation;

(ii)   elimination of the negative effects of certain monopolists, public or private, and excessive concentrations;

(iii) removal of the internal and external obstacles to a free flow and wider and better balanced dissemination of information and ideas;

(iv)   plurality of sources and channels of information;

(v)   freedom of the press and information;

(vi)   the freedom of journalists and all professionals in the communication media, a freedom inseparable from responsibility;

(vii) the capacity of developing countries to achieve improvement of their own situations, notably by providing their own equipment, by training their personnel, by improving their infrastructures and by making their information and communication media suitable to their needs and aspirations;

(viii) the sincere will of developed countries to help them attain these objectives;

(ix)   respect for each people's cultural identity and for the rights of each nation to inform the world public about its interests, its aspirations and its social and cultural values;

(x)   respect for the right of all peoples to participate in international exchange of information on the basis of equality, justice and mutual benefit;

(xi)   respect for the right of the public, of ethnic and social groups and of individuals to have access to information sources and to participate actively in the communication process.

(UNESCO, 1980)

Opposition to NWICO

The West, led by the USA, saw in the new order a 'Soviet-inspired' Third World design to control the mass media through state regulation. As a concept it was seen as one fundamentally in conflict with liberal Western values and the principle of the 'free flow of information'. The Western response was also affected by the Cold War assumptions which made them place the issues regarding the problems of global newsflow in the context of East–West rivalry.

The opponents of NWICO argued that the demand for NWICO was a pretext for Third World dictators to stifle media freedom, to impose censorship and keep away foreign journalists. Such slogans as 'cultural self-determination', 'media imperialism' and 'national sovereignty over a country's

communications', they argued, were designed to control channels of communication. The Western news organizations stoutly fought any change in
the old information order. They maintained that they were only reporting
the reality of life in the Third World – political instability, economic backwardness, human and natural disasters – and that this objective journalism
was disapproved of by undemocratic governments in the South.

Many Western observers claimed that UNESCO, the site of those heated
debates, was neglecting its true objectives by sponsoring this Third World
encroachment on international information and communication. Even the
MacBride Commission, which had members from both developed and
developing countries, was criticized for providing an intellectual justification for the reform of international communication (Righter, 1978; Jeffrey,
1978; Stevenson, 1988).

The comments of one US observer were typical of this: 'The administration's lack of vigorous opposition to the UNESCO/Soviet/Third World's
campaign for the total take-over of all means of communication is an indication that the US is abandoning its traditional values of freedom and opposition to totalitarianism' (Jeffrey, 1978: 67). The Western media viewed the
NWICO demands of 'national communication policies', 'national sovereignty over information' and 'democratisation of communications' as
'entailing too interventionist a role for the state and also as likely to result in
the exclusion of foreign journalists, with consequent restriction of information flows' (Wells, 1987: 27).

A closer scrutiny of the arguments against NWICO put forward by
Western governments and the media, reveals that the entire debate was seen
only in terms of the threat to the 'freedom of the Press' posed by Third
World governments under the new order. As Colleen Roach comments:

> To state that virtually every NWICO-related issue or subject ('social
> responsibility of the press', 'protection of journalists', 'right to com-
> municate', etc.) was reduced to the slogan of 'government control of
> the media' is no exaggeration. The reason for this strategy is not
> merely the US predilection for over-simplification of complex issues, or
> even the historical commitment to the First Amendment, although
> these factors are certainly not to be neglected. The emphasis on the
> 'government control' argument reflects, above all, the need to ensure
> that the NWICO would not reinforce government-run public sector
> communications media at the expense of the private sectors.
>
> (Roach, 1987: 38)

In the 1970s, when the superpower relations were relatively stable, the New
World Information and Communication Order was seen by Southern
leaders as an integral part of an ongoing North–South dialogue. Under
President Jimmy Carter, for whom defence of human rights was a matter of
personal commitment, the US administration appeared to take a favourable
view of the problems faced by developing countries. Facing opposition from

domestic conservative quarters, which found confusion and contradictions in Carter's human rights campaigns, limited progress was made in this North–South dialogue. However, the Carter administration played an important part in launching UNESCO's International Programme for the Development of Communications (IPDC). The fall of the Shah of Iran in 1979 as a result of anti-Western Islamic revolution, and the Soviet military intervention in Afghanistan in the same year, not only denied Carter a second term in office but also signified the abandonment of the North–South dialogue and the advent of the New Cold War.

NWICO and the New Cold War

Riding on a crest of Conservatism which thrived on anti-Soviet rhetoric, President Ronald Reagan redrafted the international agenda, dominated by ideas of a new phase in the Cold War. On the world stage, Margaret Thatcher's Conservative government in London became an important partner in this venture. The Reagan administration announced significant restrictions on development aid. 'Trade not Aid' became the catchword and the assistance that was provided was to be primarily bilateral and aimed at promoting developmental projects designed to build up the private sector in developing countries.

With regard to the information debate, which had gained momentum, the Reagan administration followed the same hardline policies. Reagan's tough line was responsible for cuts in the US allocation for various communication development programmes for the Third World undertaken by the IPDC. Under Reagan's presidency, the attacks on multilateral communication organizations, notably UNESCO, became more strident, culminating in the US withdrawal from the UN body in 1985, followed a year later by Britain. The USA opposed the MacBride Commission Report, arguing that it sought to give control of mass media to Southern governments. It would appear that the US decision was also influenced by business interests, as the memorandum of the State Department made clear: 'the divorce from UNESCO may well foster a greater willingness on the part of the US business and industry interests to support communications development projects' (Harley, 1984: 96).

Despite being the driving force behind IPDC, the USA tried to undermine the programme, demanding a greater freedom for US-based media and telecommunication corporations to explore Southern markets and help build privately owned communication infrastructure as opposed to government telecommunication monopolies (McPhail, 1987; Preston et al., 1989).

The fate of IPDC projects reflected a wider ideological shift under the Reagan–Thatcher era of right-wing governments in the 1980s, from a public service view of media and telecommunication to a privatized and deregulated industry. The 'free flow of information' doctrine, which had defined

US policy during the Cold War years received a new fillip with the neo-liberal ideology of the 'free market', expounded by ideologues such as Milton Friedman in the USA and Keith Joseph in Britain.

US communications policy during the Reagan years reflected the goals of US foreign policy. Reagan's self-proclaimed mission of fighting communism, enhanced by the US capacity to exercise control over the world information-communication order and its ability to disseminate a pro-American, anti-Soviet message globally, set the tone for an aggressive public diplomacy. In a sense, Reagan was repeating the 1950s' Cold War propaganda effort, when the American media were harnessed, together with the military–industrial complex, to give ideological justification to the US foreign policy. Thus, public diplomacy was geared to face the new communist threat and save the 'free world' from the encirclement of the Soviet Union. The International Information Committee (IIC) was established to 'plan, co-ordinate and implement international information activities in support of US policies and interests relative to national security'. Under the IIC, 'Project Truth' was set up, a campaign of an ideological war against the 'evil empire', an effort between the US Information Agency, the Departments of State and Defense and the CIA (Alexandre, 1993: 33).

In order to propagate this message abroad, the Reagan administration strengthened the Voice of America, as well as Radio Free Europe and Radio Liberty. The government started a $1.5 billion VOA modernisation pro-gramme: additional languages were included and its broadcasting hours were increased. One notable addition was the creation of Radio Marti, the VOA's daily broadcasting service to Cuba (Alexandre, 1993).

International communication at the end of the Cold War

If the East–West ideological battle characterized the Cold War years of inter-national communication, the fall of the Berlin Wall in 1989 and the break-up of the Soviet Union two years later, transformed the landscape of international politics, profoundly influencing global information and com-munication.

Television played an important role during the 1989 revolutions in Eastern Europe. (Ash, 1990), helping to bring the East–West ideological division of Europe to a close. The transition to capitalism was largely peaceful, except in Romania, where at least some of the violence was simu-lated. The 1989 Timisoara massacre in Romania was ostensibly staged for the world's TV cameras, in what the French sociologist Jean Baudrillard called, 'a hijacking of fantasies, affects and the credulity of hundreds of mil-lions of people by means of television' (1994: 69).

The August 1991 coup in Moscow, which led to the break-up of the Soviet Union, was called 'the first true media event in the history of the

Soviet Union'. The crisis had been 'profoundly and decisively shaped by the electronic eye that transformed instantly and continuously, elements of a political confrontation into meaningful scripts with their corresponding images, styles, and symbols' (Bonnell and Freidin, 1995: 44). Since the break-up of the Soviet Union, the media in the eastern bloc countries have gradually been converted to the market (Splichal, 1994; Mickiewicz, 1997).

The end of the Cold War, variously celebrated as the dawn of a 'new world order', as 'end of history' (Fukuyama, 1992) and even a 'clash of civilizations' (Huntington, 1993), profoundly changed the contours of international communication. The superpower rivalry had ended and the bipolar world, which had informed debates on international communication for half a century, suddenly had become unipolar, dominated by the remaining superpower, the United States.

Such Russian words as *glasnost* (openness) and *perestroika* (restructuring) entered the world's media vocabulary, representing a fundamental change in Moscow's thinking towards the entire gamut of international relations. The globalization of *glasnost* contributed to a greater openness in international communication, with Western journalists operating freely from behind the former iron curtain. The stridency of anti-Western rhetoric was also becoming muted in Moscow, while in the West, doubts were being raised about the relevance of Radio Free Europe and Radio Liberty (Elliot, 1988; Woll, 1989; *Time*, 1988).

This shift also affected debates on international information flows within UNESCO, which in the late 1980s, had lost its primacy as the key forum for discussing international communication issues. The focus of debate too had shifted from news and information flows to such areas as global telecommunication and transnational data flows. The Paris-based Organization for Economic Co-operation and Development (OECD), with its concern about transborder data flow and the International Telecommunication Union (ITU), through its Maitland Commission Report, and the IPDC, were becoming increasingly important international fora (Renaud, 1986). The Maitland Report, which symbolized the change in the traditional role of ITU from being a technical group to a more activist organization, gave higher priority to investment in telecommunication, especially telephones[2] (Ellinghaus and Forrester, 1985).

Another key contributing factor was the availability of new information technologies such as direct broadcasting satellites (DBS), fibre optics and microcomputers. The growing convergence between information and informatics – the combination of computer and telecommunication systems, traditionally dealt with as separate entities – made it essential to re-examine international communication in the light of technological innovations.

As the public ownership of state assets model, represented in its extreme form in the Soviet system, was dismantled, privatization became the new mantra, with the opening up of new markets in Eastern Europe and the former Soviet Union adding urgency to the privatisation project. The globalization of communication was made possible with the innovation of new information and communication technologies, increasingly integrated into a privatized global communication infrastructure. The 'time–space compression' that new technologies encouraged made it possible for media and telecommunication corporations to operate in a global market, part of an international neo-liberal capitalist system. As discussed in Chapter 3, the privatization of international communication industries became a major development of the 1990s, accelerated by the liberalization of global trade, under the auspices of the General Agreement on Tariffs and Trade (GATT).

Notes

1. The countries of Asia, Africa and Latin America were also the 'non-industrialized', 'underdeveloped' or 'developing countries'. The term 'the South' gained currency in the 1980s after the Brandt Commission report which defined 'the South' thus: 'in general terms, and although neither is a uniform or permanent grouping, "North" and "South" are broadly synonymous with "rich" and "poor," "developed" and "developing".' (Brandt Commission Report, 1981, p. 31). This division was later reinforced by the South Commission, adding, 'while countries of the North are, by and large, in control of their destinies, those of the South are very vulnerable to external factors and lacking in functioning sovereignty' (South Commission, 1990: 1).
2. The Independent Commission for World-wide Telecommunication Development, the 17-member commission headed by Sir Donald Maitland of the UK, was established in 1983 by the ITU to recommend ways to stimulate the expansion of global telecommunications. It submitted its report in 1985 (ITU, 1985).

2

Approaches to theorizing international communication

Theories have their own history and reflect the concerns of the time in which they were developed. This chapter examines some that offer ways of approaching the subject of international communication and assesses how useful their explanations are in terms of an understanding of the processes involved. This is by no means a comprehensive account of theories of communication (see McQuail, 1994; Mattelart and Mattelart, 1998), nor does it set out an all-embracing theorization of the subject, but looks at the key theories and their proponents, which together with the preceding chapter on the history of international communication, should help to contextualize the analysis of contemporary global communication systems in subsequent chapters.

It is not surprising that theories of communication began to emerge in parallel with the rapid social and economic changes of the Industrial Revolution in Europe, reflecting the significance of the role of communications in the growth of capitalism and empire, and drawing also on advances in science and the understanding of the natural world. One of the first concepts of communication, developed by the French philosopher Claude Henri de Saint Simon (1760–1825), used the analogy of the living organism, proposing that the development of a system of communication routes (roads, canals and railways) and a credit system (banks) was vital for an industrializing society and that the circulation of money, for example, was equivalent to that of blood for the human heart (Mattelart and Mattelart, 1998).

The metaphor of the organism was also fundamental for British philosopher Herbert Spenser (1820–1903), who argued that industrial society was the embodiment of an 'organic society', an increasingly coherent, integrated system, in which functions became more and more specified and parts more interdependent. Communication was seen as a basic component in a system of distribution and regulation. Like the vascular system, the physical network of roads, canals and railways ensured the distribution of nutrition, while the channels of information (the press, telegraph and postal service) functioned as the equivalent of the nervous system, making it possible for the centre to 'propagate its influence' to its outermost parts. 'Dispatches are compared to nervous discharges that communicate movement from an inhabitant of one city to that of another' (Mattelart and Mattelart, 1998: 9). At the same time, contemporary commentators were anxious about the social and cultural impact of the speed and reach of the new means of communication and the rise of a mass society fuelled and sustained by them.

In the twentieth century, theories of international communication evolved into a discrete discipline within the new social sciences and in each era have reflected contemporary concerns about political, economic and technological changes and their impact on society and culture. In the early twentieth century, during and after the First World War, a debate arose about the role of communication in propagating the competitive economic and military objectives of the imperial powers, exemplified in the work of Walter Lippmann on 'public opinion' (1922) and Harold Lasswell on wartime propaganda (1927). Lippmann's concerns were mainly about the manipulation of public opinion by powerful state institutions, while Lasswell, a political scientist, did pioneering work on the systematic analysis of propaganda activities.

After the Second World War, theories of communication multiplied in response to new developments in technology and media, first radio and, then television, and the increasingly integrated international economic and political system. Two broad though often interrelated approaches to theorizing communication can be discerned: the political-economy approach concerned with the underlying structures of economic and political power relations, and the perspectives of cultural studies, focusing mainly on the role of communication and media in the process of the creation and maintaining of shared values and meanings (Golding and Murdoch, 1997; During, 1999).

The political-economy approach has its roots in the critique of capitalism produced by the German philosopher, Karl Marx (1818–83), but it has evolved over the years to incorporate a wide range of critical thinkers. Central to a Marxian interpretation of international communication is the question of power, which ultimately is seen as an instrument of control by the ruling classes. In his seminal text, *German Ideology*, Marx described the relationship between economic, political and cultural power thus:

> The class which has the means of material production has control at the same time over the means of mental production so that, thereby, generally speaking, the ideas of those who lack the means of mental production are subject to it ... Insofar, therefore, as they rule as a class and determine the extent and compass of an epoch, it is self-evident that they ... among other things ... regulate the production and distribution of the ideas of their age: thus their ideas are the ruling ideas of the epoch.
>
> (cited in Murdoch and Golding, 1977: 12–13)

Much of the critical research on international communication has been an examination of the pattern of ownership and production in the media and communication industries, analysing these within the overall context of social and economic power relations, based on national and transnational class interests. Researchers working within the Marxist tradition were concerned, for example, with the commodification of communication hardware and software and its impact on inequalities of access to media technologies.

The influence on international communication of the growing literature of cultural studies, increasingly transnational in intent, if not yet in perspectives, grew significantly in the late twentieth century. Social-science analyses of mass communication have been enriched by concepts from the study of literature and the humanities. Cultural Studies, which started in Britain with the study of popular and mass culture and their role in the reproduction of social hegemony and inequality, is now more generally concerned with how media texts work to create meaning (on the basis of analysis of the texts themselves), and how culturally situated individuals work to gather meaning from texts (increasingly based on observation of media consumers). Cultural Studies' discovery of polysemic texts (the potential for readers to generate their own meanings) fitted well with a politically conservative era and the re-invigoration of liberal capitalism which accompanied it.

'Free flow of information'

After the Second World War and the establishment of a bi-polar world of free market capitalism and state socialism, theories of international communication became part of the new Cold War discourse. For the supporters of capitalism, the primary function of international communication was to promote democracy, freedom of expression and markets, while the Marxists argued for greater state regulation on communication and media outlets.

The concept of the 'free flow of information' reflected Western, and specifically US, antipathy to state regulation and censorship of the media and its use for propaganda by its communist opponents. The 'free flow' doctrine was essentially a part of the liberal, free market discourse that championed the rights of media proprietors to sell wherever and whatever they wished. As most of the world's media resources and media-related capital, then as now, were concentrated in the West, it was the media proprietors in Western countries, their governments and national business communities that had most to gain.

The concept of 'free flow' therefore served both economic and political purposes. Media organizations of the media-rich countries could hope to dissuade others from erecting trade barriers to their products or from making it difficult to gather news or make programmes on their territories. Their argument drew on premises of democracy, freedom of expression, the media's role as 'public watchdog' and their assumed global relevance. For their compatriot businessmen, 'free flow' assisted them in advertising and marketing their goods and services in foreign markets, through media vehicles whose information and entertainment products championed the Western way of life and its values of capitalism and individualism.

For Western governments, 'free flow' helped to ensure the continuing and unreciprocated influence of Western media on global markets, strengthening the West in its ideological battle with the Soviet Union. The doctrine also contributed to providing, in generally subtle rather than direct ways, vehicles for communication of US government points of view to international audience (UNESCO, 1982; Mosco, 1996; Mowlana, 1997).

Modernization theory

Complementary to the doctrine of 'free flow' in the post-war years was the view that international communication was the key to the process of modernization and development for the so-called 'Third World'. Modernization theory arose from the notion that international mass communication could be used to spread the message of modernity and transfer the economic and political models of the West to the newly independent countries of the South. Communications research on what came to be known as 'modernization' or 'development theory' was based on the belief that the mass media would help transform traditional societies. This pro-media bias was very influential and received support from international organizations such as UNESCO and by the governments in developing countries.

One of the earliest exponents of this theory was Daniel Lerner, a political science professor at the Massachusetts Institute of Technology, whose classic work in the field, *The Passing of Traditional Society* (1958) – the product of research conducted in the early 1950s in Turkey, Lebanon, Egypt, Syria, Jordan and Iran – examined the degree to which people in the Middle East were exposed to national and international media, especially radio. In this first major comparative survey, Lerner proposed that contact with the media helped the process of transition from a 'traditional' to a 'modernized' state, characterizing the mass media as a 'mobility multiplier', which enables individuals to experience events in far-off places, forcing them to reassess their traditional way of life. Exposure to the media, Lerner argued, made traditional societies less bound by traditions and made them aspire to a new and modern way of life.

The Western path of 'development' was presented as the most effective way to shake off traditional 'backwardness': according to Lerner:

> [The] Western model of modernisation, exhibits certain components and sequences whose relevance is global. Everywhere for example increasing urbanisation has tended to raise literacy; rising literacy has

tended to increase media exposure; increasing media exposure has 'gone with' wider economic participation (per capita income) and political participation.

(Lerner, 1958: 46)

Western society, Lerner argued, provided 'the most developed model of societal attributes (power, wealth, skill, rationality)', and 'from the West came the stimuli which undermined traditional society that will operate efficiently in the world today, the West is still a useful model' (ibid.: 47).

Another key modernization theorist Wilbur Schramm, whose influential book, *Mass Media and National Development,* was published in 1964 in conjunction with UNESCO, saw the mass media as a 'bridge to a wider world', as the vehicle for transferring new ideas and models from the North to the South and, within the South, from urban to rural areas. Schramm, at the time Director of the Institute for Communication Research at Stanford University, California, noted:

the task of the mass media of information and the 'new media' of education is to speed and ease the long, slow social transformation required for economic development, and, in particular, to speed and smooth the task of modernising human resources behind the national effort.

(Schramm, 1964: 27)

Schramm endorsed Lerner's view that mass media can raise the aspirations of the peoples in developing countries. The mass media in the South, he wrote, 'face the need to rouse their people from fatalism and a fear of change. They need to encourage both personal and national aspirations. Individuals must come to desire a better life than they have and to be willing to work for it' (ibid. 1964: 130).

The timing of Schramm's book was significant. The UN had proclaimed the 1960s as 'the Decade of Development' and UN agencies and Western governments, led by the USA, were generously funding research, often in conjunction with private companies, through universities and development bureaucracy, notably the newly established United States Agency for International Development (USAID), the United States Information Agency (USIA), and the Peace Corps, to harness the power of the mass media to 'modernize' the newly independent countries of the South.

In the 1970s, modernization theorists started to use the level of media development as an indicator of general societal development. Leading theorists of the 'development as modernization' school, such as Everett Rogers, saw a key role for the mass media in international communication and development (Rogers, 1962; Pye, 1963). Such research benefited from the surveys undertaken by various US-government-funded agencies and educational foundations, especially in Asia and Latin America for what Rogers (1962) called 'disseminating innovations'.

This top-down approach to communications, a one-way flow of information from government or international development agencies via the mass media to Southern peasantry at the bottom, was generally seen as a panacea for the development of the newly independent countries of Asia and Africa. But it was predicated on a definition of development that followed the model of Western industrialization and 'modernization', measured primarily by the rate of economic growth of output or Gross National Product (GNP). It failed to recognize that the creation of wealth on its own was insufficient: the improvement of life for the majority of the populations depended on the equitable distribution of that wealth and its use for the public good. It also failed to ask questions like development for whom and who would gain or lose, ignoring any discussion of the political, social, or cultural dimensions of development In many Southern countries, income disparities in fact increased over the succeeding thirty years – despite a growth in GNP.

Moreover, the mass media were assumed to be a neutral force in the process of development, ignoring how the media are themselves products of social, political, economic and cultural conditions. In many developing countries economic and political power was and remains restricted to a tiny, often unrepresentative, elite, and the mass media play a key role in legitimizing the political establishment. Since the media had, and continue to have, close proximity to the ruling elites, they tend to reflect this view of development in the news.

The international communication research inspired by the modernization thesis was very influential, shaping university communication programmes and research centres globally. Though such research provided huge amount of data on the behaviour, attitudes and values of the people in the South, it tended to work within the positivist tradition of what sociologist Paul Lazarsfeld (1941) had long identified as 'administrative' research, often failing to analyse the political and cultural context of international communication.

However, the outcomes of this type of research in international communication can be useful in analysing the relationship of media growth to economic development, measured in terms of such indicators as sales of communication hardware and gross national product. They are also useful in international promotion of advertising and marketing.

It is important to understand the Cold War context in which modernization theory emerged, a time when it was politically expedient for the West to use the notion of modernization to bring the newly independent nations of Asia, the Middle East and Africa into the sphere of capitalism. As Vincent Mosco comments: 'The theory of modernisation meant a reconstruction of the international division of labour amalgamating the non-Western world into the emerging international structural hierarchy' (1996: 121). It is now being accepted that some of modernization research was politically motivated. It has been pointed out that Lerner's seminal study was a spin-off from a large and clandestine government-funded audience research project, conducted for the Voice of America by the Bureau of Applied Social Research (Samarajiva, 1985).

Despite its enormous influence in the field of international communication, Lerner's research had more to do with the East–West ideological contest of those days of Cold War, when in the Middle East radical voices were demanding decolonization – Iran had nationalized its oil industry in 1951, leading to the CIA-backed coup, two years later, which removed the democratically elected Prime Minister Mohammed Musaddiq. Given the prominence of radio propaganda during the 1950s, this research could also be seen as an investigation of radio listening behaviour in a region bordering the Soviet Union. In this context it is interesting to note that Lerner had worked for the Psychological Warfare Division of the US Army during the Second World War.

One major shortcoming of the early modernization theorists was their assumption that the modern and the traditional lifestyles were mutually exclusive, and their dismissive view of the culture of the 'indigent natives' led them to believe in the desirability and inevitability of a shift from the traditional to the modern. The dominant cultural and religious force in the region – Islam – and a sense of collective pan-Islamic identity were seen as 'sentimental sorties into the symbolism of a majestic past'. The elites in the region had to choose between 'Mecca or mechanisation'. The crux of the matter, Lerner argued, was 'not whether, but how one should move from traditional ways toward modern life-styles. The symbols of race and ritual fade into irrelevance when they impede living desires for bread and enlightenment' (Lerner, 1958: 405).

What modernizers such as Lerner failed to comprehend was that the dichotomy of modern versus traditional was not inevitable. Despite all the West's efforts at media modernization, Islamic traditions continue to define the Muslim world, and indeed have become stronger in parts of the Middle East. In addition, these cultures can also use modern communication methods to put their case across. In the 1979 Islamic revolution in Iran, for example, radical groups produced printed material and audiocassettes and distributed them through informal networks to promote an anti-Western ideology based on a particular Islamic view of the world (Mohammadi and Sreberny-Mohammadi, 1994).

In Latin America most communication research, often funded by the US government, was led by proponents of the modernization thesis. However, since the gap between the rich and poor was growing, as elsewhere in the developing world, critics started to question the validity of the developmentalist project and raised questions about what it left out – the relationship between communication, power and knowledge and the ideological role of international organizational and institutional structures. This led to a critique of modernization in Latin America, most notably from Brazil's Paulo Freire, whose *Pedagogy of the Oppressed* (1970) had a major influence on international development discourse, though how far his views were adopted in devising international communication strategies remains an open question.

Southern scholars, especially those from Latin America, argued that the chief beneficiaries of modernization programmes were not the 'traditional' rural poor in the South but Western media and communication companies, which had expanded into the Third World, ostensibly in the name of modernization and development, but in fact in search of new consumers for their products. They argued that modernization programmes were exacerbating the already deep social and economic inequalities in the developing countries and making them dependent on Western models of communication development.

Partly as a result of the work of Latin American scholars, the proponents of modernization in the West acknowledged that the theory needed reformulation. Despite decades of 'modernization', the vast majority of the people in the South continued to live in poverty, and by the mid-1970s the talk was of the 'passing of the dominant paradigm' (Rogers, 1976). In a revised version of modernization theory, a shift has been detectable from support for the mass media to an almost blind faith in the potential of the new information and communication technologies – in what has been called 'a neo-developmentalist view' (Mosco, 1996: 130). Also noticeable is the acceptance of a greater role for local elites in the modernization process. However, the importance of Western technology remains crucial in the revised version too. According to this view, modernization requires advanced telecommunication and computer infrastructure, preferably through the 'efficient' private corporations, thus integrating the South into a globalized information economy.

Dependency theory

Dependency theory emerged in Latin America in the late 1960s and 1970s, partly as a consequence of the political situation in the continent, with increasing US support for right-wing authoritarian governments, and partly with the realization among the educated elite that the developmentalist approach to international communication had failed to deliver. The establishment, in 1976, in Mexico City of the Instituto Latinamericano de Estudios (ILET), whose principal research interest was the study of transnational media business, gave an impetus to a critique of the 'modernization' thesis, documenting its negative consequences in the continent. The impact of ILET was also evident in international policy debates about NWICO, particularly through the work of Juan Somavia, a member of the MacBride Commission.

Though grounded in the neo-Marxist political-economy approach (Baran, 1957; Gunder Frank, 1969; Amin 1976), dependency theorists aimed to provide an alternative framework to analyse international communication. Central to dependency theory was the view that transnational corporations (TNCs), most based in the North, exercise control, with the support of their respective governments, over the developing countries by setting the terms for global trade – dominating markets, resources, production, and labour. Development for these countries was shaped in a way to strengthen the dominance of the developed nations and to maintain the 'peripheral' nations in a position of dependence – in other words, to make conditions suitable for 'dependent development'. In its most extreme form the outcome of such relationship was 'the development of underdevelopment' (Gunder Frank, 1969).

This neo-colonial relationship in which the TNCs controlled both the terms of exchange and the structure of global markets, it was argued, had contributed to the widening and deepening of inequality in the South while the TNCs had strengthened their control over the world's natural and human resources (Baran, 1957; Mattelart, 1979).

The cultural aspects of dependency theory, examined by scholars interested in the production, distribution and consumption of media and cultural products, were particularly relevant to the study of international communication. The dependency theorists aimed to show the links between discourses of 'modernization' and the policies of transnational media and communication corporations and their backers among Western governments.

Dependency theorists both benefited from, and contributed to, research on cultural aspects of imperialism being undertaken at the time in the USA. The idea of cultural imperialism is most clearly identified with the work of Herbert Schiller, who was based at the University of California (1969/92). Working within the neo-Marxist critical tradition, Schiller analysed the global power structures in the international communication industries and the links between transnational business and the dominant states.

At the heart of Schiller's argument was the analysis of how, in pursuit of commercial interests, huge US-based transnational corporations, often in league with Western (predominantly US) military and political interests, were undermining the cultural autonomy of the countries of the South and creating a dependency on both the hardware and software of communication and media in the developing countries. Schiller defined cultural imperialism as:

> the sum of the processes by which a society is brought into the modern world system and how its dominating stratum is attracted, pressured, forced, and sometimes bribed into shaping social institutions to correspond to, or even to promote, the values and structures of the dominant centre of the system.
>
> (Schiller, 1976: 9)

Schiller argued that the declining European colonial empires – mainly British, French and Dutch – were being replaced by a new emergent American empire, based on US economic, military and informational power.

According to Schiller, the US-based TNCs have continued to grow and dominate the global economy. This economic growth has been underpinned with communications know-how, enabling US business and military organizations to take leading roles in the development and control of new electronically-based global communication systems.

Such domination had both military and cultural implications. Schiller's seminal work, *Mass Communications and American Empire* (1969/1992), examined the role of the US government, a major user of communication services, in developing global electronic media systems, initially for military purposes to counter the perceived, and often exaggerated, Soviet security threat. By controlling global satellite communications, the USA had the most effective surveillance system in operation – a crucial element in the Cold War years. Such communication hardware could also be used to propagate the US model of commercial broadcasting, dominated by large networks and funded primarily by advertising revenue.

> Nothing less than the viability of the American industrial economy itself is involved in the movement toward international commercialisation of broadcasting. The private yet managed economy depends on advertising. Remove the excitation and the manipulation of consumer demand and industrial slowdown threatens.
>
> (Schiller, 1969: 95)

According to Schiller, dependence on US communications technology and investment, coupled with the new demand for media products, necessitated large-scale imports of US media products, notably television programmes. Since media exports are ultimately dependent on sponsors for advertising, they endeavour not only to advertise Western goods and services, but also promote, albeit indirectly, a capitalist 'American way of life', through mediated consumer lifestyles. The result was an 'electronic invasion', especially in the global South, which threatened to undermine traditional cultures and emphasize consumerism at the expense of community values.

US dominance of global communication increased during the 1990s with the end of the Cold War and the failure of the UNESCO-supported demands for NWICO, Schiller argued in the 1992 revised edition of the book. The economic basis of US dominance, however, had changed, with TNCs acquiring an increasingly important role in international relations, transforming US cultural imperialism into 'transnational corporate cultural domination' (Schiller, 1992: 39).

In a recent review of the US role in international communication during the past half-century, Schiller saw the US state still playing a decisive role in promoting the ever-expanding communication sector, a central pillar of the US economy. In US support for the promotion of electronic-based media and communication hardware and software in the new information age of the twenty-first century, Schiller found 'historical continuities in its quest for systemic power and control,' of global communication (1998: 23).

Other prominent works employing what has come to be known as 'the cultural imperialism thesis' have examined such diverse aspects of US cultural and media dominance as Hollywood's relationship with the European movie market (Guback, 1969); US television exports and influences in Latin America (Wells, 1972); the contribution of Disney comics in promoting capitalist values (Dorfman and Mattelart, 1975) and the role of the advertising industry as an ideological instrument (Ewen, 1976; Mattelart, 1991). Internationally, some of the most significant work has been the UNESCO-supported research on international flow in television programmes (Nordenstreng and Varis, 1974; Varis, 1985).

One prominent aspect of dependency in international communication was identified in the 1970s by Oliver Boyd-Barrett as 'media imperialism', examining information and media inequalities between nations and how these reflect broader issues of dependency, and analysing the hegemonic power of mainly US-dominated international media – notably news agencies, magazines, films, radio and television. Boyd-Barrett defined media imperialism as:

> The process whereby the ownership, structure, distribution or content of the media in any one country are singly or together subject to substantial external pressures from the media interests of any other country or countries, without proportionate reciprocation of influence by the country so affected.
>
> (1977: 117)

For its critics, dependency literature was 'notable for an absence of clear definitions of fundamental terms like imperialism and an almost total lack of empirical evidence to support the arguments' (Stevenson, 1988: 38). Others argued that it ignored the question of media form and content as well as the role of the audience. Those involved in a cultural studies approach to the analysis of international communication argued that, like other cultural artefacts, media 'texts' could be polysemic and were amenable to different interpretations by audiences who were not merely passive consumers but 'active' participants in the process of negotiating meaning (Fiske, 1987). It was also pointed out that the 'totalistic' cultural imperialism thesis did not adequately take on board such issues as how global media texts worked in national contexts, ignoring local patterns of media consumption.

Quantifying the volume of US cultural products distributed around the world was not a sufficient explanation, it was also important to examine its effects. There was also a view that cultural imperialism thesis assumed a 'hypodermic-needle model' of media effects and ignored the complexities of 'Third World' cultures (Sreberny-Mohammadi, 1991; 1997). It was argued that the Western scholars had a less than deep understanding of Third World cultures, seeing them as homogeneous and not being adequately aware of the regional and intra-national diversities of race, ethnicity, language, gender and class. However, there have yet been few systematic studies of the cultural and ideological effects of Western media products on audiences in the South, especially from Southern scholars.

Despite its share of criticism (Tomlinson, 1991; Thompson, 1995), the cultural imperialism thesis was very influential in international communication research in the 1970s and 1980s. It was particularly important during the heated NWICO debates in UNESCO and other international fora in the 1970s. However, even a critic such as John Thompson, while rejecting the main thesis, has conceded that such research is 'probably the only systematic and moderately plausible attempt to think about the globalisation of communications and its impact on the modern world' (Thompson, 1995: 173).

Defenders of the thesis found the 1990s' debates criticizing cultural imperialism 'lacking even the most elementary epistemological precaution and sometimes actually bordering on intellectual dishonesty', arguing that the critics of this theory have often 'taken the notion out of context, abstracting it from the concrete historical conditions that produced it: the political struggles and commitments of the 1960s and 1970s' (Mattelart and Mattelart, 1998: 137–8).

With changes in debates on international communication reflecting the rhetoric of privatization and liberalization in the 1990s, theories of media and cultural dependency have become less prominent. However, Boyd-Barrett has argued that while media imperialism theory, in its original formulation, did not take into account intra-national media relations, gender and ethnic issues, it is still a useful analytical tool to make sense of what he terms as the 'colonisation of communications space' (Boyd-Barrett, 1998: 157).

One of the limits of the cultural and media imperialism approach is that it did not fully take into account the role of the national elites, especially in the developing world. However, though its influence has dwindled, the theory of structural imperialism developed by the Norwegian sociologist Johan Galtung, also offers an explanation of the role of international communication in maintaining structures of economic and political power.

Structural imperialism

Galtung argues that the world consists of developed 'centre' states and underdeveloped 'periphery' states. In turn, each centre and periphery state possesses a 'core' – a highly developed area – and a less developed 'periphery'. He defines structural imperialism as a 'sophisticated type of dominance relation which cuts across nations basing itself on a bridgehead which the centre of the centre nation establishes in the centre of the periphery nation for the joint benefit of both'. For Galtung, there is a harmony of interest between the core of the centre nation and the centre in the periphery nation; less harmony of interest within the periphery nation than within the centre nation and a disharmony of interest between the periphery of the centre nation and the periphery of the periphery nation (Galtung, 1971: 83).

In other words, there exists in the countries of the South a dominant elite whose interests coincide with the interests of the elite in the developed world. This 'core' thus not only provides a bridgehead by which the centre nation can maintain its economic and political domination over the periphery nation, but is also supported by the centre in maintaining its dominance over its own periphery. In terms of values and attitudes, the elite group is closer to other elites in the developed world than with groups in their own country.

Galtung defines five types of imperialism that depend upon the type of exchange between centre and periphery nations: economic, political, military, communication and cultural. The five types form a syndrome of imperialism, and interact, albeit through different channels, to reinforce the dominance relationship of centre over periphery. Communication imperialism is intimately related to cultural imperialism and news is a combination of cultural and communication exchange (Galtung, 1971: 93).

Periphery–centre relationships are maintained and reinforced by information flows and through the reproduction of economic activities. These create institutional links that serve the interests of the dominant groups, both in the centre and within the periphery. Institutions in the centre of the periphery often mirror those of the developed world and thus recreate and promote the latter's value systems.

According to Galtung, the basic mechanism of structural imperialism revolves around two forms of interaction, 'vertical' and 'feudal'. The 'vertical' interaction principle maintains that relationships are asymmetrical; that the flow of power is from the more developed state to the less developed state, while the benefits of the system flow upwards from the less developed states to the centre states. The 'feudal' interaction principle states that there 'is interaction along the spokes, from the periphery to the centre hub; but not along the rim, from one periphery nation to another' (Galtung, 1971: 89).

The feudal interaction structure reinforces the inequalities produced by the vertical interaction structures. Communication and information flow from the centre to the periphery and back again: for example, Southern states receive information about the North but little information about fellow developing countries.

Galtung's theory maintains that communication imperialism is based on the feudal interaction structure in which the periphery states are tied to the centre in particular ways. Information flows from different core states in different proportions, determined by capital and trade flows, as well as historical, colonial ties.

According to Galtung, the pattern of news flow exhibits these vertical and feudal patterns: news flows from the core to the periphery via the transnational news agencies, while journalists gather information in Southern countries that is eventually retransmitted via the agencies. The effect of this feudal structure is that Southern nations know virtually nothing about events in neighbouring countries that has not been filtered through the lenses of the developed media systems.

The theory argues that if the core actors are defining news according to the criteria and demand for news in the developed world market, then the demand for and criteria of news will be similar in the centre of the peripheral nation. This has been called the 'agenda-setting function' of the international media. Information is transferred to the Southern elite in such a way that primary importance is attached to the same issues the developed world sees as important. The identity of interests between the centre of the centre and the centre of the periphery greatly influences the acceptance of an international agenda and thus Galtung's theory is particularly relevant in understanding global news flow.

A striking similarity can be found in Galtung's theory of structural imperialism with Schiller's definition of cultural imperialism. Both maintain that the structure of political and economic domination exercised by the centre over the periphery results in the re-creation of certain aspects of the centre's value system in the periphery.

There is also evidence of a dependency relationship in the field of media and communication research in Southern countries. As British media analyst James Halloran notes:

> Wherever we look in international communication research – exports and imports of textbooks, articles and journals; citations, references and footnotes; employment of experts (even in international agencies); and the funding, planning and execution of research – we are essentially looking at a dependency situation. This is a situation which is characterised by a one-way flow of values, ideas, models, methods and resources from North to South. It may even be more specifically as a flow from the Anglo-Saxon language fraternity to the rest of the world.
>
> (1997: 39)

Dependency theory has enjoyed widespread influence and equally widespread criticism. It was criticized for concentrating on the impact of transnational business and the role of other external forces on social and economic development to the neglect of internal class, gender, ethnic and power relations. Theorists such as Galtung responded by examining the roles of the often unrepresentative elites in the South in maintaining and indeed benefiting from the dependency syndrome. While the globalization of new information and communication technologies and the resultant wiring up of the globe, and the emphasis on cultural hybridization rather than cultural imperialism, have made dependency theories less fashionable, the structural inequalities in international communication continue to render them relevant.

Another concern for scholars working within the political economy approach has been to analyse the close relationship between media and foreign policy. The role of the mass media as an instrument of propaganda for corporate and state power has been an important area of inquiry among critical scholars (Herman and Chomsky, 1988/1994). In their 'propaganda model' US economist, Edward Herman, and the renowned linguist, Noam Chomsky, examine through a range of detailed case studies, how news in mainstream US media system passes through several 'filters', including the size, concentrated ownership and profit orientation of media firms; their heavy reliance on advertising and dependence on business and governmental sources for information; and the overall dominant ideology within which they operate. These elements, write Herman and Chomsky, 'interact with and reinforce one another and set the premises of discourse and interpretation, and the definition of what is newsworthy' (1994: 2).

For Herman and Chomsky, a propaganda approach to media coverage suggests:

> a systematic and highly political dichotomisation in news coverage based on serviceability to important domestic power interests. This should be observable in dichotomised choices of story and in the volume and quality of coverage ... such dichotomisation in the mass media is massive and systematic: not only are choices for publicity and suppression comprehensible in terms of system advantage, but the modes of handling favoured and inconvenient materials (placement, tone, context, fullness of treatment) differ in ways that serve political interests'.
>
> (ibid.: 35)

Despite meticulously researched case studies – ranging from the US media's coverage of the war in Vietnam in the 1960s and 1970s, to its treatment of US involvement in subversive activities in Central America during the 1980s – the propaganda model has received more than its share of criticism, especially in the West. Internationally, however, *Manufacturing Consent*, a title borrowed from a phrase used by Lippmann in a 1922 publication, had a profound influence. Though criticized for its 'polemical' style, the book remains one of the few systematic and detailed studies of the politics of mass media.

Hegemony

By arguing that the propaganda model succeeds because there is no significant overt coercion from the state, Herman and Chomsky, in some ways, were following the European analyses of the role of ideology and state power in a capitalist society, articulated by, among others, the French Marxist Louis Althusser who called the media 'ideological state apparatus' (1971).

Another major influence on critical theorists as well as on cultural critics in the study of ideology is the writings of Italian Marxist Antonio Gramsci

(1891–1937). The impact of the ideas of Gramsci, who died in prison under the Fascist regime, has been widespread in critical studies of international communication. However, it was not until the translation into English of his most famous work, *Selections from the Prison Notebooks*, in 1971, that Gramsci's ideas became a major influence in the Anglo-Saxon world.

Gramsci's conception of hegemony is rooted in the notion that the dominant social group in a society has the capacity to exercise intellectual and moral direction over society at large and to build a new system of social alliances to support its aims. Gramsci argued that military force was not necessarily the best instrument to retain power for the ruling classes, but that a more effective way of wielding power was to build a consent by ideological control of cultural production and distribution.

According to Gramsci, such a system exists when a dominant social class exerts moral and intellectual leadership – through its control of such institutions as schools, religious bodies and the mass media – over both allied and subordinate classes. Social and intellectual authority is exercised by the government 'with the consent of the governed – but with this consent organised, and not generic and vague' in such a fashion that its right to govern is rarely challenged seriously. The 'state does have and request consent but it also "educates" this consent' (Gramsci, 1971).

One of the most important functions of the state, Gramsci wrote in his *Prison Notebooks*, 'is to raise the great mass of the population to a particular cultural and moral level, a level (or type) which corresponds to the needs of the productive forces for development, and hence to the interests of the ruling classes'. Schools, courts and a multitude of 'initiatives and activities ... form the apparatus of the political and cultural hegemony of the ruling classes' (Gramsci, 1971: 258–9). This, he argued, was in contrast with a situation in which the dominant class merely rules, that is, coercively imposes its will on subordinate classes. This consent thus manufactured, however, cannot simply be assumed or guaranteed and has to be renewed, indicating that hegemony is more of a process – which is to be continually reproduced, secured and lost – rather than an achieved state of affairs.

In international communication, the notion of hegemony is widely used to conceptualize political functions of the mass media, as a key player in propagating and maintaining the dominant ideology and also to explain the process of media and communication production, with dominant ideology shaping production of news and entertainment (Hallin, 1994). Thus, though the media are notionally free from direct government control, yet they act as agents of legitimization of the dominant ideology.

Critical theory

Among the substantial body of research undertaken by the Frankfurt School theorists, the concept of the 'culture industry', first used by Adorno and

Horkheimer in a book entitled *Dialectic of Enlightenment* written in 1944 and published in 1947, has received the widest international attention. Identified with the staff of the Institute for Social Research, founded in 1923 and affiliated with the University of Frankfurt, its key members included Max Horkheimer (1895–1973), Theodor Adorno (1903–69) and Herbert Marcuse (1898–1979).

Analysing the industrial production of cultural goods – films, radio programmes, music and magazines, etc. – as a global movement, they argued that in capitalist societies the trend was towards producing culture as a commodity (Adorno, 1991). Adorno and Horkheimer believed that cultural products manifested the same kind of management practices, technological rationality and organizational schemes as the mass-produced industrial goods such as cars. This 'assembly-line character', they argued, could be observed in 'the synthetic, planned method of turning out its products (factory-like not only in the studio but, more or less, in the compilation of cheap biographies, pseudo-documentary novels, and hit songs)' (Adorno and Horkheimer, 1979 [1947]: 163).

Such industrial production led to standardization, resulting in a mass culture made up of a series of objects bearing the stamp of the culture industry. This industrially produced and commodified culture, it was argued, led to a deterioration of the philosophical role of culture. Instead, this mediated culture contributed to the incorporation of the working classes into the structures of advanced capitalism and in limiting their horizons to political and economic goals that could be realized within the capitalist system without challenging it. The critical theorists argued that the development of the 'culture industry' and its ability to ideologically inoculate the masses against socialist ideas benefited the ruling classes.

Marrying the psychoanalytical theories of Sigmund Freud with Marxian economic analysis, the critical theorists borrowed the notion of commodification from Marx, who had argued that objects are commodified by acquiring an exchange value instead of their intrinsic value. In their analysis of cultural products, they argued that in a capitalist economy cultural products are produced and sold in media markets as commodities and the consumers buy them not just because of their intrinsic worth but in exchange for entertainment or to fulfil their psychological needs.

The concentration of ownership of cultural production in a few producers resulted in a standardized commercial commodity, contributing to what they called a 'mass culture' – influenced by the mass media and one which thrived on the market rules of supply and demand. In their view, such a process undermined the critical engagement of masses with important socio-political issues and ensured a politically passive social behaviour and the subordination of the working classes to the ruling elite.

Marcuse, who migrated to the USA where he had a huge influence on the labour movement, argued that technological rationality or instrumental reason had reduced speech and thought to a single dimension, establishing what he called a 'one-dimensional society' which had abolished the distance required for critical thought. One of the most incisive chapters of Marcuse's book *One Dimensional Man* (1964), discusses 'one-dimensional language' and frequently refers to media discourse.

In an international context the idea of 'mass culture' and media and cultural industries has influenced debates about the flow of information between countries. The issue of the commodification of culture is present in many analyses of the operation of book publishing, film and popular music industries. One indication of this was the 1982 UNESCO report which argued that cultural industries in the world were greatly influenced by the major media and communication companies and were being continually corporatized. The expansion of mainly Western-based cultural products globally had resulted, it argued, in the gradual 'marginalisation of cultural messages that do not take the form of goods, primarily of values as marketable commodities' (UNESCO, 1982: 10).

This emphasis on ownership and control of the means of cultural production and the argument that it directly shapes the activities of artists has been contested by several writers, arguing that creativity and cultural consumption can be independent of production cycles and that the production process itself is not as organised or rigidly standardized as stated by the Frankfurt School theorists.

The public sphere

A natural heir to the critical theorists, the German sociologist Jürgen Habermas (born 1929) also lamented the standardization, massification and atomization of the public. Habermas developed the concept of the public sphere in one of his earliest books, though it was 27 years before it appeared in English translation as *The Structural Transformation of the Public Sphere: An Inquiry into a Category of Bourgeois Society*, in 1989. He defined the public sphere as

> an arena, independent of government (even if in receipt of state funds) and also enjoying autonomy from partisan economic forces, which is dedicated to rational debate (i.e. to debate and discussion which is not 'interests', 'disguised' or 'manipulated') and which is both accessible to entry and open to inspection by the citizenry. It is here, in this public sphere, that public opinion is formed.
>
> (quoted in Holub, 1991: 2–8)

Habermas argued that the 'bourgeois public sphere' emerged in an expanding capitalist society exemplified by eighteenth-century Britain, where entrepreneurs were becoming powerful enough to achieve autonomy from state and church and increasingly demanding wider and more effective political representation to facilitate expansion of their businesses. In his formulation of a public sphere, Habermas gave prominence to the role of information, as, at this time, a greater freedom of the press was fought for and achieved with parliamentary reform. The wider availability of printing facilities and the resultant reduction in production costs of newspapers stimulated debate contributing to what Habermas calls 'rational-acceptable policies', which led by the mid-nineteenth century to the creation of a 'bourgeois public sphere'.

This idealized version of a public space was characterized by greater accessibility of information, a more open debate within the bourgeoisie, a space independent of both business interests and state apparatus. However, as capitalism expanded and attained dominance, the call for reform of the state was replaced by an effort to take it over to further business interests. As commercial interests became prominent in politics and started exerting their influence – for example, by lobbying parliament, funding political parties and cultural institutions – the autonomy of the public sphere was severely reduced.

In the twentieth century, the growing power of information management and manipulation through public relations and lobbying firms has contributed to making contemporary debates a 'faked version' of a genuine public sphere (Habermas, 1989: 195). In this 'refeudalization' of the public sphere, public affairs have become occasions for 'displays' of power in the style of medieval feudal courts rather than a space for debate on socio-economic issues.

Habermas also detects refeudalization in the changes within the mass media systems, which have become monopoly capitalist organizations, promoting capitalist interests, and thus affecting their role as disseminators of information for the public sphere. In a market-driven environment, the over-riding concern for media corporations is to produce an artefact which will appeal to the widest possible variety of audiences and thus generate maximum advertising revenue. It is essential, therefore, that the product is diluted in content to meet the lowest common denominator – sex, scandal, celebrity lifestyles, action adventure and sensationalism. Despite their negligible informational quality such media products reinforce the audience's acceptance of 'the soft compulsion of constant consumption training' (Habermas, 1989: 192).

Though the idealized version of the public sphere has been criticized for its very male, Eurocentric and bourgeois limitations, the public sphere provides a useful concept in understanding democratic potential for communication processes (Calhoun, 1992; Dahlgren, 1995). In recent years, with the globalization of the media and communication, there has been talk about the evolution of a 'global public sphere' where issues of international significance – environment, human rights, gender and ethnic equality – can be articulated through the mass media, though the validity of such a concept is also contested (Sparks, 1998).

Cultural Studies perspectives on international communication

While much of the debate on international communication post-1945 and during the Cold War emphasized a structural analysis of its role in political and economic power relationships, there has been a discernible shift in research emphasis in the 1990s in parallel with the 'depoliticitization' of politics towards the cultural dimensions of communication and media. The cultural analysis of communication also has a well established theoretical tradition to draw upon, from Gramsci's theory of hegemony to the works of the critical theorists of the Frankfurt School.

One group of scholars who adapted Gramsci's notions of hegemony were based at the Centre for Contemporary Cultural Studies at the University of Birmingham in Britain. Led by the Caribbean-born scholar Stuart Hall, 'the Birmingham School', as it came to be known in the 1970s did pioneering work on exploring the textual analysis of media, especially television, and ethnographic research. Particularly influential was Hall's model of 'encoding-decoding media discourse' which theorized about how media texts are given 'preferred readings' by producers and how they may be interpreted in different ways – from accepting the dominant meaning; negotiating with the encoded message, or taking an oppositional view (Hall, 1980).

The model was widely adopted by scholars interested in the study of the ideological role of the mass media. However, the research focus of the Birmingham School was largely British, and more often than not, its perceptions of the 'global' were based on the ethnographic studies of migrant populations – their television viewing habits, consumption of music and other leisure activities. The undue emphasis on ethnic and racial identity and 'multiculturalism', tended to limit their research perspectives, exposing them to the danger, for example, of confusing 'British Asian cultural identity' with the diverse cultures and subcultures of the South Asian region, with its multiplicity of languages, ancient religions and ethnicities.

The dominant Western view of the global South is profoundly influenced by Eurocentrism, defined by the Egyptian theorist Samir Amin as constituting 'one dimension of the culture and ideology of the modern capitalist world' (Amin, 1988: vii). Many other scholars from the developing world have argued that contemporary representations of the global South are affected by the way the Orient has been historically constructed in Western thinking, for example, through travel writing (Kabbani, 1986), literature (Said, 1978; 1993) and films (Shohat and Stam, 1994), contributing to a continuity of subordination of non-European peoples in Western imagination. The US-based Palestinian scholar Edward Said has explored how dominant culture participated in the expansion and consolidation of nineteenth-century imperialism. Taking the Gramscian view of culture, Said writes:

Western cultural forms can be taken out of the autonomous enclosures in which they have been protected, and placed instead in the dynamic global environment created by imperialism, itself revised as an ongoing contest between North and South, metropolis and periphery, white and native.

(1993: 59)

Though the cultural studies approach professes to give voice to such issues – race, ethnicity, gender and sexuality remain its key concerns – it has generally rendered less importance to class-based analysis, despite the fact that championing the 'popular' has been a major achievement of this tradition. The cultural studies approach to communication has become increasingly important, especially in the USA and Australia and with its new-found interest in 'global popular', the trend is towards the internationalization of cultural studies.

Theories of the information society

Spectacular innovations in information and communication technologies, especially computing, and their rapid global expansion have led to claims that this is the age of the information society. Breakthroughs in the speed, volume and cost of information processing, storage and transmission have undoubtedly contributed to the power of information technology to shape many aspects of Western, and increasingly, global society. The convergence of telecommunications and computing technologies and the continued reductions in the costs of computing and international telephony have made the case for the existence of the information society even stronger.

According to its enthusiasts, an international information society is under construction which will digitally link all homes via the Internet – the network of networks. The information grid of networked computers is being compared with the electricity grid, linking every home, office and business, to create a networked society, based on what has been termed as the 'knowledge economy'. These networks have become the information superhighways, providing the infrastructure for a global information society (Negroponte, 1995; Kahin and Nesson, 1997). However, critics have objected to this version of society, arguing that these changes are technologically determined and ignore the social, economic and political dimensions of technological innovation (Webster, 1995).

The technologically-determinist view of communication was promoted by Canadian media theorist Marshall McLuhan (1911–80), one of the first thinkers to analyse the impact of media technology on society. Arguing that, 'the medium is the message', he maintained that viewed in a historical context, media technology had more social effect on different societies and cultures than media content (McLuhan, 1964). McLuhan, a Professor at the

University of Toronto, was working within the tradition of what came to be known as 'the Toronto School' of thought, identified with the research of economic historian Harold Innis ([1950] 1972). McLuhan argued that printing technology, for example, contributed to nationalism, industrialism and universal literacy. Though at the time he was writing, electronic media, especially television, were confined to few Northern nations, McLuhan foresaw the impact of international television, suggesting that new communication and information technologies would help create, what he called a 'global village'. The rapid changes in international communications, spurred on by the expansion of direct satellite broadcasting in the 1980s and the Internet in the 1990s, seem to made the world shrink, generating renewed interest in McLuhan's concept of global village.

The term 'information society' originated in Japan (Ito, 1981), but it was the USA where the concept received its most ardent intellectual support. In the USA, even in the early 1960s the 'economics of information' was being considered as an important area of research activity. Fritz Machlup (1902–83), whose 1962 work, *The Production and Distribution of Knowledge in the United States,* was one of the first attempts to analyse information in economic terms. Changes in industrial production and their effect on Western societies informed the work of sociologist Daniel Bell, who became an internationally known exponent of the idea of a 'post-industrial' society – one in which the service industries employ more workers than manufacturing.

In his hugely influential book, *The Coming of Post Industrial Society*, published in 1973, Bell argued that US society had moved from an industrial to post-industrial one, a society characterized by the domination of information and information-related industries. Bell contended that not only was more information being used but a qualitatively different type of information was available. Bell's ideas were keenly adopted by the scholars who wanted to pronounce the arrival of 'the information age'. Another key figure, Alvin Toffler, though more populist than Bell, was very influential in propagating the idea of an information society, calling it the third wave – after the agricultural and industrial eras – of human civilization (Toffler, 1980).

The 'third wave' was characterized by increasing 'interconnectedness', contributing to the 'evolution of a universal interconnected network of audio, video and electronic text communication', which, some argue, will promote intellectual pluralism and personalized control over communication (Neuman, 1991: 21).

In this version of the information society, the democratic potential of new technologies is constantly stressed. However, critics such as Frank Webster emphasize 'historical antecedents', arguing that 'there is no novel, "post-industrial" society: the growth of service occupations and associated developments highlight the continuities of the present with the past' (Webster, 1995: 50). These continuities need to be underlined, especially in the global context, as the transnationalization of media and communication industries has been greatly facilitated by expansion of new international communication networks, for example, among non-governmental organizations (Frederick, 1992). The resultant 'time–space compression' is implicated in what has been called, taking up McLuhan's phrase, the phenomenon of 'global villagization' (Harasim, 1994).

With its growing commodification, information has come to occupy a central role as a 'key strategic resource' in the international economy, the distribution, regulation, marketing and management of which are becoming increasingly important. Real-time trading has become a part of contemporary corporate culture, through digital networking, which has made it possible to transmit information on stock markets, patent listings, currency fluctuations, commodity prices, futures, portfolios, at unprecedented speed and volume across the globe.

The growing 'informatization' of the economy is facilitating the integration of national and regional economies and creating a global economy, which continues to be dominated by a few megacorporations, increasingly global in the production, distribution and consumption of their goods and services. The growth of Internet-based trading, the so-called E-commerce (electronic commerce) has given a boost to what has been called 'digital' capitalism (Schiller, 1999).

In the analysis of the emerging global information society, the most significant input has come from the Spanish theorist Manuel Castells. In his trilogy *The Information Age*, Castells gives an extensively researched and detailed analysis of the emerging trends in global condition. The first volume focuses on the new social structures at work in what Castells calls the 'network society'; the second volume examines social and political processes within the context of such a society, while the third volume includes integration and information-based polarization in the international 'informational economy' in which communication becomes both global and customized.

Informational capitalism, Castells argues, is increasingly operating on a global basis, through exchanges between electronic circuits linking up international information systems. This bypasses the power of the state and creates regional and supranational units. In this 'networked' globe, he contends, flows of electronic images are fundamental to social processes and political activity, which has been progressively affected by mediated reality (Castells, 1996, 1997, 1998). Though he rejects technological determinism, his ideas are fundamentally shaped by the new technological paradigm.

It has also been claimed that new technologies have contributed to the decline of ideology. For example, a visually based medium such as television has shifted ideology from 'conceptual to iconic symbolism' (Gouldner, 1976). The growing use of computer-mediated communication could further reduce the impact of ideology in daily life, though the empowering potential of Internet could, on the other hand, create new forms of transnational ideological alliances. However, the possibilities of the Internet creating new communicative space (Poster, 1995), have been opposed with questions about access to the new technologies, within and between nations (Golding, 1998).

Some critics have been concerned with the growing commodification of personal information, from database marketing to individually targeted personalized advertising and consumer sales (Gandy, 1993). With the growing use of the Internet, companies can exploit commercially valuable data on their users, for example, by so-called Cookies (Client-Side Persistent Information). Others have raised questions about the use of new technologies for personal and political surveillance (Lyon, 1994). US dominance of global military surveillance and intelligence data gathering through spy satellites and advanced computer networks, for political, and increasingly trade-related espionage, must also be considered an integral part of the push towards creation of a global information society. The 'control revolution' (Beniger, 1986), though more pronounced in all modern organizations in 'networked societies', is in the process of going global (see Chapter 7, pp. 246–47).

Discourses of globalization

Despite the disputed nature of the utility of globalization as a concept in understanding international communication, there is little doubt that new information and communication technologies have made global interconnectivity a reality. It has been argued that 'globalisation may be the concept of the 1990s, a key idea by which we understand the transition of human society into the third millennium' (Waters, 1995: 1). The term has also been used more generally to describe contemporary developments in communication and culture.

Wallerstein (1974 ; 1980) sees globalization as a world system, a theory rejected by others on the grounds that his 'mechanisms of geosystematic integration are exclusively economic' (Waters, 1995: 25), while Robertson argues that 'globalisation analysis and world-systems analysis are rival perspectives' (Robertson, 1992: 15).

In its most liberal interpretation, globalization is seen as fostering international economic integration and as a mechanism for promoting global liberal capitalism. For those who see capitalism as the 'end' of history (Fukuyama, 1992), globalization is to be welcomed for the effect that it has in promoting global markets and liberal democracy. The triumph of democracy is celebrated through increasing emphasis on global governance (UN, 1995), 'cosmopolitan democracy' (Archibugi and Held, 1995) and even 'cosmopolitics' (Cheah and Robbins, 1998). In this dominant view of globalization, the expansion of information and communication technologies coupled with market-led liberal democracies are contributing to the creation of what has been called a global civil society, though others have identified tensions between globalization and fragmentation (Clark, 1997).

The economic conception of globalization views it as denoting a qualitative shift from a largely national to a globalized economy, in which although national economies continue to predominate within nations, they are often subordinate to transnational processes and transactions (Hirst and Thompson, 1996). The arguments for economic globalization focus on the increasingly internationalized system of manufacture and production, on growing world trade, on the extent of international capital flows and, crucially, on the role of the transnational corporations. Liberal interpretations of globalization see markets playing the key role at the expense of the states. Japanese business strategist Kenichi Ohmae, who has been included in the category of 'extreme globalization theorists', claims that, in the globalized economy the nation–state has become irrelevant and market capitalism is producing a 'cross-border civilisation' (Ohmae, 1995).

Both Marxists and world-system theorists stress the importance of the rise of global dominance of a capitalist market economy that is penetrating the entire globe – pan-capitalism is how one commentator described the phenomenon (Tehranian, 1999). With the collapse of communism, the disintegration of the Soviet Union and the eastern bloc, seen by many as alternative to capitalism, the shift within Western democracies from a public to a private sector capitalism, and the international trend towards liberalization and privatization have contributed to the acceptance of the capitalist market as a global system.

However, questions remain about the extent of globalization (Ferguson, 1992). It is argued that many of the indices of globalization are concentrated within the OECD countries, especially between the USA–EU–Japan triad, prompting scholars to talk of 'triadization' rather than the globalization of the world economy. It is beyond dispute, however, that in the post-Cold War world, transnational corporations have become extremely powerful actors, dominating the globalized economy. They must compete internationally and will, if necessary, sever the links to the nations where they originally operated, a trend which has been described as reflection of the 'global footlooseness of corporate capitalism' (Sassen, 1996: 6).

In sociological interpretations of globalization, the notion of culture is of primary importance. British sociologist Anthony Giddens (1990) sees globalization as the spread of modernity, which he defines as the extension of the nation–state system, the world capitalist economy, the world military order and the international division of labour. Waters argues that globalization is 'the direct consequence of the expansion of European culture across the planet via settlement, colonisation and cultural mimesis' (1995: 3–4).

Enthusiasts talk of a new 'global consciousness' as well as physical compression of the world, in which cultures become 'relativized' to each other, not unified or centralized, asserting that globalization involves 'the development of something like a global culture' (Robertson, 1992). Others have been more cautious, arguing that globalizing cultural forces, such as international media and communication networks, produce more complex interactions between different cultures (Appadurai, 1990; 1996). Some have made the case for considering cultural practices as central to the phenomenon of globalization (Tomlinson, 1999).

Global homogenizing forces such as standardized communication networks – both hardware and software, media forms and formats – influence cultural consciousness across the world. However, as the US-based anthropologist Arjun Appadurai argues (1990), these globalizing cultural forces in their encounters with different ideologies and traditions of the world produce 'heterogeneous dialogues'. Appadurai specifies five 'scapes' – ethnoscapes, technoscapes, finanscapes, mediascapes and ideoscapes – to describe the dynamics of contemporary global diversity.

'Ethnoscape' denotes the flow of people – such as tourists, refugees, immigrants, students and professional – from one part of the globe to another. 'Technoscape' includes the transfer of technology across national borders while 'finanscape' deals with international flow of investment. 'Mediascape' refers to global media, especially its electronic version – both its hardware and the images that it produces while 'ideoscape' suggests ideological contours of culture. Appadurai argues that the five 'scapes' influence culture not by their hegemonic interaction, global diffusion and uniform effects, but by their differences, contradictions and counter-tendencies – their 'disjunctures' (Appadurai, 1990).

Some critics see globalization as a new version of Western cultural imperialism, given the concentration of international communication hardware and software power among a few dominant actors in the global arena who want an 'open' international order, created by their own national power and by the power of transnational media and communication corporations (Latouche, 1996; Amin, 1997; Herman and McChesney, 1997). A fear of what the US sociologist George Ritzer called the McDonaldization of society, is also expressed by scholars. Ritzer says he prefers the term 'Americanization' to globalization, since the latter implies more of a 'multidimensional relationship among many nations' (Ritzer, 1999: 44).

While conceding the pre-eminence of Western media and cultural products in international communication, scholars influenced by post-structuralism dispute whether the global flow of media and cultural products is necessarily a form of domination or even a strictly one-way traffic, arguing that there is a contra-flow from the periphery to the centre and between the 'geo-cultural markets', especially in the area of television and films (Sinclair *et al.*, 1996). Ulf Hannerz contests the notion that globalization reinforces cultural movement from the 'centre' (the modern industrial West) to the peripheral 'traditional' world in a largely one-way flow, arguing that centre–periphery interactions are more complex with cultural flows moving in multiple directions, and thus the outcomes are opposite tendencies, both towards what he calls saturation and maturation, for homogenization and heterogenization (Hannerz, 1997).

Scholars broadly following this line of argument also question the assumptions about the process of homogenization as a result of the diffusion of the Western media and cultural products globally, arguing that the forces of fragmentation and hybridity are equally strong and they affect all societies. Tomlinson argues that 'the effects of globalisation are to weaken cultural coherence in all individual nation-states, including the economically powerful ones – the imperial powers of a previous era (1991: 175). Others such as Mexican anthropologist Nestor Garcia Canclini (1995 [1989]) see possibilities offered by migration and modernity to broaden cultural territory beyond the nation–state. The so-called 'deterritorialization' and the relocation of 'Third World' cultures in the metropolitan centres is considered an enriching experience for the receiving as well as the migratory cultures.

The apparent growth of alternative media and the possibilities opened up by the Internet are also seen to be a trend towards the disruption of the one-way flow of information. Robertson adopts the concept of 'glocalization', a term whose origins are in the discipline of marketing, to express the global production of the local and the localization of the global, while Nederveen Pieterse (1995) maps out how hegemony is not merely reproduced but 'refigures' in the process of hybridization.

The increased level of transnational information flows, made possible by the new technologies of communication and shifts in the institutional organization – economic, political and legal – on the means of communication, have profoundly affected global media industries. Increasingly, the emphasis is shifting from the traditional approach of considering the role of media in the vertical integration of national societies, to studying information flows which show patterns of transnational horizontal integration of media and communication structures, processes and audiences. This has become necessary because of the harmonization of international regulatory and legal frameworks and the globalization of ownership and control in the telecommunication and media sectors – including television, films and on-line media.

This horizontal communication is facilitating transnational patterns of marketing and political communication, where people are increasingly being addressed across national boundaries on the basis of their purchasing power. Transnational communication is also used by international non-governmental organizations (INGOs) whose politics and actions are being affected by the use of the Internet. The increasingly complex relations between local, national, regional and international production, distribution and consumption of media texts in a global context further complicate the globalization discourse.

Accompanying the dramatic expansion of capitalism and new transnational political organisation is a new global culture, emerging as a result of computer and communication technology, a consumer society with a wide range of products and services consumed internationally. Global culture includes the proliferation of media technologies, especially satellite and cable television, that veritably create McLuhan's dream of a global village in which people all over the world watch spectacles like the Gulf War, major sports events, entertainment programmes and advertisements which relentlessly promote free market capitalism.

With the expansion of Internet access, more and more people are entering into the global computer networks that instantaneously circulate ideas, information and images throughout the world, overcoming boundaries of space and time. What kind of international communication this is generating remains a hotly disputed subject, given that culture is an especially complex and contested terrain as 'modern' culture permeates traditional ones and new configurations emerge.

The debates about global culture have been largely ignored by many previous forms of modernization theories that tended towards economic, technological and political determinism. In classical Marxism, culture was sometimes reduced to a crass economic commodity, with scarce importance given to local forms of associations – whether based on ethnicity, religion, race or gender. It also did not take on board the issue of cultural diversity, aesthetics and spirituality, being preoccupied with the study of the production and consumption of material culture. For traditional liberalism, the advancement of the modern economy and technology was necessary for creating world markets and consumers.

Both classical Marxists and liberals predicated a borderless world – in the idealized Marxian version the proletariat across the world were to lead international communism that would eliminate nationalism, class exploitation and war, while liberal interpretations saw the market as eroding cultural differences and national and regional particularities, to produce a global consumer culture. Missing from both models has been an understanding of the complexity of the interaction of class with nationalism, religion, race, ethnicity and feminism to produce local political struggles. Despite claims for the end of ideology and history and the 'peace dividend' since the end of the Cold War, the world has witnessed a rise in ethnic and religious conflict.

The intellectual uncertainty that the end of the Cold War produced in the West and the dismantling of the last vestiges of progressive ideology in the former socialist camp, are reflected in an increasing blurring of boundaries between various strands of international communication theory. In this postmodern landscape, there appears to be a fragmentation of theories, with an emphasis on the personal and the local while macro issues affecting international communication are often ignored. Postmodernists argue that developments in transnational capitalism are producing a new global historical configuration of post-Fordism, or postmodernism as a new 'cultural logic' of capitalism (Harvey, 1989; Jameson, 1991). Yet the proliferation of difference and the shift to more local discourses and practices define the contemporary scene, and theory, postmodernists argue, should shift from the level of globalization and its often totalizing macrotheories to focus on the micro, the specific and the heterogeneous. A wide range of theories associated with postculturalism, postmodernism, feminism and multiculturalism and post-colonial studies tend to focus on difference and specificity rather than more global conditions (Lyotard, 1984; Baudrillard, 1994; Bhabha, 1994, Sreberny-Mohammadi, 1994; Garcia Canclini, 1995; Ang, 1996).

A critical political-economy for the twenty-first century

One of the significant contemporary themes in international communication research within the critical political economic tradition is the transition from America's post-war hegemony to a world communication order led by transnational businesses and supported by their respective national states increasingly linked in continental and global structures. Researchers working within this area have focused on transnational corporate and state power, with a particular stress on ownership concentration in media and communication industries world-wide – and the growing trends towards vertical integration – companies controlling production in a specific sector – and horizontal integration – across sectors within and outside media and the communication industry (Garnham, 1990; Tunstall and Palmer, 1991; Herman and McChesney, 1997; Bagdikian, 1997; McChesney, 1999).

Other scholars have supported movements for greater international information and communication equality, with concerns about incorporating human rights into international communication debates (Hamelink, 1983). Sceptical of the dominant market-based approach, many scholars have defended the public-service view of state-regulated media and telecommunication organizations and advanced public interest concerns before government regulatory and policy bodies both at national (Garnham, 1990), regional (Collins, 1998) and international levels (Mattelart, 1994).

In the twenty-first century, the focus of critical scholars is likely to be the analysis of the characteristics of the transnational media and communication corporations and locating them within the changes in international organizations such as the World Trade Organization or the International Telecommunication Union, which have played a crucial role in managing the transition to a market-driven international communication environment. The role of new technologies, especially the Internet, in international communication has also informed the critical research agenda.

The dismemberment of the Soviet Union and the advent of 'market socialism' in China and the rightward shift of the left in Europe and across the developing world, have posed a challenge to the political economic theoretical framework. However, a critical understanding of the political economy of international communication is essential if one wants to make sense of the expansion, acceleration and consolidation of the US-managed global electronic economy.

|3|

Creating a global communication infrastructure

In the 1980s and 1990s fundamental ideological changes in the global political arena led to the creation of pro-market international trade regimes which had a huge impact on international communication. The processes of deregulation and privatization in the communications and media industries combined with new digital information and communication technologies to enable a quantum leap in international communication, illustrated most vividly in the satellite industry. The resulting globalization of telecommunications has revolutionized international communication, as the convergence of the telecommunications, computer and media industries have ensured that much more information passes through a digitally linked globe today than ever before in human history.

This was made possible with the innovation of new information and communication technologies, increasingly integrated into a privatized global communication infrastructure, primarily as a result of the policy shifts – from a state-centric view of communication to one governed by the rules of the free market – among major powers and, in turn, in multilateral organizations such as the International Telecommunication Union (ITU).

Analysis of international communication has traditionally been confined to government-to-government activities where a few powerful states dictate the communication agenda, but with the growing availability of regional and global satellite networks, communication systems have become more far-reaching for telecommunications, broadcasting and increasingly in electronic commerce. Therefore, an overview of the world's satellite industry and its impact on global communication is given, to provide a framework to understand the hardware of international communication. Finally, the chapter discusses why the transnational corporations (TNCs) have benefited most from the liberalization and privatization of international communication, with Rupert Murdoch's News Corporation analysed as a case study.

The privatization of telecommunications

In the arena of telecommunications, the state was, for most of the twentieth century, the key player in providing a national infrastructure and equipment, and regulating international traffic. In the 1990s, the state monopolies of Post, Telegraph and Telecommunication (PTT) were forced to give ground to private telecommunication networks, often part of transnational corporations. This shift, which started among some Western countries, has now affected telecommunications globally, with the majority of PTTs privatized or in the process of privatization (ITU, 1999a; OECD, 1999).

Since the founding of the International Telegraph Union in 1865, regulation of international telecommunication was the subject of multilateral accord, setting common standards for telecommunications networks across the globe and prices for access to and use of these networks. These conventions were based upon the principles of national monopoly and cross-subsidization, so that national telecom operators such as the British Post Office – which had a monopoly of equipment and services within Britain – could keep the costs affordable for small users by subsidies from international telephony revenues.

In the 1980s, this regulatory framework was criticized as not taking into account technological innovations, such as computing, fibre-optic cables and fax machines. Especially significant was the blurring of the distinction between the transmission of voice and data made possible by these new technologies (Mansell, 1993). As telecommunications traffic increased, so did the demand from transnational corporations for the reduction of tariffs, especially for international services. These companies opposed national monopolies, arguing that a competitive environment would improve services and reduce costs.

In 1984 US President Ronald Reagan announced an 'open skies' policy, breaking the public monopoly and allowing private telecommunications networks to operate in the national telecommunication arena. American Telephone and Telegraph (AT&T), the biggest US telecoms company, for example, was split into 22 local companies, which enabled it to enter into new types of business. As a result, the US telecommunication sector was gradually deregulated, liberalized and privatized (Hamelink, 1994).

A year later, Margaret Thatcher's government followed suit in Britain, allowing 51 per cent of British Telecom (the former telecommunications arm of the Post Office) to be privatized, while the Japanese government permitted partial privatization of the national operator, Nippon Telephone and Telegraph (NTT). The privatization of BT and the US/UK demand to reduce the state's role in the telecommunication sector also influenced policy in Europe (Dyson and Humphreys, 1990; Curwen, 1997; EC, 1998). Martin Bangermann, European Union Commissioner for Telecommunications, conceded in his report that liberalization was 'absolutely crucial' and that the European Commission had 'got to push organizational restructuring of telecoms operators to prepare for privatization' (quoted in Venturelli, 1998: 134). However, the major European countries proceeded much more slowly in this process, with Germany's Deutsche Telekom, for example, being prepared for sale only in the late 1990s.

The general shift from the public-service role of telecommunications to private competition and deregulation had a major impact on international telecommunications policy, shaped by the USA, Britain and Europe, all of whom have companies with global ambitions.

Free trade in communication

The negotiations of the Uruguay Round of the General Agreement on Tariffs and Trade (GATT, established in 1947 to provide a framework for international trade after the Second World War), included trade in services for the first time on a par with the traditional commercial and manufacturing sectors. The agenda of this seventh round of GATT talks, which started in 1986 and were the most wide-ranging and ambitious so far, reflected the neo-liberal push towards opening up protected markets. The Final Act of the Uruguay Round, signed in 1994 in Marrakesh, Morocco, included in addition to tariff cuts of up to 40 per cent on industrial products, and liberalization commitments to remove them further, trade in services, investment and intellectual property rights.

Their inclusion in the GATT negotiations was the culmination of Western efforts to liberalize the worldwide trade in services (Drake and Nicolaidis, 1992). The USA, leading the West, argued that the world would benefit from the resulting huge expansion in investment and trade. It was estimated that the Uruguay Round, when fully implemented, could boost world income by up to $500 billion, and increase world trade volumes by up to 20 per cent (WTO, 1998).

However, there was a tension between the free-marketeers and those who argued for a more regulated system to protect domestic markets and interests. The former wanted to end state intervention in world trade and promote liberalization and privatization (Hemel, 1996). This position was strengthened with the move from GATT to the permanent World Trade Organization (WTO), which came into existence on 1 January 1995, with stricter legal mechanisms for enforcing international trade agreements (Hoekman and Kostecki, 1995).

The WTO was set up with a clear agenda for privatization and liberalization:

> The fundamental cost of protectionism stems from the fact that it provides individual decision makers with wrong incentives, drawing resources into protected sectors rather than sectors where a country has its true comparative advantage. The classical role of trade

liberalisation, identified centuries ago, is to remove such hindrances, thereby increasing income and growth.

(WTO, 1998: 38)

As part of this, the WTO also argued that dismantling barriers to the free flow of information was essential for economic growth. It was even implied that it was not possible to have significant trade in goods and services without a free trade in information. The importance of a strong communications infrastructure as a foundation for international commerce and economic development was increasingly emphasized by international organizations (ITU, 1998, 1999b, 1999c; World Bank, 1998, 1999; UNDP, 1999).

One key outcome of the Uruguay Round was the 1995 General Agreement on Trade in Services (GATS), the first multilateral, legally enforceable agreement covering trade and investment in the services sector and the one with the most potential impact on international communication, though it is also important for other sectors of global trade and investment. The services sector encompasses financial services (including banking and administration of financial markets), insurance services, business services (including rental leasing of equipment), market research, computer services, advertising, communication services (including telecommunication services – telephone, telegraph, data transmission, radio, TV and news services) (WTO, 1998).

The most significant component of this agreement for international communication was the GATS Annex on Telecommunications. Telecommunications forms one of the largest and fastest-growing service sectors and plays a dual role as a communications service, as well as the delivery mechanism for many other services. As a sector of crucial importance to all service exporters for both production and supply, the world market for telecommunications services is expected to double or even triple in the next decade. The overall network-generated revenue by 2001 is expected to reach $1 trillion (WTO, 1998).

There are interesting similarities between GATS, in particular the Annex, and the 1992 North American Free Trade Agreement (NAFTA) between Canada, the US and Mexico – the first trade agreement with commitments to reduce barriers to services trade, thus opening up Mexico's services market to US firms (Winseck, 1997). A year after the agreement was signed, Mexico's constitution was amended to allow foreign investment in Mexican media companies (Galperin, 1999).

The Annex encourages private corporations to invest in privatized telecommunication networks in developing countries and, in turn, Southern governments are encouraged to open up their markets to private telecommunications operators. It also extends the 'free flow of information doctrine' to cover both the content of communication and the infrastructure through which such messages flow.

The GATS Annex sets out the rules for trade in telecommunications and deals with access to and use of public telecommunications transport networks and services. One key guiding principle says that foreign and national suppliers of telecom facilities should be treated equally, thus exposing domestic telecommunications industries to international competition. It obliges countries to ensure that foreign services suppliers have access to public networks and services on an equal basis, both within the national market and across borders.

The rules require free movement of information, including intra-corporate communications and access to databases, with detailed guidance on acceptable conditions for access and use. To ensure transparency, information on charges, technical interfaces, standards, conditions for attaching equipment, and registration requirements has to be made publicly available. The Annex also encourages technical co-operation and the establishment of international standards for global compatibility and interoperability (WTO, 1998).

In essence, the proposed liberal global regime in telecommunication, with fewer restrictions on telecommunication flows and encouragement of investment in infrastructure in the South, aims to create the conditions to enable transnational corporations to penetrate the 'emerging markets' of Asia and Latin America, where the potential of the services sector was seen to be enormous. According to the WTO, the global trade in services is growing very rapidly (it grew 25 per cent between 1994 and 1997 alone), not least due to advances in information and communications technologies (WTO, 1998; World Bank, 1999).

Impact of WTO agreements on international communication

Three major agreements, signed in 1997 under the aegis of the WTO, are likely to have a profound impact on global trade, especially in information and communication related areas. In February 1997, 69 WTO countries agreed a wide-ranging liberalization of trade in global telecommunications services, with an annual revenue of around $600 billion. A month later, an agreement was reached to eliminate all import duties on information technology products (which include computers and communications hardware, software, and services) by 2000. Then in December 1997, 102 countries agreed to open up their financial services sector, covering more than 95 per cent of trade in banking, insurance, securities and financial information, to greater foreign competition. Altogether, these three agreements cover more than $1 trillion in international business activity.

Of the three agreements, the most significant for international communication is the GATS Fourth Protocol on Basic Telecommunications Services. The agreement, which came into force in February 1998, obliges the 69 signatories, representing more than 93 per cent of world revenues in telecommunications services, to liberalize telecommunications in their respective countries. All technological means of transmission – cable, radio and satellites – are included in the agreement, although broadcasting of radio and television programmes is excluded. It obliges the signatories to provide market access and equal treatment to international telecommunication corporations.

Within GATS, the telecommunications sector is divided into two broad categories: basic services (e.g. voice telephone, packet and circuit switched data transmission services, telex, telegraph, facsimile and leased circuits services) and value-added services (including electronic mail, voice mail, online information and database retrieval). During the Uruguay Round, most countries committed themselves to liberalize value-added services, but not basic telecommunications services, so the Fourth Protocol ensures that basic telecommunications will also be liberalized (WTO, 1998).

The Ministerial Declaration on Trade in Information Technology Products (Information Technology Agreement), the outcome of the first WTO Ministerial Conference in 1996, ruled that tariffs on information technology products should be abolished by the year 2000. Though the ITA covered six main categories – computers, telecom equipment, semiconductors, semiconductor manufacturing equipment, software and scientific equipment – Northern governments continued to demand the expansion of the agreement to include other information technology products such as audio, radio, television and video apparatus, telecommunications products and electrical/electronic machines.

As Table 3.1 shows, the USA, Japan and the EU countries dominate global exports in the information technology sector. According to the WTO, the information technology and telecommunication sectors have experienced extraordinary rates of growth in the past three decades. World annual sales of personal computers have topped the 50 million mark and now exceed the sales of cars. The cost of a unit of computing power, for example, fell dramatically between 1960 and 1990. Productivity growth in the infor-

Table 3.1 Leading exporters of IT products, 1996

Country	$billion
United States	104.62
Japan	93.93
EU	64.69
Singapore	42.35
Taiwan	35.50

Source: WTO

mation technology sector, at almost 5 per cent per year over the 1973–93 period in OECD countries, has been five times as high as overall productivity growth. As a result, this sector now accounts for one quarter of economic growth in the USA.

One billion telephones and mobile phone connections now exist worldwide, many of which are expected to be connected to the Internet. Electronic commerce over the Internet is the latest development in the emergence of an increasingly borderless global economy. It was estimated that some 300 million or 5 per cent of the world's population were Internet users at the turn of the century, and electronic commerce would amount by then to more than $300 billion (WTO, 1998: 35) (see Chapter 7, pp. 231–33)

The third major WTO agreement was made in December 1997 to open up the financial services sectors, bringing trade in this sector, worth trillions of dollars, under the WTO's multilateral rules. The Agreement on the Liberalization of Financial Services covers more than 95 per cent of world trade in banking, insurance, securities and financial information. As a result of the agreement, banking, securities and insurance services can be conducted across borders, by companies set up in one country supplying services to customers in another. For those already present in overseas markets, the conditions under which they do business will be further liberalized so that they can offer additional services. The commitments include improvements in the number of licences available for the establishment of foreign financial institutions and guaranteed levels of foreign equity participation in subsidiaries or affiliates of banks and insurance companies. More than $1.5 trillion a day is exchanged in the world's currency markets (UNDP, 1999). Given that a few, mostly Western-based corporations control this sector, the agreement raises questions about the economic sovereignty of countries, especially in the developing world.

These three agreements can be seen as the logical culmination of a process that had its origins in the 1980s' debates about what was then called transborder data flow (TDF). The developing world, concerned that such technological innovations as the integrated services digital networks (ISDNs) would make it possible for a huge amount of data to be instantly transferred in or out of countries, wanted to discuss the implications of this for their sovereignty within the UN. However, on US insistence the debate was moved to the OECD, in essence shifting the argument from national sovereignty to one about trade in global information through electronic networks. The 1985 OECD declaration on TDF was unambiguous about the need to dismantle regulations on international movement of data. The TDF, it said, will 'promote access to data and information and related services, and avoid the creation of unjustified barriers to the international exchange of data and information' (OECD, 1985). Since then even the term 'transborder data flow' has been gradually allowed to fall in disuse to be replaced by phrases with a more contemporary ring to them, such as 'information trade' (Drake, 1993). With the growing convergence between telecommunication and computer industries, the ability of privatized international telecommunications networks to transmit data across borders unhindered by national regulations became a crucial element in the globalization of financial services, especially banking and insurance and has contributed substantially to the emerging global electronic economy (see Chapter 7).

These concerns were borne out by the economic crisis in East and South East Asia in 1997. While South Korea, Thailand and Indonesia experienced an extremely serious balance of payment crisis, the Western-based financial services made huge profits. GE Capital, the world's largest non-bank financial company and part of the US conglomerate General Electric, for example, generated $3.8 billion or 40 per cent of GE's 1998 earnings. Having bought banks and other institutions in eastern Europe and during the Peso crisis in Mexico in 1994, it was aiming in 1998 at the Asian market, buying companies cheaply in Thailand and Philippines. The company estimates that its Asia-based businesses will generate 10 per cent of its global earnings by 2001, up from just 1 per cent in 1997 (Slater and Amaha, 1999).

Why services are important

International trade in commercial services has increased substantially in the past three decades. In 1970, according to the figures from the OECD, the total net trade of OECD countries in service sector was $2.8 billion, growing to $21.2 billion by 1980 and reached $30.7 billion by 1991 (OECD, 1993: 26–7). According to the WTO, world exports of commercial services amounted to $1.3 trillion in 1998. As commercial services have expanded, so has their domination by a few, mostly Western nations, not least by virtue of their financial and technological superiority.

As Tables 3.2 and 3.3 show, in international trade in commercial services, both infrastructure services (transport and telecommunication) and producer services (banking and insurance), a few rich nations or regions such as the European Union, the USA and Japan are predominant. The EU, for example, is a net exporter of telecommunications services, with telecoms revenue estimated to be 28 per cent of total world telecom revenues.

Table 3.2 World exports of commercial services, 1987–97 ($billion)

Region	1987	1990	1994	1997
Western Europe	288.1	417.6	495.5	598.1
Asia	84.2	132.4	221	297.8
North America	99.5	155.1	200.4	259.2
Latin America	20.4	29.1	41.6	51.3
Africa	13.4	18.6	22.5	27.7
World	532.8	788.8	1 036.4	1 311.5

Source: WTO

Table 3.3 Top ten exporters of commercial services, 1998

Country	Value in $ billion	Global share (%)
United States	233.6	18.1
United Kingdom	99.5	7.7
France	78.6	6.1
Germany	75.7	5.9
Italy	70.1	5.4
Japan	60.8	4.7
The Netherlands	48.3	3.7
Spain	48.0	3.7
Belgium/Luxembourg	34.7	2.7
China/Hong Kong	34.2	2.6

Source: WTO

The United States is the largest service exporter, with service exports forming almost 20 per cent of its total exports and more than 18 per cent of total world services exports. In the USA, the service sector is the fastest-growing segment of the economy, accounting for 70 per cent of Gross Domestic Product (GDP) and 80 per cent of employment (nearly 90 per cent of all new jobs are in the service sector). Employment in the USA is projected to increase by almost 25 million from 1990 to 2005, and the Bureau of Labor Statistics predicts that almost all of these new jobs will be in the service sector.

Services exports have increased steadily over the past several years – from $77 billion in 1986 to almost $182 billion in 1994. A recent US government report enthuses about the potential of electronic commerce and the information technology industries that make it possible, and the 'breathtaking speed' at which they are growing and changing. By 2006, it says, almost half of the US workforce will be employed by industries that are either major producers or intensive users of information technology products and services (US Government, 1997).

Liberalization of the telecom sector

The opening up of the global market in telecommunication services pitched the International Telecommunication Union against GATT over the regulation of telecommunications. The ethos of the ITU was based historically on the concept of telecommunications as a public utility, with operators having an obligation to provide a universal service. With a policy of co-operation, not competition, the ITU supported restrictions on ownership of and control over telecom operations, in contrast to the neoliberal telecommunication agenda, which championed privatization and deregulation.

Though initially hesitant to accept these changes, the ITU was forced to play a key part in the shaping of a new, privatized international communications regime in which the standards of universal public service and cross-subsidization were increasingly being replaced with cost-based tariff structures. One area of controversy was the renewed pressure on the ITU from Western governments to reallocate radio and satellite frequencies to commercial operators. Traditionally, ITU had administered frequency allocation on the basis of 'first come, first served'. One result of expansion of international radio broadcasting during the Cold War was that the high-frequency portion of radio spectrum became a contested area in international communication, as both Cold War blocs demanded greater access to it. The controversy was fuelled by the defence-related space race which received new momentum in 1957 with the launch of the world's first satellite – *Sputnik* by the Soviet Union, necessitating a need for space frequency allocation (Luther, 1988).

Two years later, in 1959, the UN established a committee on the Peaceful Uses of Outer Space, creating an international regulatory framework with the aim of reducing Cold War tensions and culminating in the Outer Space Treaty. Article I of this 1967 treaty, which forms the basis of international law in the field of space, stated that the exploration and use of outer space 'shall be carried out for the benefit and in the interests of all countries, irrespective of their degree of economic and scientific development, and shall be the province of all mankind', while its Article II established that outer space 'is not subject to national appropriation by claim of sovereignty, by means of use of occupation, or by any other means' (cited in Hamelink, 1994: 106).

Despite these noble sentiments, the controversy over frequency allocation continued to figure prominently in the ITU's World Administrative Radio Conferences (WARC) in 1959, 1971, 1977 and 1979. By the time of the 1992 WARC conference, held in Torremolinos in Spain, however, the political complexion had changed – superpower space rivalry had ended and the Soviet Union had been dismantled. More importantly, perhaps, in a technologically-driven environment, new advances in communications had fundamentally changed the nature of debate. The growing digitization and availability of fibre optics had made it possible for TNCs to transmit globally new communication forms and services, including satellite TV, electronic data and mobile telephony. The mobility and portability of satellite terminals ensured that international communication became much more commodified. Aware of the commercial potential for mobile telephony, the TNCs lobbied at WARC for additional use of the electromagnetic spectrum to effectively offer these new services (Sung, 1992).

In addition, with the fragmentation of the market and the proliferation of operators resulting from the processes of privatization and deregulation, the need to ensure international standards for network compatibility became increasingly obvious. Accordingly, the ITU constitution was amended at the

1998 Plenipotentiary Conference held in Minneapolis to give greater rights and responsibilities to the ITU's private-sector members. This constitutional change also ensured that private companies would have a greater role in providing advice and making decisions on technical issues. This was a culmination of a process of 'reform', made necessary by the 'changing telecommunications environment', which started at the 1989 Nice Plenipotentiary Conference and was given more concrete shape at the 1992 Geneva conference (MacLean, 1999).

The 1998 conference also agreed a 'Strategic Plan for the Union – 1999–2003', which included proposals to 'improve the structure and functioning of the radiocommunication sector, the ITU's biggest and most expensive sector, which was labouring under an increasing regulatory burden' (MacLean, 1999: 155). It also aimed at reviewing international telecommunication regulations with a view to 'adapting them to the liberalised international environment resulting from the WTO agreements' (ibid.).

The amendments made to the ITU constitution and conventions opened the organization up to private corporations interested in developing global telecommunications networks and services. ITU members, public and private, were now on an equal footing, with the same rights and obligations. In the area of 'technical recommendation', as one senior ITU official conceded, they 'effectively transfer the power to decide from government to the private sector' (MacLean, 1999: 156).

Thus, under the new international communication regime, the ITU advises countries to dismantle structural regulations preventing cross-ownership among broadcasters, cable operators and telecom companies. Since 1990, more than 150 countries have introduced new telecommunication legislation or modified existing regulation, while the percentage of international telephone traffic open to the market has more than doubled from 35 per cent in 1990 to 74 per cent in 1998; in 1990 only four countries allowed more than one operator for international telephony, by 1998, 29 countries were permitting multiple operators (ITU, 1999a).

In essence, the ITU was following the communication agenda set by the world's most powerful nations and the telecommunications corporations based in them. One indication of this was that, following the October 1998 OECD Ministerial Conference on electronic commerce, the ITU began to play a leading role among international organizations in the development of electronic commerce, particularly through standardization activities and working with developing countries, where the goal (part of the strategic plan) was to promote global connectivity to the GII (Global Information Infrastructure) and global participation in the GIS (Global Information Society) (US Government, 1995).

The United States sees the creation of a GII as critical for the success of electronic commerce, which will require, according to a policy document of the US Government, 'an effective partnership between the private and public sectors, with the private sector in the lead'. Among the governing principles behind the US administration's policy are that the private sector should lead and the government should:

> avoid undue restrictions on electronic commerce; where government involvement is needed, its aims should be to support and enforce a predictable, minimalist, consistent and simple legal environment for commerce; and electronic commerce over the Internet should be facilitated on a global basis.
>
> (US Government, 1997)

Pekka Tarjanne, the outgoing Secretary General of ITU, welcomed the participation of top telecommunications companies in global policy development. He even suggested that to make the process transparent, that the industry itself, rather than the state, should be involved in the process of regulation. The ITU, Tarjanne commented: 'will play an instrumental role in facilitating implementation of the WTO Agreement. This redefined structure and governance of the ITU will fit the landscape of 21st century telecommunications' (Tarjanne, 1999: 63).

The policy of liberalizing the global telecommunication system was greatly influenced by the 1996 Telecommunications Act, which transformed the industry within the USA, facilitating the expansion of private US telecommunications corporations to operate globally. These US-based corporations have in turn played a leading role in pushing the WTO and the ITU to further liberalize global communication. Always a champion of free trade, the United States wants to further reduce the role of its state regulatory mechanisms. The Federal Communications Commission (FCC), for example, now sees its role changing from 'an industry regulator to a market facilitator', promoting competition in the international communications market. The aim of the FCC is to refocus to meet what it calls 'the challenges of a rapidly progressing global information-age economy and an evolving global communications market'.

> Over the next five years the Commission will pursue an aggressive agenda aimed at increasing competition in communications markets around the world. Increased international competition will benefit American consumers in the form of lower rates for international telecommunications and will open new market opportunities for American companies.
>
> (FCC, 1999)

By the end of 1999, there were enough indications to show that the US Government had succeeded in building an international communication infrastructure conducive to the transnational corporations. By 1999, partly as a result of the WTO agreement, 88 countries had fully or partially privatized their telecommunications networks, with interest in free market communications varying from enthusiasm in Latin America to caution in many

Asian and Arab nations (ITU, 1999a). Although the WTO-led liberalization of international communication has transformed global communication, nevertheless demands for 'a new multilateral agreement on regulatory provision which causes the WTO Members to credibly and strongly commit themselves to open markets' have continued (Fredebeul-Krein and Freytag, 1999: 643). With the increasing privatization of global satellite networks, the satellite industry was set to benefit from liberalization of international communication.

Privatizing space – the final frontier

The extraordinary growth of global communications via satellites in the 1990s has been compared to the technological leap forward of cabling the world in the nineteenth century and, in the twenty-first century, satellites are set to become the 'trade routes in the sky' (Price, 1999). Economic growth and technological progress have fuelled a huge rise in demand for global telecommunications services of all types, resulting in the phenomenal growth of the satellite industry. Satellites are now crucial in providing the cheap, dependable and fast communication services that are essential for international businesses to operate in the global electronic marketplace, especially in such areas as transnational broadcasting and telephony, global banks and airlines, international newspapers and magazine distribution.

Ever since the mid-1960s when geostationary communications satellites first began to provide direct telecommunications links across nations and oceans, they have played a key if unsung role in the development of international communication. Complementing ground-based systems, such as cable and microwave, satellites are able to reach huge areas, unrestrained by geographical terrain. They have enabled the expansion of broadcast and telecommunications services all over the world, from metropolitan cities to the furthest flung islands and remote rural areas. These factors make satellites a lucrative and highly competitive industry in which a few big players operate, given that there are a limited number of orbital slots in the geostationary orbit and multiple satellites covering the same footprint.

To be able to fully exploit space communication services, access to the appropriate radio frequencies and orbital positions is essential. Demand is particularly high for the geostationary (and geosynchronous) orbit (GSO), some 36,000 km above the equator, where satellites move at the same speed as the earth. At this optimal location, communication satellites can cover up to one-third of the earth's surface. All satellite operators – whether global or regional – have to make use of the 180 available orbital slots (though there are 360 degrees in the orbit, geostationary satellites need at least two degrees spacing between each other, halving the number of slots available).

With communication satellites being launched by many countries, for example, India (1983), China (1984) and Mexico (1985) and by regional consortiums, Eutelsat, Arabsat, AsiaSat and Hispasat, the GSO has become very crowded. Though the ITU upholds 'equitable access to the GSO' for all countries, it continues to be dominated by a few nations. In major satellite markets such as Europe, the governments are encouraging private satellite operators. The European Commission's Green Paper on Radio Spectrum Policy, published in 1998, called for 'market-based mechanisms', a euphemism for auctions, to allocate the spectrum in an 'efficient manner' (Oberst, 1999).

More geostationary satellites have been launched in the 1990s than in any other decade combined. As Figure 3.1 shows, in just six years more satellites were launched than in the past three decades.

According to a 1998 global survey of satellites by the US-based publication *Via Satellite*, 192 Western-built geostationary commercial communications satellites were in orbit, carrying 4 241 transponders (components that receive, amplify, and retransmit a TV signal). In addition, 67 were on order, which will add another 1 918 transponders to the global supply.

Contributing to this vigorous growth were the international agreements on telecommunications in the late 1990s, especially the WTO's Fourth Protocol (see p. 86) also referred to as the Basic Agreement on Telecommunications Services, which endorsed the US position that the distinction between 'domestic' and 'international' satellite systems was no longer valid in a digitally connected world and that satellite transmissions could cross national borders.

Such has been the change in the global communication industry that even intergovernmental organizations have been increasingly driven by market

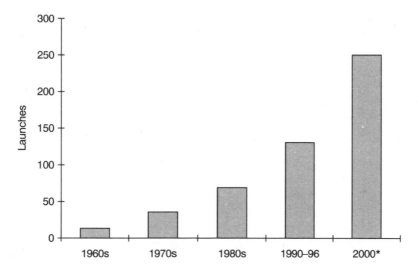

Figure 3.1 Launches of GSO communication satellites
Note: * Projected launches.
Source: Based on data from *Via Satellite*, 1998

considerations. This inevitable trend towards the privatization of intergovernmental organizations is demonstrated by the case of Inmarsat (International Marine Satellite). Based in London, Inmarsat was established in 1979 as an internationally-owned co-operative of 86 countries to serve the maritime community and is the sole provider of a broad range of global mobile satellite communications for distress and safety communication, as well as communications for commercial applications at sea, in the air, and on land.

In April 1999, it became the world's first international treaty organization to transform itself into a commercial company. Part of the company's attraction to likely investors was that it would be operating in the mobile satellite communication industry, estimated to grow to 4–8 million subscribers and to generate revenues of up to \$13 billion a year by 2002. With privatization, some of the largest national telecommunication businesses in the world, from among its former 86 member countries, have become the shareholders and backers of the new company.

Other telecommunications bodies set up along similar lines, such as the Paris-based pan-European intergovernmental organization Eutelsat, which operates 14 satellites, broadcasting more than 500 digital and analogue channels to over 70 million homes in Europe, Middle East and North Africa, are also getting ready for privatization, euphemistically called the 'restructuring process' (Sutherland, 1999b: 59). However, in an international context, a more significant change has been the gradual commercialization of the International Telecommunications Satellite Organization (Intelsat).

Intelsat

Intelsat was created in 1964 as an intergovernmental treaty organization (in the spirit of the UN) to operate a global satellite system for telecommunications services, offering affordable satellite capacity on a non-discriminatory basis. At the time of its creation commercial satellite communication did not exist and most telecommunications organizations were state-controlled monopolies, operating within a highly regulated environment. As it was the height of the Cold War, the Soviet Union and its allies inevitably saw Intelsat as a US instrument to control satellite communication.

Intelsat operated as a commercial co-operative and a wholesaler of satellite communications, providing advanced telecommunications services to its 143 member countries, and indeed to all nations. In 1971, Intelsat endorsed the landmark UN resolution on space communication, made ten years earlier, that had affirmed that satellite communication should be available to every nation 'as soon as practicable on a global and non-discriminatory basis' (Colino, 1985).

To ensure that the less developed countries could also benefit from satellite technology, Intelsat followed a policy of global price averaging, using revenues from high-traffic routes, such as North America, Europe and Japan, to subsidize the less profitable routes (Gershon, 1990: 249). However, Comsat (the Communications Satellite Corporation, a privately owned corporation with AT&T as its largest stock-holder) which represented the USA and therefore the dominant interests within Intelsat, aggressively pushed for commercial applications of satellite television. Contrary to UN resolutions, notes Schiller, the space communications development was affected by decisions 'based on market considerations emphasising capital distributions, volumes of international communications and expectations of profitability' (Schiller, 1969 [1992]: 190).

Although ostensibly a non-profit international co-operative, giving all countries access to the global satellite system, Intelsat has in fact been controlled by a few nations. As Figure 3.2 shows, eight Western countries account for half the controlling shares, with the USA holding the largest investment, followed by Britain.

The share of investment has ensured that Intelsat, like other international organiza-tions, has reflected the concerns of Western countries. In a technology-driven industry, the countries that control the technology inevitably have greater power to set and imple-ment the policy agenda.

The growth of regional satellite systems, such as Eutelsat and Arabsat, threatened the near monopoly status that Intelsat had enjoyed during the Cold War years. In 1989, the decision of the FCC to authorize a private company, Pan American Satellite Inc (PanAmSat) to provide international carrier services between the USA and Latin America, triggered the process of privatization of satellite-based international commu-nication (Frieden, 1996).

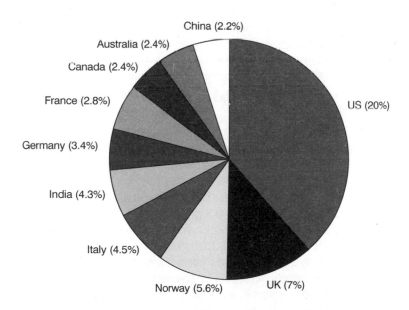

Figure 3.2 Top ten investors in Intelsat, 1999
Source: Intelsat

Commercialization received a boost with the end of the Cold War-related space race, as many eastern bloc countries, including Russia, joined Intelsat. The International Organization of Space Communications (Intersputnik), which was established in 1971 as a rival to Intelsat to provide satellite communications to socialist countries, began to negotiate with Western satellite companies for joint ventures. By June 1999, the politics of space had changed so much that a Russian rocket was used to launch the European satellite, Astra1H, with the world's first commercial Ka-band payload for use over Europe from the cosmodrome at Baikonur in Kazakhstan.

Reflecting the strides made by satellite communications globally, Intelsat massively expanded its operations in the 1990s. After an agreement with the UN in 1993 to increase satellite services globally, the pace of development was rapid. In Latin America alone, Intelsat's revenues grew from $64 million in 1994 to $130 million in 1997 (Kessler, 1998). In 1997–98 Intelsat launched five new satellites in the Intelsat VIII/VIII-A series. The Intelsat IX programme, costing approximately $1 billion, is being equipped with Intelsat IX spacecraft, built by Space Systems/Loral, the first of which will start providing services in 2000, offering more and enhanced services to operators.

In 1998, with revenues exceeding $1 billion for the first time, the organization transferred a quarter of its satellite fleet to a newly created private commercial company, New Skies Satellites, based in the Netherlands, a global system currently with five satellites. The move was justified by Conny Kullman, the new Director General and Chief Executive Officer of Intelsat, in the organization's 1998 annual report:

> The creation of *New Skies* was a fundamental step toward the full commercialisation of Intelsat, a goal we consider vital to our continued ability to prosper in an increasingly competitive and dynamic marketplace . . . . Competition breeds innovation and technological advancement, which leads to lower prices and better services for customers. The end result is a more vibrant market for all communications companies, and a confirmation that Intelsat's owners are prepared to undertake fundamental change to maximise value to shareholders and customers alike.
>
> (Intelsat, 1999a)

Testifying before the US Senate Communications Committee on Commerce, Science and Transportation in March 1999, Kullman said that '*New Skies* was the first real test of whether the Intelsat Signatories and Parties would be willing to start down the path towards privatisation. The answer was yes, by unanimous consent' (Intelsat, 1999b).

In 1999, Intelsat owned and operated a global satellite system of 19 satellites, bringing both public and commercial networks, video and Internet services to over 200 countries and territories around the world. Though more than 60 countries still depend entirely on Intelsat for their satellite-based international communications, Intelsat's position was being increasingly threatened by competition from private telecommunications transnationals both regionally and globally. As Kullman told the Third United Nations Conference on the Exploration and Peaceful Uses of Outer Space in Vienna, in July 1999, the answer was to create a 'new Intelsat', a privatized organization 'to continue our fundamental mission of providing connectivity to all countries of the world'.

We expect to obtain final approval for privatization from our owners and member governments by late 2000. New Intelsat could be established by early 2001 – in time for the new enterprise to reap the benefits of the fast-growing commercial satellite communications market.

(Intelsat, 1999c)

At their meeting in Hawaii in April 1999, Intelsat endorsed the restructuring of the organization from an intergovernmental co-operative to a fully commercial company. The General Assembly, responsible for making policy decisions relating to the treaty-based agreement which governs Intelsat, agreed to go ahead with the plan at its meeting in Malaysia in October 1999. The Assembly decided that Intelsat should be converted into a corporation, 'with an optimal tax, regulatory and operational structure without privileges and immunities'. Intelsat has targeted full privatization by 2001 (*SatNews*, 1999d).

Privatization has opened up the debate about who would have strategic control of the new Intelsat, which still runs the world's largest commercial geostationary satellite network. The US-based Comsat, the largest individual shareholder in both the Intelsat and Inmarsat satellite systems, agreed to merge with Lockheed Martin in August 1999, one of the world's biggest defence corporations. Comsat is also the largest individual owner in New Skies. Will Lockheed Martin dominate New Skies and thus take a controlling position in Intelsat?

The privatization of Inmarsat and Intelsat raises important questions about telecommunications access for the world's poorer countries. Intelsat has played a crucial role in bringing satellite technology to the South. The economies of scale coupled with innovations in satellite technology made it possible for Intelsat to progressively cut the rates charged for the use of its services. Under its policy of rate averaging – high density routes, for example between North America and Western Europe, had lower costs per circuit than low density routes – much of the developing world came under the latter category. In order to provide services to thin routes, Intelsat charged the same rate for all routes, thus in effect the high density traffic subsidized the others. The new Intelsat is unlikely to continue this practice.

Given their economic situation, it would be extremely difficult for poorer countries to afford transponder fees or to acquire other commercial satellite services. Despite its recent growth, the satellite industry demands very substantial investment and high risk, and only the large transnational corporations will be able to exploit this communication hardware. As Table 3.4 shows, in terms of satellite footprints, the most heavily covered regions are North America, followed by Asia-Pacific and Europe.

Key players in the global satellite industry

Digital technology, with modern satellites experiencing nearly 500-fold capacity increase over 1960s' spacecraft, WTO-sponsored deregulation and

Table 3.4 Global distribution of commercial satellites

Region	No. of geostationary communication satellites	
	Operational in 1998	On order
North America	44	16
Asia-Pacific	44	20
Europe	40	15
Atlantic Ocean	26	5
Latin America	10	4
Indian Ocean	10	3
Pacific Ocean	10	1
Middle East	8	2
Africa	0	1
Total	192	67

Source: Via Satellite

the rapid privatization of national telecommunications organizations, have accelerated the flow of information across national borders. This has resulted in a flourishing global telecommunications industry led by commercial international satellite and cable communications operators, offering a wider range of services at lower prices.

US companies and a French-led European consortium lead the world market for the manufacture of geostationary satellites. In 1999, the US-based Satellite Industry Association (SIA), which represents the leading US commercial satellite corporations, reported that the commercial satellite industry generated $65.9 billion in revenue in 1998, a nearly 15 per cent increase on 1997 revenue, with the US-based companies accounting for $30.7 billion of the total or about 46 per cent of worldwide revenue (*SatNews*, 1999c).

The three largest US contractors – Hughes Space and Communications, Lockheed Martin, and Loral – have between them built 68 per cent of the geostationary communications satellites in orbit, and were contracted to build 62 per cent of those on order in 1999. A European satellite consortium led by the French Aerospatiale, have built 17 per cent of those in orbit, and are building 30 per cent of those under construction (Boeke and Fernandez, 1998).

To have a better appreciation of the reach of Western satellite networks, it is useful to examine who the main international and regional satellite players are. Most of the information that follows has been obtained from the websites of the major satellite corporations and the trade press, since little academic work exists on this subject and whatever is available dates very rapidly given the changing nature of the industry.

Hughes Space and Communications Company

Of the world's three biggest satellite manufacturers, Hughes Space and Communications Company is the most significant, accounting for 40 per cent of the commercial satellite service worldwide. The Hughes conglomerate claims to be 'the most comprehensive vertically-integrated satellite firm in the world'. It includes PanAmSat (the world's largest commercial operator of communications satellites, with a network of 19 satellites in 1999) and Hughes Network Systems (a leading provider of satellite-based private communications networks for TNCs) and DirecTV, an international Direct-to-Home (DTH) operator (Hughes website).

Among Hughes' main customers is the Luxembourg-based Société Européenne des Satellites (SES), the owner and operator of Astra, Europe's leading DTH satellite system, reaching an audience of almost 75 million households in Europe. In addition, Hughes is a major supplier for the US defence services, designing and launching the Leasat satellites – launched in 1984, 1985 and 1990 – used by the US government to create a global military communications and surveillance network.

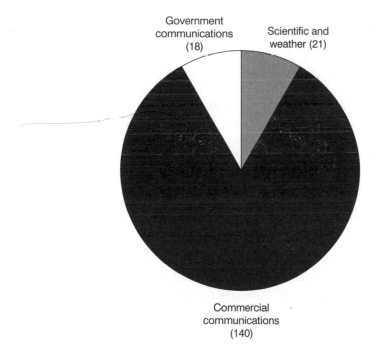

Figure 3.3 Types of satellies launched by Hughes, 1963–99
Source: Hughes website

Table 3.5 Satellites ordered from Hughes by country, 1999

Country	No of satellites
United States	62
United Kingdom	14
Japan	8
Luxembourg	7
China	7
Canada	6
Australia	6
Brazil	6
Indonesia	6
Mexico	5
UAE	2
Norway	2
Malaysia	2
Thailand	2
Sweden	1
Russia	1
Total	137

Source: Hughes website

Of the 179 satellites built by Hughes since 1963, the first 100 were launched over a period of 17 years, whereas 79 have been launched in the last nine years. Orders for satellites shown in Table 3.5 reflect the pattern of global distribution of communication hardware.

In January 2000, the US defence giant Boeing bought Hughes' satellite operations for $3.75 billion. Boeing, the largest aerospace company in the world, apart from being the world's top manufacturer of commercial and military aircraft, is also one of the biggest producers of defence-related advanced information and communication systems. The deal reinforces close links between civil and military operations among the world's top satellite corporations.

Lockheed Martin Global Telecommunications

The defence industry is also crucial for the satellite manufacturer, Lockheed Martin Global Telecommunications (LMGT), part of the Lockheed Martin corporation, the largest defence contractor in the USA. In recent years it has expanded its operations globally and is now the main actor within a privatized Intelsat. In what was termed as a space coup, Lockheed Martin formed a joint venture in 1997 with Intersputnik to launch and operate a fleet of advanced communications satellites, creating a global integrated system for communication and broadcasting services. Cash-strapped Intersputnik needed the support of one of the world's best-resourced companies, while Lockheed Martin was interested in Intersputnik's 15 highly valuable GSO slots.

By joining forces with the Russians, Lockheed Martin acquired the capacity to transmit video, data and phone services worldwide. Of particular interest were the two Intersputnik slots, registered in Cuba's name, that cover North and South America. However, the company is planning targeting first the largely untapped market of Eastern Europe, Asia and Russia, and the joint venture is expected to generate revenue of up to $500 million annually by 2001 (Mills, 1997).

In 1998, LMGT established Americom Asia-Pacific, a joint venture company, owned with GE Americom, to launch and operate a new high-powered Ku-band satellite system. Lockheed Martin is also building a regional mobile personal communications system, including a satellite, ground network and user terminals, for the Asian Cellular Satellite System, with partners in Thailand, Indonesia and the Philippines. For the crucial Chinese market, LMGT has built five satellites including ChinaStar-1 – to provide voice, data and television distribution services to one of the world's biggest markets.

In 1999, LMGT became a founding partner in Astrolink along with Telecom Italia, which will provide a Ka-band geostationary satellite system targeting the high-growth market for broadband high capacity data services. LMGT also operates Global Telecommunications Services, created in 1998 and composed of Astrolink, Lockheed Martin Intersputnik, Lockheed Martin Telecommunications and Americom Asia-Pacific, making it a major global force in the industry.

Loral Space & Communications

The third key corporation is Loral Space & Communications, one of the world's largest satellite communications companies, which, since 1957, has been awarded contracts to build 196 satellites. In 1997, as part of what the company calls 'developing the building blocks necessary to create a seamless, global networking capability for the information age', Loral acquired Skynet, then a US-provider of transponder capacity, and extended its reach to Latin America with the 75 per cent purchase of Satelites Mexicanos (SatMex).

Loral Skynet operates the Telstar and Orion satellite fleets. The Orion Network, which was bought in 1998, had licences for orbital slots covering Europe, Latin America and Asia. Loral Skynet's Telstar satellites provided coverage over most of North America, as well as trans-Atlantic coverage through the Orion 1 satellite. In the USA, Loral Skynet had links with EchoStar, the DTH service operating more than 300 channels of digital video and audio programming.

In 1999, the total combined on-orbit assets of Loral Skynet, SatMex and Loral Orion included seven satellites which, by 2002, were to be increased to 16 satellites with almost 740 transponders in its global system of networks, including two Europe*Star satellites jointly owned by a Loral/Alcatel

SpaceCom venture, to deliver services throughout Europe, South Africa, the Middle East, India and Southeast Asia.

Loral Skynet leads the Loral Global Alliance, which in 1999 had a worldwide network of satellite capacity on the North American Telstar fleet, the trans-Atlantic Orion 1 satellite, and the three-satellite SatMex fleet for South America, as well as on Europe*Star satellites. Its combined footprint covered 85 per cent of the world, providing a single resource point for broadcast and telecommunications companies around the world who can lease transponder capacity to distribute network and cable television programming to local affiliate stations. In the words of Loral Chairman and CEO Bernard L. Schwartz: 'Loral has moved aggressively to assemble the critical space and information-based building blocks that will result in a seamless, worldwide constellation of multimedia networks' (quoted in Kessler, 1998).

Regional satellite services

The deregulation and privatization of the global telecommunications market, coupled with the perceived need for a strong communications infrastructure to open up new regions to the global economy, have resulted in fierce competition in regional satellite services. Regional operators in Latin América, the Middle East and Asia are striking alliances to extend their reach and that of their customers beyond their own territories.

As a result of the gradual deregulation of broadcasting in Europe, private satellite companies have prospered. Astra (owned by Société Européenne des Satellites - SES) has seen its operations grow significantly since its launch in 1989. In less than a decade, the market share of satellite reception has risen from virtually zero to more than 26 per cent of TV households in Europe. In 1999, Astra was carrying more than 400 TV and 300 radio channels, both digital and analogue, to over 74 million homes across Europe. SES also holds a 34 per cent share of AsiaSat, Asia's premier satellite operator, providing broadcast and telecommunications services to 53 countries in the Asia-Pacific region. In 1999, the combined footprints of Astra and AsiaSat covered three-quarters of the world's population.

In Latin America, PanAmSat, the first private satellite service for the continent, launched in 1988, has made the region important for satellite manufacturers. In 1997, PanAmSat launched three satellites for the Latin American region (PAS 5, PAS 6, and Galaxy 8i) to support the DTH services operated by Sky Latin America and Galaxy Latin America, respectively. By 1999, PanAmSat, now one of the world's leading commercial providers of satellite-based communications services, was operating a global network of 19 geosynchronous satellites and seven ground facilities.

PAS 5 was the first Hughes satellite in PanAmSat's fleet to cater to the DTH services for Sky Latin America in Mexico. It was designed to provide simultaneous coverage of the Americas and Western Europe, with the potential of a comprehensive pan-American and transatlantic link using the same satellite. In 1999, PAS 5 was delivering more than 20 television channels to Latin America. Another major regional player is Galaxy Latin America, a Hughes-led Latin American venture, which since 1995 has provided a DTH service to the region, broadcasting in Spanish and Portuguese. In 1997 its Galaxy 3R was replaced with a more powerful Galaxy 8i satellite, while Galaxy 3R is used by the US DirecTV service to deliver Spanish-language broadcasting to the US market. Launched in Latin America in 1996, DirecTV is the leading DTH satellite television service in the region, reaching 26 countries, with broadcast centres in the USA, Mexico, Venezuela, Brazil and Argentina. With more than 554,000 subscribers in Latin America, DirecTV's annual revenues nearly doubled in 1999, reaching $61 million compared with $31 million in the first quarter of 1998. In the USA, DirecTV had 8 million subscribers in 1999.

There is also a trend towards the big players taking over the smaller ones, for example, Loral's 1997 purchase of SatMex, Mexico's satellite operator whose satellite system provides coverage over Mexico, the southern and eastern USA, Central America, the Caribbean and South America. This was followed by its entry into Brazil, the region's main market. In 1999, Loral's Skynet acquired a Brazilian orbital satellite slot through its local subsidiary Loral Skynet do Brasil, from which it will offer Ku-band satellite services throughout most of the Western hemisphere (*SatNews*, 1999a).

In Asia, the most significant development was the launch in 1990 of AsiaSat 1, which not only signalled China's entry into the market for launching commercial satellites, but made available, for the first time, two powerful regional beams, revolutionizing Asian broadcasting and telecommunications services. AsiaSat 1 had 24 transponders and its northern beam covered China, Japan, the Koreas, parts of Russia and Mongolia, while the southern beam stretched from Southeast Asia to the Middle East. AsiaSat 2, launched in 1995, extended the reach to cover large parts of former Soviet Union and Australia. Between them the two satellites covered 53 countries and two-thirds of the world's population. AsiaSat 3S, launched in 1999, replaced AsiaSat 1, carrying 28 C-band and 16 Ku-band high-powered transponders.

In the last decade AsiaSat has emerged as the leading regional satellite operator, whose telecommunications and broadcast facilities are used by governments, telecommunications services operators, aviation and travel services, financial institutions, news agencies and broadcasters. Without AsiaSat there would not have been a pan-Asian television network like STAR (Satellite Television Asian Region). In 1999, apart from all the main Asian channels, STAR being its biggest customer, other services available on AsiaSat included: Deutsche Welle TV and Radio, TVE Internacional of Spain, Radio France Internationale, World Radio Network, Egyptian Space Channel, Voice of America, Worldnet, BBC and Associated Press Television News.

While the Société Européenne des Satellites already held a strategic 34 per cent participation in AsiaSat in 1999, there has been speculation about PanAmSat buying stakes in the company. Given the future potential for telecommunication and DTH services in hugely populated countries such as China and India, global players such as PanAmSat have eyed the Asian market. PanAmSat, which in 1999 was considering buying a stake in AsiaSat, would have 126 transponders on four satellites in the region. In 1998, it launched PAS 8, which had 48 transponders, ensuring that, for the first time, PanAmSat was able to offer two-way Ku-band connectivity between the USA and Asia. In 1999, Loral leased the entire available transponder payload of the Apstar IIR satellite. Launched in 1997, Apstar IIR covered Asia, Europe, Africa, and Australia, including over 75 per cent of the world's population (*SatNews*, 1999b).

In the Arab world, the regional satellite operator, the Arab Satellite Communications Organization (Arabsat), established in 1976 by members of the Arab League, is also following the path of privatization. DTH services have been available to the Arab countries since the launch of Arabsat 1C in 1992. Other satellites – Arabsat 2A and 2B – whose life span is expected to last until 2012, will further improve telecommunication services in the region, while the third generation Arabsat (3A) and the Arabsat BSS1 will carry Ku-band channels covering the Arab world and Europe.

Based in Dirab in Saudi Arabia and with the Saudi government as the largest investor (nearly 37 per cent), Arabsat has also invested 10 per cent in a new commercial company – Thuraya Satellite Telecommunications Company. Founded in January 1997 with a capital base of $25 million, Thuraya grew spectacularly as the list of shareholders increased, and by August the capital base had jumped to $500 million. Though all the major telecommunication companies of the region are members of Thuraya, global players such as Hughes Space and Communications have also become involved. Thuraya was planning to provide regional mobile personal communications, based on geostationary satellite systems to be launched in 2000, covering 99 countries in Europe, North and Central Africa, the Middle East and Central and South Asia.

Though the geostationary systems continue to grow, they are being brought under the wings of large corporations through mergers, take-overs and regional alliances between major operators. From a commercial perspective, this makes market sense since large systems create economies of scale and boost the argument for further deregulation of satellite communication, especially in the DTH sector, to which several countries including India and Malaysia have been resistant. Unable to compete with global carriers, many state-run operators are privatizing their own satellite systems, as are the intergovernmental satellite operators. The net result of these changes is that the market for satellite services has become increasingly commercial, a trend which is likely to grow.

By 2003, more telecommunications deregulation will have taken place worldwide, further opening markets for Western operators. This will lead to a resurgence in the manufacturing sector, including the maturing of new technologies such as Ka-band.

According to industry estimates, sales of satellites between 1998 and 2007 are expected to reach between 276 to 348 satellites, representing a commercial value ranging from $29.7 to $38.6 billion (Crossman, 1999).

Murdoch's News Corporation – 'Around the World, Around the Clock'

> News Corp. is the only vertically integrated media company on a global scale. In the course of 24 hours News Corp. reaches nearly half a billion people in more than 70 countries.
>
> (News Corporation Annual Report 1999)

One major beneficiary of privatization of the infrastructure of international communication was News Corporation, the company owned by the Australian-born media tycoon Rupert Murdoch, whose empire straddles the globe. With wide-ranging media interests – from newspapers; film; broadcast, satellite and cable TV; digital TV; television production, to the Internet – News Corporation is a major international player in all aspects of the communications and media market.

Murdoch has made skilful use of liberalization of cross-media ownership regulations in Britain and the USA and the entry of private satellite operators into the arena of telecommunications and broadcasting. Risking an enormous amount of money by leasing time on new satellite ventures such as Astra and AsiaSat, he has been able to create a truly international media corporation, at the heart of which is satellite television. 'More than any other figure,' writes one observer, 'Murdoch has been the visionary of a global corporate media empire' (McChesney, 1999: 96). The theme for the 1999 annual report *Around the World, Around the Clock*, echoes the global nature of News Corporation. The range of its media products can best be illustrated by the following extract from the company's 1999 Annual Report:

> Virtually every minute of the day, in every time zone on the planet, people are watching, reading and interacting with our products. We're reaching people from the moment they wake up until they fall asleep. We give them their morning weather and traffic reports through our television outlets around the world. We enlighten and entertain them with such newspapers as *The New York Post* and *The Times* as they have breakfast, or take the train to work. We update their stock prices and give them the world's biggest news stories every day through such news channels as *FOX* or *Sky News*. When they shop for groceries after work, they use our *SmartSource* coupons to cut their family's food bill. And when they get home in the evening, we're there to entertain them with compelling first-run

entertainment on FOX entertainment on FOX or the day's biggest game on our broadcast, satellite and cable networks. Or the best movies from Twentieth Century Fox Film if they want to see a first run movie. Before going to bed, we give them the latest news, and then they can crawl into bed with one of our best-selling novels from HarperCollins.

It could have added, that with the successful 1998 launch of Sky Digital – a multiple-channel subscription service on British Sky Broadcasting (BSkyB), the company is set to dominate interactive digital television. Murdoch already has considerable clout in Britain (where he owns, apart from BSkyB – in 1999, it claimed to have nearly eight million subscribers – the prestigious *The Times* and *The Sun* (Britain's largest selling popular newspaper, notorious for promoting a journalism based on sex, soccer and scandal).

Apart from owning the largest number of English-language daily newspapers around the world, the company also owns Fox Network and *TV Guide* (the top selling magazine in the USA with 35 million readers every week), the first pan-Asian network STAR, the newspaper *The Australian* and television channel FOXTEL in Australia, and the publisher HarperCollins (*see* map). With worldwide operations, HarperCollins Publishing is a major global presence, with subsidiaries like HarperCollins UK, HarperCollins Canada and HarperCollins Australia. It also owns Zondervan Publishing House, the world's largest commercial Bible publisher.

Though the USA remains its primary market, accounting for 74 per cent of News Corporation's 1998 revenue, Murdoch has wide-ranging media interests in the world's two biggest consumer markets – India and China. In 1999, Hong Kong-based STAR was producing, either in partnership or alone, 23 channels in eight languages, reaching 53 countries with an estimated audience of 300 million. The STAR network spans the world's most populous continent, having a prominent position in India (where News Corp. owns STAR Plus, and partly owned, until 1999, Zee TV, the country's most popular Hindi-language private channel) and in China (where it has stakes in Phoenix, the Mandarin-language channel). As Table 3.6 and Table 3.7 show, the STAR network goes beyond the Asian region, with its signals covering a vast swathe of Asia and parts of the former Soviet Union. In the Middle East, STAR Select, the 10-channel direct-to-home service, was reaching 123 000 homes in 1999.

In the USA, News Corporation's Fox network is already well established, producing such international television hits as The *X Files* and *The Simpsons*, competing with three traditional networks – CBS, NBC and ABC. In Latin America, Sky network has agreement with Televisa, the Mexican television giant and other regional broadcasters for a DTH operation, while among News Corp.'s pan-regional Latin American programming channels are Canal Fox, 'The Hollywood Channel', one of the most widely distributed channels in the region, and Fox Kids Latin America.

This makes News Corporation one of the world's largest media empires, truly global in its reach and influence. What distinguishes it from its rivals such as Time Warner and Disney Corporation, is the fact that it is the only one created, built and dominated by one man – Rupert Murdoch, the 69-year old chairman and Chief Executive Officer of News Corporation.

The World of News Corporation
(Wholly or partially owned companies)

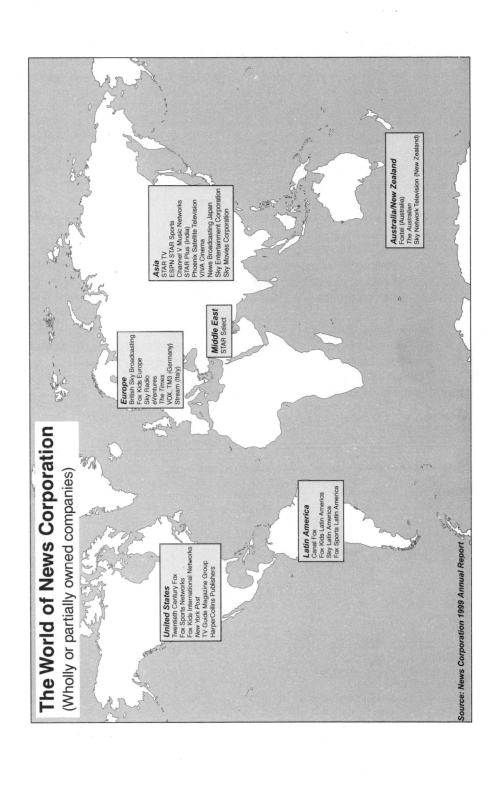

United States
Twentieth Century Fox
Fox Sports Networks
Fox Kids International Networks
New York Post
TV Guide Magazine Group
HarperCollins Publishers

Europe
British Sky Broadcasting
Fox Kids Europe
Sky Radio
eVentures
The Times
VOX, TM3 (Germany)
Stream (Italy)

Asia
STAR TV
ESPN STAR Sports
Channel V Music Networks
STAR Plus (India)
Phoenix Satellite Television
VIVA Cinema
News Broadcasting Japan
Sky Entertainment Corporation
Sky Movies Corporation

Middle East
STAR Select

Latin America
Canal Fox
Fox Kids Latin America
Sky Latin America
Fox Sports Latin America

Australia/New Zealand
Foxtel (Australia)
The Australian
Sky Network Television (New Zealand)

Source: News Corporation 1999 Annual Report

Murdoch has shown an exemplary knack in dealing with the media and entertainment business. His risk-taking attitude combined with a deep knowledge of the media industries and an uncanny ability to feel the popular pulse, account for this extraordinary success. He understood, better than any other media baron, the centrality of live sports television and therefore a crucial element of News Corporation's television strategy was its sports programming and acquiring broadcasting rights on live matches – a major earner for television. In the USA, its involvement in sports is extensive: from live broadcast of the NFL Super Bowl and baseball's World Series, to Fox Entertainment Group's ownership of the Los Angeles Dodgers – a team that draws three million fans a year to its baseball games. It has affiliations with 25 regional sports networks, which have broadcasting rights to more than 3500 live sporting events involving most teams in the National Basketball Association, National Hockey League and Major League Baseball. The company also owns part of Canada's CTV Sports Net and in Australia, FOXTEL has rights to broadcast the National Rugby League, the country's premier rugby league competition. In Latin America its cable-based FOX Sports Network boasts more than 65 million subscribers, while with a Brazilian partner NetSat it covers, among others, Brazilian and World Cup soccer and Formula One car racing.

In the UK, News Corporation's key television interests rest with its 40 per cent holding BSkyB – now Europe's most profitable broadcaster – which made much of its money by buying up the rights to telecast live top football matches and pioneered the 'pay-per-view' sports television. In 1998, Sky Sports broadcast 25 000 hours of sports on its five channels. It launched Europe's first sports news channel, Sky Sports

Table 3.6 STAR TV viewing homes, April 1999

The top five markets	Coverage (millions)
China	45
India	18
Taiwan	5
South Korea	3.5
Japan	0.5

Table 3.7 STAR regional breakdown

Region	Numbers
Greater China (China, Hong Kong, Macau and Taiwan)	50 731 000
South Asia and Middle East	19 630 000
North Asia (Japan, South Korea)	4 000 000
Southeast Asia	1 293 500
Russian CIS states and Mongolia	96 000
Other	26 000
Total	75 776 500

Source: STAR TV

News, while continuing to broadcast 60 live Premier League games a season and more than 140 other football matches. Having established a base in the UK, Murdoch expanded his business into continental Europe by establishing partnerships in Germany (VOX and TM3) and Italy (Stream). With television operations on four continents, News Corporation's reach into the world's living rooms is unequalled. Television, delivered by broadcast, cable and satellite, remains the fastest growing part of the company.

Another key area of importance was Murdoch's use of information technology. To sell its SkyDigital, Murdoch provided free digital set-top boxes and in less than a year SkyDigital had more than one million subscribers, making it the world's most successful launch of a digital platform. This was followed by Open..., an interactive service, partly owned by Sky, offering consumers home shopping, home banking and e-mail services. News Corporation also owns or has stakes in several information technology companies: NDS, the Israel-based designer and manufacturer of digital broadcasting systems; its US Internet operating subsidiary News America Digital Publishing and PDN Xinren Information Technology, a joint venture between News Corporation and the *People's Daily*, the mouthpiece of the Chinese communist party.

Murdoch's business acumen has obviously shown success – News Corporation's revenues have grown steadily (*see* Figure 3.4). The company's total assets in June 1999 were $54 billion.

Parallel to his business acumen is Murdoch's very pragmatic political agenda. Despite being critical of US big business for decades, he took US citizenship in 1984 to meet government regulations on media ownership. He withdrew BBC World Service television from the northern beam of his STAR network after the Chinese Government criticized BBC's coverage of the country.

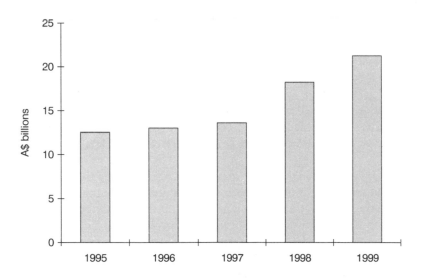

Figure 3.4 News corporation revenue growth, 1995–99
Source: News Corporation Annual Report, 1999

Murdoch's media solidly backed Margaret Thatcher in her efforts to liberalize regulations on cross-media ownership. *The Sun*'s support for Tony Blair was crucial in the 1997 election victory of the British Labour Party. This 'Murdochization' of the media has changed the media landscape in Britain and increasingly in other countries, where Murdoch has been a major player in the 1990s. In essence, this has meant an emphasis on entertainment and infotainment at the expense of the public service role of the media.

News Corporation has used an array of strategies to consolidate its position in Asia – potentially the world's biggest television market. In India, for example, its operations were co-ordinated by Rathikant Basu, a former director general of Doordarshan, India's state television network, and News Corporation Europe was launched in 1998 under Letizia Moratti, the former chairperson of the Italian state broadcasting group, Radiotelevisione Italiana (RAI).

His growing political influence as a multi-media mogul and his extensive control of both information software (program content) and hardware (digital delivery systems) make Murdoch a hugely powerful global actor. And since he was one of the first to realize the commercial importance of digital television, investing a great deal of money to get it off the ground, his empire is most likely to dominate the digital globe. With the digitization of content, which News Corp. sees as 'perhaps the most important event in business since the invention of the telephone', it has been able to produce more country-specific television channels and develop many interactive media outlets.

With the growing convergence between digital and interactive television and the Internet, News Corporation's interests are focused on developing advanced electronic programme guides, the portal of the multi-channel digital television environment. Its venture capital company, epartners, formed in 1999, was set up to exploit the new opportunities in a digitized and interactive media world.

Murdoch's worldwide presence – with operations in the USA, Canada, Britain, Australia, Latin America and Asia – makes him a significant global media player and News Corporation one of the world's largest media companies with total 1998 annual revenues of $14 billion (News Corporation, 1999).

The world of telecommunications

The expansion of global satellite networks is also having a significant impact on the international telecommunications industry. Information liberalization and the deregulation which it promotes have led to unprecedented rates of merger activity and corporate consolidation in the information and communications industries. The increasing demand for wireless technologies and mobility is spreading into all aspects of telecommunications and represents a fundamental change that is transforming international communication. These trends will converge at a single point and profoundly change the industry and the marketplace. The telecommunications and 'dotcom' industries are merging, as are the computer and media industries. A consolidation of business in these sectors is likely to lead to a global dominance of the tele-coms by 10–15 companies in operator market (*see* Table 3.8).

In 1998, the top 10 telecommunications corporations held 86 per cent of the market in telecommunications while the leading 10 computer companies controlled almost 70 per cent of the global market (UNDP, 1999). By the end of 1999, the value of mergers and acquisitions in the telecommunications industry had nearly doubled to $561 billion, mainly because of the two major deals in 1999 – the MCI Worldcom's acquisition of Sprint, and Vodafone Airtouche merger with German wireless carrier Mannesmann (*Business Week*, 2000).

The beneficiaries of such liberalization have been the major telecom operators. France Telecom's international sales grew 39 per cent as the company extended its mobile phone business to 24 countries, including major ventures in Spain and Italy. The company, which is 62 per cent owned by the government has grown more robustly since France's telephone market was deregulated in 1998. For British Telecom, 11 per cent of revenue came from overseas operations (Matlack, 1999). Ericsson, the Swedish world leader in mobile systems, connects nearly 40 per cent of the world's mobile callers in 140 countries. In 1998, the company had annual sales of $22.8 billion, with more than 95 per cent of sales originating from outside Sweden, making Ericsson the most international of all companies in the industry.

The opening up of global telecommunications services is also set to benefit the suppliers of telecommunication hardware. In 1996 exports of telecommunication and broadcasting equipment from OECD countries was $95.1 billion, an increase of 108 per cent over 1990 (OECD, 1999). The

Table 3.8 Total value of mergers and acquisitions worldwide ($ billion)

Sector	1988	1998
Computers	21.4	246.7
Telecommunications	6.8	265.8

Source: UNDP, 1999

Table 3.9 The world's top exporters of telecom equipment ($million)

Country	1990	1992	1994	1996
USA	5210	6403	10074	13025
Germany	2841	3471	5133	6957
UK	1474	1675	3250	6379
Sweden	1842	2053	2869	5423
France	1427	1800	2184	3517

Source: Based on data from ITU, 1999d

$301 billion worldwide communication equipment market, growing at 14 per cent annually, is controlled by corporations based in a few, mainly Western, countries. As Table 3.9 shows, the USA is the biggest exporter of telecom equipment (equipment used in telephony, telegraphy and radio and television broadcasting and transmission apparatus).

Japan, another leading exporter of telecom equipment, has in recent years experienced a decline in this area from the 1992 high of 899 billion yen to 695 billion in 1997 (ITU, 1999d). Other major Asian manufacturers of telecom equipment are found in Taiwan, which exported equipment worth $1729 million in 1996, Singapore, South Korea and China, but often work for Western or Japanese TNCs. The rapid growth of the Internet has also benefited the exporters of communication equipment. For example, exports of modems from the USA more than doubled between 1994 and 1997, from $501 million to $1,025 million, while sales of companies such as US-based Cisco Systems, which specializes in internetworking equipment, increased from $2.2 billion in 1995 to $6.4 billion in 1997 (OECD, 1999). Underlying long-term growth is strong in the communications industry (*see* Table 3.10 and Table 3.11). The number of fixed telephone subscribers, mobile subscribers and Internet users is predicted to reach one billion before 2004.

According to the OECD, the total revenues of the communications sector, including telecommunication services, broadcasting services and communications equipment, exceeded one trillion dollars for the first time in 1998. At the end of 1997, the total telecommunication services market in OECD countries had grown to more than $617 billion, with 64 telecommunication operators having revenue greater than $1 billion. (OECD, 1999).

Table 3.10 The top ten international telecommunication operators in 1998 by telecom revenue

Operator	Country	International telephone revenue ($ billion)
AT&T	USA	9.55
MCI Worldcom	USA	4.74
Deutsche Telekom	Germany	3.35
DGT	China	2.20
Hong Kong Telecom	HK/China	1.99
KDD	Japan	1.90
France Telecom	France	1.85
Sprint	USA	1.82
VSNL	India	1.60
Telecom Italia	Italy	1.43

Source: ITU

Table 3.11 The top ten international telecommunication operators in 1998 by telephone traffic

Operator	Country	International telephone traffic (minutes)
AT&T	USA	14 529
Deutsche Telekom	Germany	10 747
MCI Worldcom	USA	10 058
France Telecom	France	7 300
British Telecom	UK	6 350
Telecom Italia	Italy	5 289
Sprint	USA	4 470
DGT	China	4 212
Hong Kong Telecom	China	3 818
Telefonica	Spain	3 704

Source: ITU

Implications of a liberalized global communication regime

The global shift from state regulation to market-driven policies are evident everywhere. The WTO claims that the expansion of capital through the transnational corporations has contributed to the transfer of skills and capital to the global South but that it may have also contributed to widening the gap between rich and poor is not mentioned. International communication is increasingly being shaped by trade and market standards and less by political considerations, what Cees Hamelink has called 'a noticeable shift from a political to an economic discourse' (1994: 268).

The move to open up world trade by reducing tariff barriers has been unevenly applied, as India's former representative to GATT, Bhagirath Lal Das points out. After the Uruguay Agreement came into force, several developing countries made huge reductions in their tariffs: India reduced its average tariff on industrial products from 71 per cent to 32 per cent; Brazil from 41 per cent to 27 per cent and Venezuela from 50 per cent to 31 per cent. In contrast, the average tariff on industrial products in the North has been reduced from 6.3 per cent to 3.8 per cent (Das, 1998: 5).

In addition, giving priority to the service sectors – financial services, insurance, maritime transport, telecommunication – has benefited the North, while the areas where the South might have had an advantage were not given much consideration. One key such resource is labour. As Das points out, while there are specific provisions for free movement of capital associated with GATS, there is no provision for the movement of labour in a 'borderless world'. If anything, immigration laws in the European Union and the USA are being made more stringent (Das, 1998: 79).

The major trading blocs have insisted that in a globalized world economy, with growing internationalization of production and consumption, it is important to harmonize domestic laws and regulatory structures affecting trade and investment, and remove any advantage or protection for domestic industries. A global market can only be created, runs the argument, through deregulation and letting the market set the rules of international trade.

Opposition to the process of deregulation and privatization has been undermined by changes in international policy at an institutional level. International organizations, as Schiller notes, 'have either been bypassed, restructured, weakened or neutered' (1996: 123). For example, in 1992, the status of the UN Centre for Transnational Corporations (UNCTC) was fundamentally changed, making it work toward strengthening global market forces as part of the transnational corporation and management division within the UN.

The UN is positioning itself closer to the operation of international business. As part of his 'quiet revolution' to renew the United Nations for the twenty-first century, the UN Secretary-General, Kofi Annan is building a stronger relationship with the business community. A joint statement issued in February 1998 by Annan and the International Chamber of Commerce stressed the UN's role in setting the regulatory framework for the global marketplace in order to facilitate cross-border trade and investment. Among the business leaders present were executives from Alcatel Alsthom, Anglo Gold, BAT Industries, Coca-Cola, Goldman Sachs, McDonald's Worldwide, Rio Tinto, Unilever and US West. Increasingly, UN agencies are co-operating with businesses on projects, with mutual benefits. For example, the Italian fashion giant Benetton helped to design the campaign promoting the fiftieth anniversary of the Universal Declaration of Human Rights.

Who benefits from liberalization and privatization?

The biggest beneficiaries of the processes of liberalization, deregulation and privatization and the resultant WTO agreements have been the TNCs which dominate global trade. As the primary 'movers and shapers' of the global economy, the TNCs have been defined as having three basic characteristics:

- co-ordination and control of various stages of individual production chains within and between different countries;
- potential ability to take advantage of geographical differences in the distribution of factors of production (e.g. natural resources, capital, labour) and in state policies (e.g. taxes, trade barriers, subsidies, etc.);
- potential geographical flexibility – an ability to switch its resources and operations between locations at an international, or even a global scale.

(Dicken, 1998: 177)

So powerful are the TNCs that the annual sales of the top corporations exceed the GDP of many countries – for example, the 1997 annual sales of General

Motors surpassed the GDP of Thailand, while Shell Group earned more in global sales than the GDP of Greece, and Mitsui sales were higher than the GDP of Saudi Arabia – one of the world's richest countries (UNDP, 1999).

According to the 1999 *World Investment Report* from the United Nations Conference on Trade and Development (UNCTAD), in 1998, the world's largest 100 TNCs, measured in terms of foreign assets, accounted for $4 trillion in total sales and held a stock of total assets in excess of $4.2 trillion. With the exception of two corporations – Petróleos of Venezuela and Daewoo of South Korea – the other 98 were Western or Japanese firms. The TNCs are rapidly boosting their foreign activities through a variety of non-equity firms (e.g. management contracts, franchising), as well as building technology networks with local enterprises (UNCTAD, 1999).

The free-market ideology and the new international trading regime that it produced have encouraged the free flow of capital across a borderless world. Concerns about transborder data flows and their impact on national sovereignty have been replaced by the race to embrace the global electronic marketplace. According to UNCTAD, in 1998, foreign direct investment flows increased by 39 per cent over the previous year to $644 billion, mainly as a result of more cross-border mergers. In 1998, mergers and acquisitions reached an all-time record, with more than 12 500 deals totalling over $1.6 trillion, profoundly affecting companies dealing in financial services and telecommunications (*Fortune*, 1999a).

The trend continued in 1999, when the rush towards mergers and acquisitions accelerated and in the USA deals worth $570 billion were completed in the first half of 1999 while European deals, fuelled by monetary union, were worth $346 billion in the same period (*The Economist*, 3–9 July 1999). The twenty-first century opened with the world's biggest merger between America Online (AOL), the largest Internet-based company with Time Warner, the world's biggest media and entertainment corporation.

That US-based businesses have benefited most by global deregulation is clear from examining the *Fortune 500*, the annual list published by the US business magazine *Fortune* of the world's top 500 corporations. Of the seven companies with profits above $6 billion, six were American, and US corporations were among the top revenue-generating corporations in 24 out of 43 industries represented in the 1999 survey. The USA led with 185 companies (37 per cent of all companies) followed by Europe with 170 companies (Germany – 42, France – 39, Britain – 38) and Japan with 100. Of the remaining 45 corporations, Canada had 12, Australia 7 and Russia 1.

The global South was represented with just 26 companies of which South Korea had 9, China 6, Brazil 4, Taiwan 2, India, Venezuela, Malaysia and Mexico had one each. The top 500 corporations had a total revenue in 1998 of $11.46 trillion, assets of nearly $39 trillion (a 14 per cent increase over 1997) and profits of $440 billion. (*Fortune*, 1999b).

That communications industries are central to this global growth is evident from the rapid expansion of electronic-based commerce. It is

Table 3.12 The world's top ten corporations in 1999

Company	Country	Market value ($ billion)
Microsoft	USA	407.22
General Electric	USA	333.05
IBM	USA	214.81
Exxon	USA	193.92
Royal Dutch/Shell	The Netherlands/UK	191.32
Wal-Mart Stores	USA	189.55
AT&T	USA	186.14
Intel	USA	180.24
Cisco Systems	USA	174.09
BP Amoco	UK	173.87

Source: *Business Week*, 12 July 1999

indicative of the changing contours of the global economy that in the 1999 *Global 1000*, the ranking of the world's biggest corporations on the basis of market capitalization, Microsoft tops the list – its market value has surged 95 per cent in the past year. As Table 3.12 shows, high-tech corporations such as IBM, Intel and AT&T were in the top 10, eight of which were US-based companies. The US corporations, which account for 57 per cent of the world's publicly invested capital, headed the list, with nearly half of the companies listed – 494, followed by 314 European corporations and 135 from Japan (*Business Week*, 1999d).

While the liberalization of global trade has created unprecedented prosperity for some countries, the benefits are confined to a select few countries and the corporations based there. The 200 richest people in the world more than doubled their net worth in the four years to 1998, to $1 trillion (UNDP, 1999). Of the top 10 richest people in the world seven were American, with Bill Gates leading the pack with a wealth of $90 billion (*Forbes*, 1999).

But market-based progress is also causing much misery in the world. The 1999 *Human Development Report* of the United Nations Development Programme notes that the income gap between the richest fifth of the world's people and the poorest fifth, measured by average national income per head, increased from 30 to one in 1960 to 74 to one in 1997 (UNDP, 1999).

Worse still, despite claims to have created jobs and prosperity, market-based solutions and cuts to the public sector are having a devastating affect on employment, especially in the global South. According to the International Labour Organization in 1998 one billion workers – or one-third of the world's labour force – were either unemployed (150 million) or underemployed (e.g. part-time and wanting to work longer, or earning less than a living wage), while in contrast, US unemployment was at its lowest level since the early 1970s (ILO, 1998).

|4|

The global media marketplace

The deregulation and liberalization of the international communication sector in the 1990s were paralleled in the media industries and, in conjunction with the new communication technologies of satellite and cable, have created a global marketplace for media products (McAnany and Wilkinson, 1996; McQuail and Siune, 1998; Melkote *et al.* 1998). The end uses of commercial satellites (p.101), show that the largest growing application of international communication infrastructures is for the delivery of media products – information, news and entertainment. As demonstrated by the case study of News Corporation in Chapter 3, it is now imperative for media conglomerates to plan their strategies in a global context, with the ultimate aim of 'profitable growth through exploiting economies of scope and scale' (OECD, 1992: 52). The convergence of both media and technologies, and the process of vertical integration in the media industries to achieve this aim, have resulted in the concentration of media power in the hands of a few large transnational companies, with implications for global democracy (McChesney, 1999).

Convergence

Before globalization, most media corporations had distinct areas of business: Disney, for example, was primarily concerned with cartoon films and theme-park operations; *Time* was known mainly as a publishing business; Viacom was a TV syndication and cable outfit, and News Corporation was a group which owned a chain of newspapers in Australia. With the privatization of broadcasting across the globe, coupled with new methods of delivering media and communication content – namely, satellite, cable and the Internet – the distinctions between these industries are being dissolved.

With deregulation, and the relaxation of cross-media ownership restrictions, especially in the USA and Britain, media companies started to look to

broaden and deepen their existing interests and since the mid-1980s there
has been a gathering wave of mergers and acquisitions. In 1985 Rupert
Murdoch bought Twentieth Century Fox in order to acquire a base in the
USA and in 1989 Sony bought Columbia TriStar. In the same year Time Inc.
merged with Warner Communication, forming Time Warner to which
Turner Broadcasting Systems was added in 1995. Disney bought Capital
Cities/American Broadcasting Corporation (ABC) in 1995, thereby adding a
broadcast network to a traditionally entertainment company. Seagram
acquired Universal Studios in 1995 and in 1998 bought music company
PolyGram. Viacom bought Blockbuster video distribution and Paramount
in 1994 and Bertelsmann purchased Random House in 1998.

The $80 billion merger in September 1999, of two major US corpora-
tions, Viacom and Columbia Broadcasting System (CBS), created at that
time the world's largest entertainment and media company in the production, promotion and distribution of entertainment, news, sports and music.
However, it was soon to be overtaken by the megamerger of the biggest
Internet-based company America On Line (AOL), Time Warner and EMI in
the opening weeks of the new millennium, creating the world's fourth largest
corporation worth an estimated $350 billion (Waters, 2000).

In the twenty-first century, such trends towards media consolidation are
likely to reduce even further the number of corporations controlling both
content and delivery internationally. Less than ten corporations, most based
in the USA, own most of the world's media industries, with AOL-Time
Warner being at the forefront, followed by Walt Disney, Viacom-CBS,
Bertelsmann, News Corporation, Seagram, Telecommunication Inc. (TCI),
Sony and the National Broadcasting Corporation (NBC).

All the major television corporations – Disney, Time Warner, News
Corporation and Viacom – own multiple broadcast and cable networks and
production facilities. With the convergence of the media industries and integration from content origination through to delivery mechanisms, a few
conglomerates will control all the major aspects of mass media: newspapers,
magazines, books, radio, broadcast television, cable systems and programming, movies, music recordings, video cassettes and on-line services (*see*
Table 4.1, pp.126–127).

Time Warner

The New York-based Time Warner, the world's largest entertainment and
information company, has major businesses in movies, publishing, music,
and cable TV and the Internet. With the acquisition of Turner Broadcasting
it gained an international television presence in news and entertainment,
from Cable News Network (CNN), the 24-hour global news channel, which
claims to be the 'world's most extensively syndicated television news
service,' (see also p. 156) to Turner Network Broadcasting (TNT) and
Turner Classic Movies and Cartoon Network, the international children's
channel.

The publishing arm of the company is Time Inc. with its flagship international magazine *Time* and 32 other magazines, including *Fortune, Life, People, Sports Illustrated, Entertainment Weekly,* and *Asiaweek.* The total readership of the Group's magazines is estimated at 120 million. It is also a leading book publisher (Warner Books; Little, Brown) and a direct marketer of books, music and videos (Time Life).

Its music wing, Warner Music Group, whose record labels include – Warner Music International, Atlantic, Elektra, Warner Bros. Records and their affiliate labels – is one of the world's leading music entertainment companies, that owns one million music copyrights. With a growing presence overseas, Warner Music Group derived more than half its 1998 recorded music revenues from outside the USA. With its merger with EMI, Time Warner-EMI has become the world's second largest music company, accounting for 20 per cent of global market share (Teather, 2000).

The group's other major interest is in filmed entertainment through Warner Brothers, one of the world's best-known film companies, which has evolved into a global entertainment corporation with businesses ranging from film and television production and product licensing to a broadcast television network. Drawing on its vast library – 5 700 feature films, 32 000 television programmes, 13 500 animated titles, including 1 500 classic cartoons – Warner Brothers products are ubiquitous.

The group also owns TBS Superstation, which claims to have the largest audience of any cable network in the USA, and Home Box Office (HBO) cable network with 10 branded channels and more than 34 million US subscribers in 1998. Apart from being a supplier of programming, Time Warner is heavily involved in the cable industry, providing digitally compatible cable networks to households in the USA, in second place after TCI, the world's biggest cable operator. After its merger with AOL, Time Warner is set to become one of the most powerful media and entertainment corporations, with the potential to dominate all forms of media.

Bertelsmann

With annual revenues of $15.2 billion in 1998, the German media giant, Bertelsmann, is not only the world's largest publisher of books and magazines but also has interests in television, film and radio, in music labels and clubs, and in on-line services and multimedia. Bertelsmann supplies news, entertainment, music and on-line services in more than 53 countries. Nearly 60 per cent of its business is in Europe, followed by the USA, which accounts for nearly 35 per cent. Besides owning Random House, one of the world's largest publishing organizations, the company also owns many book clubs, including Britain's Book Club Associates, Doubleday Direct of the USA, and has major publishing interests in France, Spain and Germany.

Founded in 1835, the firm began as a regional publisher of religious books but expanded its publishing operations in Europe in the 1960s and

1970s, especially through book clubs (Gunther, 1998). Though the corporation has diversified its operations, the emphasis has remained on publishing, accounting in 1998 for nearly 31 per cent of its business. In 1999, Bertelsmann was the world's largest publisher, with Random House alone shipping over one million books a day. The group's Doubleday book club is one of the world's biggest, with some 25 million readers in Europe, North and South America and China. The group also owns Grüner and Jahr, Europe's leading magazine publisher, producing more than 80 magazines (magazines accounted for 20 per cent of business in 1998) and has 50 per cent equity in the Internet book retailer barnesandnoble.com.

Another major area of interest is music, accounting for nearly 30 per cent of all business in 1998. The music arm of the corporation, the Bertelsmann Music Group (BMG), produces more than 200 labels, including RCA, Arista and Ariola, along with the world's biggest music club, available in most of Europe, North America, Brazil, Australia, Japan, Singapore and South Africa. Hardware is provided by Sonopress, the world's second-largest manufacturer of CDs. This Bertelsmann company has pioneered new audio and video formats such as digital video disk (DVD). The record labels are also promoted on the net through Getmusic.com, the company's music site.

Bertelsmann has been one of the major beneficiaries both of the growth of commercial television and radio in Europe and of the privatization of the media in eastern and central Europe after the reunification of Germany. In 1997, Bertelsmann's UFA combined with the Luxembourg broadcaster CLT to form CLT-UFA. In 1999, it claimed to be Europe's highest revenue-generating media group.

Viacom/CBS

The merger of Viacom and CBS, one of the top TV networks in the USA, announced in September 1999, created another huge global media conglomerate. The operations of Viacom, one of the world's largest entertainment companies, span film, TV and publishing. The group owns Paramount Pictures, a leading producer and distributor of feature films since 1912, with more than 2 500 titles in its library, including such popular films as *The Ten Commandments* and *The Godfather* and modern blockbusters like *Forrest Gump*, *Deep Impact*, *Star Trek: Insurrection* and *Titanic* (the highest-grossing motion picture to date). United International Pictures, partly owned by Viacom, manages the foreign distribution of Paramount's feature films to over 60 countries around the world.

In television, the company has a global presence through such channels as Music Television (MTV), Nickelodeon, VH1, Showtime and The Movie Channel. Its Paramount Television is one of the largest suppliers of television programming for broadcasters worldwide, drawing on a library of 16 000 television episodes. MTV, the most widely distributed cable network in the world, reaches more than 314 million households in 83 countries, while Nickelodeon, one of the world's largest producers of children's programming, reaches more than 135 million households in over 100 countries.

The group also has interests in publishing through its ownership of Simon & Schuster, which has 34 imprints, including Scribners, Pocket Books, The Free Press and Touchstone, and annually publishes more than 2 400 titles. Following the success of MTV, in 1995 it launched the MTV Books imprint and children's books under the Nick Jr. imprint. The Simon Spotlight imprint publishes books tied to Viacom properties such as Rugrats. Simon & Schuster is also the world's largest audio publisher, owning Famous Music Publishing, one of the top 10 music publishers in the USA, whose catalogue contains over 100 000 copyrights from six decades of Hollywood films, as well as the music from Paramount's hit television shows including *Star Trek, The Odd Couple, Cheers* and *Frasier*. The group also has an interest in UCI, an international cinema chain.

The group owns Blockbuster, Hollywood's largest customer and, with more than 6 000 video and music stores in 27 countries, is one of the world's leading distributors of filmed entertainment. There are around 60 million Blockbuster cardholders worldwide, making over one billion store visits annually. Viacom's five theme parks, which feature characters from its TV programmes, are visited by more than 13 million people each year. The group has a significant and growing Internet presence, including cbs. sportsline.com, mtv.com, vh1.com, and Nick.com.

With the addition of CBS, which owns CBS Television Network and 15 CBS-owned TV stations; CBS Cable – two country networks and regional sports operations; Infinity Broadcasting Corporation which operates 163 radio stations, Viacom is set to further consolidate its international media presence, especially in the area of news. Viacom has been called 'a cradle-to-grave advertising depot' (Siklos, 1999: 72), catering to toddlers with children's channels such as Nickelodeon, to youth, by way of MTV and to the older generation through CBS.

The Walt Disney Company

The California-based Walt Disney company, the world's second largest media corporation after Time Warner, with one of its strongest brands, has interests in all the main aspects of international media. Disney owns ABC, one of the three biggest TV networks in the USA, apart from owning and operating 10 local TV and nearly 30 radio stations in the USA. The Disney Channel and Toon Disney, are two major cable channels in the USA. In addition, Disney owns Entertainment and Sports Network (ESPN) and partly owns, with Hearst and GE, Arts and Entertainment Television (A&E), as well as shares in The History Channel and E! Entertainment channel.

Disney channels also have a global presence. In 1998, there were country or area-specific Disney channels operating in Britain, Taiwan, Australia, Malaysia, France, Italy, Spain and the Middle East. In international sports, ESPN owns one third of Eurosport, the pan-European satellite service, 25 per cent of Sportsvision of Australia and half of ESPN STAR in Asia and Net STAR (33 per cent) owners of The Sports Network of Canada. The company also has Professional Sports Franchises through stakes in major US national hockey and baseball teams.

The company also had minority stakes in television companies in Germany (Tele-München), France (TV Sport), Spain (Tesauro), the Scandinavian Broadcasting System, and Japan Sports Channel. In the area of television production and distribution, the company has a global presence with Buena Vista Television, Touchstone Television, Walt Disney Television, Walt Disney Television Animation, with production facilities in Japan, Australia and Canada. The same is the case in movie production and distribution through Walt Disney Pictures, Touchstone Pictures, Hollywood Pictures, Caravan Pictures, Miramax Films, Buena Vista Home Video, Buena Vista Home Entertainment, Buena Vista International.

Its publishing arm, Walt Disney Book Publishing, produces Hyperion Books and Miramax Books and has other subsidiary groups, such as ABC Publishing, Disney Publishing, and Fairchild Publishing. The Group also publishes more than 20 magazines, including *Automotive Industries, Institutional Investor, Disney Magazine, ESPN Magazine, Video Business* and *Top Famille* (a French family magazine).

In the arena of music, Disney owns several recording labels, including Buena Vista Music Group, with its Hollywood Records (popular music and soundtracks for films), Lyric Street Records (country music label), Mammoth Records (popular and alternative music label) and Walt Disney Records. Disney is developing a presence on the net, with such major sites as ABC.com, Disney.com, ESPN.sportzone.com, Go Network. It also partly owns Infoseek, the Internet portal. The company also develops and markets computer software, video games and CD-ROMs, based on Disney characters.

Another major sphere of operations is its theme parks and resorts: Walt Disney World, Disney's Animal Kingdom, and the Magic Kingdom in the USA; Disneyland Paris and Tokyo Disneyland, and more than 660 Disney shops spread across the world, retail Disney merchandise – an estimated 14 per cent of its revenue came from merchandising and Disney Store sales in 1998 (Grover, 1999: 47).

Sony

Another global conglomerate is the Tokyo-based consumer electronics and multimedia entertainment giant, Sony, with 72 per cent of its sales and operating revenues from overseas sales. The USA is Sony's biggest market, followed by Europe. In 1999, its total sales and operating revenue stood at $56.62 billion (Sony, 1999). Sony is an interesting example of expanding into content creation from a base in hardware and equipment.

Since its founding in 1946, the Sony corporation has grown to become a global producer of communication hardware, especially electronics products, which accounted for 64 per cent of sales in 1999 at $36 billion. Among its major products are MD systems, CD players, stereos, digital audio tape, recorders/players, DVD-video players, video CD players, digital still cameras, broadcast video equipment, videotapes, digital TVs, personal computers, cellular phones, satellite broadcasting reception systems and Internet terminals.

Another area in which Sony has a global dominance is the computer game market, accounting for more than 11 per cent of sales and operating revenue at $6.3 billion in 1999. Since the sale of the first PlayStation game console in 1994, this sector of Sony has grown extremely fast, with sales and revenue demonstrating a more than 200-fold increase in the period 1995–99. By developing new genres of software, with advanced computer graphic technology, Sony is set to make video games a major leisure activity among the youth across the globe – by 1999, cumulative production shipments worldwide of PlayStation reached 54.4 million units (Sony, 1999).

Sony's global business interests in music and music publishing accounted for more than 10 per cent of its sales and revenues in 1999, at nearly $6 billion. Through its global network of label affiliations, Sony tapes and CDs are sold in their millions in all the major regions of the world. In 1998, for example, the album by Mariah Carey and the soundtrack from the film *Titanic*, sold more than eight million, while the soundtrack of the Indian blockbuster film *Kuch Kuch Hota Hai* sold over five million copies worldwide. Ricky Martin's *La Copa de la Vida*, the official song of the World Cup France '98, was a number one single in more than 30 countries (ibid.).

Sony is also a major player in the international entertainment business by virtue of owning Columbia TriStar, one of the world's top film and television production company, which includes Columbia Pictures, Screen Gems, Sony Pictures Classics and Columbia TriStar Film Distributors International. Sony's television interests include Columbia TriStar Television, producer of such internationally adapted game shows as *Wheel of Fortune*, the highest-rated game show in the USA for the past 13 years; Columbia TriStar International Television and Game Show Network, while its home video operations are conducted through Columbia TriStar Home Video.

Besides operating more than 900 cinema screens around the world, Sony is also involved in local-language film production in the UK, Germany, France and Hong Kong and television programming in eight languages. In 1999, it had more than 25 international channels with a global audience of approximately 120 million. Revenues from licensing films and programmes from Columbia's library of more than 3 500 films and 40 000 television episodes,

Table 4.1 Media convergence and integration – the top six players

Area of interest	Time Warner	Disney	Sony	Bertelsmann	Viacom	News Corp.
TV channels	CNN, TNT, Cartoon Network HBO	ABE, Disney Channels, ESPN, History Channel (Joint Venture)	Sony Entertainment Television – more than 25 international channels	CLT-UFA-22 TV channels including RTL, RTL II (Germany) M6 (France), RTL 4 (Holland) RTL 7 (Poland) and 18 radio stations in ten European countries	CBS, MTV Nickelodeon, Showtime Networks	Fox Networks Fox Sports Networks Fox Kids Canal Fox Sky Channels Star TV Channel [V] Phoenix (JV)
TV production	Warner Bros TV	Buena Vista TV Touchstone TV Walt Disney TV	Columbia TriStar International Television, Game Show Network.	CLT-UFA, Europe's largest film producing enterprise	Paramount TV Spelling Television	Twentieth Century Fox TV
Film	Warner Bros	Walt Disney Pictures, Touchstone Pictures, Miramax Pictures, Buena Vista International Pictures	Columbia TriStar Columbia Pictures, Screen Gems, Sony Pictures Classics		Paramount Pictures	Twentieth Century Fox Films
Newspapers and magazines	*Time, Life Fortune, Sports Illustrated, Entertainment Weekly* and 27 other magazines	More than 20 magazines including *Disney Magazine* and *ESPN Magazine*		Grüner + Jahr – Europe's largest magazine publisher, producing more than 80 magazines		More than 160 newspapers in 6 countries, including *The Times* (London), *New York Post, The Australian TV Guide*

Table 4.1 continued

Area of interest	Time Warner	Disney	Sony	Bertelsmann	Viacom	News Corp.
Book publishing	Warner Books, Book-of-the-Month Club, Little, Brown and Co.	Walt Disney Book Publishing, Hyperion Books, Miramax Books		Random House, Berlin, Goldmann and Siedler (Germany), Transworld (UK), Springer Scientific Publisher, Book clubs including, BCA (UK) and Doubleday Direct (US)	Simon & Schuster Group	HarperCollins Publishing Group
Music	Warner Music International	Walt Disney Records, Buena Vista Music Group, Hollywood Records	Sony Music	Bertelsmann Music Group, produces more than 200 labels, including RCA, Arista and Ariola		
Hardware	TV Cable		Electronics products	Sonopress, the world's second largest manufacturer of CDs.		Digital decoders
1998 Revenue	$26.83 billion	$22.97 billion	$56.62 billion.	$15.2 billion	$18.9 billion	$13.6 billion

have more than doubled between 1995 and 1998. Already operating its own international channels, such as Sony Entertainment Television (India), the company is expanding its action channel AXN into Spain and Japan and starting a Japanese animation channel - ANIMAX. In 1999, Sony was planning a children-oriented family entertainment unit 'to create and acquire properties and characters we can market across all lines of business' (Sony, 1999).

With its experience in information technology, Sony is well placed to exploit new forms of digital content and distribution – it is already a producer of new and library films in the DVD format and is using the advent of Internet technologies and digital distribution to promote its record labels.

Other major players

Apart from these top global players, TCI, NBC (owned by General Electric) and the Canadian entertainment company Seagram have a significant international presence. The Montreal-based Seagram, which runs one of the largest distilleries in the world, is also a major entertainment corporation with global presence, offering movies, television programmes, music and theme parks. With 1998 revenue of $9.7 billion, its Universal Studios (formerly MCA), produces and distributes films, television, home video products, music and operates theme parks and more than 500 retail gift stores. In addition to 84 per cent ownership of Universal Studios, the company owns PolyGram, the largest record company in the world, which it acquired in 1998. Universal produces and distributes films worldwide in the theatrical, television, home video and pay television markets. In addition, it licenses merchandising rights and film property publishing rights. It also has interests in multiplex cinema chains, for example, United Cinemas International Multiplex.

Synergies

As is clear from Table 4.1, a few large conglomerates dominate the global media industries and the exponential growth in the reach of the media coupled with diversification of its forms and modes of delivery have made convergence a reality. The media conglomerates can promote their products across virtually all media segments, including broadcast and cable television, radio and on-line media. For example, *The Times* of London can be used to promote Murdoch's television interests in Britain, while TNT films can be advertised on the CNN networks. The exploitation of synergies – the process by which one company subsidiary is used to complement and promote another – by media conglomerates has greatly increased their power over global news, information and entertainment.

Much of the global film and television production and distribution is in the hands of a few Hollywood studios – Paramount Pictures (part of

Viacom); Universal Studios (part of Seagram);Warner Brothers (part of Time Warner); Disney; Twentieth Century Fox (part of News Corporation) and Metro-Goldwyn-Meyer (MGM). The California-based MGM company has a library of 4 000 films and more than 8 200 TV episodes and it includes MGM Studios, United Artists, Goldwyn Entertainment and Orion Pictures.

These companies develop, produce and distribute film and television programmes, soundtracks, cartoons and interactive products for a global audience. They also make money by charging for the rights to use the characters, titles and other material, and rights from television and films and other sources are licensed to manufacturers and retailers. Typically, a film is first distributed in the theatrical, home video and pay television markets before being made available for worldwide television syndication. Some made-for-TV films are licensed for network exhibition in the United States and simultaneously syndicated overseas. After its showing on a network, a series may be licensed for broadcast on cable.

The film soundtrack albums are released by the music publishing arms of the corporations, who also license music from their copyright catalogues for a variety of uses including recorded music, videocassettes, videodisks, video games, radio, television and films. Concerts and live events are presented at and promoted by the corporation's television channels.

This synergy can be illustrated by the following example: Viacom capitalizes on the strength of its internationally known brand name MTV to launch MTV Books, an imprint launched with company's publishing arm Simon & Schuster's Pocket Books; MTV Films produces and develops film and TV programming, including *Beavis and Butt-head Do America* with Paramount Pictures, owned by Viacom. These films are sold by its 6 000 Blockbuster video stores across the world. A variety of programming-based CD-ROMs and a host of home videos, albums and products from more than 50 international licensees are then promoted, including on the Internet, at MTV On-line.

Another example of cross-promotion is the phenomenally popular Paramount Television's *Star Trek* franchise, which has generated three more television shows, including *Star Trek: Voyager;* nine *Star Trek* films from Paramount Pictures; more than 65 million copies of *Star Trek*-related books from Simon & Schuster; four CD-ROM titles for Simon & Schuster Interactive; and *Star Trek: The Experience* at the Paramount theme park.

Disney has its own central synergy department charged with maximizing company product sales, through cross-selling and cross-promotion strategies involving hundreds of media markets round the world. It publishes a series of books based on Disney characters; its own magazines, videos, CD-ROMS, on-line programmes; it produces top-selling toys, and promotes its products through Disney theme parks and retail stores.

The model has been compared with a wheel:

At the hub lies content creation. The spokes that spread out from it are the many different ways of exploiting the resulting brands: the movie studio, the television networks, the music, the publishing, the merchandising, the theme parks, the Internet sites. Looked at this way, the distinction between manufacturing and distribution begins to blur, because the various ways of selling the brand also serve to enhance its value.

(The Economist, 1998: 8)

Despite intense competition among major corporations to control distribution and production to feed satellite and cable channels worldwide, they have many overlapping operations. Media rivals can share content through programming consortiums like Latin America Pay TV (News Corp., Universal, Viacom, MGM), HBO Ole and HBO Brasil (Time Warner, Sony, Disney), and HBO Asia (Time Warner, Sony, Universal and Viacom) (Rose, 1998: 50).

Likewise, Disney shares programming with TCI in E! Entertainment and News Corp. in ESPN Star Sports in Asia. Sony has aligned itself with Canal Plus, Europe's leading pay-TV company. In movies, Paramount frequently splits costs with studios like Miramax, owned by Disney. Viacom TV stations are major buyers of Sony broadcasting equipment, while Sony Music can be promoted on MTV, owned by Viacom.

Many commentators have expressed fears about the possibility of so much of power being concentrated in so few corporations and that these few mainly American conglomerates may act like a cartel in production and distribution of global information and entertainment (Herman and McChesney 1997; Bagdikian, 1997; McChesney, 1999). Monitoring this trend towards concentration, in his 1983 book *Media Monopoly*, the US media scholar Ben Bagdikian argued that the US media were dominated by 50 private corporations. By 1997, when the book was republished in its fifth edition, the number of corporations controlling most of US media had dropped to just 10. In the twenty-first century, it would appear the US-led global media is in the grip of a new communications cartel.

The growing involvement of industrial conglomerates in the media business, including such major defence industry players as General Electric (NBC) and Westinghouse (CBS, before it merged with Viacom), also has implications to what is covered by global media and how (Bagdikian, 1997). In 1998, for example, Disney's ABC news division dropped a critical report about Disney's theme park from its broadcast (*The Economist*, 1998). As one commentator noted:

A market system of control limits free expression by market processes that are highly effective. Dissident ideas are not legally banned, they are simply unable to reach mass audiences, which are monopolised by large profit-seeking corporations that offer programmes supported by advertising, from which dissent is quietly and unobtrusively filtered out.

(Herman, 1999: 18)

Global trade in media products

The global trade in cultural goods (films, television, printed matter, music, computers) has almost tripled between 1980 and 1991, from $67 billion to $200 billion and is growing at a rapid pace with the liberalization of these sectors across the world (UNESCO, 1998b). The United States is the leading exporter of cultural products and the entertainment industry is one of its largest export earners. Table 4.2 lists the world's top five entertainment corporations, three of which are based in the USA, while the other two have substantial US business and corporate connections.

Television

As Table 4.3 shows, for several leading media companies, a significant proportion of their revenue comes from television. Most of the world's entertainment output is transmitted through television, which is increasingly becoming global in its operations, technologies and audiences (Smith, 1998). One of the most significant factors is the growth in satellite television, which cuts across national and linguistic boundaries, creating new international audiences. In 1998, according to the *Screen Digest*, more than 2 600 television channels were operating in the world, the majority of which were private channels (*Screen Digest*, May 1998). The number of television

Table 4.2 The world's top five entertainment corporations, 1998

Company	Country	Revenues ($m)	Profits ($m)
Walt Disney	USA	22 976	1 850
Time Warner	USA	14 582	168
News Corporation	Australia	12 995	1 153
Viacom	USA	12 096	(122)
Seagram	Canada	10 734	946

Source: Fortune, 1999b

Table 4.3 The sultans of the small screen

Company	1998 total revenue ($ billion)	1998 TV revenue ($ billion)	% of total revenue
Time Warner	26.83	18.46	69
TCI	7.35	7.35	100
Walt Disney	22.97	7.14	31
CBS	6.80	4.91	72

Source: Based on data from *Television Business International* July/August 1999

sets in the world has tripled since 1980, with Asia showing the highest growth, as demonstrated in Figure 4.1.

The potential of this market, especially in China and India, can be seen from Table 4.4, showing the levels of TV ownership and the penetration of cable and satellite television internationally.

The volume of US trade in cultural products and its capacity to produce and distribute to an international audience ensure that US-based networks are the most prevalent in the global television system. In most countries outside the USA, imported programming forms a significant part of the

Table 4.4 World's biggest TV markets, 1997

Country	TV households (millions)	Cable homes (millions)	Satellite homes (millions)
China	340	57	0.80
USA	98	66	8
India	79	19	2.5
Russia	45	14.5	0.35
Japan	41	14	12
Germany	37	19	11
Brazil	36	1.3	2.4
Britain	24	2.3	4.3
Indonesia	20	0.02	3
Italy	19	0.01	0.76

Source: Based on data from *Screen Digest,* May 1998

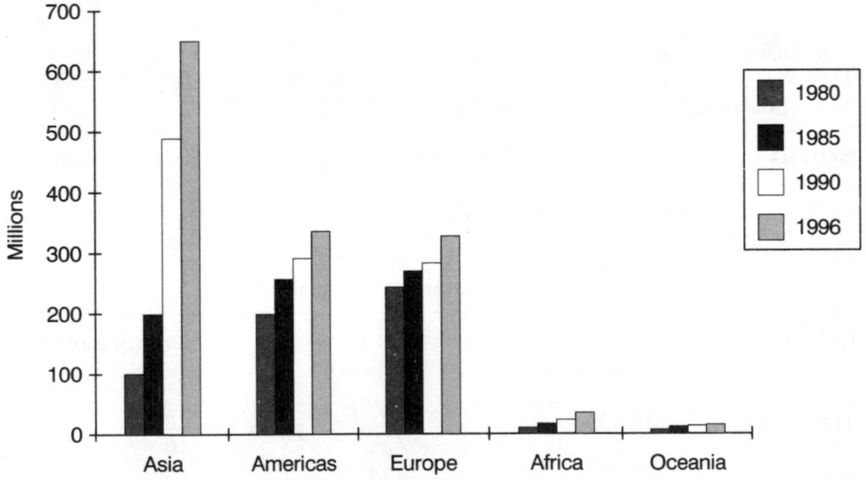

Figure 4.1 Growth in TV sets, 1980–96
Source: UNESCO, 1998

television schedule, making the USA a 'world provider' of television programmes (Dunnett, 1990). Table 4.5 lists the main players in global television, ranked in terms of the number of households where these networks are available.

US entertainment programmes – drama serials, soaps and shows, such as *Star Trek, Baywatch, Friends, ER,* and *The X Files* are shown on television channels all over the world. In addition, syndication companies also sell 'format rights' for programmes that are more nationally specific, such as game shows. The formats of such US-made shows as *Family Feud* and *Wheel of Fortune* have been adapted for production in many countries (Blumenthal and Goodenough, 1998). Some genres of television, notably animation, music, wildlife documentaries and live sporting events, are relatively easy to sell into different cultural contexts. Wildlife programmes, for example, can translate easily into other languages, since they often do not have a visible presenter and therefore it is cheaper for voice-over track to be laid down.

The US-based Discovery network, making factual programmes about history, science and technology, art and natural history, is the key player in this genre. From its modest beginnings in 1985, it has grown to become the world's biggest producer of documentaries, reaching 144 million households in more than 140 countries. Half owned by Liberty Media Group, the Discovery Networks International (DNI), its international network and programme distribution division, includes Discovery Channel, Discovery Kids, Discovery Home & Leisure, and two joint-venture channels with the BBC – Animal Planet and People+Arts. With 1999 revenues at $1.1 billion and its services being translated into 24 languages, Discovery was planning to launch a travel and a health channel as well as Discovery Civilisation and Discovery Science channels on a digital platform, which is estimated to increase the company's value to around $14 billion (*Business Week*, 1999b).

Table 4.5 Global TV in 1998

Network	Type	Ownership	No. of households (millions)
MTV Networks	Youth Music	Viacom, US	310
ESPN	Sport	Walt Disney, Hearst Corp	250
CNN International	News	Time Warner, US	221
NBC	News	NBC, US	200
Discovery Channel	Documentaries	Discovery Comm.	144
CNBC	Financial news	NBC	142
TNT	Films	Time Warner	140
Cartoon Network	Cartoons	Time Warner	125
BBC World	News	BBC	60

Sources: Based on data from *Advertising Age International*, 8 February, 1999 and company websites

In addition, through its chains of Discovery Channel Stores it sells catalogues, videos, books and travel packages.

National Geographic Television, which has a business partnership with NBC since 1996, and had its overseas debut in Britain in 1997, broadcasts to 54 countries, reaching 40 million households in nine languages (Fannin, 1999a). The History Channel, owned by the A & E Television, has a 50–50 joint venture with BSkyB in Britain. The Sci-Fi channel brings latest science and technology news and science fiction to viewers across the world. One reason for the international expansion of such channels is that most of their tailoring to local markets is dubbing and sub-titling and the content is portable and generally non-political.

In the global adult TV market, Playboy TV International, is pre-eminent. This joint venture between Playboy Enterprises and Latin American media giant Cisneros Television Group, owns and operates nine Playboy-branded channels, available in Latin America, Europe and Japan. The channel also has international rights to its huge programmes library of adult television material and it aims to set up new Playboy channels across the world (Tobin, 1999a).

The USA also is a major player in religious television, which is being increasingly commercialized and globalized. The Family Channel, which was launched in 1977, the first 24-hour religious cable network, as the Christian Broadcasting Network, and which since 1997 has been part of Fox Network, is a major player, along with the 24-hour Trinity Broadcasting Network, founded in 1973, and carried by thousands of cable affiliates in the USA, also owns, or is affiliated with, more than 530 broadcasting stations throughout the world (Schreiber, 1999). The Eternal Word Television Network, 'the global Catholic network' which claims to be the world's largest Catholic television, founded in 1981, now reaches more than 55 million homes in 38 countries in Europe, the Pacific Rim, Africa and the Americas. In Europe the biggest player is the British-based Christian Channel Europe, available in 22 million homes across 24 countries including Russia and countries of North Africa (Callard, 1999).

Two major areas of international television are sport and popular music, which reach across national barriers of language and culture, delivering the largest audiences for US networks, ESPN and MTV. MTV, part of the media giant Viacom, is the world's most widely watched television network, which with its local and regional channels, dominates global youth music, while ESPN, with 24 networks is the global leader in sports television, claiming to reach 250 million households in 21 languages.

Televising sport globally – ESPN

A major factor in the expansion of satellite and cable television internationally has been television's unique ability to transmit live sports events. As a genre, sports programmes cut across national and cultural boundaries. Live coverage of a prestigious football league match is as much a media event in Cameroon as it is in the Czech Republic. Unlike films, which the consumers can rent from video outlets, the live nature of sports coverage makes it suitable for pay-television, a fact which media companies are using as an incentive for subscribing to pay-TV.

Sport is increasingly becoming a major industry and advertisers are keen to exploit the reach of TV channels dedicated to sport. During the 1998 World Cup soccer some games were watched by over a billion people. FIFA which licenses the World Cup, sold the global rights for the 2002 and 2006 tournaments for $2.24 billion – in 1998 the same rights were sold for $230 million (Blumenthal and Goodenough, 1998). This reach is making television an expensive proposition. In 1949, the BBC paid just £5 387 for Britain's FA Cup, by 1998 ITV paid $51 million for the same rights. Such has been the change that when FA Premiership announced a $6.17 billion five-year joint deal with BSkyB and the BBC it did not seem to evoke much surprise (Ryan, 1999).

The cost of global TV rights for the Olympic Games has increased ten-fold from the Moscow games of 1980 to Atlanta in 1996. As indicated by Table 4.6, only broadcasters from the media-rich regions can afford to pay TV rights for major sporting events like the Olympics. US networks have provided up to 75 per cent of total Olympic revenue from TV rights and production costs, with NBC being one of major networks to benefit from this commercialization of sport.

One consequence of the soaring cost of rights for sports coverage is the creation of new contests by media giants. In 1998, the Milan-based Media Partners tried to establish a new European Super League football tournament and in the same year Manchester United, the world's most profitable football club, launched its own channel MUTV, jointly owned by BSkyB, Granada Media Group and the Club. For a major domestic sporting league such as National Football League (American Football) ESPN has signed a $2.2 billion annual fee sports rights agreement with ABC and Fox, for the period 1998–2006.

The increasing commercialization and 'media-ization' of sport are also reflected in commercial sponsorship of the games and teams themselves. The 1996 Olympics in Atlanta, for example, set records by selling more than $1 billion in corporate sponsorship (Real, 1996: 252). Merchandising such as baseball caps in the USA and football shirts in Europe, along with corporate public relations and cross-marketing have

Table 4.6 TV rights payments for the Olympic Games ($ million)

	Moscow 1980	Los Angeles 1984	Seoul 1988	Barcelona 1992	Atlanta 1996
USA	72	225	300	401	456
Europe	6	20	28	90	255
Japan	5	18	52	63	100
Australia	1	11	7	34	30

Source: Based on data from *Screen Digest*, June 1996

become an integral part of televised sports. Apart from selling company products, the trend is towards marketing of sport stars themselves. A US basketball player Michael Jordan has become an international icon by selling Nike shoes, while Indian cricket captain Sachin Tendulkar is the best salesman Pepsi ever had.

A symbiotic relationship has evolved between global sport and the international television industry. Given the profit involved, sport networks have to find new and innovative ways to fill their international channels and keep the advertisers happy. ESPN, for example, is investing in promoting its X Games, started in 1995, featuring the world's top athletes in several sport categories. There are plans to expand the 'X' franchise with several events throughout the world – an Asian X Games Qualifier and a new Junior X Games, co-developed by the Disney Channel and televised by Disney around the world. ESPN International will televise six original hours from the qualifier on several networks.

The Entertainment and Sports Network (ESPN) is the world's leading sports television broadcaster and one of the world's most profitable networks, 80 per cent owned by Disney Corporation, with the remaining 20 per cent owned by the Hearst Corporation. In 1999, it was reaching 242 million households across the globe.

ESPN has a share in the pan-European sports network Eurosport, of which it owns 33 per cent, the rest being owned by EBU, TF1 and Canal Plus, and reaching 80 million homes in 47 countries in Europe and the Middle East. ESPN's Latin American operation has a viewership of 9 million, while with its 50 per cent ownership of Star Sports, part of News Corporation, the ESPN network claims to reach nearly 91 million viewers across Asia. This global television audience is made possible by PanAmSat satellites which act as its global programme distribution network. ESPN's cable affiliates downlink its customized signals from five PanAmSat satellites, serving the USA and the Atlantic Ocean, Pacific Ocean and Indian Ocean regions.

Apart from its highly popular domestic cable networks in the USA (ESPN, ESPN2, ESPN Classic, ESPNEWS – presents coverage of 195 live news events and press conferences each month), the network has been steadily increasing its global presence since it launched ESPN International in 1988. In 1999, ESPN International had 20 international networks and syndication, including – Sports-i ESPN (Japan), ESPN Asia, ESPN Taiwan, Sky Sports (New Zealand) and ESPN Australia. It owns 50 per cent of ESPN Brazil and one-third of Net STAR, owners of The Sports Network of Canada, and a quarter of Sportsvision of Australia.

Syndicated programming from ESPN Radio is broadcast globally while Hearst Group distributes ESPN Magazine. ESPN.com is one of the most popular sport websites. In addition, ESPN also has a number of real and on-line shops, selling ESPN digital games, books, music, videos and CD-ROMs. There is even an ESPN credit card and ESPN Visa card. The company has developed global strategies to exploit the explosion of channels on satellite television and the potential of multi-million dollar sponsorship from transnational corporations, using television to promote their products (Bellamy, 1998).

In the area of supplying sports news and features a key player is TransWorld International (TWI), the world's largest independent supplier of sports programming. In 1996, TWI launched a joint venture with AP, Sports News Television (SNTV), a sports news video agency, which serves more than 100 broadcasters worldwide.

Apart from promoting corporate products does the globalization of sports television have more significant ideological implications? It has been argued that televised sport can be used to further political aims (Riggs, Eastman, and Golobic, 1993). Given that ESPN is the world leader in televising sport, it is conceivable that only those sports that are sponsored by big corporations and of interest to the widest possible audience will be encouraged. The new global media-sport industry offers interesting sites for future research.

Public service to private profit – European broadcasting

The international success of the US-originated commercial model of television has had a profound effect on broadcasting in Western Europe, the world's second biggest media market and home to a public service ethos of broadcasting (Atkinson and Raboy, 1997; Tracey, 1998). The privatization of the European airwaves, a process which started in the late 1980s, had by the beginning of the twenty-first century, transformed the media landscape (*see* Table 4.7), epitomized by the entry into international commercial television arena of the world's first and most famous public service broadcaster – the BBC.

The BBC is now Europe's largest exporter of television programmes: in 1997, it licensed 27000 hours of programming to 554 broadcasting organisations in 67 countries (Brown, D. 1998: 77), with sales from TV programme exports in 1998 accounting for £135 million (BBC, 1999b). Through its commercial arm, BBC Worldwide, formed in 1994, the BBC has entered into the competitive world media market through its wholly-owned channels and joint ventures, in the UK and globally.

In 1998, BBC Worldwide channels (both wholly-owned and joint-venture) were being watched by 230 million households worldwide, up from 115 million in 1997, providing outlets for BBC programming (ibid.). Nevertheless exports accounted for only 36 per cent of total programme sales, 12 per cent to the USA and 24 per cent to the rest of the world. Unlike US-based media TNCs, much of BBC's sales come from within the UK market. Also, it was publishing ventures, not television, that accounted for 61 per cent of the sales.

While BBC World, its 24-hour international news service has yet to make a profit, BBC Prime, its international entertainment channel, has been more successful. Launched in 1992, as a joint venture with the Pearson group, one of Britain's biggest media corporations, it offers English-language programming, primarily beamed at Europe. Through such joint ventures with commercial companies, the BBC has gradually expanded into the international markets. These partnerships are based on mutual benefit: the commercial channels gain by association with the BBC brand, while a cash-strapped

BBC can access more resource to produce programmes. Through its joint venture with Flextech – partly owned by TCI – the BBC has five pay-channels available on Sky Digital's package: UK Gold (comedy and drama), UK Horizons (factual entertainment), UK Arena (arts entertainment), UK Style (leisure and lifestyle) and UK Play (music and comedy).

In 1998, the BBC joined forces with the Discovery channel to launch a natural history and wildlife channel, Animal Planet, available in North America, Latin America and Asia. In the USA, the BBC also has a deal on sharing programmes and co-production with Boston broadcaster WGBH on behalf of US public television, and has also co-produced programmes with the A & E network.

Recognizing that imported programmes often do not receive prime-time slots in national broadcasting schedules, BBC Worldwide has launched branded blocks such as BBC Animal Zone, BBC Britcom and BBC Learning Zone. This strategy seems to work well as indicated by the success of BBC Exclusiv in Germany. Such an approach has allowed the BBC to raise its international profile and brand name and promote BBC products. In addition, the BBC can capitalize on its rich library of programmes, selling footage and specialist programme to broadcasters worldwide, accounting for more than £10 million in 1998. The BBC also sells specialized packages such as in-flight programming, sports programming and programme formats.

Apart from the BBC, one of the largest British-based media companies is Pearson Television, which has a wide range of entertainment programmes in production in more than 30 countries. Owning the largest selection of game-show formats in the world, it is also a major producer of serial dramas. It owns businesses in US syndication, international distribution and British transmission, a 24 per cent stake in Britain's Channel 5 and 20 per cent stakes in UKTV in Australia and M-RTL in Hungary. In 1998, Pearson Television made operating profits of £61m on sales of £343m.

The opening up of the audio-visual market both to pan-European and international operators has changed the television landscape in Europe, with a six-fold increase in the number of channels available to European audiences in the past decade, as shown in Table 4.7.

English was the most widely used language of television in Europe with 160 channels in operation in 1999, followed by French 120, German 80, Italian 78 and Arabic nearly 30. Among the pan-European channels, the top three in terms of distribution were in the categories of documentary, sport and music (*Screen Digest*, May 1999).

In the German-speaking market, the KirchGruppe is a major player. After its 1990 launch of the pay-TV channel Premiere, in collaboration with Bertelsmann and the French television company, Canal Plus, Kirch has become the main programme provider for European television channels. In 1999, KirchGruppe was the majority shareholder in SAT 1, the second-largest German private broadcasting company, DSF (Deutsches SportFernsehen), Germany's first commercial sports channel, and the digital

Table 4.7 Expansion of TV channels* in Europe

Channel type	1990	1998
Entertainment	37	149
General	42	114
Movies	7	94
Sport	2	32
News/Business	4	31
Music	4	30
Documentary	2	29
Children	3	26
Shopping	1	20
Lifestyle	0	17
Ethnic	0	16
Adult	0	13
Travel	0	12
Cultural	1	11
Total	103	594

*cable, satellite and digital terrestrial
Source: Based on data from *Screen Digest*, May 1999

pay-TV channel Premiere World. With more than 85 000 hours of programmes (feature films, serials, documentaries, children's TV, music) the KirchGruppe possesses one of the world's largest film and TV libraries, making it the leading European programme exporters.

The group also deals with German and international licensing rights for film and television. It has long-term licensing agreements with major studios such as Sony/Columbia, Viacom/Paramount, MCA/Universal, Warner Brothers and Disney/ABC. One key earner is its position as a leading trader of sporting rights – it won the broadcasting rights for the soccer World Cup in 2002 and 2006.

With 22 television stations and 18 radio stations in ten countries, Bertelsmann's CLT-UFA claims to be Europe's biggest broadcasting corporation. According to company figures, every day more than 120 million Europeans watch a CLT-UFA channel – RTL, RTL II or Super RTL in Germany, M6 in France, Channel 5 in Britain, RTL 4 in the Netherlands, RTL Klub in Hungary and RTL 7 in Poland. CLT-UFA is also one of Europe's largest television producer, making nearly 1 000 hours of programming every year, while the Hamburg-based *UFA Sports* has partnerships with soccer organisations, broadcasters and sponsors, marketing 200 European franchises and 40 national teams worldwide.

Programmes from major French companies such as Canal Plus International also have a pan-European viewership: in 1997 it had five million subscribers on the continent, with its biggest markets in Germany (1.5 million) and Spain (1.4 million). Outside Europe, the French presence is particularly strong in the Francophone regions of Africa where *Canal Plus*

Horizon had more than 110 000 subscribers in 1997, its key markets being Ivory Coast, Morocco, Senegal and Tunisia. The company's revenues rose from $1.45 billion in 1994 to $2.47 billion in 1998 (Williams, 1999).

According to *Screen Digest*, between 1992 and 1996 France managed to increase its exports of TV programmes by 20 per cent (*Screen Digest*, November 1997). Since 1998, the French-language international channel TV5 – jointly owned by a collection of French, Canadian, Swiss and Belgian public service broadcasters, has collaborated with Canal France International (CFI), to export French programmes. TV5, mostly financed by the French Foreign Ministry, broadcasts 24-hours a day on 5 000 cable networks across the world and is available on 23 satellite platforms which can reach a potential audience of 500 million (Vulser, 1999).

CFI supplies programming to 98 TV channels, mostly in Africa, but also in Eastern Europe and Haiti, Vietnam, Laos, Cambodia and Lebanon – with historical links with France. In Africa it supplies eight hours of programming, mainly sports and entertainment programmes – to 46 channels. In 1998, CFI television partners rebroadcast 24 000 hours of programmes, out of which 20 360 hours accounted for the African broadcasters (CFI website).

Other countries such as Brazil, Mexico, Egypt, India and China also export television programmes. Exports of television programmes from China's state broadcaster China Central Television (CCTV), nearly tripled – from 919 hours in 1993 to 2 880 hours in 1996 – most of this being used by satellite television channels aimed at the Chinese diaspora (*see* Chapter 6, pp. 212–14).

The international film industry

Though more films are produced in India than in the USA (*see* Table 4.8), global cinema and television screens are dominated by Hollywood: Hollywood films are shown in more than 150 countries, earning more than $30 billion worldwide in 1997. Half of Hollywood's revenue comes from overseas markets, up from just 30 per cent in 1980. The US film industry provides the majority of pre-recorded video cassettes seen on millions of television screens around the world. In 1996, it claimed nearly 70 per cent of the European and 83 per cent of Latin American market (UNESCO, 1998b). In 1990, world cinema box-office revenue was $11.8 billion and by 1999 it was approaching nearly 17 billion dollars and it is estimated that the value of the world cinema market is likely to reach $20 billion by 2003 (*Screen International*, October 1999).

Internationalization defined Hollywood for much of the twentieth century (Guback, 1969; Jarvie, 1992; Vasey, 1997), a trend which is likely to grow given the proliferation of new ways of delivery of films and films-based programming. Since at least the Second World War, US film corporations

Table 4.8 The world's top ten film-producing nations

Country	Number of films (1989–98 annual average)
India	787
USA	591
China (including Hong Kong)	296
Japan	255
Philippines	160
France	148
Russia	124
Italy	105
Thailand	73
South Korea	73

Source: Based on data from *Screen Digest*, June 1999

have planned their marketing strategies with an international audience in mind. A film like Stanley Kubrick's controversial 1999 work *Eyes Wide Shut* was a top earner in such culturally diverse countries as France, Japan, Australia and Mexico (*Screen International*, 8 October 1999). Blockbusters such as *Forrest Gump* and *Mission Impossible* generate more box office receipts internationally than in the USA: the 1998 film *Titanic* grossed more than $1.8 billion in worldwide sales.

According to OECD figures, US international trade in films has grown substantially in the past three decades. In 1970, the US earned $31 million from global rental of films, a figure which was $335 million in 1981, touching $1 482 million in 1991, in that year it imported only $36 million worth of films while exporting $1 518 million (OECD, 1993: 90–1).

One reason for the presence of US films worldwide is its distribution network. Viacom, for example, can use its synergies to promote its films and other products globally. Paramount Pictures, part of Viacom, distributes its films in over 60 territories in Europe, Asia and Africa. Cinema International BV, Paramount House Video's international distribution arm, distributes videos and CR-ROMs from Simon and Schuster Interactive, MTV and Nickelodeon Home Videos, as well as Paramount Home Videos, throughout Europe, Asia, Africa and Australia. In the retail end of the chain, Viacom's Blockbuster's 6000 video stores cover 27 countries around the world (Hindes, 1999).

In 1998, the worldwide video market was worth $15.6 billion and Figure 4.2 shows US video sales by region, the key markets being in Western Europe and in Japan, with the top ten markets (*see* Table 4.9 and Figure 4.2) accounting for three-quarters of all sales.

The structural links between producers, distributors and exhibitors of the US film industry and its ties with global banking industries (Aksoy and Robins, 1992) and extension of such connections to the cable TV industry (Wasko, 1994) all contribute to the pre-eminent position of the USA in the global image market.

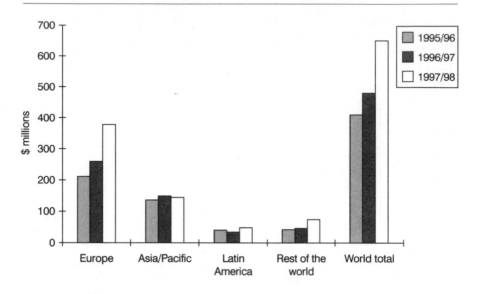

Figure 4.2 US revenue from video sales, 1995–8
Source: Based on data from the American Film Marketing Association

Table 4.9 Top ten markets for US videos in 1997–98

Country	Sales ($ million)	% of global sales
Germany	96.9	15.1
Japan	85.3	13.2
United Kingdom	63.3	9.8
Italy	50.5	7.7
Spain	47.2	7.3
France	45	7.0
Australia/New Zealand	28.1	4.3
Canada	23.8	3.5
Scandinavia	19.5	3.0
Argentina	19.4	2.9

Source: Based on data from the American Film Marketing Association

International book publishing

In the world of book publishing, though China and Germany rank first and third in the highest number of titles produced in 1996, English-language publishing is predominant. The global market for English language books is valued at around $20 billion a year and set to grow as the demand for English language books and publications increases worldwide (*see* Table 4.10). The USA leads the world's book export market, closely followed by Britain. The

US publisher, the Readers Digest Association, for example, has an international market for its well-known editions of condensed books, books on do-it-yourself, home improvement, cooking, health, gardening and children's books. In recent years, the company has expanded into newer markets such as Eastern Europe, South America and China, where it is planning to launch a direct market book business. The British-based Miller Freeman, a subsidiary of United News & Media PLC, is one of the world's largest publishers with divisions in Europe, Asia, South America and North America, producing nearly 300 publications in 49 countries.

As Table 4.11 shows, of the top ten exporting nations, eight are Western and the remaining two closely associated with Anglo-American publishing. Three major exporters in the list – France, Belgium and Netherlands nevertheless imported more than they exported in 1995, with France running a deficit of $43 million, Belgium a deficit of $53 million, and the Netherlands of $31 million.

Recognizing the growing market for English-language books, in 1998 Bertelsmann took over US-based Random House, the world's largest English-language trade publisher. With subsidiaries and affiliated companies in Canada, Britain, Australia, New Zealand and South Africa, its publishing groups include Ballantine, Bantam Books (one of the largest mass-market publishers in the USA), Broadway, Crown Publishing, Dell Publishing, Doubleday, Fodor's Travel and Knopf Publishing. Among its main imprints are: Arrow, Bodley Head, Chatto & Windus, Century, Ebury, Heinemann, Hutchinson, Jonathan Cape, Pimlico, Secker & Warburg, Sinclair-Stevenson and Vintage. Bertelsmann also owns TransWorld International, a major British publisher, with many well-known imprints.

Another major international presence is that of McGraw-Hill, part of the US-based McGraw-Hill group (1998 sales, $3.7 billion), publishers of *Business Week*. It is a global publishing operation, with offices in more than

Table 4.10 Global book production – the top ten

Country	Number of titles in 1996
China	110 283
United Kingdom	107 263
Germany	71 515
United States	68 175
Japan	56 221
Spain	46 330
Russia	36 237
Italy	35 236
France*	34 766
South Korea	30 487

Note: Figures for 1995
Source: Based on data from UNESCO *Statistical Yearbook, 1998*

Table 4.11 The world's top ten book exporters, 1995

Country	Exports ($ million)
United States	1 991
United Kingdom	1 786
Germany	975
France	594
Italy	585
Spain	573
Singapore	403
Hong Kong	380
Belgium	353
The Netherlands	235

Note: Figures rounded
Source: Based on data from UNESCO *Statistical Yearbook, 1998*

32 countries. Among its international publishing operations are – McGraw-Hill Ryerson (Canada); McGraw-Hill Interamericana (for Latin America); McGraw-Hill Spain; McGraw-Hill Europe, Middle East, Africa; McGraw-Hill Asia/Pacific; McGraw-Hill Australia and Tata/McGraw-Hill (for India) (Mcgraw-hill.website). In 1999, McGraw-Hill was one of the two major publishers in Latin America, the other being Pearson Education (Taylor, 1999b).

Created in 1998 through the merger of Simon & Schuster and Addison–Wesley Longman (AWL) education businesses, Pearson Education is a leading publisher of books in the school, university and professional markets around the world with 1998 sales of £2.4 billion. Among its main publishing arms is Prentice Hall, the main educational publisher in the USA and across the world. Its 1998 sales were £702 million, with North America being its biggest market. Pearson also owns the Penguin Group, one of the world's best known English-language general interest publishers, with subsidiaries in the USA, Britain, Australia, New Zealand, Canada and India.

Thomson Learning, formerly known as Thomson International Publishing, is another major international educational publisher, operating in more than 100 countries around the world. Among its publishing arm and imprints are – International Thomson Business Press, ITP Asia, ITP Nelson (Canada), ITP Spain / Paraninfo, Nelson ITP (Australia) and Thomas Nelson, UK.

In the field of scientific, professional and business publications Reed Elsevier – formed after the merger of Reed International and Elsevier NV – is one of the largest in the world, with annual sales of $4.5 billion. Reed Elsevier's principal operations are in North America and Europe and include: Butterworths, Lexis Nexis, Cahners Publishing Company, Elsevier Business Information, Editions du Juris, Classeur, Reed Business Publishing, Elsevier Science and Reed Educational and Professional Publishing.

Elsevier Science is the world's leading publisher of scientific information, with headquarters in The Netherlands and operations throughout the world. The group publishes more than 1 200 journals, including *The Lancet,* one of the world's most respected medical journals, in the physical, life, social and medical sciences, and operate an international network of medical communications services. The group's legal division includes the Butterworths group of companies, covering the legal markets in Britain, Australia, Canada, New Zealand, South Africa and South East Asia. LEXIS-NEXIS is a provider of legal and professional information to the legal, corporate and government markets mainly in North America, while Reed Educational & Professional Publishing serves the British schools market as well as the international professional and academic sectors (Reed-Elsevier website).

Another global player in specialized areas such as legal, medical or scientific publishing, is the Amsterdam-based Wolters Kluwer, operating in 26 countries. Legal and tax publishing accounted for 44 per cent of sales in 1998 – 82 per cent of its sales were generated from overseas. Apart from Europe and North America, the company is operational in Australia, Hong Kong, Japan, Malaysia, New Zealand and Singapore. Among its international outfits are Wolters Kluwer International Healthcare Publishing and Kluwer Academic Publishers. Its net sales have increased from 854 million Euro in 1989 to 2 739 million Euro in 1998.

The reach of these publishing giants is global: via networks of local affiliates, their books and journals are sold in virtually every country in the world. These groups and their imprints publish fiction and non-fiction, both original and reprints and they appear in all formats – including hardcover, paperback, as well as audio, electronic, multimedia, and other forms for the widest possible international readership.

The international print media

The US–UK 'duopoly' seems to dominate global newspaper and magazine markets as well. Though six Japanese and two Chinese newspapers figure among the world's top 10 newspapers in terms of circulation (*see* Table 4.12), they are rarely read outside their countries of origin. In contrast, as noted below, the Anglo-American press have global reach and influence. Some publications such as the British weekly news magazine *The Economist,* in fact, sell more copies outside Britain.

One of the most well-known newspapers with an international readership is the Paris-based *International Herald Tribune,* jointly owned by *The New York Times* and *The Washington Post.* Distributed in 186 countries, 'the world's daily', as it calls itself, has a worldwide circulation of 638 000, more than 60 correspondents around the world, and is printed in London, Tokyo, Hong Kong, Jakarta, Singapore, Kuala Lumpur, Taipei and Bangkok. As Table 4.13 shows, in terms of global circulation seven out of eight top publications originate from the USA.

Table 4.12 The world's top ten newspapers by circulation, 1998

Title	No. sold (million)
Yomiuri Shimbun (Japan)	14.5
Asahi Shimbun (Japan)	12.6
Sichuan Ribao (China)	8
Mainichi Shimbun (Japan)	5.8
Bild (Germany)	5.6
Chunichi Shimbun (Japan)	4.3
The Sun (Britain)	3.7
Renmin Ribao (China)	3
Sankei Shimbun (Japan)	2.8
Nihon Keizai Shimbun (Japan)	2.7

Source: Based on data from *Editor and Publisher*, 1999

Two American news weeklies – *Newsweek* and *Time* – have shaped global journalism for half a century. *Newsweek* is distributed in more than 190 countries and has various editions and a network of local-language publications (*Hankuk Pan* in Korean and *Nihon Ban* in Japanese). With its six regional editions, *Time* reaches more than 28 million readers globally. Its European edition alone has a readership of over two million. The London-based *The Economist*, which sells double the number of copies overseas than at home, primarily in the USA, claims to have a global readership of three million senior decision-makers. The circulation figures of *The Economist*, according to the Audit Bureau of Circulation, have shown a 96 per cent growth in the past decade – from 349 030 in 1988 to 684 416 in 1998. Of this North America had 301 806 followed by Europe at 147 539, while the domestic circulation was 119 400.

Table 4.14 makes it clear that the US–UK publications lead the field of global business journalism. *Business Week* tops the league with a global

Table 4.13 The world's top newspapers and magazines, 1998

Publication	Ownership	Global circulation (millions)
Reader's Digest	Reader's Digest Association, USA	26
National Geographic	National Geographic Society, US	9
Time	Time Warner, USA	5.6
Elle	Hachette (French)	5.1
Newsweek	The Washington Post, USA	4.2
PC World	International Data Group, USA	3.6
USA Today	Gannett Co., USA	2.2
International Herald Tribune	The New York Times/ The Washington Post	0.63

Source: Based on data from company websites and the trade press

Table 4.14 The world's top international business newspapers and magazines, 1998

Publication	Ownership	Global circulation
The Wall Street Journal	Dow Jones, USA	4 300 000
Business Week	McGraw-Hill, USA	1 080 000
Fortune	Time Warner, USA	915 000
Forbes Global	Forbes USA	860 000
The Economist	Pearson, UK	684 420
Financial Times	Pearson, UK	385 000

Source: Based on company websites and the trade press

readership of 6.3 million. *Fortune*, the world's leading biweekly business magazine has a global readership of five million. The other major publication in this area is *Forbes*, whose 1998 launch *Forbes Global Business and Finance*, 'edited for a new generation of ambitious men and women who are embracing the forces of market capitalism to create unprecedented business opportunities worldwide', (as *Advertising Age International* commented), has already reached a circulation of 75 000 outside the USA.

The Wall Street Journal is the largest circulation daily in the USA and the flagship publication of Dow Jones, the world's leading business publishers. It is read by five million affluent Americans and its regional editions make it a major global player. *The Wall Street Journal Europe*, which reaches more than 300 000 business readers in Europe, and *The Wall Street Journal Asia*, the leading pan-regional business newspaper published since 1976 in Hong Kong, with editions in Tokyo and Singapore have a dedicated readership among the business elite. It publishes articles running the same day in the USA, Europe and Asian editions of the *Journal*. Its nearest competitor, the London-based *Financial Times* has a readership of over one million and is distributed to 140 countries worldwide.

In the category of general interest magazines, *Reader's Digest* with its 48 editions in 19 languages, occupies the premier place. The family monthly has a global readership of 100 million and the company which owns Reader's Digest had worldwide revenues in 1998 of $2.6 billion, more than 55 per cent of the revenues generated outside the USA. As Table 4.15 indicates, Germany is the largest exporter of magazines, Bertlesmann's Grüner and Jahr being the major player, with internationally popular titles, such as *Best* and *Hello!* being published in many language editions.

International advertising

The global expansion of television and other media could not have been possible without the support of advertisers, central to a commercial broadcasting culture. Given the historical importance of advertising in the American domestic commercial radio and television, the USA is the world's

Table 4.15 Top global exporters of newspapers and magazines, 1995

Country	Exports ($ million)
Germany	991
United States	847
Britain	619
France	482
Italy	225
The Netherlands	180
Finland	173
Spain	169
Belgium	145
Canada	144

Note: Figures rounded
Source: Based on data from UNESCO *Statistical Yearbook, 1998*

biggest advertising market, three times bigger than its nearest rival, Japan in terms of spending on advertising, as Table 4.16 makes clear.

Though print advertising still leads among the top ten markets, television remains one of the fastest growing advertising media, especially internationally, with the proliferation of television channels across the world. According to Zenith Media, the global media spend is set to rise from $289 billion in 1997 to nearly $349 billion in 2001, with North America accounting for $133 billion of that, followed by Europe with $96 billion and Asia Pacific with $77 billion.

TV networks in the USA carry 6 000 advertisements a week, up 50 per cent since 1983, so that American viewers see on average 38 000 commercials per year. Some cable channels air as many as 28 commercials per hour, devoting a quarter of the prime time hours to advertisement (Lloyd,

Table 4.16 Top ten global advertising markets

Country	Total ad spending ($ billion)	TV	% by medium Print	Radio	Other*
USA	117	39	49	10	2
Japan	35.7	44	37	5	14
UK	20.8	33	58	4	5
Germany	20.3	23	70	3	4
France	9.7	35	46	7	12
Brazil	8.8	65	29	3	3
Italy	7.2	55	36	5	4
Australia	5.5	34	53	8	5
Canada	5.4	38	46	13	3
South Korea	5.3	25	51	3	21

*Note: Includes cinema and outdoors. Figures, 1999 estimates
Source: Based on data from *Advertising Age International*, May 1999

1999: 92). Partly because of this experience, US-based advertising agencies also dominate the global advertising industry (*see* Table 4.17).

As the table shows, just four countries dominate the global advertising industry, with US-based corporations being the most important. The close links between many top level advertising and marketing organizations further limit the number of corporations active in global advertising. The Japanese advertising giant Dentsu, one of the oldest advertising agencies in the world, has close business alliances with American and French advertising agencies (Mattelart, 1991). Through a network of their national subsidies they influence the international advertising industry, reckoned to be worth $435 billion annually.

The opening up of new markets has ensured that advertising conglomerates can expand their operations without restrictions, installing new networks and facing fewer problems in repatriation of royalties or profits. Having grown substantially during the 1980s as a result of deregulation of television, primarily in the USA (Mattelart, 1991), the advertising industry has been transformed into a transnational marketing service for conglomerates. In this new role, the advertising industry has gone beyond its traditional business, offering a global package which includes advertising, marketing, promotion, media services, public relations and management consultancy (Dicken, 1998).

A survey of the world's top advertisers shows that often the same TNCs are the main users of advertising in different regions. For example, in 1998, Procter and Gamble were the top advertisers in Europe, Latin America and the Middle East while Toyota led the advertising spending in the Asia-Pacific region. Unilever was the leading advertiser in such diverse countries as Britain, Italy, Argentina, Turkey, Thailand, India and South Africa, while Procter and Gamble led the advertising markets in Russia, Germany, Hungary, China, Mexico and Egypt (*Advertising Age International*, November 1999) (*see* Table 4.18).

Table 4.17 The world's top ten advertising organizations, 1997

Organization	Country where based	Gross worldwide income ($ billion)
Omnicom Group	USA	4.15
WPP Group	Britain	3.64
Interpublic Group	USA	3.38
Dentsu	Japan	1.98
Young & Rubicam	USA	1.49
True North Communications	USA	1.21
Grey Advertising	USA	1.14
Havas Advertising	France	1.03
Leo Brunett	USA	0.87
Hakuhodo	Japan	0.84

Source: Based on data from *Advertising Age International*, April 1998

Table 4.18 The top ten global marketers by advertising spend, 1998

Advertisers	No. of countries where advertised	Worldwide ad spending ($ billion)
Procter & Gamble (USA)	68	4.7
Unilever (The Netherlands/Britain)	67	3.4
General Motors (USA)	39	3.1
Ford Motors (USA)	45	2.2
Philip Morris (USA)	51	1.9
DaimlerChrysler (Germany/USA)	35	1.9
Nestle (Switzerland)	65	1.8
Toyota (Japan)	41	1.6
Sony Corp. (Japan)	52	1.3
Coca-Cola (USA)	69	1.3

Source: Based on data from *Advertising Age International*, November, 1999

As Table 4.18 demonstrates, the major conglomerates are the advertisers and the advertising agencies are themselves part of major conglomerates, both of which are global in their strategies and approach (Jones, 1999). Some advertisers can also play an important part in television programme production. With its historic role as the originator of the 'soap opera', Procter and Gamble still co-produces programmes, such as *Sabrina: The Teenage Witch* (Blumenthal and Goodenough, 1998). There is, therefore, a community of interest between the advertisers and advertising medium.

The trend is towards global branding, as Mooij comments:

A global brand is one which shares the same strategic principles, positioning and marketing in every market throughout the world, although the marketing mix can vary. It carries the same brand name or logo. Its values are identical in all countries, it has a substantial market share in all countries and comparable brand loyalty. The distribution channels are similar.

(1998: 16)

Given the increasingly international nature of advertising and marketing, the concept of Globally Integrated Marketing Communications has been proposed, arguing that co-ordinated global management of products across country offices and disciplines was essential in contemporary international interactions (Gould and Grein, 1996).

Global news and information networks

In the realm of international news, US/UK-based media organizations produce and distribute much of the world's news and current affairs output. From international news agencies to global newspapers and radio stations, from providers of television news footage to 24-hour news and documentary channels, the US/UK presence seems to be overwhelming.

News agencies

As collectors and distributors of news to newspapers, magazines and broadcasters globally, news agencies play a central role in setting the international news agenda. It has been argued that news agencies contributed significantly to the globalization and commodification of international information (Boyd-Barrett and Rantanen, 1998). Though traditionally the news agencies sold news reports and still photographs, today they have diversified their operations, for example, by offering video news feeds for broadcasters and information and financial databases. Most countries in the world have a national news agency – in many cases state-owned or a government monopoly. However, there are only a few transnational news agencies and these continue to be owned by US and British companies. As Table 4.19 shows, two of the world's three biggest news agencies are British or American, with AP leading the trio.

Associated Press

In terms of overall news output, the Associated Press is the world's largest news-gathering organization, serving more than 15 000 news organizations worldwide with news, photos, graphics, audio and video, claiming that 'more than a billion people every day read, hear or see AP news'. AP operates as a not-for-profit co-operative with its subscribing member organizations, supplying news, photographs, graphics, audio and video to an international audience. It also has a digital photo network – supplying 1 000 photos a day worldwide to 8 500 international subscribers, a 24-hour continuously updated on-line news service, a television news service (APTN) and AP Network News (largest single radio network in the USA).

Table 4.19 The world's top three news agencies

	Associated Press (USA)	Reuters (UK)	Agence France-Presse (France)
Worldwide bureaux	237	183	140
Countries covered	112	157	165
Languages used	6	23	6
Journalists employed	3 421	2 072	1 200
News output (words per day)	20 million	3 million	2 million

Source: Based on data from company websites

Apart from English, AP's service is available in German, Swedish, Dutch, French and Spanish, while subscribers translate its stories into many more languages. As newspapers, radio and television stations have cut back or folded, AP has endeavoured to sell selected, packaged news to non-members, such as governments and corporations, for example, by AP Online, a group of subject-specific news wires, tailored to each client's industry and news needs. Since 1995, AP has operated an on-line service called The WIRE.

Reuters

In the world of news Reuters remains a major actor, supplying news, graphics, news video and news pictures to a global audience (see Chapter 1). However, Reuters Holding, the company which owns the news agency, deals in 'the business of information', making its main profit in transmitting real-time financial data and collective investment data to global financial markets. Over 519 000 users in 57 720 locations access Reuters information and news worldwide (Reuters, 1999). In 1999, Reuters provided news and information to over 225 Internet sites reaching an estimated 12 million viewers per month and generating approximately 130 million pageviews. With regional headquarters in London, New York, Geneva and Hong Kong, and offices in 217 cities, Reuters employs more than 16 000 people of 40 nationalities.

Agence France Presse (AFP)

The third global news agency is the Paris-based Agence France-Presse, with subscribers including businesses, banks and governments, apart from news-papers, radio and TV stations across the world. Though subsidized by the French government, AFP claims to provide 'accurate, speedy, quality reporting' of world events. Every day it distributes two million words, 250 news photos and 80 graphics in English, Spanish, French, German, Arabic and Portuguese. AFP is particularly strong on coverage of the Middle East and Africa, perhaps reflecting French geo-economic interests. It has regional centres in Washington, Hong Kong, Nicosia and Montevideo. Apart from news, AFP produces on average 20 graphics each every day in English, French, Spanish and German. Its ImageForum offers Internet or ISDN access to AFP's international Photo Service – 150 000 digital images are available. It has also launched an email service la carte news, tailored to client specifications.

According to UNESCO, the three main news agencies are the source of about 80 per cent of the public's information worldwide and they operate in a commercial environment: though it is a not-for-profit organization, AP's mission states unambiguously that the agency 'is in the information business'. The dominant position of Western news agencies is based on professional output – a reputation for speed and accuracy in the coverage of international events, though their interpretation may often reflect Western, or more specifically, US editorial priorities.

Other major agencies

United Press International (UPI) 'the world's largest privately owned news service' which was considered one of the 'big four' until the 1980s, is another US-based news agency with international influence. For most of the 1990s the majority of shares in UPI were owned by Saudi media interests but in 2000 it was taken over by the Rev Sun Myong Moon's Unification Church ('the Moonies'). In 1999, it had 600 correspondents in 90 bureaux worldwide, distributing on average 1 000 stories daily.

Other major Western news agencies with notable international presence include Germany's DPA (Deutsche Presse-Agentur), particularly strong in eastern Europe, and EFE of Spain, with close links in Latin America. China's Xinhua news agency, founded in 1931, has expanded steadily since the country began to open its doors for business in 1978. It has four regional offices in the Pacific region, Latin America, Africa, and the Middle East and branches in more than 100 countries. Its average daily output is 250 stories.

TASS, the official Russian news agency renamed, in 1992, ITAR-TASS (*Informatsionnoe telegrafnoe agentstvo Rossii-Telegrafnoe agentstvo Sovetskogo Soiuza*), had 74 bureaux and offices in Russia and other former Soviet republics and 65 bureaux in 62 foreign countries, distributing on average 105 stories daily. ITAR-TASS also co-operates with more than 80 foreign news agencies and operates a photo service, the largest of its kind in Russia and has also entered into joint ventures in operating private and corporate telecommunication networks based on satellite, fibre-optic, microwave, radio and cable lines. It also produces multimedia products to clients in Russia and abroad. The English-language service of Japan's news agency Kyodo, established in 1945, produces 200 stories per day, accounting for some 100 000 words.

Financial news services

In the globalized free-market world of the twenty-first century, speedy and regular transmission of accurate financial intelligence has become very important for news organizations. According to a UNESCO report, the global market for financial news stood at some $5 billion in 1996. The growth of televised financial news market has made this sector even more lucrative (UNESCO, 1997). The blurring of boundaries between financial news and financial data has contributed to news screens carrying news and financial information side by side or even on a single screen.

Reuters, which changed through the 1970s and 1980s, from being merely a news agency to an international electronic data company, is the leading international player in financial news and data. In 1999, it was providing data for over 940 000 shares, bonds and other financial instruments as well as for 40 000 companies. In the past five years, financial information products revenue accounted for 64 per cent of the company's total, while media and professional products revenue accounted for just 7 per cent (Reuters, 1999).

Other global key players in financial journalism are AP-DJ economic news service, formed as a result of AP's teaming with Dow Jones and the recently launched AFX News, an agency providing real-time news service with a European focus, and produced by AFP and *The Financial Times*. However, the most important new player is Bloomberg which has emerged as a major rival to Reuters financial market.

Bloomberg

Started in early 1980s by Mike Bloomberg, a former employee of Salomon Brothers, Bloomberg offers a 24-hour, worldwide real-time financial information network of news, data and analyses of financial markets and business (Bloomberg, 1997). By 1999, it was providing financial information to more than 140 000 users in 91 countries. Its news service, Bloomberg News, available in five languages – English, French, Spanish, German and Japanese – is syndicated in over 250 newspapers around the world. Bloomberg Radio, syndicated through more than 100 affiliates worldwide, reports market news every hour while Bloomberg Television – a 24-hour news channel that reports market news, is broadcast throughout the world in seven languages. Apart from producing its own business programmes, it also provides syndicated reports to television stations. In addition, it produces two monthlies *Bloomberg Personal Finance* and *Bloomberg Money* for investors. Bloomberg Press publishes business books while its website draws select content from the financial service and its media products to provide up-to-the-minute information.

Other major international players in financial news are Knight-Ridder Financial, an international news service that reports on business, finance and economics from around the world. Among business-related regional agencies are AsiaInfo Services, a joint venture between US-based BDI Group and Wanfang Data Inc, China's largest database company, providing daily abstracts of news from China; and Sydney-based Asia Pulse, a joint venture, formed in 1996, by major news and information organisations, including Xinhua, Press Trust of India and Antara of Indonesia, to distribute business intelligence on Asia.

Many financial news services make revenue from large-scale trading in shares and currencies and a fluid and insecure financial market is good news for them since they take commission from billions of dollars worth in weekly currency trading. This raises questions about whether their role is promoting and sustaining free-market liberalization of financial markets.

International television news

Two of the world's biggest wire services – AP and Reuters – are also the two top international television news services. These two companies largely control global flow of audio-visual news material, thus influencing global television journalism. In the realm of television news – both raw footage and complete news channels – the US-UK predominance is obvious, as is indicated in Table 4.20.

Reuters Television (formerly Visnews) one of the world's two largest television news agencies, remains a key player in global trade in news footage, and is used by major news organizations such as CNN and BBC. Reuters also owns 20 per cent of the London-based Independent Television News (ITN). Its rival is Associated Press Television News (APTN) which was launched in 1998 following the acquisition from ABC of TV news agency Worldwide Television News (WTN) by AP, integrating it with the operations of APTV, the London-based video news agency launched by the AP in 1994. This development indicates further narrowing of international television news sources – just two organizations now supply most of the news footage to broadcasters worldwide. ABC News, part of the Disney empire, had a 80 per cent stake in WTN (formerly UPITN) since 1998, while 10 per cent was owned by the Nine Network Australia and the rest by ITN. Why it sold such a powerful resource – the second largest provider of international television

Table 4.20 News on television

Global News Channels				
	Viewership	Bureaux	Correspondents	Ownership
CNN International	221 million homes	32	150	AOL-Time Warner
BBC World	135 million homes	42	250	BBC

Global TV News Agencies			
Agency	Subscribers	Countries	Ownership
APTN	330	110	Associated Press
Reuters	310	93	Reuters Holdings

Source: Based on data from company websites and trade press

news pictures – is a matter of speculation. Perhaps Disney's priorities are in
the entertainment business, as news and current affairs, though very influential, can struggle for revenues.

Given their access to global satellite networks, APTN and Reuters
Television offer satellite news-gathering deployments around the world.
Their feeds are sent, both with ready scripts to allow immediate broad-
casting, or with natural sound which can be re-edited with local voice-overs.
Through dedicated 24-hour uplinks in Beijing, Hong Kong, Moscow,
Jerusalem, New York and Washington, APTN offers individual regional
services for Europe, North America, Latin America, Asia Pacific and the
Middle East.

International news channels

In the category of news channels, the Atlanta-based Cable News Network
(CNN) is undoubtedly the world leader. CNN, 'the world's only global, 24-
hour news network', best symbolizes globalization of American television
journalism, influencing news agendas across the world and indeed shaping
international communication.

CNN – The 'world's news leader'

Started by Ted Turner in 1980 as the world's first 24-hour dedicated television news
channel, CNN grew, in just over a decade, to become a premier global news network.
From its rather modest origins – CNN was derogatorily referred to by rivals as 'Chicken
Noodle Network' – it was able to start an international service within five years of its
launch.

One reason for the rapid expansion of CNN was its use of satellite technology. Satellites
gave CNN first a national audience in the USA, and CNN was one of the first international
broadcasters to take advantage to 'blanket the globe', using a mixture of Intelsat,
Intersputnik, PanAmSat and regional satellite signals (Flournoy and Stewart, 1997).

Its move from a national to a global news organization was also due to its aggressive strategy of covering live international news events, through news exchange programmes with more than 100 broadcasting organizations across the world. The
resultant *CNN World Report*, started in 1987, was a key factor in its initial acceptance
among international broadcasters and its eventual growth (Volkmer, 1999). UNTV, the
United Nations television unit, was one of the most prolific contributors to *CNN World
Report* – perhaps related to Turner's 1997 announcement of $1 billion gift to the UN –
the largest such award the organization has received in its 55-year history.

CNN played an important role in integrating the media systems of the former socialist
countries into the Western fold – it was involved, for example, in the 1993 launch of TV
6, the first private television network in Russia; it entered into an agreement with China's

CCTV to receive and selectively distribute its programmes, and CNN was one of the first Western news organizations to open a bureau in Cuba. Such moves have won accolades from many including former US President Jimmy Carter: 'CNN has done more to close the gaps of misunderstanding between the world's people than any enterprise in recent memory' (Carter, in Flournoy and Stewart, 1997: vii).

CNN shot to international fame during the 1991 Gulf War, when its reporters in Baghdad beamed live the US bombing of the Iraqi capital, thus contributing significantly to making it the world's first 'real-time' war, in which television became 'the first and principal source of news for most people, as well as a major source of military and political intelligence for both sides' (Hachten, 1999: 144).

CNN's on-the-spot reporting of global events gave it unparalleled power to mould international public opinion and even contributed to influencing the actions of people involved in the events it was covering. Chinese students protesting against authorities in Beijing's Tiananmen Square in 1989 were aware that through CNN the world was watching the unfolding events – the Chinese government pulled the plug on the CNN transmission before its crackdown on protesting students. Similarly, politicians such as Boris Yeltsin astutely used the presence of CNN cameras during his very public opposition to the 1991 coup in Russia, which acted as a catalyst for the break-up of the Soviet Union. Such instances show that networks like the CNN can contribute to a new version of TV-inspired public diplomacy, presenting 'opportunities to constantly monitor news events and disseminate timely diplomatic information' (Hoge, 1994: 136). There is little doubt that CNN established the importance of a global round-the-clock TV news network, a concept which 'certainly changed the international news system – especially during times of international crisis and conflict' (Hachten, 1999: 151).

As it gained respectability CNN also expanded its operations, facilitated by it becoming part of the TimeWarner group in 1996. A financial service CNNfn was started in 1995 to provide coverage of the stock, bond and commodities markets; and especially breaking stories about business news; a 24-hour sports TV news service CNN-SI (Sport Illustrated) was added to the CNN platform a year later. By the late 1990s, CNN had regional versions for audiences and advertisers in Europe/the Middle East, Asia-Pacific and Latin America and the United States.

Europe remained one of its key markets and in 1998, CNNI had become Europe's most watched news channel, reaching 79 million households, broadcasting 24 hours a day to 37 countries, with 4.5 hours a day of programming from its London centre (Callard, 1998). In 1997, it launched CNN Deutschland, a half-hour daily German language slot for the German market. In Japan, the number of localized transmissions in Japanese through simultaneous translation, on the JCTV cable system, Tokyo was doubled to 86 hours in 1999.

Reflecting that there is a greater need for local news in local languages (Parker, 1995) and already operating, since 1997, CNN en Español, a Spanish language channel based in Atlanta for the Latin American market, in 1999, CNN launched CNN Plus in Spain, its first branded local-language version in collaboration with Sogecable, the cable operator owned by media group Prisa. This was followed by CNN Turk, a Turkic channel started in autumn 1999. CNN is also aiming to expand the localization process in other major non-English markets.

CNN has spawned imitators across the world. By the end of 1990s other dedicated round-the-clock global news services – BBC World and CNBC were in operation. Regionally too networks such as Middle East Broadcasting Centre (MBC) aspire to be 'CNN in Arabic' (Amin, 1996: 114). In the USA, where CNN was being distributed to 77 million homes in 1999, the established three networks – ABC, NBC and CBS – have had to adapt their operations to the 24-hour channel, while Fox network, part of Murdoch's empire, has already launched a 24-hour news channel (Schreiber, 1998). In Britain, apart from Murdoch's Sky News, BBC was also operating News 24 – a round-the-clock service for the domestic audience, launched in 1997. State broadcasters in both India's Doordarshan and China's CCTV have launched dedicated 24-hour news channels. Among private round-the-clock channels were Murdoch's India-based English-language Star News, the Hindi-language Zee News, and Brazil's Globo News, launched in 1996, all available outside the countries of their origin.

Though CNN is watched by a relatively small proportion of viewers, they fall into the category of what CNN calls 'influentials' – government ministers, top bureaucrats, company chief executives, military chiefs, religious and academic elites (Flournoy and Stewart, 1997). Perhaps more importantly, it is constantly being monitored by journalists and news organizations worldwide for any breaking news stories. It is the only network capable of covering international news instantly, given its wide network of correspondents – in 1998 it had 32 international bureaux with 150 correspondents and its communications resources – in 2000 it was beaming its programmes through a network of 23 satellites to cover the entire globe.

However, it remains an advertisement-based channel whose output may sometimes lack depth in its desire to catch up with the speed and delivery of stories, and veering towards infotainment. Larry King, host of one of its most watched chat-shows *Larry King Live*, has no hesitation in calling himself an infotainer. As competition grows and more and more national all-news channels appear with the expansion of digital broadcasting, the pressure to be first with the news – TV news is a $3 billion business – is likely to grow. Already, there is a discernible tendency among television news channels to sacrifice depth in favour of the widest and quickest reach of live news to an increasingly heterogeneous global audience. In the era of live and instant global communication there is a danger that 'by making the live and the exclusive into primary news-values, accuracy and understanding will be lost' (MacGregor, 1997: 200). For some the 'CNNization' of television news has become a model for expanding 'American news values around the world' (Papathanassopoulos, 1999: 22).

For many non-Americans, CNN was and remains the voice of the US Government and corporate elite, despite its international presence, its multinational staff (usually US-educated or domiciled) and its claims to be free from US geo-strategic and economic interests.

At the start of the twenty-first century, CNN was available in more than 150 million television households in more than 212 countries and territories worldwide. CNN News Group was one of the largest and most profitable news and information companies in the world. Available to more than 800 million people worldwide, the group's assets included: six cable and satellite television networks (CNN, CNN Headline News, CNN International, CNNfn, CNN/SI and CNN en Español); two radio networks (CNN Radio and a Spanish version CNN Radio Noticias); 11 web sites on CNN Interactive; CNN Airport Network, the only live TV service broadcast to travellers in US airports; and CNN Newsource, the world's most extensive syndicated news service, with more than 200 international affiliates. By virtue of the AOL-Time Warner merger of 2000, CNN has become part of the world's biggest media and entertainment conglomerate, whose significance in international communications is likely to grow and its version of world events – more often than not an American one – is likely to define the worldview of millions of viewers around the globe.

After CNN, the BBC is the second most important global television news broadcaster. BBC World, its 24-hour global news and information channel, can be seen in more than 55 million homes across 187 countries and territories. Distributed through a global network of broadcasters, satellite packages and cable operators, BBC World offers separate feeds for European, Asian and Latin American viewers, all of which contain regional coverage. It was launched in Europe in 1995 and claims to be Europe's fastest growing news channel, which broadcasts hourly news, as well as current affairs, documentaries, lifestyle and travel features. Although BBC World plans to regionalize its service in terms of programme scheduling, it will continue to broadcast only in English, with the exception of Japan where it broadcasts six hours of dubbed programming per night (Callard, 1998).

The news channel can draw on the reputation of BBC World Service Radio. In addition, the Reading-based BBC Worldwide Monitoring provides a unique news service based on media reports edited by journalists at BBC Monitoring, part of the BBC World Service. Originally created in 1939, BBC Monitoring has an international reputation for authoritative coverage of political and economic developments in more than 140 countries. With bases in Tashkent, Baku, Kiev, Moscow and Nairobi, its news is drawn from international and national media sources and among the users of its material are government offices and embassies, international businesses, investment houses and banks.

Though not as influential as CNN or the BBC, Sky News was the first 24-hour news channel to broadcast to Britain and Europe when it was launched in 1989 (Horsman, 1997). In 1999, it was available to 70 million people across 40 countries, though most of its audience was in Britain where its main rival was BBC News 24, launched in 1997. Though originally intended as a British news service it has increased its international coverage through alliances with other broadcasters including CBS, ABC and Bloomberg Television. Sky also has an alliance with Reuters, which provides all its news gathering. As part of News Corporation, it can also draw on the resources of Star News in India, and Fox News in the USA. There has been speculation that the news operations of the three news networks may be merged to form a formidable international news organization to compete against CNN.

Euronews provides a 20 hour daily service broadcasting via cable and satellite TV to over 32 million homes in 41 countries, as well as a further 64 million via terrestrial public-service broadcasters. Euronews is the only pan-European news channel to broadcast simultaneously in more than two languages – English, French, German, Spanish and Italian, with an Arabic service transmitted at peak times. It does not have its own network of news bureaux across the world but instead uses the Eurovision News Exchange, a 66 member consortium of public broadcasters, for its programming.

The British presence in the European news market was strengthened in 1997 when ITN bought a 49 per cent managing stake in Euronews. ITN is owned by Carlton Communications (20 per cent), Daily Mail and General Trust (20 per cent), Granada Group (20 per cent), Reuters (20 per cent) and United News and Media (20 per cent). With the 1998 merger of Carlton and United News and Media, creating one of Britain's biggest media companies, ITN is likely to become more important internationally. A proportion of Euronews is owned by a consortium of 18 public broadcasters – Italy, Spain and France provide 52 million of the 64 million homes reached, by terrestrial broadcasts via RAI, RTVE and France Television, respectively.

Television news exchange among regional public-service broadcasters such as the European Broadcasting Union's Eurovision and Arabvision of Arab States Broadcasting Union (ASBU) shows that the flow is one-way – European news providing the main input to television channels in Arab countries. This dependence is more pronounced in the case of Afrovision the regional exchange mechanism of the Union of National Radio and Television organization of Africa (URTNA) (Hjarvard, 1998).

Among the dedicated financial news television channels the most important is CNBC, formed after the merger of NBC and European Business News (EBN) (which is owned by Dow Jones) and its sister channel Asia Business News (ABN). CNBC is almost exclusively devoted to business news from the world markets. It covers Europe in the mornings from CNBC's studios in London, then moves to CNBC US at lunch time to cover the opening of the Wall Street and all the day's trading action. From 0.30 it shows CNBC Asia's live market coverage, through to the morning. In 1999, it claimed to reach more than 140 million households worldwide. As one senior executive of CNBC said. 'CNBC provides unique coverage of business news which can't be presented without full global resources. National news services focus on general news, and in that regard aren't competitors to CNBC' (Callard, 1998).

Global radio

Though radio has given way to television as the main medium of international communication, it still remains an important source of information, especially in the South. An indication of this importance is the fact that major governments continue to support overseas broadcasting (*see* Table 4.21).

Table 4.21 Major international radio stations, 1999

Station	Founded	Languages	Journalists	Weekly listeners
BBC World Service	1931	44	1037	143 million
Voice of America	1942	53	1137	86 million
Deutsche Welle	1953	35	1700	—
Radio France Int.	1975	18	—	30 million

Source: Based on data from company websites

In 1999, the BBC World Service was reaching, on average, 143 million listeners a week, of which 120 million listen directly, while about 31 million listen to rebroadcasts on local stations. Of these South Asia accounted for 57.5 million, Sub-Saharan Africa 34.5 million, Europe 16 million, America 9 million, the Middle East and North Africa 7 million and the Asia-Pacific region 6.5 million. Of the global total, 35 million listen in English (BBC, 1999a). Calling itself 'the world's reference point', the BBC World Service is the world's best-known international broadcaster whose aims include 'promoting the English language and interest' and 'projecting Britain's values' worldwide.

BBC World Service's 'reputation for authoritative, comprehensive and impartial news' was underscored by events in the Balkans. BBC World Service combined extra broadcasts on short wave and satellite with the new on-line services. Listeners in Serbia, Albania, Macedonia and Bulgaria could hear BBC World Service programmes on the Internet.

Through its language services the VOA programming reaches more than 1 100 affiliate radio stations, most of these receive programming via one of the 42 satellite circuits that deliver VOA broadcasts worldwide. In areas of the world where television has not yet penetrated to a great extent, like Africa, radio remains an important medium. The VOA's Africa Service, formed in 1963, in the wake of the retreat of European colonial powers, produces 31 hours of English broadcasts each week, reaching up to 15 million listeners weekly in 19 countries. VOA has also built a network of 16 affiliate radio stations in 10 countries that carry its programmes on local private commercial stations. Its French to Africa Service broadcasts to the Francophone African countries, sometimes competing with Radio France International. It also provides VOA-Hausa for Nigeria, Swahili Service for eastern and a Portuguese service for Lusophone regions of Africa.

Given the growing economic importance of China, the Mandarin service of the VOA broadcasts 12 hours a day, to China, Taiwan and to overseas Chinese. In 1999, 41 radio stations in China were receiving VOA Mandarin service materials. The VOA's Korean Service broadcasts to the communist North Korea with affiliated stations such as Christian Broadcasting System. Since 1994, VOA began distributing its programmes in 19 languages, via the Internet. During the March 1999 NATO bombing in Yugoslavia, as the

Yugoslav government shut-down Belgrade's Radio B-92 and other independent media, the VOA expanded its daily Albanian and Serbian language broadcast.

Another international radio broadcaster is World Radio Network (WRN), formed in 1992, which carries live audio newscasts 24 hours a day from 25 of the world's leading public and international broadcasters. WRN claims to provide 'the global perspective on the world's news' from its source, operates an international satellite network broadcasting to Europe, North America, the Middle East, Africa and the Asia Pacific. Network One, the European service in English began on the Astra satellite, in 1993. A year later, WRN North America was launched, followed, in 1996, by a service for the Middle East, Africa and Asia. Programming on WRN is offered free to non-commercial stations for rebroadcast. It also operates distribution services on the Astra and Eutelsat satellites for Vatican Radio, Radio Telefis Eireann and Radio Canada International.

Radio Moscow, which was rechristened as The Voice of Russia after the Cold War, broadcasts in 32 foreign languages 77 hours a day. Its 24-hour world service in English is broadcast daily to all continents. The French Service covers Europe, Africa, the Middle East and North America; the Spanish Service broadcasts to Latin America and Europe; the Portuguese Service is received in Europe, Africa and Latin America; the European Service broadcasts in German, and other major European languages; the Middle East Service broadcasts in Arabic, Pushtu, Dari, Farsi and Turkish while the Asian Service broadcasts in Hindi, Bengali, Urdu, Chinese, Japanese, Vietnamese, Mongolian, Korean, and Nepali.

Another major international radio broadcaster is Deutsche Welle (The German Wave), broadcasting in 35 languages and, since 1992, also operating Deutsche Welle TV, a 24-hour daily television service in German, English and Spanish. Though a latecomer to overseas broadcasting, starting only in 1954 in English, French, Spanish and Portuguese, by 1999 Deutsche Welle was reaching a global audience via satellite networks. Its influence in Eastern Europe increased after 1990 with the merger of its operations with Radio Berlin International, the leading broadcaster in the Eastern bloc during Cold War years.

The French international station, Radio France Internationale (RFI), though its precursor was established in 1931, was not formally launched until 1975. Its presence is particularly strong in Francophone Africa. In all, 250 radio stations take RFI's 24-hours a day service. Since it took over Radio Monte Carlo, a private radio station catering to the Middle East, its audience share has increased to reach a total of 30 million. In 1999, RFI was broadcasting in 18 languages, including Arabic and had also started an FM service to Africa.

Though not as influential as Western radio, China too has an extensive international broadcasting network. The first international service of Chinese radio started in 1941. By 1999, Radio Beijing had 43 language services, broadcasting 192 hours of programming every day to an estimated 10 million listeners. It had 29 overseas bureaux and was employing nearly 1 000 journalists (information received by email from Ying Lian, English Service).

Setting the global news agenda

It is clear from the preceding discussion that the West, led by the United States, dominates the world's entertainment and information networks. These mainly Western corporations are the major global players in most sectors of the media – book publishing, news agencies, international newspapers and magazines, radio and television channels and programmes, music, advertising and films. Apart from showing the validity of the arguments of dependency theorists and the proponents of the NWICO, the evidence presented suggests that Western control and its ability to set the agenda of international communication debates have, in fact, increased.

During the 1970s and 1980s the debates about global cultural flows were mainly concerned with news agencies (see Chapter 1), but with the expansion of television – a medium which transcends language and literacy barriers – the Western way of life is in the process of being globalized. Though there are more producers of images and information, the global entertainment and information flow between Africa, Latin American and Asian, is still mediated, to a large extent, through content provided by Anglo-American news organizations, who share information, visuals and even journalists. It is not unusual to find an ITN report on CNN or CNN visuals on the BBC news. For nearly 40 years, between 1954 and 1993, NBC had an arrangement to share news pictures with the BBC. These exchanges also include magazines and newspapers, given the linguistic, political and cultural affinity between the USA and Britain (Hess, 1996).

A market-led global media system benefits TNCs on whose advertising support the media edifice is based. As noted in Chapter 3, the TNCs have increasingly taken an active role in promoting a global privatized international network. Corporations have used their media power to placate governments, some have even used it to acquire direct political power. One prominent example was Italian media magnate Silvio Berlusconi, owner of the AC Milan football club, who used his popular appeal and his media empire, crucially satellite channels, to launch his political party Forza Italia that vaulted him, in 1992, to Rome as Prime Minister of a right-wing coalition government.

Media organizations are often part of major entertainment conglomerates. Does the corporate nature of the global media industry affect its content? Sometimes, broadcasters themselves exercise self-censorship when dealing with sensitive issues. In May 1999, NBC, which claims to reach a global audience, took a last-minute decision to redub the two-part adventure drama *The Atomic Train* to delete all references to nuclear waste, in what critics said was NBC acting out of deference to its parent company, General Electric, a major investor in the nuclear industry (Kettle, 1999).

It is tempting to wonder how people would react if the world's books, visual media and journalism were controlled, for example, by the Chinese. Would they be concerned that such concentration of media power could lead to globalization of a Chinese perspective on world events? However, unlike the media in China, the US media, despite close links with officials, are independent of government control, a fact which adds to their international credibility. At the heart of this credibility is the ability to consistently provide accurate, fast and authoritative news and information to an international audience, something which has been earned over two centuries of journalism – indeed, it has been argued that journalism itself is an Anglo-American invention (Tunstall, 1992; Chalaby, 1996).

Though the French and the Germans may dispute this assertion, there is little doubt that from its inception, the mass media has operated in a market system. In an age of privatized global communications is it possible that the Western media is becoming conduits for promoting Western consumerism and a free-market ideology? In the new media landscape, observes one commentator: 'Consumerism, the market, class inequality and individualism tend to be taken as natural and often benevolent, whereas political activity, civic values, and anti-market activities tend to be marginalised or denounced' (McChesney, 1999: 110).

There is a danger that rather than being used by governments for propaganda purposes, as was the case during the Cold War years when anti-communism defined the Western media's ideological orientation, in the era of globalization and increasing corporate control of the channels of international communication, the media may become the mouthpiece of global corporations and their supporters in governments. It has been argued that in Western democracies a symbiotic relationship exists between the media and governments. 'Information is power in the foreign policy sense ... and one may grant the necessity for governments to manipulate it on occasion as they would other instruments of national power,' wrote Bernard Cohen in his famous book, *The Press and Foreign Policy* (1963: 279).

If during the heydays of radio, governments could use the airwaves to promote their viewpoint, in the era of round-the-clock global news, they have refined their public diplomacy to the extent that it can be marketed successfully to international publics. This is true as much for the Bush Administration's attempts to 'sell the war' during the 1990–91 Gulf crisis as for the subsequent 'humanitarian interventions' which have defined US foreign policy in the 1990s (Seib, 1997). The world's view of US military interventions were, to a very large extent, moulded by the US-supplied images of Operation Just Cause in 1989 in Panama; Operation Provide Comfort (in Northern Iraq, following the Gulf War in 1991); Operation Restore Hope in Somalia in 1992 and Operation Uphold Democracy in Haiti in 1994.

A recent study of how television news can influence foreign policy, based on US 'peacekeeping' operations in Iraqi Kurdistan, Somalia, Haiti, Rwanda and Bosnia, argues that the relationship between the government and media is more complex than is sometimes believed.

> The CNN effect is highly conditional. Images and written accounts of the horrors of the post-Cold War world that stream into the offices of government officials do not dictate policy outcomes. Sometimes they suggest policy choices ... at other times media reports become an ally for an entire administration, or individual member of it, seeking to pursue new policies.
>
> (Strobel, 1997: 211)

Others have maintained that US media have let the government set the terms of military policy debate in the news and American journalists rarely criticize US military interventions (Mermin, 1999).

In the market-driven media environment there is also a discernible tendency to simplify complex international issues into what may be called easily digestible 'sightbytes', given the proliferation of 24-hour TV and on-line news culture. In such an environment, the coverage of the South, already 'deplorably infrequent and misleading' may be further reduced (Paterson, 1998: 96).

Already, US networks have cut back on their foreign coverage (Utley, 1997). Partly as a result of this and partly as a consequence of depoliticization in many postmodern Western societies, only certain parts of the world – where the West might have geo-political and economic interests – and particular types of stories, which have wide appeal, are given prominence. So for example, the ethnic conflict in Sri Lanka barely gets a mention in mainstream media while when the West decides to bomb Yugoslavia – Operation Allied Force – to defend Albanian communities in Kosovo, the coverage is almost wall-to-wall. It is not just a question of the quantity, also crucially important is how issues impinging on Western geo-political interests are covered by mainstream Western, and by extension, global media, especially television.

The 1999 bombing of Yugoslavia by the North Atlantic Treaty Organisation (NATO) was presented by the media as the only course of action to stop 'ethnic cleansing' in its Kosovo province. The media generally omitted to comment on the fact that it was the first incidence of NATO actively interfering in the internal affairs of a sovereign nation, thus rewriting the rules of international law. However, the bombing may have more to do with changing the character of the Western military alliance from a relic of Cold War into a 'humanitarian force' which with its rapid reaction units can be deployed anywhere in the world. Already, NATO's remit has been extended to allow it to operate out of area. However, this crucial aspect was rarely discussed in the mainstream media, which focused on the humanitarian aspect of the crisis and how a benevolent West was resolving it.

Despite protestations from Western media organizations, such double standards in reporting are not uncommon and have been well documented in the context of Vietnam (Hallin, 1986), East Timor and Central America (Herman and Chomsky, 1988) and Iraq (Mowlana *et al.*, 1992; Taylor, 1992).

In the post-Cold War era communism seems to have been replaced in the media by 'Third World threats', especially emanating from Islamic fundamentalism, which often receives more negative coverage than other forms of fundamentalism, namely Christian, Hindu or Jewish (Said, 1997). The news discourse is also biased in terms of nuclear issues – if a developing country aspires to join the exclusive nuclear club, as India has tried to do, the US media, reflecting the US Government's position, tend to argue that such moves would threaten world peace. Exhortations of moral rectitude from the only country which has used nuclear weapons – in Hiroshima and Nagasaki in 1945 – and not balked at dropping chemical weapons in Vietnam, air-fuel explosives in Iraq and bombs tipped with depleted uranium on civilian populations – most recently in Yugoslavia, may not be universally acceptable. Yet, in the absence of a credible alternative media system, the US position – given the reach and influence of the Western media – often becomes the dominant position, whether on nuclear issues, trade policy, human rights or international law.

| 5 |

Communication and cultural globalization

The analysis of the effects of the explosion in international communication has been mainly preoccupied with the economic dimensions of globalization at the expense of cultural aspects of interactions between and among the world's peoples (Carey, 1988; Tomlinson, 1999). Is globalization another term for Americanization? The general pattern of media ownership indicates that the West, led by the USA, dominates the international flow of information and entertainment in all major media sectors. But what is the impact of such one-way flows of global information and entertainment on national and regional media cultures? It has been argued that international communication and media are leading to the homogenization of culture, but the patterns of global/national/local interactions may be more complex. The issue of hybridity – how global genres are adapted to suit national cultural codes – is analysed through the case study of Zee TV, India's biggest private multimedia network.

Globalization of Western culture?

As detailed in Chapter 4, the global communication hard and software industries are owned by a few transnational corporations, notably those based in the USA. It is US entertainment (films, television programmes, advertising) and information networks (news, documentaries, on-line information) that have the widest international appeal. Some argue that such globally transmitted programming will promote a shared media culture, based on the English language and Western lifestyles and values (*see* p. 77).

The globalization of the privatized, advertisement-driven model of Western commercial television has brought consumer culture to living rooms across the world. As a visual medium, television has a much wider reach than the print media, as even at the beginning of the twenty-first century, millions of people still cannot read or write. The international dissemination of images transcends linguistic barriers, and global television has 'created a space of its own through a unique merger of entertainment and information technologies' (Schneider and Wallis, 1988: 7). Television is thus central to what Stuart Hall has called a 'global mass culture', one dominated 'by the image, imagery, and styles of mass advertising' (Hall, 1991: 27).

This mass culture may be influencing the way people think about their regional or national identities, as they are increasingly exposed to global, which in most part are American, messages. As British cultural geographer Kevin Robins argues, audio-visual geographies are 'becoming detached from the symbolic spaces of national culture, and realigned on the basis of the more "universal" principles of international consumer culture' (1995: 250).

The globalization of consumerism has been variously described as 'Coca-Cola-ization' or 'McDonaldization' (Ritzer, 1993), creating a credit-card global society modelled on US commercial culture epitomized by Nike and McDonald's and their promotion by celebrities like Michael Jordan, America's most famous sportsman (LaFeber, 1999). It has been argued that one reason for the global appeal of US popular culture is its openness and mingling of a multiplicity of cultures, many of which are themselves imports from outside the USA, and that 'this intercultural density may constitute part of the subliminal attraction of American popular media, music, film, television' (Nederveen Pieterse, 1996: 1393).

In their well-known cross-cultural study of the popular American serial *Dallas*, Katz and Liebes propose three reasons for the worldwide success of US television:

> the universality, or primordiality, of some of its themes and formulae, which makes programmes psychologically accessible; the polyvalent or open potential of many of the stories, and thus their value as projective mechanisms and as material for negotiation and play in the families of man; and the sheer availability of American programmes in a marketplace where national producers – however zealous – cannot fill more than a fraction of the hours they feel they must provide.
>
> (Katz and Liebes, 1990: 5)

Since this study, the demand for programme content has risen exponentially with the explosion of television channels worldwide and market logic may be a more powerful explanation of why the US is pre-eminent in global television and popular culture. The fact that *Star Trek* is the world's most profitable media franchise, or that *Baywatch* is the most widely syndicated television programme globally is not necessarily because of their intrinsic entertainment quality or interest but rather that they are promoted by the huge media conglomerates. Part of this marketing success is also to do with establishing global branding and the internationalization of the advertising industry.

According to industry estimates, one-third of the world's wealth can be accounted for by brands and could account for 50 per cent of global wealth

Table 5.1 The world's top ten brands in 1999

Brand	Country	Brand value ($ billion)
Coca-Cola	USA	83.8
Microsoft	USA	56.6
IBM	USA	43.7
General Electric	USA	39.6
Ford	USA	33.1
Disney	USA	32.2
Intel	USA	30
McDonald's	USA	28.2
AT&T	USA	24.1
Marlboro	USA	21

Source: Based on data from Interbrand/Citibank

within the next 25 years. More than 1.2 billion people use a Gillette product daily, while 38 million people eat at a McDonald's restaurant each day (Clifton and Maughan, 1999). Table 5.1 shows the leading brand names – all ten are US-based conglomerates.

Two groups particularly targeted by advertising and branding are children and young people. The Jesuitical principle of catching children at a young and impressionable age, it would appear, has been well learnt by advertisers, as well as media producers, who, with the proliferation of channels by satellite and cable can now together target this audience and exploit the synergies between television and toys. With the boundaries between age groups ever blurring, international popular music is another vehicle for producing susceptible proto-consumers via entertainment, as the case of MTV demonstrates.

Children's Television – catching them young

Before liberalization of the media market, the international distribution of children's programming was restricted by the number of TV outlets available and the existence of quotas on foreign material in operation in many countries. With the proliferation of television channels globally, dedicated children's channels have become an integral part of the international television market. According to *Screen Digest*, of the 87 children's channels in operation across the globe in 1999, 50 were launched in the past three years alone, with 33 channels using English-language programming (*Screen Digest*, 1999).

The four major players in global children's television are all US-based – Nickelodeon, (part of Viacom-CBS), Cartoon Network, owned by Turner Networks, part of AOL-Time Warner; the Disney Channel, launched in 1984; and Fox Family Worldwide, owned by Fox Broadcasting, part of News Corporation, with Saban Entertainment. The global expansion of these companies, often through joint ventures with local television channels, has been a major factor in the growth of children's channels worldwide. In 1999, outside the USA there were 39 channels or feeds offered by Nickelodeon, Fox Family Worldwide, Cartoon Network and Walt Disney.

For historical reasons the US television companies are the largest producers of children's programmes (Barrier, 1999), a significant proportion of which is animation. One advantage for children's television channels is that animation translates well in overseas markets, since cartoons require minimum of cultural interpretation, based as they are on stylized characters. As this type of programming also has a much longer shelf life, these companies, with their large film and programme libraries, are well positioned to supply material to meet the growing worldwide demand. When released in 1937, the Disney classic *Snow White* earned $8.5 million at the box office. Subsequent re-releases have added $300 million and the *Snow White* video release earned the company more than $500 million in profit (Parkes, 1999). In Britain too, animation has been a key export – *Thomas the Tank Engine* has been translated into 11 languages and seen in 120 countries.

The United States has been a leading exporter of children's programmes – a series like *Sesame Street* is broadcast in over 115 countries and has 500 internationally licensed products. The USA was also the first country to have a specialized children's channel in 1979, when Nickelodeon was launched. By 1999, Nickelodeon reached 137 million households in over 100 countries with dedicated channels in the USA, Britain, Australia, Latin America, the Nordic Region and Turkey. It also had Swedish, Danish, Norwegian, Turkish, Hungarian and Japanese channels as well as Spanish and Portuguese for the Latin American market. In 1998, Nickelodeon launched a 24-hour Russian language channel available in eight countries in the Baltic region and in Central Asia. Nickelodeon can also be seen in the Middle East, as a 12-hour daily block on the Showtime DTH package. In 1999, it added Sub-Saharan Africa, with a daily service on Multichoice direct-to-home satellite platform and signed an agreement with India's Zee network to enter the large Indian market.

Fox Family Worldwide's Fox Kids International Networks have experienced significant growth in Europe and Latin America. By 1999, Fox Kids European Network was broadcasting in 24 European countries in 10 languages, reaching more than 15 million households, the fastest growing children's channel in Europe since its launch in Britain in 1996. Fox Kids Latin America, a 24-hour channel, transmitted in Spanish, English and Portuguese, reaches more than 6 million households in 17 countries in the region. The network now provides programming to 50 countries in 14 languages, extending the Fox Kids brand globally.

Similarly, Disney launched its first channel in Britain and Taiwan in 1995 and since then has opened many channels across the globe. In 1999, Disney had feeds in Spanish, German, French, Italian, Cantonese and Malay. Disney also has a 23 per cent share in Germany's RTL-2 as well as a 50 per cent stake in Super RTL, the family entertainment channel. In 1999, Cartoon Network was reaching 125.5 million households globally with, in addition to its English-language market, channels in Japanese, Mandarin, Cantonese and Thai for Asia; French, Italian, Dutch, Polish, Danish and Swedish for European markets and Spanish and Portuguese for Latin America.

Most of these organizations will also have a children's magazine, and audio and video units, on-line shopping and recreation. Nickelodeon, for example, is also a global entertainment brand, with businesses in programming, production, consumer products, on-line, recreation, publishing and feature films. Nickelodeon Consumer Products has over 100 licensees worldwide, and sells nearly 500 products through mass merchandisers, toy and gift retailers and theme parks.

Saban Entertainment, established in 1983, is a global corporation marketing children's programmes and merchandise to the world market. Its programmes especially *Mighty Morphin Power Rangers* has been screened in more than 100 countries. The idea originally imported from Japan, became an international success and videos and interactive stories on CD-Roms were produced by Saban and a motion picture was made by Twentieth Century Fox.

Children's television has to be seen in its close relationship with the global toy market. It has been argued that TV is central to the expanding demand for new toys – children are most likely to buy the merchandise based on their favourite television characters and the products advertised on the channels they watch with great attention. The US toy industry is among the most successful retail areas involved in licensing. While this is not a new development – between 1933 and 1935, more than 2.5 million watches with the licensee Mickey Mouse character were sold in the USA (Pecora, 1998) – globalization has ensured that these are now global products. Licensed characters offer an easily identifiable toy or story line, a series of accessories or collectable items and extra income through royalties.

Within a fortnight of its release, Disney's *The Lion King* had sold 2.88 million tickets in 11 countries, while Nickelodeon's first animated feature film, *The Rugrats Movie*, based on the television series, grossed nearly $90 million in worldwide sales (*Screen Digest*, May 1999). As Norma Pecora comments: 'No longer are limits of the marketplace defined by national boundaries; rather, the global market is considered foremost in decisions about programme production and distribution, motion picture release, and the marketing of toys and merchandise' (1998: 150).

The toy company Mattel, for example, has licensing arrangements with Walt Disney, Fox and Nickelodeon (Pecora, 1998). One implication of this is that toy companies in other countries cannot compete with such global giants as Toys R' Us and Mattel, and become vulnerable to aggressive marketing by US companies. In addition, it has been argued that since children's preferences are not well established, they are more vulnerable to the advertising of US-based international brands such as McDonalds's, Barbie and Coca-Cola, which are then favoured over indigenous products (McNeal, 1992).

With their powerful marketing resources and huge programme libraries, the commercial children's channels can provide schedules of new services at low cost, with which local television companies find it hard to compete. In Britain, for example, Nickelodeon and Cartoon Network had a larger proportion of the children's audience share – at 9.1 and 8.5 per cent, respectively – than other domestic terrestrial channels such as BBC2 and Channel 4 (Knowles and Price, 1998). However, some companies are also realizing that they can reach a wider audience by producing national programming often with local television companies. In 1998, Disney UK launched a comedy drama *Microsoap* – a co-production with Children's BBC, while Nickelodeon UK spent nearly 38 per cent of its programming budget on original production for the British market in the same year, and announced it was going in for coproduction deals with Granada Media, Britain's most prolific programme maker (Knowles and Price, 1998).

MTV Music Television

When this network was born, it forever changed American music and television. Now it's the biggest network in the world.

(MTV)

Since its launch in 1981, as the world's first 24-hour video music network, Music Television (MTV) has emerged as the most visible symbol of globalization of Western popular music and youth culture. With its slogan of 'Think globally', act locally', MTV networks are targeted to suit the musical tastes, lifestyle and sensibilities of 12–24 year-olds throughout the world. By 1999, MTV, part of the media giant Viacom-CBS, was reaching more than 314 million households in 83 countries, and claiming to be 'the most widely distributed network in the world'. Table 5.2 lists the main elements of MTV's global networks. MTV's 1998 revenues were $1.85 billion. With a presence from Asia to Latin America and from eastern Europe to North America this channel has also spawned a range of imitations from national popular music television channels that copy its irreverent style. Though the music charts can be determined locally, there is a predominance of English-language popular or rock music videos on its networks.

Asia is the biggest market for MTV networks, with more than 107 million households in 20 countries watching its programmes regularly. The Asian operations are managed by MTV networks from its regional headquarters in Singapore and co-owned

Table 5.2 MTV's world

Network	Launch year	Language	Subscribers (million)
MTV	1981	English	72
MTV Network Europe*	1987	English	83
MTV Brasil	1990	Portuguese	17
MTV Latin America	1993	Spanish	9
MTV Asia†	1995	English/Mandarin	107
MTV2	1996	English	11
MTV Australia	1997	English	2
MTV Russia	1998	Russian	13
Global total			314

Notes: * Includes figures for MTV UK, launched 1996, and MTV Nordic, launched 1998.
† Includes 44 million of Mandarin service and 23 million English-language listeners of Southeast Asian service, launched in 1995; and MTV India, launched in 1996.
Source: Viacom

with music giant PolyGram. MTV in Asia was launched with MTV Mandarin in 1995, reaching via satellite on Apstar 1, Taiwan, Brunei, China, South Korea and Singapore. In the same year MTV Southeast Asia was launched which can be seen via satellite on Palapa C2 throughout the region including Brunei, Hong Kong, Indonesia, Malaysia, Papua New Guinea, Philippines, Singapore, South Korea, Thailand and Vietnam. A year later, the English-language MTV India, was delivered via satellite on PanAmSat4 to Bangladesh, India, the Middle East, Nepal, Pakistan and Sri Lanka. In the world's most populated continent, MTV's major rival is Channel V, owned by News Corporation in conjunction with EMI, Sony, Time Warner and Bertelsmann, which is part of the STAR platform and claims to reach 72 million households in Asia.

The second biggest market for MTV is Europe, where, in 1999, the network was being distributed via satellite and cable by digital platforms, reaching 83 million homes in 41 countries. In 1996, MTV created four separate services – MTV in Britain and Ireland, MTV Central (Austria, Germany and Switzerland), MTV Europe (35 countries including Belgium, France, Greece, Israel, Romania) and MTV Southern (Italy) A fifth service, MTV Nordic, was launched for the markets of Sweden, Denmark, Norway and Finland.

MTV's Spanish language service MTV Latin America offers 24-hour programming in 19 countries in Latin America, besides the US Hispanic market, via, among others, PanAmSat 3. With regional headquarters in Buenos Aires and Mexico City, and operating headquarters in Miami, the network's northern feed is distributed to Bolivia, the Caribbean, Central America, Colombia, Ecuador, Mexico, the USA and Venezuela while the southern feed is distributed to Argentina, Brazil, Chile, Paraguay, Peru and Uruguay.

MTV has also entered into strategic licensing agreements with national companies: MTV Brasil, distributed from Saõ Paulo in collaboration with the Abril Group; MTV Russia, a free-to-air service, available in major Russian cities after a deal with Russian company BIZ Enterprises and MTV Australia, a result of an agreement with Optus Vision, are examples of this trend. MTV also owns the VH1 international music channel, which was reaching 90 million households in 1999. Its VH-1 Germany, launched in 1995, is aimed at 25–49-year-olds in the German-speaking parts of Europe, while VH-1 UK caters to the British market. As it is in English, the channel is also exported or adapted for export to 28 other countries, including France, Hungary, Israel, Portugal, Norway, Russia, South Africa and Spain.

As in other transnational media operations, synergies are exploited in MTV, using the brand name to promote a range of Viacom entertainment businesses. The network is used to launch home videos, CD-ROMs, albums, consumer products (from more than 50 international licensees) and books, featuring MTV programming and personalities, as well as on-line services offering music information and an interactive version of its programmes, MTV2, specializes in interactive television.

This makes sense for international advertisers, often record companies, that want to use its global reach and brand name to sell their products. As Banks comments, a service 'targeting youth throughout the world would be much sought after by advertisers seeking to expand their share of the world market for specific consumer goods of interest to youth, including jeans, designer clothes, watches and soft drinks' (1996: 105).

Among its main advertisers have been Coca-Cola, which paid $1 million in 1986 to acquire the sole sponsorship rights to the World Music Video Awards, one of the network's most watched television events. For major recording labels and Hollywood companies, the USA is no longer the primary market and the product has to be sold globally. Therefore major Hollywood films and record labels use MTV networks to promote a new film or music video through commercials and related music videos featuring songs from the soundtrack and clips from the movie playing simultaneously on all of MTV's channels, reaching a global audience.

The flow of international television programmes

The global flow of consumerist messages through international television has been seen by some as evidence of a new form of cultural imperialism, especially in the non-Western world (Schiller, 1996). One reason why these messages have become global is largely due to the extensive reach of the US-based media, advertising and telecommunications networks, helping the USA to use its 'soft power', to promote its national interests (Nye, 1990).

The flow of international television programmes from the West (mainly the USA) to other parts of the world, documented by UNESCO (Nordenstreng and Varis, 1974; Varis, 1985) has become more pronounced in the era of multi-channel television. Both studies confirmed that there is generally a one-way traffic, mainly in entertainment-oriented programming, from the major Western-exporting nations to the rest of the world. Though some peripheral countries (Sinclair *et al.*, 1996) have emerged as exporters of television programmes and films, the USA continues to lead the field in the export of audio-visual products.

In Latin America, for example, virtually all imports in this sector are from the USA. Even in countries where a strong domestic television industry exists, such as Brazil, Mexico and Argentina, more than 70 per cent of films and television series are imported from the USA, and US programmes occupy more than 50 per cent of prime time. In 1993, for example, more than 62 per cent of all the programming in Latin America and the Caribbean, some 1 506 hours of television, was from the USA – mostly entertainment. Nearly 30 per cent (721 hours) of programmes were from other countries in the continent, while Europe accounted for 6 per cent (145.6 hours) and just over 2 per cent of programming came from the rest of the world – Asia, the Arab world and Africa (UNESCO, 1998b: 166).

Even in a country like Britain, with substantial earnings from exporting its own television programmes, the US television presence is still significant, as demonstrated by the balance of trade figures for television programmes shown in Table 5.3.

Table 5.3 UK–US balance of trade in TV programmes (£million)

	1991	1992	1993	1994	1995	1996
Exports						
Europe	66	90	90	116	109	128
North America	38	48	49	68	52	49
Rest of world	38	46	43	71	84	57
Total	142	184	182	255	245	234
Imports						
North America	177	189	199	212	238	273
Europe	58	79	43	77	119	190
Rest of world	21	22	26	28	43	33
Total	256	290	268	317	400	496
Balance of trade						
North America	-139	-141	-150	-144	-186	-224
Europe	8	11	47	39	-10	-62
Rest of world	17	24	17	43	41	24
Total	-114	-106	-86	-62	-155	-262

Source: Based on data from *Screen Digest*, December 1996 and November 1997

With a fourfold growth in commercial television channels in a decade, the US presence on European television has increased substantially, especially in film-based programming, which is often dubbed into local languages. One reason for this, it has been argued, was that no "lingua franca" unites European television viewers in front of their screens, and if there is a media "cultura franca", it is based on American-style popular entertainment forms – soaps, game shows, talk shows, hospital and detective series – but preferably with nationally specific themes and settings (Richardson and Meinhof, 1999: 174–5).

The balance of trade in television programmes between the EU and the USA more than tripled between 1989–93, as Table 5.4 makes clear and total European programming exports to North America were only $100 million in 1996, leaving the Europeans with a trade deficit in television of almost $2 billion (Echikson *et al.*, 1997: 27).

Table 5.4 EU-US balance of trade in TV programmes ($million)

	1989	1990	1991	1992	1993
Imports	614	1289	1458	1648	1559
Exports	139	94	69	95	90
Deficit	-475	-1195	-1389	-1553	-1469

Source: Based on data from *Screen Digest*, July 1995

Table 5.5 Major US TV networks in Europe and the Middle East, 1998

Network	Ownership	No. of households (million)
CNN International	Time Warner	103
MTV Network Europe	Viacom	77
CNBC Europe	NBC/Dow Jones	52
Cartoon Network	Time Warner	43
TNT	Time Warner	39
Discovery Europe	Discovery	18
National Geographic Europe	News Corp/National Geo	16

Source: Based on data from *Advertising Age International*, 8 February, 1999

With a forecast growth in digital satellite subscribers across the continent, the US programme intake is likely to grow. Table 5.5 gives the major US-based television networks operating in Europe and the Middle East.

In Sub-Saharan Africa, the poverty of the region makes it difficult for local television channels to make their own programmes, forcing them to depend technically and financially on international organizations or Western media corporations. Public service broadcasters such as BBC World Television, Deutsche Welle TV, Canal France International and Worldnet also provide programmes to African broadcasters as free-to-air or in a subsidized form.

The same dependence affects the broadcasting of programmes, 'more than 70 per cent of which are of foreign origin' (UNESCO, 1997: 180). Countries like Cape Verde and Djibouti import more than 90 per cent of their programmes. Local production is usually limited to television news bulletins, news magazine and a few entertainment programmes.

Hollywood hegemony

Even in countries with developed local film-production networks and markets, US films represent a majority of imports, as Table 5.6 shows, and given the proliferation of dedicated film channels across the world, it is unlikely that the dependence on US cinema will decrease.

One of the most contested issues in global film exports has been the trade in films between the USA and Europe, one of the world's richest media markets. As Table 5.7 indicates, in 1996 US films accounted for nearly 64 per cent of the European market while European films made up only around 2 per cent of box-office revenue in the USA.

According to an European Commission report, the audio-visual market in the EU remains overwhelmingly dominated by American productions, with annual EU trade deficit with the US in this sector approaching 7 billion Euro (approx. $7 billion). American productions account for between 60 to 90

Table 5.6 US presence in major film-producing countries

Country	Latest data year	Total film imports	US imports (%)
Israel	1993	152	80
India	1991	141	72
Australia	1995	239	72
Egypt	1994	220	71
Germany	1995	197	69
Hong Kong	1995	177	66
Italy	1995	247	64
Japan	1993	352	60
Mexico	1995	268	59
Russia	1995	118	59
France	1995	235	57
Spain	1995	346	55

Source: Based on data from 1998 UNESCO *Statistical Yearbook*

per cent of member states' audio-visual markets (receipts from cinema ticket sales, video cassette sales and rentals and from sales of TV fiction programmes), while the respective EU share of the American market is of the order of 1 to 2 per cent (EC, 1999).

The process of trade deregulation and expansion in the US film and television industry in the 1990s has also, it is argued, undermined the heavily subsidized European film industry (Nowell-Smith and Ricci, 1998) and, since the end of the Cold War, has profoundly affected film production in countries of the former Eastern bloc. In the former Soviet Union and among many Eastern European countries, which had a well-developed film industry, globalization has changed the volume and types of films being produced, as major Hollywood studios take control of the new markets. The leading Russian studio, Mosfilm, which used to produce up to 50 films a year in the 1970s and 1980s, released only three films in 1997 (UNESCO, 1998b: 160).

As Table 5.8 shows, Mexico's film industry experienced a dramatic fall in production between 1988 and 1998, possibly affected by the introduction of the NAFTA, and in Japan, another key US market, film production has halved in the past three decades.

Table 5.7 US vs. Europe – share of the film market, 1996

Country/region	US films	British	French	German
Europe	63.5%	6.4%	9.4%	3.3%
Box office revenue ($m)	2 818	283.4	418.2	145.8
US	96%	1.5%	0.5%	0.0%
Box-office revenue ($m)	5 675	88.7	29.6	0.6

Source: Based on data from *Screen Digest*, August 1997

Table 5.8 Hit by Hollywood? Feature film production (selected countries)

Country	1968	1978	1988	1998
France	117	160	137	183 (81)
Germany	107	57	57	119 (30)
Spain	117	104	63	65 (18)
UK	88	54	40	108 (40)*
Poland	22	36	30	14 (4)
Mexico	90	63	112	7
Brazil	47	101	88	40
Indonesia	8	81	84	15
Hong Kong	156	135	139	92 (20)
Japan	494	326	265	249 (8)
South Korea	219	117	87	43
Thailand	64	150	–	30
Egypt	40	51	60	16*
South Africa	12	19	52	10
USA	180	241	617	661(9)

Note: *Data for 1997. Figures in brackets indicate co-productions.
Source: Based on data from *Screen Digest*, June 1999

Although production has risen in some European countries, this is often because film producers are developing joint ventures to deal with this problem. In France, for example, 81 out of 183 films produced in 1998, were co-productions with other European and international partners. For Spain, Germany and Britain this is also a preferred method of dealing with US competition, although in the case of Britain, most joint ventures involve US film companies. In developing countries, many of whom have no film industry of their own, Hollywood films account for a majority of their film imports (*see* Table 5.9).

The demand for films is likely to grow, given the expansion of film-based channels in new markets such as China, potentially one of the world's largest

Table 5.9 The Hollywood hegemony

Country	Latest data year	Total film imports	US imports (%)
Ecuador	1991	215	99.5
Barbados	1991	190	97.8
Costa Rica	1995	49	95.9
Gabon	1993	55	94.5
Zimbabwe	1991	215	90.2
Cyprus	1995	179	88.8
Sri Lanka	1993	116	88.5
Syria	1993	122	86.1
Madagascar	1991	19	84.2
Lebanon	1993	277	83.0

Source: Based on data from 1998 UNESCO *Statistical Yearbook*

movie markets. In 1999, China Central Television (CCTV) announced that it was investing $6 million for the production of 100 made-for-TV movies to ensure an adequate supply for its dedicated film channel CCTV 6, the second most popular of the national broadcaster's eight channels (launched in 1995). An estimated 400 million people watched the movie channel in 1998, while its advertising revenues for the same year hit $36 million, double the 1997 figure (Li, 1999b).

Concerns for cultural diversity

The standardization of programmes on the world's cinema and television screens 'under the influence of impoverishing, reductive content which trivialises everything', risks the disappearance of cultural and linguistic identities which many societies consider to be a 'basic component of their national sovereignty' (UNESCO, 1997: 17). Aware that television, like other cultural products, possesses intrinsic qualities which distinguishes it from other commodities, many countries have regulations on maintaining a certain level of programming on television dealing with local content, though increasingly these are being fought over by global television companies. The domestic content requirements can vary – for example, on Canadian Broadcasting Corporation (CBC), at least 60 per cent of entire broadcasting time must be Canadian programmes. In France, for films and audio-visual programmes, at least 60 per cent must be European programmes and at least 40 per cent must be original French-language programmes (OECD, 1999).

At the time of its inception in 1947, GATT recognized the role of audio-visual products in reflecting national cultural values and identities and permitted governments to impose national screen quotas. However, during the Uruguay Round of GATT negotiations in the 1980s, the USA argued that, like other sectors, audio-visual products should follow free market principles, ending the national import quotas and state subsidies common in Europe. Such quotas were considered by many countries, especially France, as vital to protect the domestic film and television industry from US-style commercialization. The French film and television industry, vocally behind this position, protested against the inclusion of audio-visual products in the final text of the GATT and EU opposition succeeded in excluding audio-visual services from rules of national treatment and market access.

However, these exemptions have since been undermined by the growth of TNC subsidiaries in other countries, for example, if a big US media conglomerate has a subsidiary company based in a country in the European Union, it has to be given the same access to the market as a 'national' company. The EU went on to negotiate these issues within the European context. Through its Television without Frontiers directive, adopted in 1989 and amended in 1997, the EU has created a pan-European audio-visual area within which a set of common rules concerning advertising, sports coverage and promotion of European products has been established (Machet, 1999).

It is not surprising that the EU restrictions on market access through quotas were contested by the Americans as Europe is one of the three biggest audio-visual markets with the USA and Japan, who together account for $173 billion, with the USA accounting for 51 per cent of the world audio-visual market compared with 31 per cent for Europe. With the rapid development of a wide range of new products and services as a result of digital technology (pay-per-view, interactive TV, video-on-demand, web TV), the audio-visual industry is one of the fastest growing within the EU and it is estimated that the EU workforce in this sector might approach four million by the year 2005. Apart from the economic significance, such dependency can have implications for cultural and linguistic identities. The European Commission considers the audio-visual industry as a 'cultural industry *par excellence*', which has 'major influence on what citizens know, believe and feel and plays a crucial role in the transmission, development and even construction of cultural identities' (EC, 1999: 9).

The EU's position, however, is likely to be called into question during negotiations due to begin in 2000, since Article XIX of the GATS contains a built-in agenda for further liberalization in audio-visual services. In addition, though GATS exempted the broadcasting, film and cable industries, convergence in the industry, with multi-media conglomerates offering video programming, computing and telecom networks over the same technological infrastructure, has blurred the distinction between broadcasting and telecommunications, further strengthening the position of the champions of free trade in the audio-visual sector. It is likely that the lobbyists will continue to pressure the US Government to use its economic and diplomatic muscle to open foreign filmed entertainment markets and push for liberalization of the audio-visual sector in the new round of world trade negotiations (EU, 1999).

From the European Union to the Islamic world, to China and India concerns have been raised about the impact of media globalization, often equated with Americanization, on national cultures. The Malaysian Prime Minister Mahathir Mohamad's speech at the UN General Assembly in September 1996, blaming a handful of Western corporations for destroying 'all our cherished values and diverse cultures ...' is only one example of such rhetoric (quoted in Berfield, 1996).

UNESCO's *World Culture Report* gives many reasons why it is important to preserve cultural diversity, which it sees as a 'manifestation of the creativity of the human spirit', and is required 'by principles of equity, human rights and self determination'; it is needed to 'oppose political and economic dependence and oppression' for 'sustainability' and it is 'aesthetically pleasing to have an array of different cultures', it 'stimulates the mind' and can provide a 'reserve of knowledge and experience' about good and useful ways of organizing society (UNESCO, 1998b: 18).

Concerns about the impact of the US domination of international communication and media on culture are inextricably linked with the question of language and cultural identity and, in particular, the rise of English as the global language (Crystal, 1997).

Global English

English has emerged in the past two hundred years as the *lingua franca* of global commerce and communication. As was discussed in Chapter 1, the cabling of the world in the nineteenth century by the British gave them an early advantage in promoting their language and their control of global telegraph networks led to English becoming the main language of international trade and services. Until 1923, Britain controlled half of the world's telegraph cables, a position that it lost to the USA as other media forms developed (Headrick, 1991). The US assumption of this pre-eminent position, however, ensured the continuation of English as the key language of global communication, with significant implications for the future of the world's other languages.

At the start of the twenty-first century, English tops the hierarchy of international languages, being the main language of multinational interactions and the United Nations system, transnational corporations, international media, including the Internet and scientific and technological publishing. Given the extent of British domination of the globe in the nineteenth and the first half of the twentieth century, the English language has acquired the status of being the language of power and prestige, especially in the territories which once formed part of the British Empire (Phillipson, 1992). Even though it is used by the tiny minority of the political and cultural elite, English continues to have a disproportionate influence among many Commonwealth countries, especially in education and literature.

This is particularly noticeable in the field of book publishing, where English-language publishers set the literary agenda globally, which is often detrimental to the interests of many Southern writers. Only those authors who can write in English, or whose works are translated into English are considered 'international'. Cultural globalization implies a two-way relationship but more often this is skewed by international power relations, as one Indian novelist observed: 'I have yet to hear that there is any writer in the West who is waiting with trepidation to hear what a critic in India has to say about her/him' (Deshpande, 2000).

This is a view shared by many others in India, who argue that languages are 'the real repositories of our thought, sensibility and culture'. Writing in the official journal of India's national academy of letters, *Sahitya Akademy*, one prominent Indian author reflected:

English, preferably American English, the chief language of the computer and the internet and the accepted vehicle of global communication, if not command, is slowly beginning to replace our languages and make them irrelevant. Encyclopaedias and anthologies of world literature have already begun to be silent on the literatures in India's native languages, taking up for discussion only Indian writing in English: the first death-knell for Indian languages has already been struck.

(Satchidanandan, 1999: 10)

Although such assertions may be contested by those who see the language of the colonial rulers having been adapted, expanded and enriched by Indian literary tradition, with some of the finest writers of contemporary English fiction belonging to the Indian sub-continent, yet it cannot be ignored that those who are not writing in English are at a disadvantage. Translations, where they exist, are not always of high standard, a contributing reason for why the world's most frequently translated authors of fiction belong to the works published in the West, as Table 5.10 demonstrates.

Of the ten most translated authors of fiction in the world (whose books have been translated into 25 or more languages), as many as nine originally wrote in English. It is interesting to note that of 119 works mentioned in the UNESCO's *World Culture Report,* only four were published in the non-Western world – one each from India, Iran, Columbia and Mexico. The last two were writing in a European literary form (novels), the first two – Acharya Rajneesh, known more for his 'sex therapy' than spiritualism and the *Arabian Nights* are publications which fit in Western perceptions of the Orient, conforming to all its exotic features.

Books published in other major languages of the world, especially from the major book-producing nations in the global South – China, South Korea, Brazil, Iran, India and Egypt – do not have an international

Table 5.10 The world's most frequently translated authors, 1994

Author	No. of translations	No. of countries translating
Agatha Christie (UK)	218	21
Danielle Steel (USA)	131	19
Victoria Holt (UK)	120	15
Patricia Vandenberg (USA)	112	2
Stephen King (USA)	110	17
Jules Verne (France)	109	20
Barbara Cartland (UK)	98	9
Robert L. Stevenson (UK)	96	18
Enid Blyton (UK)	95	12
William Shakespeare (UK)	93	19

Source: UNESCO (1998b)

readership and are rarely given any attention in global media or academic circles. This is as much true of popular fiction as of serious literature. A look at the list of the winners of the Nobel Prize for Literature will show that since its inception in 1902, of the 96 winners of the prize only 10 came from the developing world. Apart from poet-philosopher Rabindra Nath Tagore, who composed poetry in Bengali and Naguib Mahfouz of Egypt, who writes in Arabic, all the other award winners from the developing world wrote in a European language.

Not since Tagore – the first non-European to win a Nobel Prize, in 1913 – has any writer from the Indian sub-continent been considered worthy of the award. Hindi short story writer Premchand, Urdu poets Muhammad Iqbal and Faiz Ahmed Faiz and Bengali novelist Sarat Chandra Chatterjee are some of the many other major omissions. Authors belonging to other ancient cultures, for example, China, where printing was invented, Iraq or Turkey, the cradle of human civilization, do not figure in this coveted list, while many obscure European or American writers have been awarded the prize. Instead, what is in evidence is the literary fashion for 'Third World' literature, which lumps together a rich diversity of literatures from many countries and cultures. As Aijaz Ahmad has eloquently argued, literature from the global South only becomes visible internationally after it has been 'selected, translated, published, reviewed, explicated and allotted a place in the burgeoning archive of "Third World Literature" ' – a process controlled by the First World (Ahmad, 1992: 45).

English has also been blamed for loss of indigenous languages in the English-speaking countries – Canada, USA and Australia – and for contributing to undermining national languages in the former British colonies. Writing in the early 1990s, one scholar lamented the loss of linguistic diversity: 'I consider it a plausible calculation that – at the rate things are going – the coming century will see either the death or the doom of 90 per cent of mankind's languages' (Krauss, 1992: 7).

While English is promoted as a universal language, and widely used on the Internet, this does not reflect the linguistic variety of a world in which, according to UNESCO, 6 700 languages are spoken. Of the 34 countries with a rich multilingual tradition (i.e. more than 50 languages in daily use), two-thirds are to be found among the countries of Sub-Saharan Africa, South-East Asia and the Pacific region, while not a single European nation belongs to this category (UNESCO, 1998b). There is also concern that the varieties of spoken English will be affected by the single 'world English'. When the US giant Microsoft launched, in 1999, a new 'global English' *Encarta* dictionary, the move was received sceptically even by such traditional guardians of the English language as the publishers of the authoritative *Oxford Dictionary*.

The growth in multi-channel television, filled with American programming or its local clones, is likely to extend an American version of English language to all parts of the world. Will global audiences eventually accept programmes in English and become at least passively competent in the language? Communicating in the same language can help acquire a collective understanding and even cultural identity. In countries like France, which fear being swamped by US popular culture, attempts have been made to legislate to protect the French language, requiring that public and private companies should not use English expressions in public activities where a French equivalent existed.

Regionalization and localization in the media market

Although there is enough evidence of the globalization of Western media products to raise profound concerns for cultures outside the USA and UK, there is also a trend towards the regionalization and localization of media content to suit cultural priorities of audiences, and fears of a homogenized world culture may be premature.

Just as market logic leads McDonald's to develop a vegetarian version of the Big Mac in Delhi and the McCarnaval in Brazil, so international media organizations are increasingly becoming conscious of the varying tastes of their consumers in different parts of the world in a gradually fragmenting global market. As they now operate in a global market, adapting their products and services to local cultural conditions has become a commercial imperative.

The global media conglomerates tend to make use of local cultural resources in order to promote their products, being influenced not so much by any particular regard for national cultures but by market forces. They realize that people prefer to watch programmes in their own languages; it is also cheaper to dub, for example, Cartoon Network programming into Hindi or a holiday programme into Mandarin, than to produce country-specific television. For broadcasters in the developing world, it makes sense to localize global programming through dubbing or sub-titling, as the cost of indigenous production is prohibitive. Even in Europe, regionalization has become a commercial imperative for international broadcasters (Sutherland, 1999a). Adaptation of US programming is easier in the countries where English is widely used, as in Scandinavia, but in France and Italy subtitled or dubbed programmes do not seem to work.

Though some see this regionalization of products as a sign of global-local cultural syncretism, others, for example in the context of the Arab world, define it as a

> subcontracting of market niches to local companies better equipped to deal with audiences which possess special characteristics which create special expectations at the level of the message: language, the place of music and dance, history, religion, and a certain way of coding relations between the sexes, generations and social classes.
>
> (Chevaldonne, 1987: 145)

As a result, there is a trend towards publishing regional or local editions of newspapers or magazines; transmitting television channels in local languages and even producing local programming. The strategies adopted to sell these products can have a distinctly local flavour, for example, using national languages to promote cable television programmes through innovative and customized marketing. This regionalization takes place also in terms of the price paid by broadcasters in key territories for various genres of US television programming. According to the US trade weekly *Variety*, a feature film can be sold for between $200 000 to $3.5 million in Germany to $5 000 in Egypt, while a TV drama per hour can be priced for the Canadian market at $50 000 or just $2 000 for India. Similarly prices for a 30-minute children's programme vary a great deal from $12 000 in France to $700 in Russia (*Variety*, 27 September – 3 October, 1999).

Even the BBC channels, only available in English, which 'is almost part of their selling proposition' (Brown, D. 1998: 81), have regionalized their content after attempts to run a BBC Arabic television service and a Hindi language television channel for India failed. In 1998, the BBC introduced local editions of BBC magazines for the first time in Australia and established seven branded blocs with broadcasters in Hong Kong, Japan, South Korea, Singapore, Taiwan and Thailand, mainly in the factual and natural history genres and began to regionalize publishing in Asia, managing book, video and audio sales in Hong Kong and exports in Sydney.

BBC programmes have traditionally done well in countries like Canada – *Antiques Roadshow* is one of the highest-rated shows on CBC. The BBC comedy hit *The Fast Show* was re-titled *Brilliant* in the USA while an American version of its popular children's series *Noddy* was adapted for the US market in 1998 as *Noddy in Toyland*. Some version of the British game show *Who Wants to Be a Millionaire?* which captured 73 per cent of the market when it was launched in 1998, has been shown in more than 50 countries (Brockes, 1999). British TV programme *Till Death Us Do Part* was remade in the USA as *All in the Family* and ran for eight years, while Australian ABC's sitcom *Mother and Son* was adapted by Australian television company Grundy (since 1995 owned by Pearson group) for Chilean market as *Madre e Hijo* (Moran, 1998).

Australian Broadcasting Corporation (ABC) has adapted British formats for many programmes including the current affairs slot *Panorama* and *Tomorrow's World*. In the other direction, Grundy, makers of *Neighbours*, an Australian soap which is very popular in Britain, has also produced shows such as *How Do They Do That?* for the BBC. It adapted its popular game show *Going for Gold* for French television as *Questions pour le champion*. A version of the popular British soap *Coronation Street* became *Lindenstrasse* (Linden Street) on German television while British sitcom *Man About the House* was adapted as *Three's Company* in the USA (Moran: 1998).

Local versions of the Disney Club have been in existence for over a decade and, in 1998, 35 versions tailored to individual countries were operating. Since 1995, major US studios are increasingly going for local production facilities in Europe, Asia and Latin America. Columbia TriStar, Warner Brothers and Disney have set up international TV subsidiaries to produce English-language co-productions, to be followed by country-specific programming. Sony is contributing to local-language film production in Germany, Hong Kong, France, and Britain, and television programming in eight languages (Sony, 1999).

In other genres of television, such as the chat and game shows there is also evidence of extensive adaptation. The US game show *Wheel of Fortune*, first broadcast in 1975 on NBC, had been shown in 55 countries, with more than 100 million viewers watching it every week, in such diverse countries as Japan, Canada, Ghana and Singapore, making it the most popular TV game show. It has been licensed to 60 countries and in Germany it becomes *Glucksrad*; in Columbia it goes by the name of *La Rueda De La Suerte*; in Malaysia it is christened as *Roda Impian* and in Turkey the programme is called *Carkifelek* (Armstrong, 1999).

In the Middle East, key Western television channels, such as Star Select and Showtime, are increasingly localizing their contents to go beyond the expatriate constituency in the Gulf region. Showtime, a DTH operation, for example, has undergone changes 'to make its output more friendly to Arabic ears and eyes' (Woodman, 1999: 38). This 'Arabization' has included subtitles on The Movie Channel and on other channels such as Style. Since depiction on TV or in films of nudity and sex is particularly objectionable to the censors in the Islamic countries, the global media channels have to edit out the sections which may be censored by the authorities. However, such US serials as *The Bold and the Beautiful*, *Dallas*, and *Santa Barbara* which portray the brighter or glamorous side of life, have been popular in the Arab world.

Star is a major player in Asia, the world's most populous continent, with a huge potential for growth. The regionalization of all the major global channels is clearly demonstrated in Table 5.11. ESPN STAR Sports, for example, the result of STAR's agreement with ESPN to provide coverage of pan-Asian and international sport events, has become Asia's most widely watched channel.

In Asia, STAR TV has aggressively adopted the policy of indigenization, with localized channels including, STAR Chinese Channel (for Taiwan), STAR Plus Japan, STAR Plus and STAR News (for India which makes programmes both in English and Hindi) and VIVA Cinema for the Philippines. The BBC has also expanded into Asia, with the 1998 launch of Animal Planet, its joint venture with Discovery. Global media companies are particularly keen to consolidate their position in the two major markets in Asia – China and India. Increasingly Asian languages are being used, with Columbia (owned by Sony) making programmes for the vast Chinese and Indian markets. Of the 2 000 hours Columbia produced in Asia in one year, about 1 300 was Hindi language programming made for Sony Entertainment Television (SET), launched in 1995 (Walker, 1998).

Table 5.11 Major US television networks in the Asia-Pacific region, 1998

Network	Ownership	No. of households (millions)
ESPN STAR Sports	Disney/NewsCorp.	76
STAR TV Network	News Corporation	72
MTV Mandarin	Viacom	44
Discovery Asia	Discovery	34
CCN International	Time Warner	25
MTV Southeast Asia	Viacom	23
TNT/Cartoon Network	Time Warner	17
CNBC Asia	NBC/Dow Jones	13
NBC Asia	NBC	6

Source: Based on data from *Advertising Age International*, 8 February 1999, figures rounded.

In Latin America, traditionally considered as within the 'sphere of influence' of the USA, the American networks dominate television, with CNN in the lead. According to UNESCO's World Culture Report, 62 per cent of television programmes shown on Latin American channels originate from the USA (UNESCO, 1998b). Since the launch of the 24-hour movie channel TNT Latin America, in 1991, the first pan-regional network in Latin America, available in English, Spanish and Portuguese, US-based television companies have considerably expanded into the Latin market, often using innovative marketing techniques. To promote itself in Latin America, Discovery, for example, organized an interactive promotion through its Latin American affiliate Net Brazil, in which consumers travelled through a large interactive tunnel in which they experienced the different genres available in Discovery programming – nature, science, technology and culture. Having travelled through the tunnel the public were given the opportunity to sign up for cable subscription (Wright, 1998).

One of the most popular channels in the region is Canal Fox, a 24-hour pan-regional general entertainment channel, launched in 1993 and available to over seven million homes, in Spanish, Portuguese and English. Fox's other major regional interests are Fox Kids Network, broadcast in the region in Spanish, Portuguese and English, and Fox Sports Americas, an all-Spanish 24-hour sports network. CNN En Español, CNN's first independently produced 24-hour network in a language other than English is seen throughout Latin America and among the Hispanic Americans. Columbia is making gameshows for TV channels in Mexico and Chile (Walker, 1998) (*see* Table 5.12).

However, the dream of a single Spanish-speaking market place of 300 million, made up of 260 million Latin Americans and 40 million Spaniards, is not matched by the reality. Each country has its own version of the mother tongue with its own colloquialisms and linguistic and cultural differences. International schemes such as *Ibermedia*, launched in 1997, with Portugal,

Table 5.12 Major US-based TV networks in Latin America, 1998

Network	Ownership	No. of households (millions)
CNN Latin America*	Time Warner	14.2
USA Network	USA Network Int.	10.5
Cartoon Network Latin A.	Time Warner	10.3
Canal Fox	News Corp.	10.2
Discovery Latin America	Discovery	10.1
TNT	Time Warner	9.8
ESPN	Disney/ABC/Hearst	9.2
The Warner Channel	Time Warner	8.9
Fox Sports Americas	News Corp./TCI	8.9
MTV Latin America	Viacom	8.7

Note: *Includes CNN en Español
Source: Based on data from company websites and trade press

Spain, Argentina, Brazil, Colombia, Mexico and Venezuela, to fund joint programme productions, have not been very successful (Davies, 1999).

In America's own Hispanic market – 30 million strong with a majority under 35 years of age – the two major players are Univisión (owned by a consortium which includes Televisa, the world's largest producer of Spanish language programming) and Telemundo (owned by Sony and Liberty Media Group). Telemundo broadcasts Spanish-language cartoons produced by Nickelodeon. In 1998, Liberty Media Group launched an eight-channel digital network – Canales n, including Discovery en Español, Fox Sports Americas, CBS TeleNoticias and CNN Español (Ballestero, 1999).

In Africa, the launch, in 1995, of PanAmSat4, heralded the arrival of DTH satellite operators such as Multichoice's DStv, in the continent. As a result, the number of commercial satellites covering Africa has increased substantially, though most programming is in English language. The South Africa-based ATV (Africa Pay Television) is a major player in the continent, carrying CNN, TNT, Cartoon Network, Canal + Horizon, whose programmes are also widely available in Francophone Africa.

Since satellite services still remain out of the price range of much of Africa's population, the growing introduction of Multipoint Multichannel Distribution (MMDS) technology or 'wireless cable' has made this expansion possible, coupled with deregulation of major markets such as Nigeria and South Africa (*Screen Digest*, 1995; Haddow, 1999). The opening up of the media as a result of restricting government control of broadcasting is likely to contribute to the continent's gradual integration with global media culture, from which it is mostly cut off at present.

Regionalization in print journalism

To cater to the needs of regional and national audiences, many global media corporations produce regional editions of their newspapers and magazines, claiming to provide a regional perspective on issues relevant to their respective readerships. In Europe, Asia and Latin America, as Tables 5.13–5.16 demonstrate, such publications have a wide circulation. Many of these are produced in English with a regional content focus, while some are also published in other languages.

In the Asia-Pacific region, the US–UK-based magazines and newspapers are a significant presence. Although English is used by a small minority of the population in Asia and the mass market in newspapers and magazines is dominated by Asian languages, pan-Asian newspapers and magazines are only published in English and are owned by major global conglomerates. Though some of the circulation figures are not large, such international publications are read by the small but influential groups of businessmen, financiers and politicians. The regional editions of major US business publications such as the *Asian Wall Street Journal,* for example, are essential reading for the Asian business elite.

Asia's leading news magazines, the *Far Eastern Economic Review,* published since 1946 from Hong Kong, and *Asia Week* – the former owned by Dow Jones and the latter part of Time Warner, also have significant readerships among affluent groups in Asia. *Fortune* magazine has also launched *Fortune Asian* edition and, more recently, *Fortune China.* As Table 5.15 demonstrates, the top ten publications in Asia in terms of advertising revenue are all Anglo-American.

In Latin America, the global players are present in significant number, with *The Wall Street Journal Americas* published as a supplement in leading newspapers in nine Spanish-speaking countries in Latin America, and

Table 5.13 Major US–UK print media in Europe

Publication	Ownership	Regional circulation
Reader's Digest	Reader's Digest Association, USA	7 300 000
Cosmopolitan	Hearst Corp	2 500 000
PC World	IDG	1 800 000
National Geographic	National Geographic Society, USA	1 100 000
Time	Time Warner, USA	663 370
Newsweek	The Washington Post, USA	340 000
Financial Times	Pearson, UK	286 670
The Economist	Pearson, UK	285 680
Network World	IDG	246 880
International Herald Tribune	The New York Times and The Washington Post	206 370

Source: Based on data from *Advertising Age International*, 8 February, 1999

Table 5.14 US–UK print media in the Asia-Pacific region, 1998

Publication	Ownership	Regional circulation
Reader's Digest	Reader's Digest	1 900 000
Cosmopolitan	Hearst Corp	1 100 000
Computerworld/Infoworld	IDG	486 565
National Geographic	NG society	479 679
PC World	IDG	423 710
Time	Time Warner	327 086
Newsweek Asia	Washington Post	240 000
Asiaweek	Time Warner	128 125
Far Eastern Economic Review	Dow Jones	92 506
The Economist	Pearson	79 500
Business Week	McGraw-Hill	67 000
Fortune	Time Warner	66 127
Asian Wall Street Journal	Dow Jones	59 309

Source: Based on data from *Advertising Age International*, February 1999

weekly in eight countries including three Portuguese language newspapers in Brazil (*see* Table 5.16). *Time* also produces a pan-regional newspaper supplement in Latin America in Portuguese and Spanish, called *Time Americas*, whose 1998 circulation was 865 000, published in Brazil, Mexico, Argentina, Chile, Columbia, Venezuela, Ecuador and El Salvador. *AmericaEconomia*, a Dow Jones publication, is Latin America's leading pan-regional business magazine, published biweekly in Spanish and Portuguese since 1986, with editions in cities including Santiago, Mexico City and São Paulo. *Fortune* also has a Latin American edition, *Fortune Americas* with a readership of 1.5 million.

Tables 5.13–5.16 show the extent to which US-based magazines and newspapers are predominant in regional print media. While it is arguable

Table 5.15 Asia's top ten publications in terms of advertising revenue

Publication	Total 1998 advertising revenue ($ million)
Time Asia	49.4
The Asian Wall Street Journal	39.1
Newsweek Asia	36.4
AsiaWeek	28.7
International Herald Tribune	20.5
Far Eastern Economic Review	20.0
Reader's Digest	15.9
Business Week	17.7
The Economist	12.8
Fortune	12.8

Source: Based on data from *Advertising Age International*, 12 April 1999

Table 5.16 Major US print media in Latin America, 1998

Publication	Ownership	Regional circulation
The Wall Street Journal Americas	Dow Jones	2 400 000
Reader's Digest Latin America	Reader's Digest	1 700 000
Fortune Americas	Time Warner	1 400 000
Computerworld/Infoworld	IDG	800 000
PC World	IDG	270 000
National Geographic	NGS	137 150
AmericaEconomia	Dow Jones	123 790
Time Latin America	Time Warner	102 340
Newsweek Latin America	Washington Post	77 000
Newsweek en Español	Washington Post	54 100

Source: Based on data from company websites and trade press

whether they promote an Asian or Latin perspective on world issues, it is undoubtedly true that such regional editions have contributed to more coverage of Asia and Latin America, albeit from a business perspective and for the consumption of an English-speaking elite.

Apart from the news publications mentioned above, many international media brands publish local editions of leisure magazines, for example, the three glossy titles published by Hearst Corporation. In 1999, *Esquire* had ten editions including one each for Japan, Britain, South Korea, China and Czech Republic. *Harper's Bazaar* had 16 country-specific editions, including Britain, Australia, Russia, South Korea, Mexico, Czech Republic, Greece and Turkey, while the women's monthly *Good Housekeeping* was published in over a dozen countries, including Japan, Britain, Russia, Mexico and the Philippines. Other women's magazines such as *Marie Claire* is available in 28 countries, including France, Germany, Italy, Japan, Poland, Australia and Brazil and *Vogue* in a dozen countries, including Russia, South Korea, Japan, Germany, Britain, Australia and Brazil. The adult magazine *Playboy* is available in 19 countries, with major markets in Brazil, Russia, Germany, Taiwan, Poland and The Netherlands, while its rival *Penthouse* has 17 editions worldwide.

A publication like the *National Geographic*, which specializes in wildlife, the environment and travel adventure, has more than 20 million readers worldwide. Given their subject matter, such magazines translate well for foreign readers, accounting for 20 per cent of its revenue from overseas. Since its international expansion, started with the launch of a Japanese edition in 1995, the magazine has opted for many regional and country-specific editions with local partners. Its Latin American edition is published with *Editorial Tele*, while its European editions – German, Spanish, Italian, Greek – are brought out in collaboration with Germany-based publisher Grüner & Jahr, part of the Bertelsmann group. In 1999, it already had a

Hebrew edition while a Polish and a Portuguese edition were planned (Fannin, 1999a: 29).

Regionalized advertising

Since most of the regional media discussed above are sustained by advertising, it is also important to assess how advertising is being regionalized to cater to national and regional priorities. The localization of advertising and marketing is now received wisdom. A survey of top executives of the US-based global advertising agencies found that 'the main issue of global communications is not thought to be standardisation versus adaptation *per se* but rather organisational coordination which recognises and encourages global strategies while working with local managers and markets' (Gould, Lerman and Grein, 1999: 13). As Table 5.17 shows, this strategy is being used in different parts of the world, with a few select agencies operating the regional marketing networks, sometimes through local subsidiaries or by virtue of joint ventures.

As Table 5.17 shows, regional marketing corporations are increasingly using regional and national languages and different cultural values to sell consumer and other products through the various media. The United States, the country where media advertising had its birth, has already exported its style to various countries, suitably adapted in accordance to local tastes and values. In China, the market research sector, non-existent at the beginning of 1990s, has shown extraordinary growth. Set up in 1992, the earnings of the Horizon Market Research Group Inc, China's largest and most successful privately-owned market research agency, multiplied ten-fold between 1993 and 1997. Horizon's research findings are used by more than 600 companies in China and around the world, including such giants as Microsoft, Ericsson, Mitsubishi and Coca-Cola. The TNCs need this local input, especially in such areas as media measurement. Another research agency, the Central Viewer Survey & Consulting Centre, owned by CCTV, has teamed up with the French agency Sofres (Li, 1999a).

In India, Pepsi featured India's top-ranking film star Shah Rukh Khan and ace batsman Sachin Tendulkar in an advertisement to run its promotional campaign, launched in May 1999 to coincide with the Cricket World Cup. The advertisement, on every television channel during the tournament, had the punch line 'Pepsi Player Ke Dil Se' (from the heart of the Pepsi player), cashing in on the twin passions in the country – films and cricket.

Regionalization of pop music

Some genres of international media messages are more global than others. Being less dependent on language and specific cultural traditions, popular

Table 5.17 Top regional marketing networks in 1998

Region and agency	Regional gross income ($ million)
Europe	
Euro R& Co Worldwide	647.4
BBDO Worldwide	634.8
McCann Erickson Worldwide	627.5
Publicis Worldwide	586.8
Young & Rubicam	516.3
Asia	
Dentsu	1561
Hakuhodo	716.5
Asatsu-DK	300.9
McCann Erickson Worldwide	263.4
J. Walter Thompson	181.2
Latin America	
McCann Erickson Worldwide	260.8
J. Walter Thompson	134.5
Young & Rubicam	112.8
DDB Needham Worldwide	84.3
Foote, Cone & Belding	81.3
The Middle East	
Promoseven (49% McCann Erickson Worldwide)	33.5
Intermarkets (part of TBWA International)	22.4
TMI (part of J. Walter Thompson)	20.8
PubliGraphics	20.5
Impact/BBDO (44% BBDO Worldwide)	16.3
Africa	
TBWA International	31.3
McCann Erickson Worldwide	26.4
Ogilvy & Mather Worldwide	14.2
Jupiter	11.8
Leo Burnett Co.	10.2

Source: Based on data from *Advertising Age International*, June 1999

music is one such genre, which has arguably helped to create a global youth audience and culture. Western popular music has always drawn on different cultures and traditions, many present within the USA itself, and in the last two decades, has appropriated musical forms from around the world, from Mali to Bali in the fashioning of a 'world music'. The availability of new technologies such as FM radio, satellite and cable television and Internet has facilitated this fusing of musical forms. The flow of rap music and the hip-hop culture in 1990s, originating from US inner cities to virtually every part of the globe, is an example of this cultural movement (Lull, 1995). This 'world music' has then been packaged and resold back to the world by the recording companies. (Burnett, 1996).

As noted in Chapter 4, the global music industry is run by a few Western and Japanese conglomerates, which control 80 per cent of the world market. The globalization of such Western television networks as MTV has given a boost to Western popular music. According to the International Federation of Phonographic Industries, the sale of recorded music is estimated to grow in the ten years to 2001 by more than 130 per cent. However, as Table 5.18 shows, in the past decade there has been a significant shift in the geographic pattern of demand, with a high growth in developing countries and a decline in the West. In Africa and Latin America the share of sales tripled, while in Asia, excluding Japan, there was a fourfold increase.

Major music companies such as Sony, Warner-EMI and Bertelsmann's BMG are taking advantage of this interest, with Bertelsmann acquiring national music companies such as Fun House (Japan), Elite Music (Taiwan) and Music Impact (Hong Kong) (Gunther, 1998). While in most countries in the North, international (generally Anglo-American) music is most popular, in non-Western cultures with a strong indigenous tradition of popular music, such as India and China, the opposite is the case – in China the latter accounts for 95 per cent (*see* Table 5.19).

Given the preference for local popular music in many countries, media conglomerates are increasingly becoming conscious of the need for localization of their products. To keep up with the growing demand, Warner Music International, with a roster of more than 1 000 artists, is increasing its efforts to sign local artists. MTV has been forced to customize programmes according to local cultural priorities: it has tied up with Vijay TV to bring the MTV brand to the Tamil-speaking audience, by producing regional programmes (Kamath, 1999).

In major markets, for example, in China, MTV Mandarin's music list consists of up to 70 per cent music videos from China, Taiwan and Hong Kong while MTV India's programming consists of only 30 per cent foreign music, the rest is Indian film music. In other parts of the world often local

Table 5.18 Global music – share of music recording sales by region

Region	1991	1996	2001*
Europe	38%	38%	30%
North America	34%	33%	28%
Asia	22%	23%	30%
Latin America	2%	6%	7%
Africa/Arab world	0.5%	2%	2%
World sales value	$26.5bn	$39.7bn	$61bn

Note: *Projected.
Source: Based on data from IFPI

Table 5.19 Distribution of popular music – selected countries, 1996

Country	International (%)	Domestic (%)
Canada	85	10
Australia	83	12
South Africa	71	23
Germany	50	40
France	45	47
UK	42	51
Nigeria	35	65
Brazil	33	66
Turkey	21	79
Egypt	17	83
Russia	12	85
India	5	95
China	4	95

Source: UNESCO, 1998b. Figures do not add up to 100 per cent as they exclude classical music.

VJs are employed to retain ratings – this is the case in MTV's Portuguese language network for Brazil and MTV Russia. Likewise, in 1998, BBC launched *Top of the Pops* in Japan and in Thailand, re-hosted in Thai. To cater to the upwardly mobile Chinese youth, Channel V signed in 1999 Martell Fusion (part of the Seagram distillery empire), as sponsor of a new prime time show, *Martell Urban Fusion* hosted in Mandarin with the aim of 'positioning Martell Fusion as a drink for individualistic and stylish people who dare to be different'.

Global media – local audience?

As noted, the providers of global media messages are primarily Western, though they employ an array of regional and local strategies to maximize their audiences and advertising revenues. The influence of international communication is often indirect – Western media texts bring with them images of lifestyles, expected social relations and ways of representing the world, which go beyond verbal communication and which survive translation. Most television programmes in India, for example, with their middle-class characters, are aimed at middle classes with burgeoning aspirations to a 'modern' lifestyle and the disposable income to buy consumer items advertised on various channels, which would enable such living (Varma, 1998). There have been concerns that the ideological messages that US-made programmes may promote, such as individualism and hedonism, will damage traditional values such as respect for elders and the family. The images are also of a very unrepresentative, wealthy urban elite, excluding the vast majority of the population. Speaking to the nation on the eve of the Golden Jubilee of the Indian Republic, the President of India K. R. Narayanan said:

> advertisement-driven consumerism is unleashing frustrations and tensions in our society. The unabashed, vulgar indulgence in conspicuous consumption by the nouveau riche has left the underclass seething in frustration. One half of our society guzzles aerated beverages while the other half has to make do with palmfuls of muddied water.
>
> (quoted in Khare, 2000)

While the presence of imported television products on screens in the South and in Europe is undeniable, the consumption of them is by no means a passive, receptive process. Evidence suggests that there is a 'discount' factor at work with foreign programming and that, where it has been measured, domestic programming tops the ratings (Hoskins and Mirus, 1988). In addition, Western programming is still watched by a relatively small percentage of the population in much of the non-Western world. In many countries in Africa, satellite and cable TV have not yet penetrated vast sections of society, while in other developing countries Western programming is confined to off-prime-time slots.

In many traditional societies, the interactions with mediated Western culture can produce complex results. Martin-Barbero has argued that people 'first filter and reorganise what comes from the hegemonic culture and then integrate and fuse this with what comes from their own historical memory' (1993: 74). This plurality of interpretation of media messages is borne out by the studies of television, the most powerful global medium. International comparative research of family viewing of television (Lull, 1988) and of international news (Jensen, 1998) show that routine viewing in one particular cultural and political context may vary considerably between and within nations. Other forms of differentiation in terms of rural/urban, male/female and class distinctions, also influence media consumption within and between nations. As Lull has argued, 'symbolic messages are polysemic and multisemic and social actors interpret and use the symbolic environment in ways that advance their personal, social, and cultural interests' (1995: 174).

However, it is important to emphasize that though the number of people watching CNN or reading *Time* magazine in developing countries may be tiny, they are often those with power and influence. It could be argued that international communication is promoting a globalized, 'westernized' elite which believes in the supremacy of the market and liberal democracy, as defined by the West. A pan-Asian cross-media survey in 1999 found that CNN, Discovery and MTV were the most popular channels among 'the affluent sections of society' in Asia (Madden, 1999: 36).

The reception and consumption of media in a cross-cultural context remain a complex and contested terrain of academic inquiry, made more difficult with the paucity of many empirical studies. Much more research, especially from a Southern perspective, has to be undertaken to ascertain the impact of Western television on non-Western cultures and vice versa.

Rather than creating a homogenized culture, globalization of Western culture may be producing 'heterogeneous disjunctures' (Appadurai, 1990). The global-local cultural interaction is leading to a hybrid culture, one, it has been argued, which blurs the boundaries between the modern and the traditional, the high and low culture and the national and the global culture. Robertson (1992) called such a phenomenon 'glocalization', characterized by cultural fusion as a result of adaptation of Western media genres to suit local languages, styles and cultural conventions, using new communication technologies. A prime example of this cultural hybridity can be found in the case of Zee TV, India's first private Hindi-language and most successful satellite channel.

Zee TV and hybrid television

Launched, in 1992, by the Essel Group of Indian entrepreneur Subhash Chandra, only a year after STAR started beaming through satellite Western programming to India, Zee TV began by offering Hindi-language programmes. Unlike transnational broadcasters whose largely US-made programmes were watched by the English-fluent urban middle classes, with aspirations to Western way of life, Zee targeted the mass market, making programmes in a language that majority of Indians used in their everyday life.

With its pioneering movie-based television entertainment, Zee TV broke new grounds in nationally produced entertainment, skilfully adapting and developing local-language derivatives of Western programme formats such as game-and-chat shows, leisure programming and quiz contests. Another case of indigenizing global TV products was its Music Asia channel, an Indian version of Western music channels – MTV and Channel V. By launching the first dedicated music channel, broadcasting Indian film music mixed with a new genre called Indipop, a pale imitation of Western pop music, Zee became very popular among the youth in India.

One outcome of the availability of Western television was the mixing of English and Hindi and the evolution of a hybrid media language – Hinglish. Though a form of Hinglish had been in existence in urban north India for decades, it was Zee TV that popularized it. The extensive use of Hinglish on Music Asia, contributed immensely to the popularization of Hinglish, particularly among the youth. Zee was also the first network to elevate this new language by using it in the more serious genre of news, which had traditionally been either in pure Hindi or in 'BBC English' (Thussu, 1998). Such was the impact of this hybridization of languages that by 2000 most private television networks, often aimed at a younger 'westernized' urban audience, used Hinglish regularly in their programming.

By using English words, Zee aimed to expand its reach beyond the Hindi-speaking regions of India to cater to regional audience, and the South Asian diaspora, who may be more amenable to a hybrid variety of television. Like other commercial channels,

Zee is dependent on advertisers, and is therefore acutely aware that language can influence people in their buying choices, a contributing factor why it used Hinglish, the language of the urban middle class. The role of television, therefore, has been very important in fusing Hindi and English and creating a popular and youthful new *lingua franca*, and making such television programme titles as *Superhit Muqabala* (competition) and *Chalo* (let's go to) *Cinema,* a part of television schedules.

The deployment of an approach of cultural hybridity has been a contributory factor in the expansion of Indian television outside the borders of the country. There is a certain amount of empathy with hybridized languages and culture among the South Asian diaspora. The members of this ethnically, linguistically and religiously diverse group, scattered around the globe, want to keep up cultural links with their countries of origin. Though these groups speak a myriad of languages, most of them at least understand some Hindi, due largely to the popularity of Hindi films. Among the second and third generation South Asians who have grown up within other cultures, Hinglish is the language they can relate to relatively easily.

Zee was among the first to recognize the potential of overseas markets for its programming. After STAR TV purchased 50 per cent of Asia Today (the Hong Kong-based broadcaster of Zee TV) in 1993, it became Zee's partner in India, facilitating the Zee network's overseas expansion. Following their 1992 launch in the Middle East, Zee TV entered the lucrative British market in 1995, when it bought TV Asia, a loss-making channel catering to the British Asians (Tobin, 1999c).

In 1999, it became one of the first channels to go digital in the UK, offering programming in Hindi and other South Asian languages, namely Bengali, Urdu, Gujarati and Punjabi. It was available on the Sky network and claimed to have one million subscribers in Britain and continental Europe. Zee also became available to subscribers in Africa after it entered into a joint venture with a South Africa-based platform operator, MultiChoice, in 1997.

By 2000, Zee claimed to be 'the world's largest Asian television network', covering Asia, Europe, the USA and Africa, catering to the 25 million strong Indian diaspora. In Asia the network spans more than 43 countries and offers round the clock programming on four channels – Zee TV, Zee Cinema, Zee TV India and Music Asia. Having reached more than 23 million homes in the Indian sub-continent and United Arab Emirates, Zee's strategy now is to expand its operations in the lucrative North American market. To cater to the new subscribers the channel now increasingly uses English subtitles in its Hindi programmes.

After STAR started making programmes in Hindi, it became a direct competitor for Zee, creating business rivalry between the two operations of News Corporation in India. In September 1999, in an unprecedented action, Zee bought back STAR's 50 per cent share in the company for $300 million, ending years of acrimony and establishing Zee as a major media player in its own right (Rangnekar, 1999).

In 1999, Zee Network unveiled 'Alpha', an umbrella brand for its pay channels in regional languages – Marathi, Bengali, Punjabi and Gujarati. Though some of the programming on these channels will be original, the bulk will come from recycling content by dubbing programmes from Zee's huge library of 15 000 hours of programmes and 2 200 Indian movies. With this, says the network, Zee has 'the first and last word in

Indian TV entertainment' (quoted in *Cable and Satellite Television,* September 1999).

Zee's concern to make programmes in Indian languages may be dictated by market considerations. It recognizes that, despite the influence of the English language in India, the biggest media growth is in regional languages – the 1999 National Readership Survey in India reported that not one English-language daily could be found in the top ten newspapers in terms of their readerships (Swami, 1999).

Though Zee has adapted American TV genres and hybridized them to suit Indian tastes – a recent example of programme poaching is *Hello Friends*, an Indian version of the hugely popular youth-oriented American sitcom *Friends*, started on Zee TV in 1999 – they have not been the most popular programmes, since they portray a lifestyle with which only a small minority of Indians can identify.

It is no coincidence that the two most popular programmes on Zee TV have a very Indian sound to them. The first one is *Sa Re Ga Ma*, a music programme where vocalists compete in rounds devoted to classical, folk and film songs before a panel of some of India's best known classical musicians. Another major success has been *Antakshari*, a traditional song-based game, a challenging test of Hindi film music lore. Launched in 1993, *Antakshari* has been extremely popular in India and increasingly in South Asia. These programmes have also been hosted in Middle East, Britain, South Africa, and the USA and helped find new musical talents in India and among the South Asian diaspora.

Taking a cue from its former business partner Murdoch, Zee has also invested heavily in making sure that the company owns communication hardware as well as programming. With this in view, in 1999, Zee announced the construction of Agrani, the regional satellite project which when operational in 2002, will provide direct to home satellite TV and long-distance telephony to consumers in South Asia. This was followed by Zee acquiring a 25 per cent share in British satellite telecommunication company ICO (International Communications Ltd) which is to have a network of satellites beaming voice and data signals around the world. Such control will make Zee a major global player (Kriplani, 1999). Its sister company, Siticable, that has the majority share of cable TV homes in India, is moving into Internet service provision. Zee is also investing $92 million in E-Connect, an Internet service provider and portal operator (Lall, 1999).

At the beginning of the twenty-first century, Zee is poised to become a major player in international communication. Its success is reflected in the network's financial gains – in 1999 it recorded revenues of $100 million, rising about 30 per cent annually (Kriplani, 1999). Given its growing global presence and wide-ranging media and communication interests – that include cable distribution, satellite channels, TV and film production units, publishing ventures and satellite telephones – Zee had become 'a multimedia empire' (Ninan, 1999).

6

Contraflow in global media

The globalization of Western media has been a major influence in shaping media cultures internationally. While there are forces for convergence and homogenization, the spread of the US model of professional, commercial television has also brought beneficial changes to some national and regional media industries, leading to a revival of cultural nationalism. The availability of digital technology and satellite networks has enabled the development of regional broadcasting, as with the pan-Arabic Middle East Broadcasting Centre (MBC) and the Mandarin language Phoenix channel, which caters to a Chinese diaspora. This has also enabled an increasing flow of content from the global South to the North, for example, the Brazilian television giant TV Globo, which exports its *telenovelas* to more than 100 countries, while the Indian film industry is an example of a non-Western production centre making its presence felt in a global cultural context.

Seeing the big world on a small screen

With the developments of the 1990s, television has come to dominate the media scene in virtually every part of the world and such icons of global television as CNN and MTV have become ubiquitous. The role of television in the construction of social and cultural identities is now much more complex than in the era of a single national broadcaster and a shared public space, which characterized television in most countries in the post-war years. Though national broadcasters continue to be important in most countries, still receiving the highest audience shares, the availability of a myriad television channels has complicated the national discourse. In the multi-channel era, a viewer can have simultaneous access to a variety of local, regional, national, and international channels, thus being able to engage in different levels of mediated discourses.

In Russia, for example, since the end of the Cold War, global television has helped promote Western consumerist culture. The secret of the success of the new privatized Russian television, says a recent UNESCO report, 'is a mix of American and Latin American soap operas, games inspired by channels in the West, talk shows and occasionally sensational news bulletins' (UNESCO, 1997: 178). At the other end of the world, the Australian Broadcasting Corporation provides loans and technical support to the island nations of the Pacific region to ensure that they can download their TV signals and retransmit Australian programming and Australian products (Varan, 1999).

Global television has created a new phenomenon of 'media events' – the live broadcasting of 'historic' events around the world – Olympic Games, Tiananmen Square violence, the Gulf War, natural or human disasters (Dayan and Katz, 1992). The global coverage of the 1995 televised trial of US sportsman O. J. Simpson, television's treatment of the death of Princess of Diana in 1997, 'Monicagate' in 1998 and the millennium celebrations in 1999, can be added to the list of such shared global media experiences.

Transnational corporations, governments and militant groups have harnessed the power of television to put across their case. In Venezuela, President Hugo Chavez has used the medium to have his own three-hour face-to-face TV show, with live phone-ins from the audience, which attracted more than 11 million viewers in a country of just 23 million (Gamini, 1999). In Malaysia, the Prime Minister, Mahathir Mohamad, Asia's longest-serving leader, commissioned a 33-part soap opera based loosely on his life, called *Unfinished Struggle* (Harrison, 1999).

When rebel gunmen stormed the parliament and killed Armenian Prime Minister Vazagen Sarkissian in October 1999 as he was addressing the parliament on TV, they did not shoot the television crew, aware that their pictures and messages were being broadcast live in the country and through national broadcasters and thanks to modern digital technology, beamed across the newsrooms through global TV channels.

The Kurds have established their own satellite channel MED-TV, which broadcasts in three main Kurdish dialects – Kirmanci, Sorani and Zazaki – and in Turkish and Arabic to Kurds living in Kurdish regions of Turkey, Iran, Iraq and Syria and those of Kurdish diaspora in Europe. The station which operated from London from 1995 took its name MED from Medes, the ancient people from whom the Kurds are descended, now the world's 'largest stateless nation' (Ryan, 1997: 45). The Turkish government alleges that MED-TV is a mouthpiece for the PKK, the Turkish Workers Party, which has been waging a guerrilla war for the past two decades in eastern Turkey.

Visual media have tremendous power to influence people's political and social attitudes. As Reeves and Nass observe: 'Media can evoke emotional responses, demand attention, threaten us, influence memories, and change ideas of what is natural. Media are full participants in our social and natural world' (1996: 251). Television images of emotionally charged funerals of soldiers, broadcast on Indian news channels during the 1999 border conflict with Pakistan, labelled as 'India's first conflict in the information age,' created 'a direct impact on policy makers, the armed forces, the families of the dead – and the public opinion' (Halarnkar, 1999: 20).

The globalization of such a powerful visual medium has tended to increase Western cultural influence but other models do exist, argues UNESCO World Culture Report, based on 'a different cultural institutional and historical backgrounds and such alternatives are likely to multiply in the era of globalisation, in spite of appearances, which may paradoxically witness greater diversity than uniformity' (UNESCO, 1998b: 23).

As Chapter 5 noted, the US-led Western media conglomerates have used an array of strategies, including regionalization and localization of their content to extend their reach beyond the elites in the world and to create the 'global popular'. The proliferation of satellite and cable television channels, made possible with digital technology and growing availability of communication satellites, has undoubtedly made the global cultural landscape much more complex.

While their well-publicized commercial agenda has been criticized, the globalization of Western or Western-inspired television also has benefits. It has contributed, for example, to the creation of jobs in media and cultural industries. As localization becomes part of the business strategy of media transnationals, it is likely more jobs will be created in these industries in many developing countries to make programmes taking on board cultural specificity. At the beginning of the 1990s there was no television industry worth the name in India, which until 1991 had just one state-controlled channel, little more than a mouthpiece of the government and notoriously monotonous. By the end of the 1990s, there were 70 channels, more than 20 national, others regional, some joint ventures with international operators. This expansion demanded new programme content – from news to game-and-chat shows, from soap operas to documentaries, which has been provided by a burgeoning television industry.

It has also been argued that the extension of Western media, and with it 'modernity', across the globe has a liberatory potential that can contribute to strengthening liberal democratic culture (Dunn, 1992; Elster, 1997) and promoting gender equality and freedom from the 'national strait-jacket' (Kapur, 1997). There is little doubt that digital technologies have made it possible to beam a range of specialized channels across the world, some in local or national languages, which are giving more choice to consumers and opening up their window on the world (Noam, 1993). This is particularly the case in many developing countries, where the media, especially broadcasting, had been under state control and where often unrepresentative and sometimes unelected governments could use the airwaves to control their populations, severely restricting plurality of opinions and possibilities of open discussion.

The Western style of professional television journalism, essentially based on independence from government control, has influenced programme-making in many countries. Examples of the adoption of this kind of journalism are the current-affairs programmes such as *Aap Ki Adalat* (Your Court) on Zee TV in India, and critical investigative programmes such as

Jiaodian Fangtan (Focal Report) on China's CCTV, which in the words of one Chinese scholar, has 'proved that television can play a role in being the people's and not just the Party's mouthpiece' (Zhao, 1999: 303). In Turkey, the privatization of television has challenged the monopoly of the state-run national broadcaster Turkish Radio and Television Authority (TRT), and brought 'openness and plurality' to the airwaves (Catalbas, 2000: 144). There is also more evidence of liberalism in the press. After the advent of 'multi-partyism' in Africa, there has been a rapid increase in the number of privately-run small newspapers and magazines (Kasoma, 1995). As state after state moves towards democracy this trend is likely to grow. In Indonesia, for example, more than 730 press publication licences were issued in 1998–99, compared with a total of 289 during President Suharto's 32-year one-party rule (Richardson, 1999).

In other areas of the media too, examples can be given of how globalization has improved the quality of media products. Expansion of Western publishing houses in the global South has had some positive impact. For example, after NAFTA, US publishing giants such as McGraw-Hill and Prentice Hall entered the Mexican publishing market, opening up new avenues for Mexican writers as they become popular in the USA, with many more being translated into English. The English translation of the Mexican author Laura Esquivel's novel *Coma agua para chocolate*, sold more than a million copies in the USA as well as 200 000 copies in the Spanish market in the USA, leading to what one Mexican scholar called, surely as a hyperbole, the 'Latinization of the United States' (UNESCO, 1998b: 164). Similarly, since the launch of Penguin India, in the early 1990s, many books on Indian politics, economics and culture, including a series of translations of Indian classics, have been produced to international publishing standards and are also available for a wider global market, given the vast marketing network of Penguin.

Global culture's discontents

Despite such welcome developments, the growing Western cultural presence in the developing world has also produced unease in some quarters. In many developing countries, Western influence is bringing mixed results. The Islamic revolution that overthrew the Shah of Iran in 1979 was not spurred by modernization as much as by opposition to what Iranian intellectuals called 'westoxication', the adoption and flaunting of superficial consumerist attributes of fads and commodities, originating in the USA. Though Iran may be an extreme case of an anti-Western cultural backlash, degrees of xenophobic reaction emerging in response to such superficial elements of Western way of life, often mediated through television, can be found in many other non-Western cultures – the ideological revival of *Hindutva* (Hinduness) in India is a case in point (Panikkar, 1999).

Countries such as China, Singapore, Saudi Arabia and Iran have tried to restrict the reception of Western satellite television by introducing licensing regimes. Iran banned Western television on the grounds that it was culturally inappropriate in an Islamic nation, primarily because of the sexual content and orientation of Western television programmes, films and advertising. In other traditional societies like India, worries have been expressed about the representation of women in the media, especially advertising. 'The commodification of women so evident in the West during the 1960s', wrote two observers of India's media scene, 'is likely to become far more virulent in India' (Joseph and Sharma, 1994: 300).

There is also a feeling that in the McWorld, culture is being commodified to the extent that it impacts on religious sensibilities of various communities (Barber, 1995). In Asia, Western culture, based on individualism and mediated primarily through television, is seen as undermining traditional Asian values, revolving round the family and the community (Goonasekera, 1997; Goonasekera and Lee, 1998). Disney's animation film *The Hunchback of Notre Dame* drew criticism from many in France for its trivialization of Victor Hugo's famous novel, while its *Hercules* offended many Greeks. The release in China of Disney's 1998 feature *Mulan* was delayed by the government which was unhappy with the portrayal of aspects of Chinese culture in the film. It is interesting to note that despite its theme and supposed cultural sensitivity *Mulan* did not do very well in China (Parkes, 1999). Hindu groups in the USA took exception to the portrayal of Hindu deity Krishna in an episode of a popular New Zealand-made and globally syndicated television serial *Xena: Warrior Princess* (Tsering, 1999).

Partly as a reaction to perceived Westernization of their cultures and partly as a reaction to the alleged distortion in representations of non-Western cultures in the global media, many countries have experienced a cultural revival, often influenced by religious groups and encouraged by political establishments, acting as a barrier to the flow of Western media products. In India, for example, the phenomenal success of two television serials based on the Hindu epics *Ramayan* and *Mahabharat*, telecast in 1988, have arguably contributed to the rise of a Hinduized version of Indian identity, undermining the secular basis of Indian society (Mitra, 1993). Eleven years after they were broadcast on India's official television network *Doordarshan*, repeats of both *Mahabharat* and *Ramayan* were being shown on Zee TV and Sony TV, respectively, still managing very high ratings. The exceptional popularity of such programmes has led to the production of many more religious serials. At their height in 1997, nearly a dozen 'mythologicals', as they were called, were being shown on television, representing an alliance between what an observer aptly called 'godland and adland' (Jain, 1997). Such was the popularity of those godly serials that in 1999 a 130-episode *Gita Rahasya* started beaming from the Indian state broadcaster (Shahryar, 1999).

In China, the revival of the traditional *Beijing opera* and the screening of classics on television have contributed to a renewed interest in the country's history and culture, after half a century of its denigration under Maoist ideology. Episodes of the TV series *Outlaws of the Marsh*, screened on CCTV, drew 900 million viewers and by 1998, three further leading Chinese classic novels, *Journey to the West, A Dream of the Red Mansions* and *Romance of the Three Kingdoms* had been adapted for TV (Chengxiang, 1998). The popularity of the *mau lum* (song-story) in Thailand and the *telenovela* in Latin America are other examples of the trend towards capitalizing on the popularity of mediated tradition.

In the Muslim world, where a majority of the populations perceive Islam as a civilization rather than a culture (Mazrui, 1997), Western liberalism has its most robust resistance. This is reflected not merely in the political discourse characterized by anti-Western rhetoric but also in the symbolism of interactions with Western cultural artefacts. In 1996, Iran released Sara, who wears Islamic dress – its answer to the glamorous US doll Barbie, which has iconic status among young girls across the world. The Bosnian Muslims have also introduced their own doll called Amina and, in 1999, Arab nations introduced an Arab doll, Leila. In Malaysia, for example, the reaction to Western popular music has been in the form of the growing popularity of the Islamist music groups such as Huda – an all-female group whose music, promoting family values, has been very successful.

These examples show that fears of a global harmonization of culture due to the globalization of Western television forms and formats may not be entirely justified. Although Western domination of the global media and communication industry remains overwhelming, the cultural interactions between Western media products and non-Western societies are deeply complex. There is little doubt about the existence of American cultural products worldwide, though how these are used and interpreted by various cultures remains largely unexplored, given the limited number of concrete case studies which systematically examine these issues (Tomlinson, 1991).

Often the discussion has focused on the media consumption of the ruling elites in developing countries, ignoring how the majority of populations for whom Western products – be that Hollywood films, pop music or computer-related leisure activities – are inaccessible and, even if available, with which they cannot relate easily. Not surprisingly, people prefer entertainment in their own language, catering to their own cultural priorities – one key reason why most of imported programmes rarely make it to prime-time slots in the world's television schedules. Audiences can critically negotiate with an imported programme – something more than many have given them credit for.

The tendency to lump the 'third world' as one homogenized Other in many Western discourses – unfortunately within both the critical and liberal traditions – is partly responsible for such an omission. Obvious unfamiliarity or limited and often distorted understanding of history, traditions, languages and cultures of many developing countries leads to such undifferentiated view of the 'majority world'. One only has to look at the popularity of the Indian film industry, discussed below, in South Asia, or the *telenovelas* in Latin America to discount notions of hapless 'traditional' viewers in the developing world. Some critical scholars seem to have given far too much credit to the media's capacity to shape a nation's cultural agenda. To just give one example – despite 200 years of British colonial subjugation, a vast majority of Indians practise their own religion, speak their own languages and pursue their traditional culture. It is therefore unlikely that a CNN or an MTV will achieve what the British Empire failed to do. This is not to argue that US-led media are not influential but to submit that the interaction is much more complex and there are aspects of Western media and culture which have been easily adapted and assimilated by non-Western cultures.

Global counterflow of television

A more nuanced understanding of the complex process of international cultural flow will show that the traffic is not just one way – from North to South, even though it is overly weighted in the favour of the former. Evidence shows that new transborder television networks are appearing, some from the periphery to the metropolitan centres of global media and communication industries. The extension of satellite footprints and the growth of DTH broadcasting have enabled networks such as Zee to operate in an increasingly global communication environment. Such groups represent Southern media organizations which are becoming visible across the globe, and feeding into and developing what has been referred to as the emergent 'diasporic public spheres' (Appadurai, 1996).

The deregulation of broadcasting, which has been a catalyst for the extension of private television networks, has also made it possible for private satellite broadcasters to aim beyond the borders of the country where the network is based. Traditionally, state broadcasters have seen their roles confined to the borders of a nation–state. Apart from major powers, whose broadcasting had an international dimension, most countries have had to make programmes for a domestic audience. This was particularly the case in the South. In contrast, the private channels, primarily interested in markets and advertising revenues, had a more liberal media agenda. This basic difference between the state-centric and market-oriented broadcasting has been a key factor in the expansion of many Southern broadcasters to the lucrative Northern markets, aiming to reach the diasporic communities. Being part of global conglomerates, such as Phoenix and Zee until 1999, has given them the technical and managerial support to operate as a global channel.

Cultures of diaspora

One reason for the proliferation of such transnational channels is the physical movement of people – what Appadurai has called 'ethnoscape' – from one geographical location to another, carrying with them aspects of their culture. Cultures have always been affected by external influences as a result of trade, proselytization and migration, from the expansion of Christianity and Islam to colonialism and decolonization. In the twenty-first century there are significant populations of South Asians in Britain, North Africans in France, Turks in Germany, and Latin Americans in the United States. Over 20 million people have been forced to leave their countries of origin in the last ten years as a result of conflicts or poverty. The bulk of migration has taken places within the countries of the South: 90 per cent of the population of the United Arab Emirates, for example, consists of foreign workers, a majority of them coming from the Indian sub-continent. This has made the oil-rich Gulf region a key target for media organizations based in India, with television channels, video and audio tape companies and film distribution networks vying with each other to provide cultural goods to what remains a rich market. In addition, there is an increasing internationalization of a professional workforce, employed by the transnational corporations, international non-governmental organizations and multilateral bureaucracies. As a result, with a few exceptions, most nations of the twenty-first century have sizeable minorities and many countries are multilingual. Among the major geo-cultural markets based on language are – English, Spanish, Chinese, Hindi, Arabic and French.

It is, however, the Southern presence in the metropolitan centres of the world brought about by a process of what has been called 'deterritorialization', which Garcia Canclini has described as 'the loss of the "natural" relation of culture to geographical and social territories' (1995: 229) that has received most attention. The issue of identity is central to migrant lifestyle, living as they often do 'between cultures' (Bhabha, 1994). The duel between the dual identity of the host country and the aspiration to be part of the culture of the country of origin, sometime an imaginary 'homeland', makes them susceptible to accepting cultural hybridity (Anderson, 1991). The nature of cultural mixing, as Martin Barbero has argued, can lead to a hybridization of cultures. Iranian cable television in Los Angeles, for example, has had to tread a careful line between providing programmes which retain traditional Islamic way of life with those which display the local consumerist lifestyle in the USA (Naficy, 1993).

In the past, diasporic communities have used different types of media to keep in touch with their culture – from letters, books, newspapers and magazines, to, more recently, audiotapes and videos of films. Satellite television opens up possibilities for transnational broadcasters to cater to specific geo-linguistic groups. For example, the Chinese minority in Malaysia can receive programming from China or the Algerians in France can watch Algerian and other Arabic channels. The demand for such channels also reflects the lack of provision for minority communities by mainstream media and national broadcasters.

New communication technologies have made it possible for broadcasters from many developing countries to successfully export their media products. Turkey's TRT launched TRT-INT in 1990 to transmit via Eutelsat programmes to Turkish-speaking populations in Western Europe, mainly aimed at the two-million strong Turkish population in Germany. Two years later, in 1992, it launched a transborder broadcasting channel TRT AVRASYA TV, aimed at the Turkic-speaking populations in Central Asia, who share language, religion and cultural affinities with Turkey and whose cultural sovereignty was undermined by decades of domination under Soviet communism. With the launch of Turksat 1 in 1994, the flow has increased.

In 1999, reruns of the Indian mythological serial *The Ramayan* were being broadcast by Sony UK, Sony US, by East-Net (part of M-Net, Africa's biggest pay channel network) and on satellite channels in Sri Lanka, Nepal, Malaysia, Indonesia, Surinam and British Guinea. *The Ramayan* has been dubbed into English, Mandarin, Cantonese, Thai, Sinhalese and Bhasa Indonesia; while *Mahabharat* – which was also broadcast by the BBC in the early 1990s was dubbed into Persian for telecast in Iran. Reruns of *Mahabharat* were being shown, in 1999, on Zee TV in the UK and the USA with English subtitles, the serial having been telecast in, among others, Thailand, Indonesia, Mauritius, Nepal, Canada, Trinidad, Uzbekistan, Sri Lanka, Singapore and Malaysia (*Times of India*, 14 October 1999).

Such expansion has been possible because of availability of satellite platforms. In Britain, South Asian channels – Zee, Sony, Asianet, B4U – were being made available on Sky's digital network. The US-based International Channel Networks (ICN), whose platform is providing a distribution outlet for European and other channels, launched a digital language channels for ethnic communities. These include ART (Arabic), CCTV-4 (Mandarin, Cantonese and English) and TV Asia (Hindi) (Sutherland, 1999a). It is a popular fallacy that the growing availability of such channels has contributed to a greater awareness of cultural differences in the world's metropolitan centres and a trend towards multiculturalism. However, these channels are not watched by the majority of the population, even though some advertisers have found it a useful means to target a niche audience, further leading to the fragmentation of the audience and ghettoization of minorities.

The following case studies examine two examples of regional media actors, who are playing an increasingly important role in international communication. The two networks discussed – Middle East Broadcasting Centre (Arabic) and Phoenix (Mandarin) – represent distinct geo-linguistic categories, though their influence and reach are wider than just among the speakers of the particular language group towards which they are primarily targeted. Channels like Phoenix and MBC are aiming at a specific demographic/linguistic segment of populations in various different countries and thus they represent attempts at creating supranational public spaces, based on cultural and linguistic affinities.

Middle East Broadcasting Centre (MBC)

Among the regional geo-linguistic areas, the growth of pan-Arabic television is one of the most important media developments of the 1990s. In the Arab world, where media has traditionally been under the direct control of the state, the growing popularity of international television has raised questions about the suitability of some of its programming in what remains one of the world's most conservative areas with strict regulations, especially about the depiction of women on television or in cinema. Most Arab television systems are under direct government control, dependent on state support rather than advertising (Amin, 1996).

Partly as a reaction to the availability of Western television in the region, pan-Arabic channels such as Middle East Broadcasting Centre (MBC) have emerged on the Arab broadcasting scene. The primary objective of these channels is to broadcast Arabic-language programmes to Arab nationals living in Europe and North America – an estimated five million Arabs live in Europe and another two million in North America. This well-established and wealthy diaspora has created new foreign markets for Arab broadcasters.

Intra-Arab communication was first established by the international Arabic newspapers, written with datelines across the Arab world, edited in London and printed in major world capitals, using satellite communications. The newspapers such as *al-Sharq al-Awsat* (started in London in 1978), *al-Hayat* (originally a Beirut newspaper which was resurrected in London in 1988 but only became famous in 1990 with Saudi funds) and *al-Quds al-Arabi*, (unlike the other two, this is a radical newspaper and supports the PLO) cover issues of importance to Arab readers and are available on the day of publication in most Arab capitals. In 1998, *al-Hayat* was being printed in eight cities, including Riyadh, London, Frankfurt and New York, with a combined circulation of 168 000 copies (Alterman, 1998).

Prior to the availability of satellite television, regional broadcasting was largely about exchange of government propaganda between Arab state-regulated broadcasters through such organizations as the Arab States Broadcasting Union (ASBU). In the 1990s with the rise of a privatized Arab satellite broadcast television, a new type of pan-Arabic television emerged, challenging state monopolies that had characterized broadcasting in the Arab world. The success of round-the-clock news such as CNN after the 1991 Gulf War made the Arabs look for a new market of broadcasting, influenced by American journalistic and production values.

The launch of a new generation of satellites helped broadcasting. Arabsat, a consortium comprising the members of the Arab League, launched its first communications satellite in 1985. In the 1990s, the development of new satellite technology, especially the new Ku-Band, set aside specifically for direct-to-home broadcasting, have ensured more traffic on satellites which is making them cheaper to run (Marghalani *et al.*, 1998).

The expansion of Arabsat has ensured that pan-regional satellite television can prosper in the region, given the linguistic, religious and cultural affinities among Arab countries. Increasingly, Arab citizens who live in the global North are also being linked to this shared experience.

To cater to this generally prosperous diasporic community, the London-based Middle East Broadcasting Centre (MBC) has emerged as the key pan-Arabic television channel. Owned by the Saudi-based ARA Group International and started in 1991, aimed at a middle-class audience with an interest in pan-Arabic and international affairs, MBC has emerged as a major voice projecting an Arab viewpoint in the world.

Launched with a capital of $300 million, MBC started broadcasting across Europe and North Africa via Eutelsat II and across the Middle East through Arabsat. In contrast to state-run TV, it has higher production values and professional standards and a potential viewership of more than 100 million in the Arab world. By 1999, it was one of the most widely viewed channels in the Arab world, claiming an audience of between 100 and 120 million viewers, in 50 million households across the Middle East. Many of its programmes are then rebroadcast on terrestrial television in Arab countries.

MBC has given a new professional touch to Arabic news and current affairs output, modelling its news programmes on US television networks. Through a wide network of correspondents, MBC provides a detailed analysis of developments in the Arab world – in 1999, it had correspondents in most Arab countries as well as in the United States, France, Germany, Russia, India, Italy, Sweden and Bosnia. Such journalistic resources have helped MBC to cover the Arab countries not through the viewpoint of Western news agencies but by on-the-spot reporting from Arab journalists, reporting in Arabic for an pan-Arabic audience. A more liberal news agenda has helped to make it a major regional broadcaster – it was the first Arab television company to open a Jerusalem bureau.

In addition to its news and current affairs output, MBC also features talk shows, music, films and serials. It was a partner with the Voice of America in a pioneering series of programmes, started in 1995, called *Dialogue with the West*, which brought together for a discussion experts and officials from the Middle East and the USA for 80 episodes, lasting two years. It has also broadcast political documentaries made by Western television networks on locally sensitive issues, for example, a five-part BBC documentary *The Fifty-Year War – Israel and the Arabs*, in 1998, causing political ripples in some Arab capitals (Alterman, 1998).

MBC has benefited from being owned by Shaikh Walid al-Ibrahim, a Saudi entrepreneur and relation of King Fahd. The Shaikh also partly owned the news agency UPI, thus combining a dose of US-style journalism with the financial resources of the Saudi royal family, enabling the company to invest in latest satellite technology and other broadcasting equipment. MBC's location in London, a global media centre even in this 'post-imperial age', also helps raise its profile as an international media player.

In the arena of news and current affairs, MBC faces its main rival, the Doha-based Qatari all-news channel Al-Jazeera, which started broadcasting in 1996 and has developed a reputation for independent and critical reporting of Arab issues. In the field of entertainment, it faces the Lebanese Broadcasting Corporation (LBC), whose light entertainment programming is popular in the Arab world, making it a profitable broadcaster. It has emerged as an amalgam of Arab and Western (mainly US) culture, and perhaps a harbinger of what Arab television would look like as a purely commercial venture and not one financed (and often subsidized) by conservative Gulf Arabs.

Other major entertainment channels in the region are the Cairo-based Arab Radio and Television (ART), owned by Saudi billionaire Prince al-Waleed bin Talal, whose holdings include part of EuroDisney, Citicrop and Apple Computer (Serwer, 1999) and Lebanon's 24-hour channel Future International, which since its launch in 1994, has steadily grown in the region and claims to be the first 'to create a melange between Oriental and Western melodies and ideas'.

MBC also has to compete with other major pan-regional channels such as Orbit and Showtime. Orbit, launched in 1994 and owned by the Mawarid Group, a multi-billion dollar Saudi conglomerate controlled by Prince Khalid bin Abdallah, features locally adapted versions of ESPN and the Disney Channel, US films, and US situation comedies. In addition to its English-language offerings, Orbit broadcasts Arabic films (or Western films dubbed into Arabic) and an Arabic light entertainment programming channel. Orbit also provides regional access to STAR Select, part of STAR TV's Middle Eastern service, which supplies mainly US programming aimed at expatriate Western workers in the Gulf region and Westernized Saudi businessmen By 1998, Orbit was claiming to reach 180 000 'viewing points', many of them hotels.

Though Western television – through such channels as Showtime and STAR Select and Orbit – offers US entertainment, it is the Egyptian soap operas which are hugely successful in the Arab world. Egyptian programming is a substantial source of revenues for Egyptian Radio and Television Union (ERTU), responsible for all public service channels in the country, producing 3 900 hours of television programming every year. In 1995, television fiction earned more than $18 million for the ERTU (UNESCO, 1997: 205). It is interesting that the two most successful channels in the Arab world are al-Jazeera and ART (considered the 'most Arab' of the broadcasters) and are based in the region, in which by 1999, more than 150 TV channels were operating.

Satellite broadcasters have two sources of income – advertising revenue and subscription fees. Though advertising is less well developed in the Arab world than in other Southern regions, in recent years it has increased substantially. MBC's advertising and subscription revenues in 1998 were $80 million. To increase its reach among the Arab youth, in 1999 MBC launched programmes such as *Pepsi Muzica*, a weekly youth music programme sponsored by Pepsi – the MBC logo is also stamped on cans of Pepsi sold in the region (Koranteng, 1999). In 1998, the advertising spend in the Middle East was $1.93 billion, a rise of 21 per cent over the previous year, with regional satellite channels accounting for 46 per cent of that growth.

Although the Saudis own nearly 75 per cent of all satellite television in the region, the issue of cultural immodesty is always to the fore and they have threatened to impose current ban on satellite dishes. According to the Dubai-based Pan-Arab Research Centre, MBC is likely to account for nearly 40 per cent of viewers share in Saudi Arabia, with its nearest rival being LBC–Lebanese Satellite at 37 per cent and Egypt Space Channel at 26 per cent.

By providing news and entertainment to the Arab world and among the Arabic diaspora, channels like MBC could help shape a new kind of Arab identity – one based on a regional or geo-linguistic rather than national identity. As the wealthiest market and the dominant owner of satellite television in the region, Saudi Arabia has a major role in the Arab media. However, it also is one of the world's most conservative countries – the BBC Arabic Service was abandoned in 1995 when the BBC aired stories that Saudis found objectionable, including coverage of the activities of London-based Saudi dissident Muhammad al-Mas'ari, and a report on its flagship current affairs programme *Panorama* that explored the issue of capital punishment in the Kingdom.

The growing popularity of regional actors such as MBC raises questions about the ability of Arab governments to control regional media, perhaps widening the terms of debate in what remains an undemocratic part of the globe. However, it is also important to remember that some of the major players in this region are pro-Western nations such as Saudi Arabia, the real power behind ventures like MBC. And given the nature of the state in that country – dynastic rule – it is possible that only certain types of discussion would be allowed on pan-Arabic channels.

Broadcasters like MBC have helped to strengthen a moderate and pro-Western Arab public opinion. A recent policy paper recommends that the USA should engage with this new media run by the Westernized Arab elite:

> At a time when the U.S. government's standing in the region is at low ebb, a concerted and sophisticated effort to engage the regional Arab media, and through them the Arab world at large, could reap great rewards. The media world is, after all, one that the United States had a large role in creating and which the US government understands well. Success in this field could vastly facilitate the execution of US policy in the region.

(Alterman, 1998: 79)

Phoenix Chinese Channel

With a population of 1.2 billion and one of the world's fastest-growing economies, China is a prize media market. By 1999, China had an estimated 320 million television sets, more than the USA, the world's biggest TV market (Lawrence, 1999). In the past quarter of a century, the TV audience in China has increased exponentially – from a mere 18 million in 1975, to 540 million in 1985 to 1 020 million in 1995. TV stations have also grown substantially from 30 in 1978 to 980 in 1995 (Hong, 1997).

It is scarcely surprising, then, that major media corporations have endeavoured to enter this lucrative market. However, the language barrier and the tight control of airwaves by the Chinese government, have made it difficult for transnational media players to operate in China. News Corporation's launch in 1996 of Phoenix Chinese Channel, the round-the-clock, Mandarin language channel was an attempt to get round these barriers by localizing the media product. Though partly owned by Murdoch, the channel has most of its programming in Mandarin and the top management, including Executive Chairman and CEO, are Chinese. More than other media tycoons, Murdoch has realized that it is local programming that sells best. Therefore his priority is to make original programming in Chinese for the Chinese mainland and for the Chinese diaspora – estimated to be more than 30 million – mainly concentrated in south-east Asia but also present in sizeable numbers in North America.

This Hong Kong-based, general entertainment channel offers Chinese and international programming, including news, sports, music, drama, movies and variety shows.

A joint venture between STAR TV, Hong Kong-based *Today's Asia* and China Wise International, Phoenix, is broadcast via AsiaSat 3S and Palapa C2 satellites. A 24-hour movie channel, Phoenix Movies Channel, was launched in 1998, broadcasting every month more than 280 Chinese and Western classics and blockbusters, with sub-titles.

Given its mix of entertainment and infotainment, Phoenix has reported a 20 per cent rise in programme ratings throughout the Asia-Pacific region and a steady increase in revenues. In 1999, it claimed to be reaching more than 47.5 million households in mainland China. The channel could reach almost two billion viewers in more than 30 countries in the Asia-Pacific region, including 550 000 homes in Hong Kong. Like Zee TV in India, Phoenix has shown that entertainment in local language sells. One of the most popular programmes on the Chinese channel is *Perfect Match*, the match-making/dating show, which was named Entertainment Programme of the Year 1998 by China's *New Weekly* magazine.

Claiming to blend traditional Chinese culture with the Westernized ethos of Hong Kong, which until 1997 was a British colony, Phoenix has attracted TV personnel from Hong Kong, Taiwan, the mainland China and among the Chinese diaspora. More importantly, it has been able to attract multinational companies to advertise on the channel. According to *Advertising Age International*, among the key advertisers on the channel in 1998 were such world brands as Nokia, Philips and BMW (*Advertising Age International*, 8 February 1999).

Phoenix is benefiting from the gradual opening up of China, traditionally a closed society and for half a century a communist country. A Gallup Poll published in *Fortune* magazine in 1999 showed that nearly half of all urban Chinese had eaten Western fast food and watched Western films, while 30 per cent said they had bought Western music and 23 per cent had read Western books, magazines and newspapers (*Fortune*, 1999c: 61).

Having established itself in the region, the channel has ambitions to go global. In its first step to move beyond Asia, in August 1999 Phoenix launched Phoenix Europe, in collaboration with London-based Chinese News and Entertainment (CNE) to bring entertainment and news programming in Chinese to European audiences. There are also plans to enter the lucrative US market, home to a large and financially well-off Chinese community. Operating from London since 1992, with a programming mix of news and current affairs and entertainment, CNE claims to reach more than 56 million homes worldwide.

Phoenix may have to compete or cooperate with the state Chinese television CCTV, whose main channel reaches over 84 per cent of the population of China, with the number of regular viewers exceeding 900 million. In addition, it also has two international channels – CCTV-4, a round-the-clock satellite channel serving overseas Chinese and broadcasting mostly in Mandarin, and since 1997, the English-language CCTV-9 channel, whose programmes include news, *China Business Guide*, *Learning to Speak Chinese* and *MTV China*.

Television played an important role in China in legitimizing and popularizing its policy of economic liberalization, introduced in late 1970s, after the death of Mao Tse Tung, the leader of the 1949 communist revolution. As one commentator wrote: 'Television has irreversibly altered the consciousness of the Chinese public' (Lull,

1991: 170). The gradual glasnost detectable in Chinese news and current affairs pro-grammes, can also be attributed to the economic liberalization (Chang *et al.*, 1998).

Since China is increasingly keen to integrate with global financial and information markets, the accent of news and information programmes is on economic and trade issues. The change of attitude is also discernible in the way authorities deal with the foreign media. Though still in control of information channels, the communist party has given up its rhetoric of the 1980s which saw the West as source of 'spiritual pollution' and 'bourgeois liberalization'. Instead, the party now happily embraces what it calls market socialism, with CCTV keenly promoting consumerism through retail program-ming – CCTV2 launched a direct retail programme *Dianshi Gouwu* (TV Shopping) in 1998 (Zhao, 1999).

For their part, transnational media corporations have to tread a careful line in dealing with what is still a one-party state. Especially sensitive are news and current affairs issues, for example, the Chinese definition of human rights may differ consid-erably from that of the US government. Such sensitivities were behind STAR TV's summary removal in 1994 of the BBC from its northern beam covering China after the Chinese government complained of the BBC's coverage of human rights issues in the country.

Since then, News Corporation has undertaken many measures to placate the Chinese government, including setting up in 1995 an information technology joint venture with the *Peoples Daily*; publishing (under HarperCollins imprint) the English translation of a biography of the Chinese leader Deng Xiaoping and showing on Phoenix, in 1997, a series of 12 one-hour episodes on the life of Deng, made by CCTV.

In 1998, Murdoch cancelled a HarperCollins contract to publish the memoirs of Chris Patten, the controversial last governor of Hong Kong. More recently, when the Chinese Prime Minister Zhu Rongji visited the USA on an official visit in April 1999, Phoenix broadcast live coverage of events throughout his trip. In May 1999, within days of the NATO bombing of the Chinese Embassy in Belgrade in which three Chinese journalists were killed, Phoenix organized a concert in Shenzhen, named *It's Time to Say NO*, in memory of the journalists, with participation from musical groups from China, Hong Kong and Taiwan. News Corporation was the first major international media company to open an office in Beijing in 1999, the year when for the first time on Chinese mainland *Channel [V] Chinese Music Awards* were held in Shanghai.

As a regional Chinese television channel, backed by one of the world's biggest media conglomerates and sympathetic to the government in China, Phoenix is an important vehicle for international advertisers, though its capacity to raise critical issues and fight censorship – overt and covert – remains extremely limited. Apart from their economic value as champions of consumerism, such channels can also create a greater sense of cultural solidarity among the Chinese-speaking peoples in the region. Particularly significant will be its role in narrowing political differences between China and Taiwan, which Beijing refuses to recognize as a separate nation. Phoenix can con-tribute towards closer cultural ties among people of Chinese descent, one based on cultural and linguistic affinity rather than nationality.

Media exports from the South to the North

Apart from the regional broadcasters discussed above, which are likely to become more important in the coming years, there are also international players from the global South, whose presence is increasingly being felt in international cultural communication. In the evolution of channels like MBC and Phoenix, global, regional and national experiences interplay and produce something which is unique and whose impact on media globalization is yet to be assessed. The following case studies offer two main examples of this contraflow of cultural products from the South – Brazil's TV Globo and the Indian film industry. TV Globo reflects the international acceptance of a genre like the soap opera, which has evolved from its origins in French and English serial novels – through serializations in magazines and newspapers, to their adoption by US radio and television and then its adaptation as a genre at a global level (Allen, 1995).

TV Globo

One key example of cultural export from the South to the North is the Latin American soap opera, the *telenovela*, and the Brazilian media giant TV Globo is the primary exporter of this popular genre of television across the globe. The *telenovela*, whose origins lie in radio soaps, thrives on melodramatic and often simplistic narrative which can be understood and enjoyed by audiences in different cultural contexts.

Though US-generated programmes, films and cartoons are widely shown on Brazilian and other South American television channels, the prime time is dominated by *telenovelas* (Fox, 1997). Globo, along with Mexico's Televisa, the world's largest producer of Spanish-language television programmes, are two major regional players in the continent. Though developed as a genre by other Brazilian channels, it was TV Globo which made *telenovela* into a export product (Mattelart and Mattelart, 1990).

TV Globo is part of Rede Globo, one of the world's largest multimedia conglomerate which owns Brazil's leading newspaper *O Globo*, founded 1925; Globosat satellite; the Globo radio system, inaugurated in 1944; a publishing firm; a music company and a telecommunications firm. In 1999, Globo television network had 113 broadcast and affiliate stations and an audience share of 74 per cent, while it absorbed 75 per cent of all Brazil's advertisement revenue.

Launched in 1965 in collaboration with the US-based Time-Life group, TV Globo was instrumental in building a national network, based on the commercial television culture of the USA. With US financial, managerial and technological help, Globo was able to bring television to the masses in Brazil, one of the biggest consumer markets in Latin America. Though Time-Life withdrew in 1968, the US model continued to be the guiding principle for TV Globo. In the early years, the *telenovelas* were sponsored by transnational corporations such as Procter and Gamble, Colgate-Palmolive and

Unilever. Gradually however, production was taken over by Globo. This was made possible partly because of massive support from the Brazilian government.

TV Globo was clearly aligned with the successive authoritarian governments following the 1964 military coup. The right-wing military dictatorships, which dominated Brazilian politics until 1985, used this powerful medium to legitimize their rule and shape public opinion. In return the Globo group received special treatment from the generals, who besides investing heavily in Brazil's telecommunications infrastructure – including national satellite networks – gave TV Globo most of government advertising. The launch of Brazil's first telecommunications satellite, Brazilsat, in 1985, facilitated the further expansion of TV Globo. Such government support not only enabled the commercialization of television but also helped create a sense of Brazilian national identity (Mattelart and Mattelart, 1990). As a result of the close ties with the military regime the Globo group was allowed to have a virtual monopoly on media in Brazil, restricting alternative viewpoints to emerge in a country deeply divided in social and economic terms (Mader, 1993).

As part of an array of new cable and satellite TV services targeted at Brazil's 36 million TV households, Globo News, a 24-hour news channel, was launched in 1996. In 1999, TV Globo's programmes were available in Japan on Sky PerfecTV! and on DTH platform on Sky in Chile, Columbia and Mexico, with plans to extend them to other parts of Latin America, Canada and Europe.

Telenovelas in the 1970s had already pushed the American canned programmes to less popular hours (Oliveira, 1993). While imported programmes in 1972 occupied approximately 60 per cent of the total programme share, they decreased to 30 per cent in 1983 (Rogers and Antola, 1985). TV Globo entered the international market in 1975 with exports of *telenovelas* to Portugal. *Gabriela*, a *telenovela* based on an adaptation of a best-selling novel, telecast daily in Portugal, was a major hit, leading to the charge of 'reverse colonization' (Lopez, 1995). In subsequent years, Brazilian *telenovelas* became extremely popular in Portugal and their style was adapted for domestic production (O'Donnell, 1999). However, *telenovelas* were less than successful in former Portuguese colonies in Africa and to reach a bigger audience in Latin America, TV Globo started dubbing its programmes in Spanish, the most widely spoken language in Latin America and also one of the fastest-growing languages in the US. The availability and popularity of Latin American *telenovelas* in the US have also been called 'reverse media imperialism' (Rogers and Antola, 1985).

One of TV Globo's biggest international successes was the historical romance *Escrava Isaura* (Slave Girl Isaura), which was a great hit in Italy, France, the former Soviet Union, and, particularly, in China, where 450 million viewers watched the series. The Chinese translation of the book on which it was based sold 300000 copies (Oliveira, 1993).

Globo opened sales offices in New York, Paris and London as television channels proliferated in the wake of the satellite revolution. Since 1993, Globo has been exporting television formats to even well-established broadcasters such as the BBC, whose game show *Do the Right Thing* was adapted and licensed from TV Globo and was based on the Brazilian format *Voce Decide* (You Decide). By 1996, this interactive game show had been adapted in 37 countries as diverse as China and Angola, with the

Spanish-language version being broadcast in 12 countries, including the USA, 18 productions in Europe and six in the Middle East (Moran, 1998).

Virtually all the Rede Globo programmes are produced in-house. In 1999, the group claimed to produce a total of 4 420 hours of programming annually, including news and current affairs, entertainment and soap operas, making it one of the world's largest television programme producer. *Telenovelas* are edited to make them intelligible with fewer specific Brazilian references. Many *telenovelas* are dubbed in different languages, especially in Spanish for other Latin American countries, still the biggest market for such a genre. In 1999, TV Globo's programmes, mainly entertainment oriented, were being exported to 130 countries across the globe. In 1998, Globo had a total revenue of $4.4 billion, of which nearly 32 per cent of the total company's revenue – $1.4 billion – was TV revenue (*Television Business International*, July/August 1999).

The international success of TV Globo is primarily based on its commercial nature. In the crudely advertising-driven media environment with few regulations on what can be advertised, TV Globo has consistently used its programmes to promote consumer products, from Coca-Cola to ladies underwear. 'Merchandising' is integrated into the narrative, either by actors directly advertising a product or through product placement, when the consumer items appear in the programme (Tufte, 2000). Apart from such crass commercialism, TV Globo also claims to use what it calls 'social merchandising', weaving public information – such as awareness of gender rights and birth control – into the plots. International organizations such as UNICEF have acknowledged the importance of such methods in reducing the infant mortality rate in Brazil.

It is debatable to what extent TV Globo reflects the realities of Brazilian life. Is it a localized version of US television, a 'creolization' of US commercial culture? Such a form of programming, common in much of Latin American television, it has been argued, could be seen as legitimizing free market capitalism, substituting the government's hegemony by private initiative, which is also projected as the key link between national and international culture (Martin-Barbero, 1993).

Globo is one of the strongest media corporations in Latin America and in 1995 established a consortium of DTH broadcasters with News Corporation, Televisa and TCI to provide a range of programming to the continent. However, it is important to remember that unlike US media giants, TV Globo's primary market is local and among the Latin countries, and none of its *telenovelas* have had the international impact comparable with US soaps such as *Dynasty*, *Dallas* or the cult following of an *X Files* or a *Friends*. The challenge that organizations such as Globo pose to the traditional dominance of the USA in the world audio-visual trade is, as one observer notes 'more conceptual than real: that is, it has more to do with our theoretical common wisdom about that dominance than with the actual degree of commercial threat' (Sinclair, 1996: 51). Indeed, it can be argued that television channels such as TV Globo are instrumental in legitimizing consumerist values and are more often than not complementary rather than oppositional to the US-based media transnationals.

The other Hollywood – the Indian film industry

India is among the few non-Western countries which have made their presence felt in the global cultural market. Particularly significant, though largely ignored in mainstream international scholarship and journalistic writing on films, popular music and television, is India's 50 billion-rupee Hindi film industry based in Mumbai (formerly Bombay), the commercial hub of India. In addition to productions from 'Bollywood', there are strong regional centres making films in India's other main languages, notably Tamil, Bangla, Telugu and Malayalam. Though more films are made in India each year than Hollywood – in the decade 1989–98 India produced 787 feature films against 591 produced in the US (*see*, Figure 6.1. See also Chapter 5, Table 5.6) – its influence is largely confined to the Indian subcontinent and among the South Asian diaspora.

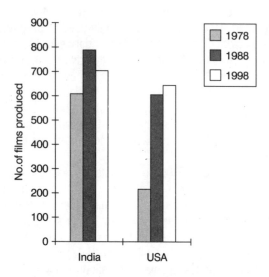

Figure 6.1 Hollywood vs. Bollywood
Source: Based on data from *Screen Digest*, June 1999

Within months of the invention of the motion picture by the Lumière brothers in France in 1895, films were being shown in Bombay and film production in India started soon afterwards, in 1897. In 1913, Govind Dhundiraj Phalke, better known as Dadasaheb Phalke (the father of the Indian film industry, in whose honour India's highest award for films is named) launched the first full length feature film *Raja Harishchandra*, based on the life of a mythological king of ancient India. In the silent era (1913–31) more than 1 200 films were made in India (Rajadhyaksha and Willemen, 1994).

In 1931, India entered the sound era and the first sound film – talkie – was Ardeshir Irani's *Alam Ara*. By the end of that year, 28 full-length feature films in three languages were released – of which 23 were in Hindi, four in Bangla and one in Tamil. Since then the growth of feature films has been remarkable – from 84 in 1932 to 173 in 1942 to 233 in 1952 to 315 in 1962 (Rajadhyaksha and Willemen, 1994). Hindi films dominated these productions but there were other major regional film industries notably, Tamil, Bangla, Telugu and Malyalam. In 1999, India boasted of being home to the largest film industry in the world, producing the highest number of films than any other country. Given the size of India's one billion population and the place that cinema has among people's leisure activities, cutting across regional, class, gender and generational divisions, it remains the most popular form of entertainment. Table 6.1 shows how many people visit cinemas in India – not only in urban and sub-urban areas but also in rural parts of the country, often in makeshift cinema houses.

Table 6.1 Cinema in India

	1995	1996	1997	1998
Admissions (millions)	3 380	3 380	3 580	2 860
Net box office ($million)	418	516	537	430

Source: Based on data from *Screen Digest*, July 1999

The unprecedented expansion of television in the 1990s has also been a boost for the movie industry, as many dedicated film-based pay-channels have emerged. In addition, advancements in technology and the availability of satellite and cable television have ensured that Indian films are regularly shown outside India, dominating the cinema of South Asia and defining popular culture in the Indian subcontinent. Hindi films are also very popular in the Arab world, in central Asia and among many African countries. Table 6.2 shows the extent of some of the international audience for Hindi films. Only the countries where Indian film imports account for a quarter or more have been included. Other countries, notably United Arab Emirates, Russia and Malaysia, are also major markets for Indian films.

Table 6.2 Indian films in the global market

Country	Latest year	Total film imports	Indian imports (%)
Tanzania	1991	71	62
Kenya	1993	364	52
Uzbekistan	1993	53	49
Tunisia	1996	110*	48
Côte d'Ivoire	1993	86	42
Benin	1993	219	35
Mauritius	1993	50	34
Guinea	1991	394	27
Morocco	1996	382*	26
Tajikistan	1995	66	24

Note: *total films released.
Source: Based on data from 1998 UNESCO *Statistical Yearbook*

However, in terms of earning revenue from film exports, India is no match for the USA – in 1993, for example, the USA earned nearly 750 times the revenue that India earns from film exports (Pendakur and Subramanyam, 1996). One reason for the popularity of Indian films among other developing countries is their melodramatic narrative style, often a storyline which emphasizes dichotomies between the poor-pure-and-just vs. rich-urban-and-unjust, enlivened with song and dance sequences (Dissanayake, 1993). Films have also contributed to the burgeoning popular music industry and a mainstream Indian film is inconceivable without prominent musical support (Manuel, 1993). Although most of the films are social and family-oriented dramas, Indian filmmakers have also experimented with other major genres of cinema, such as historical, mythological, comic, supernatural and 'Western'.

Even before India became an independent nation, films from India were being exported to south-east Asian and African nations (Barnouw and Krishnaswamy, 1980). In fact, within a year of the launch of sound movies, the Motion Picture Society of India (which in 1951 became the Film Federation of India) was established and a Hindi film weekly *Cinema Sansar* (Cinema World) had been launched.

The formative years of Indian cinema were profoundly influenced by the anti-colonial movement (Kaul, 1998). A progressive message of communal harmony and national integration was fostered through films – extremely important in a country of very low literacy. Of particular significance was the contribution of the Indian People's Theatre Association (IPTA) whose 1946 film *Dharti Ke Lal* (Children of the Earth), directed by prominent progressive writer Khwaja Ahmad Abbas, was the first film to receive widespread distribution in the Soviet Union, while the 1957 feature *Perdesi* (foreigner) was the first Indo-Soviet co-production.

By the 1950s the mainstream Indian cinema was producing internationally known films which have since acquired the status of classics. Prominent among these were Raj Kapoor's 1955 sentimental and moral tale with progressive overtones, *Shri 420* (Mr 420), which became immensely popular in the Soviet Union; Guru Dutt's 1957 film *Pyaasa* (The Thirsty One), a tense melodrama and the prominent director's 1959 autobiographical work *Kaagaz Ke Phool* (Paper Flowers), India's first cinemascope film, known for its brilliant camerawork. Mahboob Khan's 1957 national epic *Mother India* was a landmark commercial success, which acquired the status of an Indian *Gone with the Wind.* The first partly coloured movie, K. Asif's 1960 epic *Mughal-e-Azam*, based on the legend of princely romance during the reign of Mughal emperor Akbar, is often considered India's most accomplished historical film.

There has always been a progressive tradition within film-making, addressing such issues as exploitation based on class, caste or gender. Three prominent examples of this trend are Bimal Roy's 1953 realist drama *Do Bhiga Zameen* (Two Bhiga of Land) about land reform; Shambhu Mitra's 1957 film *Jagte Raho* (Stay Awake), which won the Grand Prix at Karlovy Vary Film Festival that year and *Garam Hawa* (Hot Winds), directed by M. S. Sathyu, a powerful 1973 film about communal issues in the wake of India's partition.

However, it was not the star-studded movies but a low-budget film in a regional language – Bangla – which put India on the international cinema map. Satyajit Ray's debut film *Pather Panchali* (Song of the Little Road), released in 1955, won international critical acclaim and continued to run for more than seven months in New York, setting a new record for foreign films released in the USA (Garga, 1996).

The film is part of the Apu trilogy, based on the works of noted Bengali novelist Bibhuthibhushan Bandhopadhyaya – the other two films in the trilogy were *Aparajito* (The Unvanquished), 1956, and *Apur Sansar* (The World of Apu) released in 1959. Ray's only non-Bengali feature was the 1977 film *Shatranj Ke Khiladi* (The Chess Players), based on a story by eminent Hindi writer Premchand. Ray was more than just an outstanding film-maker – he excelled in other creative areas too, being an author, painter and editing and illustrating the children's magazine *Sandesh* (Message) (Robinson, 1989). He was presented with *Legion d'honneur* by the French President François Mitterand in 1990 and, in 1992, just a few weeks before his death, awarded an Oscar for lifetime achievement in film.

Ray's influence was profound, inspiring a new generation of film-makers, contributing to a trend of 'parallel' cinema which started with the 1969 film *Bhuvan Shome*, directed by noted Bengali film-maker Mrinal Sen, and followed by two other releases in the same year – Basu Chaterjee's *Sara Akash* (The Whole Sky), and *Uski Roti* (Our Daily Bread) directed by Mani Kaul. Other prominent films in this genre were the 1972 film *Maya Darpan* (Mirror of Illusion) directed by Kumar Shahani, *Ankur* (The Seedling) directed in 1973 by Shyam Benegal and the critically acclaimed 1980 film *Aakrosh* (Cry of the Wounded) by Govind Nihalani.

Among the regional films this trend was to be seen in such films as Pattabhi Rama Reddy's 1970 Kannada feature *Samskara* (Funeral Rites) and in *Shantata! Court Chalu Aahe* (Silence! The Court is in Session), the 1971 political film directed by noted Marathi playwright Vijay Tendulkar. Internationally acclaimed regional film makers include Ritwik Ghatak, the Bengali genius, best known for his 1960 film *Meghe Dhaka Tara* (The Cloudcapped Star) and Adoor Gopalakrishnan from the southern state of Kerala, best known for his 1977 film *Kodiyettam* (The Ascent).

Though critically acclaimed nationally and internationally and funded by state organizations such as the Film Finance Corporation (renamed the National Film Development Corporation in 1980), the so-called 'parallel cinema' has hardly made a dent in popular choice in films which continues to revolve around musical films with an undemanding script, and increasingly, foreign locales. Most Indian and indeed foreign viewers of Indian films are more comfortable watching a fast-paced action movie such as the 1975 megahit *Sholay* (Embers), a massively popular adventure film directed by Ramesh Sippy, or a musical family drama *Hum Aapke Hain Koun* (Who am I to you) directed in 1994 by Sooraj Barjatya.

Domestically, films continue to exert extraordinary influence, including political clout. Several film stars have entered politics and thrived. Many are members of parliament – Amitabh Bachchan, India's most popular actor during the 1970s and 1980s became a Member of Parliament in 1984. In the 1980s, the Telugu superstar N. T. Rama Rao was elected the Chief Minister of Andhra Pradesh, while in neighbouring Tamil Nadu two former Chief Ministers have been leading actors in the Tamil film industry. Such was their popularity that when M. G. Ramachandran the Tamil megastar and Chief Minister, died in 1987, his funeral was attended by two million people (Rajadhyaksha and Willemen, 1994).

The globalization of Indian television has ensured that more and more Indian films are being watched by a varied international audience (Kazmi, 1999). This has made it imperative for producers to invest in sub-titling to widen the reach of Indian films. The changing global broadcasting environment and the availability of digital television and online delivery systems will ensure that Indian films will be available to new audiences. In August 1999, B4U or Bollywood for You, Britain's newest round-the-clock digital television channel for Hindi movies, 'the first South Asian digital channel in the northern hemisphere,' (Ahmed, 1999), was launched. Indian films makers are aiming to reach the coveted Northern markets. The hitherto unexplored Asian niche in the entertainment market came to light when the 1998 love story *Kuch Kuch Hota Hai* (Something is Happening), directed by Yash Johar, featured in British weekly top 10 film lists. Since then, Indian films are being seen as a serious export earner.

In February 1999, the Indian government passed a law exempting export earnings from films from tax. Subhash Ghai's love story *Taal* (The Beat), and Barjatya's 1999 musical, extolling the virtues of extended family *Hum Saath Saath Hain* (We Stand United) had the distinction of being the first Indian films to make it to the top 20 slot in the US film trade magazine *Variety*'s box office chart. Within the first ten days of its release in the USA, the latter film had earned $1.2 million at the box office (*Variety*, 1999). Indian film exports, which were barely 200 million rupees in 1988–89 jumped to 4 billion rupees in 1998–99 – a 20-fold increase in a decade, with the Indian Motion Pictures Producers' Association predicting that film exports would cross 10 billion rupees by 2000 (Singh, 1999).

Plans are afoot for joint ventures between Indian film producers and Hollywood giants as they discover the Indian version of the tinsel world (Chohan, 1999). These will receive a boost with the decision of the Indian government, announced in February 2000, to allow foreign companies to invest in Indian film industry. Though this may make Indian films more visible in the global market, there is a danger that they might lose their cultural distinctiveness.

These examples of a counter-flow of cultural products in no way show that the Western media domination has diminished. There is a temptation, even a valorization, of seeing such a flow having a potential to develop counter-hegemonic channels at a global level to balance this. Indeed, as seen in the case of Zee in Chapter 5 and TV Globo and Phoenix in this chapter, all three channels were modelled on transnational corporations and Phoenix is still part of a top media conglomerate. Their output too is relatively small and their global impact is restricted to the diasporic communities, their primary target market. They are all market-driven private organizations for whom the most important consideration is to make a profit. Therefore, the emergence of regional players contributing to a 'decentred' cultural imperialism, is not likely to have a significant impact on the Western hegemony of global media cultures.

Nevertheless, there does exist a blurring of boundaries, mixing of genres, languages and a contraflow of cultural products from the peripheries to the centres. The process of what has been called 'transculturation, hybridity and indigenisation' (Lull, 1995: 153) has sometimes made scholars enthuse about the possibilities of developing parallel cultural discourses. At the beginning of the twenty-first century, though the West continues to set the international cultural agenda, non-Western cultures are more visible than ever before. The international interest in Chinese cinema (Corliss, 1996); the globalization of Afro-Caribbean style of music, and the growing popularity of Karaoke (Mitsui, and Hosokawa, 1998) point to this trend. Japanese computer games, for example, are a major influence among the youth in the West – the Japanese fighting monsters, *Pokemons*, emerged as the most popular toy in 1999. Japanese animation has been exported worldwide while its serial dramas have been shown on television in Arab countries and in Canada (Singhal and Udorjpim, 1997).

Today, Indian film-maker Shekhar Kapur can direct *Elizabeth*, a quintessentially English feature film, while a Taiwanese born, US-educated Ang Lee is director of Jane Austen's *Sense and Sensibility*. Indian film musician A. R. Rahman recorded a duet *Ekam Satyam* with Michael Jackson in 1999 and after the success of his music for the film *Taal*, whose album entered the top 20 of the UK audio charts, he was offered a chance to collaborate with British composer Andrew Lloyd Weber on a musical *Bombay Dreams* (Kazmi, 2000).

West African beats mingle with Arabic tunes which are adapted in Indian film songs – Brazilian soap operas are watched by Ghanaians; Tai Chi is becoming a popular activity with many Westerners – all these are indications of what has been called the postmodern sensibility. Such categories as 'world music', 'world cinema' and 'global culture' are routinely mentioned in media and academic discourses. Yet the desire to experience the new is balanced by that to protect cultural sovereignty. As Mahatma Gandhi, voted the Man of the Millennium in a BBC on-line poll, once remarked:

> I do not want my house to be walled in on all sides and my windows to be stuffed. I want the culture of all the lands to be blown about my house as freely as possible. But I refuse to be blown off my feet by any.
>
> (cited in UNESCO, 1995)

7

International communication in the Internet age

Communication technologies were crucial in the establishment of European domination of the world during the era of colonial empires. The new technologies of the nineteenth century 'shattered traditional trade, technology, and political relationships, and in their place they laid the foundations for a new global civilisation based on Western technology' (Headrick, 1981: 177). If trains and ships facilitated the movement of manufactured products from one part of the world to another, fibre optics, satellites and the Internet can trade information, instantly, and across the globe. From telegraph to telephone, from radio to television, from computer and direct dial telephony and DBS to the Internet, international communication has been greatly affected by technological innovation. The convergence of telecommunication and computing and the ability to move all type of data – pictures, words, sounds – via the Internet have revolutionized international information exchange. At the same time, information processing has become far cheaper and faster, resulting in what the *Business Week* has called the dawn of 'the Internet age' (*Business Week*, 1999d).

The digitalization of all forms of data – text, audio and video, words sounds and pictures – has increased exponentially the speed and volume of data transmission compared with analogue systems. At first the introduction of digital communication was closely linked to the laying down of new fibre optic cable for telephones and television but even this constraint has been removed with the move to wireless transmission via satellite. Digitalization has had a major impact on international telephony: by 1997, for example, 89 per cent of telephone lines among the world's most industrialized countries were digital. In the use of fibre optic cable, the USA leads the way with 19.2 million cable miles deployed by 1997 (OECD, 1999). The impact on capacity can perhaps be most easily seen in television with the numbers of channels increasing from units to hundreds. Combined with the exponential growth in computing capacity and concomitant reduction in costs, the convergence of computing and communication technologies opens up potential for global interconnectedness such as that offered by the Internet. As Craig Barrett, Intel's Chief Executive points out, 'We are moving rapidly towards one billion connected computers. This does not just represent an online community: it represents the formation of a "virtual" continent' (quoted in Taylor, 1999a).

The dawn of the Internet age

The origins of the Internet lie in the US Department of Defense's Advanced Research Projects Agency Network (APRANET), created in 1969 as a communication network linking top defence and civilian branches of the US administration in case of a Soviet nuclear attack. In 1983, APRANET was divided into military and civilian sections, with the latter giving rise to the Internet. For the next decade this operated as a network among US universities and research foundations (Hafner and Lyons, 1996). The explosion in the use of the Internet took off with the establishment of the World Wide Web (WWW) in 1989, which began as a network of servers using a set of common interface protocols developed by a British computer specialist Tim Berners-Lee of CERN in Geneva. Any individual using these protocols could set up their own 'home page' on the web. This involved giving each page or website a unique address or URL (universal resource locator) and using the hypertext transfer protocol (http) which enabled the standardized transfer of text audio and video files, while the hypertext mark-up language (html) inserted links from one document to another anywhere on the web (Berners-Lee and Fischetti, 1999).

In the history of communication, it took nearly 40 years for radio to reach an audience of 50 million and 15 years for television to reach the same number of viewers – but it took the WWW just over three years to reach its first 50 million users (Naughton, 1999). By 2000, it had become a global medium, with 320 million users. According to a 1999 survey of the World Wide Web by US-based Inktomi, there were one billion unique Web pages. The instantaneous and relatively inexpensive exchange of text, sound and pictures has made a huge impact on international communication. The Internet, 'the fastest-growing tool of communication', with the number of users expected to grow from 150 million in 1999 to more than 700 million by 2001, is making this possible. As Figure 7.1 shows, the growth of the Internet has been remarkable.

At the end of the 1990s, IP (Internet Protocol) traffic was rising by 1 000 per cent a year, compared to a growth of less than 10 per cent on the Public Switched Telephone Network (PSTN), and if new technologies can meet the demand for bandwidth, IP traffic will surpass PSTN traffic. The proposed Internet 2, backed by major communications companies such as IBM, will give more speed to global communication and thus a boost to e-commerce – trade that takes place over the Internet. A much higher data transmission

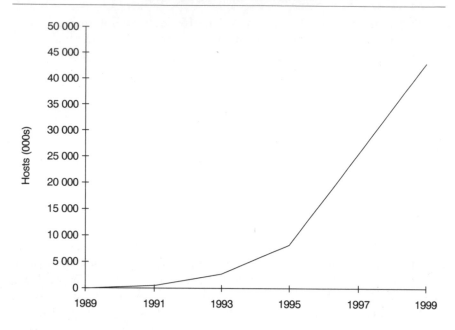

Figure 7.1 Growth of the Internet, 1989–99
Source: Internet Software Consortium (http://www.isc.org/)

capacity will enable Internet 2 users to communicate at speeds as much as 1 000 times faster than regular Internet users (Taylor, 1999a).

The new wireless world

The next stage of convergence is that of the Internet and mobile telephony, combined with the development of mobile satellite communication. The birth of the wireless Internet is being heralded as a new telecommunications revolution. There is increasing realization that despite the continuing expansion of telephone companies and cable-TV providers to connect users to higher-speed lines, it would be cheaper for consumers to receive entertainment and information by satellite. Satellite communication also offers the widest possible customer base, given that even in heavily wired Western Europe and North America an estimated 30 per cent of customers are far from major population centres. By 2003, there will be thousands of satellites in low, medium and geostationary orbits, providing universal voice data, multimedia and 'Internet in the sky' services across the planet (Wooldridge, 1999).

For businesses, one of the most significant technological developments has been the ability of the new mobile telephones to offer Internet access and high-speed wireless data services. Such 'value-added' services have contributed to the exponential growth of mobile telephony. While the fixed telephone networks took more than 130 years to reach one billion subscribers, at the current rate of growth, the mobile industry will take just over two decades to reach that many subscribers. By the late 1990s, it had emerged as an industry in its own right, with revenues of around $155 billion and more than 300 million subscribers around the world, up from just 11 million in 1990. In 1998, mobile cellular accounted for one-third of all telephone connections – there were almost twice as many new mobile subscribers as fixed ones and, by 2005, according to ITU forecasts, the number of mobile cellular subscribers will surpass conventional fixed lines (ITU, 1999e). As Tables 7.1 and 7.2 demonstrate, major global operators of mobile telephony and its equipment manufacturers, are concentrated among the world's richest countries.

Table 7.1 The world's top ten mobile equipment manufacturers in 1998

Company	Mobile revenue ($billion)	Foreign sales (%)
Motorola (USA)	17.9	59
Nokia (Finland)	14.7	94
Ericsson (Sweden)	14.5	95
Lucent (USA)	4.3	26
Nortel (Canada)	3.7	36
NEC (Japan)	3.7	5
Qualcomm (USA)	3.3	34
Matsushita (Japan)	3.1	51
Siemens (Germany)	3.0	69
Alcatel (France)	2.1	83

Source: Based on data from ITU

Table 7.2 The world's top ten mobile cellular operators in 1998

Company	Subscribers (millions)	Revenue ($bn)
NTT DoCoMo (Japan)	23.9	26.2
TIM (Italy)	14.3	7.2
AirTouch (USA)	14.1	5.2
Vodafone (UK)	10.4	5.4
BAM (USA)	8.6	3.8
BellSouth (USA)	8.2	4.7
AT&T (USA)	7.2	5.4
SBC (USA)	6.8	4.2
China Telecom (China)	6.5	3.2
Omnitel (Italy)	6.2	2.8

Source: Based on data from ITU

Third-generation mobile systems will enable Internet access at high speeds, and with the huge demand for mobile access to data services, this is creating a new industry (ITU, 1999f). In 1999, Motorola, the world's biggest manufacturer of mobile telephone equipment, announced an alliance with leading network equipment company Cisco Systems to invest more than $1 billion over the next four years to build a wireless Internet. The two companies will develop hardware and software to simplify connection of wire devices to the Internet. Microsoft has an alliance with British Telecom to create a wireless Internet service, based on devices using Microsoft's Windows CE operating system. Ericsson, the world's third largest mobile phone maker, has also joined forces with Microsoft to develop an Internet web browser and e-mail access from mobile phones and hand-held computers. Ericsson, along with Motorola, Nokia and Matsushita, is involved in the Symbian venture, which is working on the next generation of smart mobile phones and palm-top computers with Internet access. To make this a success, the wireless and computer companies have collaborated with major corporations like Microsoft in the Wireless Application Protocol (WAP) Forum in order to develop a common protocol that allows users to gain easy access to the WWW (Wooldridge, 1999).

Many international telecom companies have joined forces to exploit the potential of a global communications system based on mobile satellites. Global Mobile Personal Communications by Satellite (GMPCS) systems will allow users to make and receive calls via mobile handsets from virtually anywhere in the world. Satellites in Low-earth Orbits (LEOS), 500–1200 miles above Earth, can be reached by a new generation of mobile phones with a much smaller aerial. As they do not remain stationary relative to the earth, like geostationary orbits, LEO satellites will not experience delay in routing calls from one LEO satellite to another. In 1999, the US-based cable company NTL merged with Cable and Wireless of Britain and towards the end of the year the German mobile giant Mannesmann merged with the British company Orange in the race to become a long-distance operator. The most significant corporate development in this area was the takeover in February 2000 of Mannesmann by Britain's Vodafone, creating a 'global telecommunication behemoth' with a market capitalization of $340 billion (Wallace, 2000: 72). In 1999, BT and AT&T entered into an alliance to integrate their services and networks so that mobile phone users could send and receive voice and other data using the same handset on both sides of the Atlantic (Baker *et al.*, 1999).

Transnational telecom corporations are most interested in the so-called B2B (business to business) transactions, as businesses are by far the biggest data users and mobile wireless communication offers a cheap and speedy way for remote offices to connect to their corporate centres. In early 2000, Hughes announced that its focus would be on wireless broadband opportunities and the emphasis on business-to-business communication, to cater to what, in industry jargon, is called 'enterprise' customers. Spaceway, backed by Hughes, is a two-way, interactive broadband service providing high-speed data communications, beginning in 2002 (Matlack *et al.*, 1999). By the late 1990s, US telecom giant MCI WorldCom was spending one billion dollars per year to link businesses to high-speed networks that circle the globe (Baker, *et al.*, 1999). Motorola, along with other telecommunication giants, such as Boeing and Microsoft, have started Teledesic, which plans a network of 200 satellites, at the cost of $10 billion each, to become operational by 2004.

In the new wireless world, the electronic organizer, personal computer and mobile phone will all be combined into one portable gadget connected to the Internet via satellite, enabling users to buy or sell shares, book tickets, shop online, listen to music, watch a video, receive the latest news or play online games. By early 2000, Japan's top mobile communications operator NTT DoCoMo was offering i-mode cellular phones with many such services. With interactive digital television, consumers can dial up the programme of their choice or a film they have missed in the cinema and pay for what they watch. Or if they are watching a live sporting event they will be able to pause and get instant replay at any time. Electronic programme guides will select and inform viewers about programmes in which they might be interested. Tapeless VCRs, where images are 'streamed' onto the computer, can also be set to record the user's favourite programmes or programmes on particular subjects, even without the user's knowledge. Although this will offer viewers greater choice and freedom to use television in a more active way, such technology will also make consumers vulnerable to exploitation by direct marketing and advertising as well as having implications for security and privacy.

Another, quicker and cheaper technology for delivering multimedia information is the Data Broadcasting Network (DBN), which allows data services to use the existing infrastructure of DTH satellite broadcasters to distribute electronic content directly to personal computers. It uses a DBS broadcasters' extra satellite transponder space to broadcast content into the home via the consumer's satellite dish. With the satellite's footprint, many subscribers can be reached from just one transmission, making Data Broadcasting cheaper than upgrading the public telephone networks to be able to provide the high bandwidth required for multimedia services. This also opens up possibilities for DTH operators of new revenue streams. At the heart of the technological push to provide seamless communications is the potential use of the Internet as a global marketplace.

Harmonizing global technical standards

The unprecedented growth in the volume of international communication and possibilities of increasing businesses through the Internet has made it imperative for transnational corporations to demand the harmonization of standards of equipment and frequencies so that telecommunication and broadcasting equipment can be used across national borders. They are taking a lead role in setting worldwide standards in new communication technologies, since the standardization of equipment and frequencies is an essential basis for servicing a global market.

The USA, in co-operation with the ITU (which defines global telecommunication standards) and the Geneva-based International Organization for Standardization (ISO), is creating a global communication system to include, for example, mobile telephony which is affected by 'an anarchy of standards', as different systems operate in various parts of the world (ITU, 1999f). In the early 1980s, the EU decided to impose a common standard within its borders – the Global System for Mobile Communications (GSM), which has become the standard of choice in 118 countries, with 324 networks serving more than 150 million subscribers – or 40 per cent of the world's mobile phones (Wooldridge, 1999).

The Nordic region, home to some of the world's leading mobile networks, was among the first to establish a cellular standard (the Nordic Mobile Telephone system, NMT), creating a market for regional equipment manufacturers. Even though NMT never became the dominant standard globally, it provided Nokia with experience in producing mobile phones. Japan has also developed its own standard – Personal Digital Cellular (PDC). Until 1999, the USA had failed to establish a national standard for digital; the USA is a battle ground between warring technologies and the policy has been to grant regional licences instead, with the Federal Communications Commission (FCC) carving out cellular markets.

In mobile telephony, as in other communication arenas such as the Internet, the US Government supports the private sector development of technical standards, set up and guided by 'the requirements and processes of the marketplace', and opposes efforts by governments to impose standards or to use standards for electronic commerce as non-tariff trade barriers (US Government, 1997 and 1999; FCC, 1999). In 1997, the Steering Committee of Global Standards Conference, comprising TNCs as well as governments, endorsed private sector leadership in standards development. One internationally recognized initiative was the US-inspired Advanced Encryption Standard. The challenge to standards development and implementation was summarized in a 1999 report: 'timely and appropriate standards are critical to the long-term commercial success of the Internet, as they allow products and services from different vendors or industry sectors to work together, facilitate competition, and assist towards enabling the global electronic marketplace' (US Government, 1999).

Internationally, cellular networks have evolved from 'first-generation' analogue networks to 'second-generation' digital systems. The existing cellular landscape consists of a mix of analogue and digital systems with different networks often co-existing in the same country. The ITU did not issue technical recommendations for first or second-generation mobile systems. However, the growth of mobile cellular networks has forced the ITU to create a global standard for 'third generation' wireless, using a much higher frequency than the current generation. This is intended to produce a quantum leap in the capacity available, making it possible to download data at high speeds and preparing the way for new services, such as interactive games, and also to eliminate existing incompatibility between rival standards. The ITU's International Mobile Telecommunications-2000 (IMT-2000) initiative will bring together different types of networks – cellular, cordless, wireless and satellite systems – and thus enable the possibility of seamless global roaming in which users can communicate across borders, using the same telephone number and handset. The IMT-2000, expected to be launched in Japan in 2001 and in Europe a year later, will offer higher transmission rates and standard service delivery via fixed, mobile and satellite networks (ITU, 1999f).

It is in the interests of the countries and corporations that dominate global trade to ensure that electronic commerce operates in a free-market environment. Within the WTO, the USA has been arguing that new regulations should not be imposed upon online service providers that might hinder e-commerce. Under US pressure, in May 1998, the WTO's Ministerial Conference adopted a declaration committing members to refrain from imposing customs duties on electronic transmissions. The USA was working towards a more inclusive Information Technology Agreement II, to further liberalize global trade in information technologies. Its policy is unambiguous: 'enforce existing agreements and secure new agreements to make electronic commerce 'a seamless global marketplace' to ensure 'a free flow of commerce' (US Government, 1999).

From a 'free flow of information' to 'free flow of commerce'

Technological developments, combined with the liberalization in trade and telecommunications, have acted as catalysts for e-commerce. This has been made possible largely because of the opening up of global markets in telecommunications services and information technology products that are 'the building blocks for electronic commerce' as a result of the WTO agreements discussed in Chapter 3. Trade on the Internet has taken hold very quickly – in 1998, companies did $43 billion in business with each other over the Internet (*Business Week*, 1999d). So important had e-commerce become by 1999, that the American business magazine *Fortune* had started *The Fortune e-50 index*, to be published every quarterly, unlike its annual *Fortune 500* listing of the world's biggest corporations.

The growth of electronic commerce has outpaced even the most optimistic predictions and is now expected to exceed $1.4 trillion by the year 2003, according to a 1999 report from the US Government (US Government, 1999). Though electronic payments made up only about 1 per cent of all consumer settlements in 1999, the predictions were that they would grow to 5 per cent by 2005. The top 300 companies doing business on the Internet in 1999 had an average market capitalization of $18 billion (McLean, 1999) (*see* Table 7.3).

Table 7.3 Trading on the Net (selected industries)

Industry	E-business in 1999 ($ billion)
Computing and electronics	52.8
Retailing	18.2
Financial services*	14
Travel	12.8
Energy	11
Telecommunications*	1.5

Note: *Business-to-business only
Source: Based on data from *Business Week*, (1999d)

The Internet has dramatically lowered transaction costs and facilitated on-line transnational retail and direct marketing. The 'e-corporations' operating in a 'net-centric world' break every business free of its geographic moorings (Hamel and Sampler, 1998). According to *Business Week*, in 1998 corporations did $43 billion worth of business with each other over the Internet, predicted to rise to $1.3 trillion by 2003, or nearly 10 per cent of total business-to-business sales. The Internet is still in its 'Stone Age' and the scope for colonizing cyberspace is virtually limitless, as AOL chairman Steve Case admitted after his company bought Time Warner: 'We're still scratching the surface' of the Internet's potential (Waters, 2000). As Table 7.4 shows, major web-based corporations have reached respectable revenue levels within a surprisingly short period of time, as the date of their Initial Public Offering (IPO) demonstrates.

Table 7.4 The world's top E-companies

Company name	1998–99 revenue ($ million)	IPO date
America Online (on-line services)	4777	1992
Charles Schwab (Stock trading)	4113	1987
Amazon.com (e-retailing)	1015	1997
E*Trade Group (financial services)	621	1996
Knight/Trimark Group (stock trading)	618	1998
Yahoo! (Most important portal)	341	1996

Source: Based on data from *Fortune*, 6 December 1999

Though most of e-trading is between businesses, it is also having a profound effect on the retail market – on-line business is undermining off-line transactions. Increasingly, global trade in computer software, entertainment products, information services and financial services is taking place using the Internet. In 1999, 39 million Americans shopped on-line and computer software, airline tickets and books were among the main products bought. The so-called 'webonomics' favours the world's rich countries. Nearly 75 per cent of all e-commerce in 1999 took place within the USA, which also accounted for 90 per cent of commercial websites (Peet, 2000). As monetary transactions via the Internet become more secure and new services are offered, e-commerce is set to go global. Already, cyber loyalty schemes are in operation, such as Beenz, ipoints and flloz, which pay customers who visit Internet sites in credits which can be spent on-line.

One of the biggest potential growth areas for e-commerce is in Asia, which had just over 14 million people on-line in 1998, but by 2000 their estimated numbers had reached nearly 40 million, with Singapore, China, Japan and South Korea having the highest net penetration in the continent. On-line advertising was predicted to grow in Asia at an unprecedented rate – from $10 million in 1998 to $1.5 billion in 2001 (Fannin, 1999b). China, in particular, is emerging as a major market for e-commerce. The Chinese economy has been steadily growing for the last two decades, and by joining the WTO and integration with the global economy, it is set to become an important global player. China is the world's fifth largest PC market and Internet use in the country has jumped from 1 600 in 1994 to an estimated six million in 2000.

In recognition of this, US corporations have struck deals with Chinese companies – Yahoo!, the most popular portal in China, launched a Chinese site in 1998, while News Corporation has been involved in developing two websites, ChinaByte and CSeek. In 1999, the most popular Chinese-language portal Sina was backed by Goldman Sachs, Sohu by Intel and Dow Jones, while China.com was supported by AOL (Einhorn and Roberts, 1999: 28). Youjing Zheng, Director of the Centre for Information Infrastructure and Economic Development in Chinese Academy of Social Sciences argued: 'Informatisation is the foundation for China's economic modernisation; information resources is one of the most basic and important inputs for modern economic development; information industry should become the fundamental sector of China's economy' (quoted in Tan, 1999: 264). In 1998, China merged all the information and telecommunication related regulatory institutions into one single regulator – the Ministry of Information Industry (Tan, 1999).

Media on-line

According to the industry outlook for 2000 published in *Business Week*, the Internet was the fastest-growing part of the media sector. With the reducing cost of computers and telephone networks, more and more people are connecting to the Internet, making it a major source of revenue. A 1999 survey by *Publishers Weekly* of the on-line bookselling market, covering four major e-retailers, reported that on-line book sales rose 322 per cent in 1998 to $687 million. The largest on-line bookseller, Amazon.com, had total sales of $610 million, while the fastest-growing site was Barnesandnoble.com, where sales jumped 419 per cent to $61.8 million (Milliot, 1999).

With the convergence between the Internet and television, media corporations are developing strategies that include the new electronic media. For example, News Corporation's *TV Guide*, (the bestselling US television listing magazine), in its deal with United Video Satellite Group (provider of electronic and interactive programme guides), has created a leading television news and listings service, operating across multiple platforms. In the future the *TV Guide Channel* will become a portal, similar to that of existing Internet search engines. News Corporation's US new media unit, News America Digital Publishing, is providing high speed Internet access and also delivering FOX news and sports content. Its E-Direct develops databases of customer information, opening up the e-commerce opportunities in book, video and 'merchandise sales already flowing from this knowledge are enormous' (News Corporation, 1999).

The creation of an Internet-based media giant valued at around $350 billion, a result of the merger of America Online and Time Warner, is indicative of the commercial potential of this new medium. Signed just weeks into the new millennium, the deal marks the coming of age of the Internet as the next stage of communication, bringing together television, film, radio, publishing and computing into one accessible medium. In this marriage of the old and the new media, AOL will provide its Internet subscriber service via Time Warner's huge cable network, while the media giant will use AOL's customer base to gain new consumers for its various media products.

Time Warner's extensive fibre-optic cable networks in the USA mean that AOL can offer a service 100 times faster than traditional phone lines, cutting the time needed to download movies, music and 3-D graphics. Coupled with Time Warner's enormous stock of information and entertainment products, the new group is poised to dominate global communication. AOL-Time Warner can draw from the huge library of more than 5 700 Warner Bros. feature films, or thousands of record labels produced by Warner-EMI, the world's second biggest music company. For children it offers Cartoon Network and for sports fans, the leading magazine *Sports Illustrated*. In the area of news and current affairs, the group has such global brands as CNN, *Time* as well as *Fortune*.

Founded only in 1985, America Online has become the world's biggest Internet company, whose stock value has increased from just $5 billion in 1996 to $164 billion at the beginning of the twenty-first century. Already America's largest Internet service provider (ISP), AOL also owns another well-known ISP, CompuServe, as well as Netscape, the most widely used browser among 'net-izens' worldwide. Its informal style helped to make AOL famous, promoting on-line 'chat rooms' for people looking for romance. It gave the world the message 'You've got mail!', later the title of a successful Hollywood film about a love story blossoming in virtual space. Not surprisingly, the Warner Bros. film was extensively promoted by AOL to its 20 million subscribers.

With the number of Internet users expected to rise rapidly, all the major media and communication companies are scrambling to get on-line. By sharing their resources, AOL and Time Warner can dominate the cyberworld and encroach on the market share of rivals in media, entertainment and the Internet access business.

The world's top media corporations see the potential of using the new medium to exploit synergies between their print, broadcast and on-line operations in a multimedia environment, in which cross-promotion is the norm. According to Bob Eggington, editor of BBC Online, in global terms, the three major news websites were CNN, BBC and Yahoo!, the last, though not a primary news provider, but a 'news aggregator', which acquires news content from world's top news agencies, newspapers and other organizations (Eggington, 2000). The BBC on-line service is trying to exploit the BBC brand to develop e-commerce revenue around the world (Barrie, 1999). The BBC World Service has steadily extended its on-line presence with plans to operate interactive websites in twelve languages. Its first interactive programme, *Talking Point*, which enables Internet and radio audiences to join live debates, is becoming popular globally.

Within a year of the development of the WWW, most major newspapers in the USA had started a web edition and all the major broadcasters had a presence too on the Internet. In the initial years these were seen more as a supplement to the main newspaper or magazines rather than entities in their own right, though apart from the *Wall Street Journal* no newspaper on the web has as yet made a profit (Katz, 1999). By 2000, this had become a normal phenomenon and a web presence was an integral part of media organizations, not only in the media-rich North but increasingly across the world. As in other sectors of the media, major corporations such as CNN also dominate on-line journalism. CNN Interactive, for example, had eleven web sites in 2000: CNN.com, CNNSI.com, a CNN and Sports Illustrated sports news site, CNNfn.com, a unit of CNN Financial News, AllPolitics.com, a US political news site operated in conjunction with *Time* and *Congressional Quarterly, Custom News*, CNN's news personalization product with Oracle and CNN's web sites in Swedish, Spanish, Portuguese, Norwegian, Danish and Italian.

With mobile telephones linked to the Internet, news has become instant and personalized. Now the news will come to subscribers rather than the other way round. With the arrival in 1999 of WAP, phones can offer direct access to the Internet, making the newsroom redundant. CNN, which gave the world the concept of *Headline News*, launched in 1981 in the USA to update viewers on news issues every 30 minutes, has taken the lead again by providing a personalized service through its alliance with Nokia to offer news that has been specifically designed for phones. In 1999, CNN was running myCNN, a personalized news service. Other Internet content providers too are tailoring their products for phone users and 'distilling long-winded news stories into the bald facts' (Wooldridge, 1999: 14). Already question are being raised about the relevance of traditional journalism 'in an online world where brevity and speed seem far more important than elegance or intelligence' (Katz, 1999: 2). By 2000, Ananova, the world's first virtual newscaster which CNN called 'a personality designed to rival flesh and blood anchors', had already become a feature of on-line media. In the digital media age the future of newspaper itself was in doubt, with the US company Xerox announcing in 1999 that it will be producing electronic paper – which unlike ordinary paper can be scrubbed and reused.

In the new media environment the boundaries between advertising and programming are constantly blurring. The growth of cable and satellite television has already made the task of selling products less cumbersome and the development of interactive television and on-line retailing means that advertisers will no longer have to conduct expensive and time-consuming market research but will have access to relevant information about individuals' leisure and consumption habits. In the age of narrowcasting, the consumers are self-selected on such specialist channels as MTV, ESPN, Disney or CNN and their purchasing patterns and predilections will in the future be relatively easy to monitor for advertisers.

The international media survive on advertising. Programme production on television would be prohibitive if it were dependent on subscribers only, while newspapers and magazines would have to double their cover price if they were not supported by advertising. However, advertising on the Internet can be more complex. Surfers may just ignore the advertisers' logos on the margins of the screen, unlike TV, where advertisement breaks in the middle of movies or TV programmes are the norm. Not surprisingly, Internet revenue from advertising was just 0.2 per cent of all media advertising in 1999 (*see* Table 7.5).

Table 7.5 Internet advertisement revenue forecasts ($ millions)

Region	1998	1999	2000	2001	2002
North America	1 300	2 340	3 995	5 425	7 890
Europe	105	235	525	1 050	1 840
Asia-Pacific	80	130	250	475	815
Latin America	20	45	110	230	420
% of media advertising	0.1	0.2	0.4	0.7	1.1

Source: Based on data from Forrester Research

Despite accounting for a very small proportion of global advertising, the growing commercialization of the Internet and its increasing use among consumers are likely to make it a sought-after advertising medium. Already, 'dot.com advertising' has become a regular feature on television and print – in 1999 the on-line magazine *Salon* launched a $4 million TV campaign (Eisenberg, 1999). Given the nature of the Internet, on-line advertising can be used by corporations to record not only every transaction but also which advertisement the consumer clicks on and how long they stay on it (Peet, 2000). Apart from making one-to-one marketing possible, this type of information has security and privacy implications since it can also be misused by corporations or governments. By being able to monitor and record pattern of Internet use, the governments can control citizens' political activities while businesses can have access to private information – about bank accounts, insurance details and spending habits of consumers, which can be traded for marketing purposes.

Protecting intellectual properties in a digital era

A significant proportion of e-commerce, such as music, video or publishing, involves the sale and licensing of intellectual property. To promote this trade, sellers must feel sure that their intellectual property will not be stolen and buyers must know that they are obtaining authentic products. International agreements to establish effective copyright, patent, and trademark protection are therefore necessary to prevent piracy and fraud. While technology, such as encryption, can help combat piracy, a legal framework is necessary to protect intellectual property, and to provide effective recourse when piracy occurs.

For TNCs it is critical that the legal framework for electronic commerce is governed by principles valid across international borders. Protection of copyrighted works – including motion pictures, computer software, and sound recordings – disseminated via the Internet, performances and sound recordings in the digital environment have brought the issue of intellectual property to the fore. New formats for storing music, especially MP3, make it very easy to share over the Internet recordings that can be played, in full stereo, on PCs. In 1998, listeners downloaded billions of songs from websites free of charge, threatening the $38 billion-a-year recording industry (Mardesich, 1999). The merger of EMI and Warner Music, announced in January 2000, was partly influenced by the realization that more and more people were downloading music from the web and Warner Music – part of the AOL-Time Warner group – has a good Internet base.

Digital technologies make the tracking of copyright infringements more difficult as any intellectual property encoded as a digital data stream can be copied perfectly via the Internet. Digital technology also threatens traditional methods of distribution, when text messages, images, audio, video can all be distributed electronically. This issue is not completely new: in the 1960s, publishers tried to restrict photocopies, the recording industry fought hard to stop development of magnetic cassette recorders and film-makers tried to stop the spread of low-cost video cassette recorders.

International treaties for the protection of copyrights, notably the Berne Convention for the Protection of Literary and Artistic Works, provide nations with a means of protecting copyrighted works under their own laws. In 1996, the World Intellectual Property Organization (WIPO), a UN specialized agency, which promotes the protection of intellectual property rights, updated the Berne Convention and provided new protection for performers and producers of sound recordings by adopting two new treaties – the WIPO Copyright Treaty and the WIPO Performances and Phonograms Treaty. Both treaties include provisions relating to technological protection and copyright management information and facilitate the commercial applications of on-line digital communications.

The USA has consistently tried to force countries to implement the WTO's Agreement on Trade-Related Aspects of Intellectual Property (TRIPS), which came into force in 1996, and to join the two WIPO treaties. It has demanded that all countries establish laws and regulations that provide protection for copyrighted works, and that these are implemented and enforced. Another significant effect on electronic commerce is the issue of legal protection for databases.

One major lobbying group demanding stringent regulations to protect intellectual property is the International Intellectual Property Alliance (IIPA). It was formed in 1984 to represent US copyright-based industries – films, videos, recordings, music, business software, interactive entertainment software, books and journals. The IIPA consists of the American Film Marketing Association; the Association of American Publishers; the Business Software Alliance; the Interactive Digital Software Association; the Motion Picture Association of America; the National Music Publishers' Association and the Recording Industry Association of America. According to a 1999 report, *Copyright Industries in the U.S. Economy*, prepared for the IIPA, the estimated trade losses due to piracy were $12.5 billion in 1998 (*see* Table 7.6).

Table 7.6 Intellectual property loss by US companies in 1998 ($ million)

Sectors	Estimated loss
Business applications	4 837.4
Entertainment software	3 429.0
Records and music	1 792.5
Motion pictures	1 781.5
Books	685.9
Total	12 526.3

Source: IIPA

The significance of intellectual property in the US economy can be gauged from the fact that the intellectual property income of the US jumped from $1.10 billion in 1970, to $4.80 billion in 1983 and $13.81 billion in 1991 (OECD, 1993). In 1997, in the USA the copyright industries accounted for $348.4 billion or 4.3 per cent of the GDP. The foreign sales and exports of the copyright industries were $66.85 billion. Between 1977 and 1997 their share of GDP grew more than twice as fast as the remainder of the economy, while employment in these industries more than doubled to 3.8 million (IIPA, 1999).

Another major area for concern is the possibility of conflict between Internet domain names, which function as a source identifier on the Internet, and trademark rights, if the same or similar trademarks for similar goods or services are registered in different countries. Countries may also apply different standards for determining infringement. As the use of domain names as source identifiers has increased, the courts have attributed intellectual property rights to them. The US Government played a crucial role in the privatization of the Internet domain name system (DNS), when in 1998, in alliance with TNCs, it created the Internet Corporation for Assigned Names and Numbers (ICANN) to take over its management of the domain name system. Under a 1999 agreement signed with the US Government, ICANN can accredit domain name registrars from around the world to provide competitive registration services for the .com, .net, and .org domains.

Organizations such as the IIPA were instrumental in including TRIPS into the Uruguay Round of GATT and, accordingly, by 2000 most developing countries were obliged to be in full compliance with TRIPS requirements. The extension of this international intellectual property regime has raised concerns among many developing countries which see these as new taxes on knowledge, aimed to benefit the TNCs – according to the UN, industrialized countries hold 97 per cent of all patents worldwide (UNDP, 1999). This can block the access to new technologies' innovation and knowledge diffusion and restrict the competitive power of developing countries (Raghavan, 1990). A more stringent international patent regime, argues one observer, 'will greatly facilitate the process of global commodification of human intellectual and artistic creativity,' leading to 'an even greater concentration of copyright ownership in the hands of the global cultural industries' (Bettig, 1996: 226).

The Microsoft monopoly?

The world's computer software industry is dominated by the US-based Microsoft Corporation. Like the aspiration of the nineteenth-century colonial traders who dreamt of a common global currency, Microsoft has created a common computer language for worldwide use. In 1998, nearly 90 per cent of the world's PCs were using its office applications and 88 per cent its operation systems, as well as 44 per cent of its Internet browsers. As worldwide computer use increases, driven by e-commerce, the issue of who controls and sets the agenda of on-line technology has acquired great significance.

Microsoft, the largest maker of PC software and the world's biggest corporation in terms of market value, was founded in 1975 by Bill Gates in partnership with Paul Allen. Within five years of its founding it was chosen by IBM to create an operating system for its first PC. The software, which runs the machine's basic functions, was called MS-DOS. In 1983, Microsoft introduced the Word word-processing programme and within two years it launched the first version of Windows, which improved MS-DOS with graphical icons that make PCs easier to use, followed by its spreadsheet programme, Excel, introduced in 1987. Microsoft has seen its revenue grow at an astonishing rate, from an initial turnover of just $16 005 in 1975, to $197.5 million in 1986, when it became a public company (*see* Figure 7.2), and its revenues in 1999 were $19.7 billion.

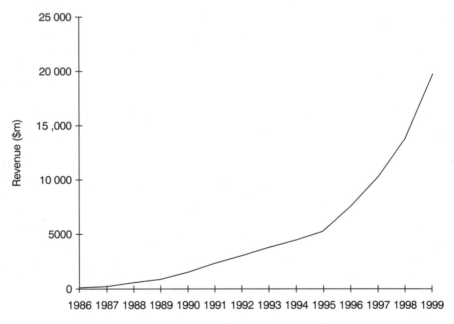

Figure 7.2 Microsoft's revenue, 1986–99
Source: Microsoft

So powerful had it become by the early 1990s, that in 1991 the US Federal Trade Commission began to investigate claims that Microsoft was monopolizing the market for PC operating systems. The European Commission anti-trust investigators also started investigations into monopoly charges. These forced Microsoft to rethink its strategy and in 1994 it agreed to change contracts with PC makers and eliminate some restrictions on other software makers, ending the US and European anti-trust investigations. However, in 1995, a Microsoft deal to buy Intuit, maker of a personal finance software, was blocked by the US Justice Department, on the grounds that it could reduce competition in the computer industry.

Microsoft was one of the first major corporations to launch a cybermag – *Slate*, in 1996. Later in the same year Microsoft launched MSNBC, the 24-hour news and information network with NBC News. In 1998, *Slate* became the first Internet-based magazine to join *The New York Times* global news distribution service, which includes content from *The Economist* and *Le Monde*. The entry of Microsoft into the world of journalism raised fears among many that it would use its enormous financial power to undermine well-established media organizations.

Critics see Microsoft as a giant which has tried to stifle software from its competitors such as IBM, Intel and Apple. Partly in response to such criticism, the US Justice Department filed a case in 1997, alleging that Microsoft had violated a 1994 decree dealing with licensing the Windows operating system to computer manufacturers. It asked the court to stop Microsoft linking the use of its Windows 95 operating system, which sold more than one million copies within the first few days of its release in 1995, to the use of its Internet browser, a tool to navigate the Internet. Microsoft launched Internet Explorer to rival Netscape and its Internet Explorer 2.0, the first browser to support advanced multimedia and 3-D graphics capabilities, was widely available for free downloading, after its launch in 1995. In 1997, Microsoft also bought WebTV Networks, offering consumers access to the Internet via television. Though, in 1998 Microsoft agreed to offer the newest version of its Windows 95 operating system without requiring easy access to its Internet Explorer software, the Justice Department sued Microsoft, alleging it illegally thwarted competition to protect and extend its monopoly on software. The antitrust trial which lasted for a year labelled Microsoft as a monopoly.

Despite these setbacks, Microsoft continues to overwhelmingly dominate the global PC software, selling a new version of its Windows operations and its Office desktop-applications software – products which provide nearly three-quarters of Microsoft's revenues and even more of its profits. Its focus has shifted to exploring Internet business to facilitate e-commerce through its Windows NT, which Microsoft wants to make the standard for nearly every size of computer (Nee, 1999). Renamed as Windows 2000, it was released in February 2000.

With offices in 50 countries, Microsoft employs more than 30 000 people to develop products, available in 30 languages for most PCs, including Intel microprocessor-based and Apple computers. By 1999, Microsoft had total assets of $37.1 billion, revenue of $19.7 billion and net income of $7.7 billion. Gates has acquired the status of an international icon, especially among the younger generation – his 1995 international best-selling biography *The Road Ahead* was published in more than 20 languages. *Forbes* magazine in 1999 declared him the world's richest man with a total net worth of $90 billion. Such has been the attraction of computers for youth that even pre-school children are getting hooked on to the new technology. The three-year-old Ajay Puri, Microsoft's 'youngest software executive' in the world, was comfortable working on the computer using a variety of software (Vidyasagar, 1999).

The emphasis is now on e-commerce, using mobile phones and satellites to access the Internet in a business environment where prices will be driven down by the consumer's ability to shop around, a phenomenon dubbed by Gates as 'frictionless capitalism'. With this in view, Microsoft was among the backers of Teledesic, the company which is building the new breed of satellite systems for Internet use (Matlack et al., 1999). Microsoft has stakes in telecom operators and is allied with AT&T, America's biggest telecommunication corporation. It is also developing, with Ericsson, an Internet web browser and e-mail access for mobile phones and handheld computers. As the demand for wireless services increases with the availability of new technologies, Microsoft is set to become a major player in this field too. The deal has implications for the entire wireless industry – Ericsson has handsets and Microsoft has operating systems and the two together are likely to dominate the wireless communication industry. Microsoft is trying to ensure that Windows CE, a slimmed-down version of the system that runs most PCs, finds its way into the world's mobile phones. It wants to turn Windows CE into the operating system for a whole range of devices, from set top boxes for cable television to notebook computers.

It is also working towards revolutionizing electronic publishing. Its Microsoft Reader will bring to the screen clean type, uncluttered format like books and one would be able to download books directly from the Web, while electronic news kiosks would allow readers to download newspapers and magazines onto mobile computers with flexible screens. A corporation which has effectively monopolized the global computer software industry may also turn out to be the portal controller of electronic publishing.

The Internet as a political tool

Once hailed as a democratizing and even subversive communication tool, the commercialization of the Internet is perceived by some as betraying the initial promise of its potential to create a 'global public sphere' and an alternative medium. In its early days, the Internet was seen as a mass medium whose fundamental principles were based on access to free information and a decentralized information network. For many the Internet had opened up possibilities of digital dialogues, across the world (Negroponte, 1995), and given freedom of speech its biggest boost since the US Constitution got its first amendment (Naughton, 1999). As *Time* magazine wrote in 1994: 'Most journalism is top down, flowing from a handful of writers to the masses of readers. But on the Net, news is gathered from the bottom up – the many speaking to many – and it bears the seeds of revolutionary change' (Elmer-Dewitt, 1994: 56).

However, the Internet has also provided a platform for extremist organizations. In the USA, for example, supremacist groups have created bulletin boards such as Aryan Nation Liberty Net, which has created international links with other such groups in Europe and other parts of the world, electronically transmitting hate literature. The British National Party's sites offer essays on far-right issues, Nazi merchandising and hate propaganda (Ryan, N., 1999).

Others, such as radical Palestinian groups, operate anti-Zionist websites, while the Tamil Tigers continue their battle with the Sri Lankan government on to cyberspace through such sites as Eelam.com, Tamilnet.com and Tamileelam.net. The world's 'first informational guerrilla movement' was the Zapatista National Liberation Army which fought for self-rule in Mexico's Chiapas state. Subcommandante Marcos, the leader of the uprising in 1994, became something of an international hero. This status was largely gained through the movement's use of the Internet to promote their cause (Castells, 1997).

Internationally, the most significant political role that the Internet has played is in promoting links between community groups, non-governmental organizations and political activists from different parts of the world. One major success of such activism was the use of the Internet to mobilize international support against Multilateral Agreement on Investment (MAI). The MAI, which was being discussed within the OECD, if approved, would give extraordinary powers to TNCs, especially with regard to freedom to move capital from one country to another. Through a concerted international effort which included flooding the relevant ministries of the OECD governments, major TNCs and other intergovernmental organizations with e-mails, the activists were able to stop the agreement to go ahead (Kobrin, 1998). The Internet also played a major role in organizing and publicizing the very public opposition to growing corporate control of global trade, leading to the scuppering of the WTO's ministerial meeting in Seattle in November 1999. This type of activism has been termed by the US military as 'social netwars' being used by NGOs, though they also fear the involvement of computer-hacking 'cyboteurs' (Vidal, 2000).

The Internet has influenced the mass media in a substantial way: not only has it provided a new platform for media organizations to reach consumers but it has also changed the time frame of news production and distribution. In an era of real-time news, journalists are under increasing pressure to provide up-to-minute information, while ordinary citizens now can access the world's top news organizations – news agencies, 24-hour news channels, once available only to journalists – without being mediated by editorial control of news organizations. During the 1999 NATO bombing of Yugoslavia the Internet was widely used by both sides. The independent Serbian radio station B-92 used its website to provide information about the war, free of Yugoslav government control and the Voice of America website became very active during the first days of bombing – between March 21 and 28, over one million hits were registered, nearly four times the normal.

The Internet has also greatly influenced the speed with which news is disseminated, making it more difficult for governments or corporations to suppress information. One key example of this was the 1998 revelation about US President Bill Clinton's affair with a White House intern Monica Lewinsky on *The Drudge Report*, which catapulted US journalist Matt Drudge into global spotlight. Within hours of the story breaking on the Internet, millions of Americans had knowledge of what turned out to be the one of the biggest sexual scandals in US political history, leading to the impeachment of the President. The story had become so widespread that the mainstream media had little option but to cover it. The Internet was instrumental in the publication in late 1998 of the report by President's Prosecutor Kenneth Starr, which was made available first on the Internet, and thus to 55 million people, even before its official release. So pressured were the media to cover it live that networks like CNN had a correspondent reading it straight from text scrolling on the screen. This was an early example of how Internet had the potential to loosen, if not abandon, editorial control over media content.

It is undoubtedly the case that the Internet has been an extraordinary source of information for journalists – from government documents, to TNC annual reports, to NGO viewpoints – all are available to journalists with computer and telephone access. This has meant that they can research a story at greater detail, and given the global nature of the Internet, they can also investigate an issue taking on board 'foreign' views. Most major media organizations now regularly provide background information on contemporary issues through their webpages.

The new medium has also contributed to journalists becoming connected to each other, reading about other countries through websites or watching their television channels. This can happen both in a regional and an international context. The information about the October 1999 military coup in Pakistan was posted by an anonymous person on a website for Indian media professionals, eight days before General Parvez Musharraf seized power in Islamabad (Chakraborty, 1999). Another significant development was the publication in January 2000 by the US-based International Consortium of Investigative Journalists, exposing the involvement of the London-based British American Tobacco, the world's second largest cigarette company, in illegally selling cigarettes to Latin America. The detailed reports on 'duty not paid tobacco' were also carried by *The Guardian* (Leigh, 2000).

The downside of the new journalism is its stress on speed, with the danger that in the race to be first with the news, a news organization may sacrifice depth in a story. Already journalists are being criticized for their often superficial and sensationalist slants on news stories (Postman, 1985; Franklin, 1997). The competitive multimedia environment is likely to make news more prone to infotainment. Even as well established a newspaper as *The Financial Times* was considering revamping its web edition after the US-based *TheStreet.com*, an on-line financial newspaper described 'as a combination of news agency and financial newspaper produced in real time', was launched in London in 1999 (Snoddy, 1999).

Corporate consolidations such as AOL with Time Warner and new types of synergies that will inevitably follow are likely to increase, triggering concerns among consumer groups about reduction of choice, as a few megacorporations control all forms of media content and their delivery systems. There are enough indications to show that this is already happening. The gateways to the Web, opening up the information highway for all to use, are increasingly being controlled by the big players. As the smaller ISPs are swallowed up, this new medium, which has been used by a myriad of alternative media and political groups and non-governmental organizations, is in danger of being further commercialized. The AOL-Time Warner merger sparked off speculation about similar deals between other Internet and media companies. As one commentator predicts:

> In a world where attention is increasingly scarce, the voices of many of the Internet's early beneficiaries – individuals, non-profit, and small businesses – may, like the voices on ham radio or public-access cable channels, become lost in cyberspace, drowned out by the din of speech that is paid for by the highest bidder.
>
> (Shapiro, 1999: 16–17)

In many countries the growing use of the Internet and its potential power to provide alternative viewpoints and exchange of information beyond the national borders have generated anxiety. In the digital era, some have argued, filtering software and protocols may in fact make censorship easier. Governments do not have to confiscate printing presses producing subversive propaganda from underground bunkers, they can simply route all Internet traffic through electronic gateways, which they can control (Shapiro, 1999). A country such as Saudi Arabia, which has state controlled media, did not give its citizens on-line access until it had effectively tinkered with the code of the Net to filter out all 'objectionable' material, while Iran programmed the chat rooms of its online network so that only two people could speak to one another at a time (Shapiro, 1999).

Singapore and China require Internet service providers to filter 'objectionable' material – mainly sexual or political content. China blocked access to some Western websites including *BBC Online* and in 1999, a Chinese software entrepreneur was given a two-year sentence for supplying e-mail addresses to US-based pro-democracy activists. Security and defence issues have been a key concern for Chinese authorities, especially after the information about China's first unmanned spacecraft was revealed on a Chinese website two days before its launch in November 1999. In January 2000, the government announced new measures to control on-line activities to check publication of state secrets on the web. It ordered that 'all organisations and individuals are forbidden from releasing, discussing or transferring state secret information on bulletin boards, chat rooms or in Internet newsgroups' (Gittings, 2000: 3).

Unlike in the West, privacy laws in many developing countries are non-existent or not applied rigorously, making it easier for authoritarian governments to monitor e-mail traffic. The generally small number of approved Internet providers in any individual country can help monitor and control Internet access, making it difficult for Internet activity to escape government purview. In Saudi Arabia, for example, Arabia Online, a Saudi-owned company, runs a number of 'gateway' sites. In the Islamic world new information and communication technologies can undermine state censorship. DTH television has already restricted government's power to censor or control viewing habits. The growing popularity of the Internet is likely to increase this trend. As a recent study predicts: 'With ever-growing amounts of information circulating at increasing speeds and decreasing costs, political systems predicated on restricting the information available to individuals will be sorely tested' (Alterman, 1998: xii).

Issues concerning financial security have also come to the fore with electronic commerce. It has been argued that economic intelligence on global trade can be manipulated through faulty analysis or misinterpretation of commercial data. Referring to the foreign-exchange crisis in Thailand, Mexico and Brazil in the late 1990s, one US observer comments, 'much of the sea of information on which modern markets float is polluted with misinformation' (Rothkopf, 1999: 95). If the USA, which dominates the global information and financial networks is worried about the possibilities of such manipulation, the economies of the developing countries are much more vulnerable.

Global electronic surveillance

The struggle over control of international information has been a main tenet of international communication. As was noted in Chapter 1, the international means of communication – cables and radio – have always had important strategic functions in war. More than 70 per cent of satellites launched during the Cold War years were used for defence purposes – both superpowers used satellites to spy on each other's nuclear capabilities. In the post-Cold War era there is a growing realization by the US military that information and communication technologies are an important element in their arsenal. In recent 'humanitarian crises', increasingly, a 'central role is being given to Psychological Operations (PSYOPS)' (Taylor, 1997: 148).

Electronic warfare would also be a key element in a cyberwar. Advanced spy satellites could provide intelligence about what has been called 'information battlespace', while unmanned electronic warfare planes could jam enemy radar or feed it false images as well as block or intercept telephone or television transmission. Enemy computer systems, especially those running a country's financial networks can be disabled with 'email bombs' and viruses. The US Army is developing a 'Land Warrior' equipped with computer radio – a PC-based system with a pentium processor, protective clothing and a helmet with high-tech optics (Palmer, 1998). During the 1999 NATO bombing of Yugoslavia – termed as the first war on the Internet – hackers from both sides disrupted Serb and NATO websites, while American 'Information Operations' disabled the Yugoslav government's e-mail system (Dinnick, 1999; Borger, 1999).

In keeping with the times, the satellite imagery industry has also been gradually privatized as a sign of greater civilian–defence co-operation. The

US Government permits its defence forces to use satellite intelligence from commercial companies. Now the general public in the USA can buy computer simulation developed for the army or download satellite imaging from the Internet. Space Imaging, a US-based company formed in 1994, by Lockheed Martin and Raytheon is moving into the commercial satellite imaging market, with predictions that the industry is likely to grow by 56 per cent to $2.5 billion by 2003 (Robinson, 1998).

The USA already has an extensive international surveillance operation Echelon, run by the US National Security Agency. Through a combination of spy satellites (such as Orion/Vortex for telecom surveillance and Trumpet to intercept cell-phone calls) and sensitive listening stations, it eavesdrops on international electronic communication – phones, faxes, telexes, e-mail and all radio signals, airline and maritime frequencies. Established in 1948 after a secret pact between major Anglo-Saxon countries – the USA, Australia, Britain, Canada and New Zealand – in 1999, Echelon system's main bases were Menwith Hill and Mowenstow in Britain, Yakima on the Pacific coast and Sugar Grove on the east coast of the USA, Leitrim in Canada, Shoal Bay and Geraldton in Australia and Waihopai in New Zealand. In the post-Cold-War era, spying is designed primarily for non-military targets, with business intelligence becoming very important in the world of electronic commerce. The US/UK domination of this area of international activity – for example, NASA's biggest base for electronic spying is at Menwith Hill in Britain, jointly operated with the UK's Government Communications Headquarters (GCHQ) – can give a competitive advantage to Anglo-American corporations, which has generated some resentment among other industrial countries, especially France (Port and Resch, 1999).

After Boeing's take-over of Hughes' satellite operations in 2000, the defence role of satellites has increased. A combination of Hughes' satellite business, which has a special position in reconnaissance, surveillance and imaging systems, and Boeing's pre-eminent position in integrated space, air and terrestrial information and communications systems, should ensure that US control over international communications – both soft entertainment and hard espionage – is likely to grow.

Boeing, NASA's leading contractor, is developing the next generation of global positioning system satellites, known as GPS IIF. Industry projections indicate that the space and communications market will grow from its current $40 billion to $120 billion annually by 2010, primarily driven by growth in commercial and government information and communications systems and services (Hughes website).

The global digital divide

The global imbalance in access to information must be viewed within the overall context of international inequality. The fifth of the world's people living in the highest income countries has 86 per cent of world GDP, 82 per cent of world export markets, 68 per cent of foreign direct investments and 74 per cent of world telephone lines: the bottom fifth, in the poorest countries, has about 1 per cent in each sector (UNDP, 1999).

Inequality between the information-rich North and information-poor South was central to the 1970s' demands for a NWICO (see Chapter 1) but with the globalization of new information and communication technologies the issue of access to information has once again become significant (Golding, 1998). A recent UN report explores innovative financing arrangements involving public and business partnerships for promotion of access to new information and communication networks. Conceding that the costs of building new information infrastructures are prohibitive for developing countries, the cost of not so doing would risk exclusion from the global electronic economy (Mansell and Wehn, 1998) (*see* Table 7.7).

Table 7. 7 The North-South Divide

	Newspaper circulation per 1 000 people (1994)	Newsprint consumption per person (tons)	Radios per 1 000 inhabitants	TV sets per 1 000 inhabitants	Internet use %
North	286	21.2	1 045	544	88
South	44	1.8	198	153	12
World	96	6	379	236	—

Source: Based on data from UNESCO *Statistical Yearbook* (1998) and *Human Development Report* (1999). Figures for 1996.

As Table 7.7 makes clear, the information divide between the North and South remains as pronounced in the late 1990s as it was during the NWICO debates. In 1957, the UN General Assembly endorsed the objective of universal access to basic communications for all, but the global information and communication disparity in terms of vast differences in access to telecommunications remains. Though 'the right to communicate', was promoted in 1996 by the ITU as a fundamental human right, the organization, which claims to be committed to redress global inequity in telecommunication, admits the existence of an information poverty gap between the North and the South. The most common measure of telecommunication access, teledensity or the number of main telephone lines per 100 inhabitants, shows that in 1996, teledensity ranged from 0.07 in Cambodia to 99 in Monaco. When the Maitland Commission published its report, three billion people, more than half the world's population, were living in countries with a teledensity of below one. The commission envisaged that by the first decade of the twenty-first century, everybody should be brought within easy reach of a telephone. However, by 1996 there were nearly 800 million people in 43 countries with a teledensity of below one (ITU, 1998).

Many developing countries lack affordable access to information resources and their telecommunication systems need technological upgrading. The biggest dilemma they face is that in order to widen access, telephone tariffs need to be reduced and the sector opened to international operators, thus undermining the often subsidized domestic telecoms. As the UN statement on Universal Access to Basic Communication and Information Services proclaims:

> We are profoundly concerned at the deepening maldistribution of access, resources and opportunities in the information and communication field. The information and technology gap and related inequities between industrialised and developing nations are widening: a new type of poverty – information poverty – looms.
>
> (ibid.)

Supporters of communication technologies argue that such information poverty will be reduced with the deployment and distribution of new tools and technologies, yet this disparity is still in evidence (Cairncross, 1997). According to the ITU, in 1998 the worldwide volume of international telephone traffic was more than 90 billion minutes and nearly 75 per cent of international outgoing traffic was generated in 23 Northern countries, which also accounted for 57 per cent of international incoming traffic (ITU, 1999e). Though mobile telephony offers possibilities of improving telecommunication access in the South, as systems can be installed relatively cheaply and more rapidly than fixed-line networks, nearly 80 per cent of mobile subscribers are in developed countries, while China, Brazil, South Korea and Turkey account for another 12 per cent. In more than 100 countries, which between them only accounted for 8 per cent of mobile communication access, mobile telephones are priced beyond the reach of the average citizen. In addition, frequency constraints and the high level of initial investment in developing networks are further barriers to telecoms in poorer countries. Therefore coverage in many developing countries is typically limited to major towns (ITU, 1999e).

Alternative communication

Though the Internet has the potential of evolving into a new and relatively cheaper medium for alternative communication, the tradition of providing an alternative viewpoint to the mainstream media has a long history – from radical pamphleteers in Europe and the USA, to anti-colonial newspapers and magazines in Asia, to alternative media organizations using video, fax, satellite and now, the Internet.

In the USA, such organizations as PeaceNet, established in 1985, to co-ordinate peace activists internationally through computer networks, and the New York-based Deep Dish TV Satellite Network, which has been providing programming since 1986, to public access channels, have contributed to an alternative media discourse (Lucas and Wallner, 1993). In Britain, video-based networks such as Undercurrents, have sold their footage to more than 120 TV stations in 15 countries on subjects like environment and genetic engineering (McGuire, 1999: 26), while OneWorld Online, launched in 1995, has emerged as a site dedicated to providing alternative voices on issues of global importance (Vittachi, 1998).

In the context of the South, alternative communication has taken the form of development journalism, partly as a result of the NWICO debates (Aggarwala, 1979). Initially developed in Asia, this journalism claimed to pursue a news agenda different from the mainstream media, steeped in the so-called 'coups and earthquakes' syndrome (Rosenblum, 1979), and investigate the process behind a story rather than merely reporting the news event itself. In a market-driven news environment there is a discrimination against news that cannot be 'sold', resulting in a distorted presentation of events to make them more marketable (Galtung and Ruge, 1965; Somavia, 1976; Masmoudi, 1979).

The civil war in Angola – one of the world's longest-running conflicts dating back to 1970s – is a case in point. Whenever it is covered in the international media, the focus seem to be on the inability of Angolans to live in peace while their 'traditional' tribal rivalry, and ethnic nationalism are often emphasized. Rarely, if ever, are economic factors adequately covered – in this case, control over the country's diamond industry.

An analysis of British television's coverage of the 1994 genocide in Rwanda, which claimed one million lives in a country of only seven million, within just three months, found that it became a television story only after it was framed as a humanitarian crisis, with an emphasis on Western support for refugee camps. The study from Britain's Glasgow Media Group reported that most of the coverage was devoid of historical or political context. 'Through this distortion,' it found, 'the media unwittingly helped Western governments hide their lack of policy on genocide behind a mask of humanitarian zeal' (Philo *et al.*, 1999: 226). However, such coverage may be rooted in racism in reporting – it is worth reflecting how British television would have reacted if the dead were not black Rwandans but white South Africans.

Such distortions in the media's coverage of crises in developing countries can affect the understanding of the South in the North and among the countries of the South since most of the newsflow continues to be from North to South and limited South–South news exchange takes place. Worse, in most of the developing world, the media generally caters to the requirements of the urban readership, with little contact with the villages where the majority of the population live. The acceptance of Western definitions of what constitutes news by most journalists in the South can affect the coverage of development issues directly and adversely.

One reason why a Southern-oriented news agenda has not emerged is that in much of the developing world governments have sought to use the media to promote their viewpoints, in the name of providing 'positive news'. Historically the media in the Third World formed part of the anti-colonial nationalist movements. After independence the anti-colonial press assumed, by and large, a supporting attitude towards the new states. In many African countries, for example, journalists were part of information bureaucracies as newspapers and the electronic media were wholly or partly controlled by the state or the ruling parties (Bourgault, 1995). Not surprisingly then, the news Third World agencies put out, often referred to as 'protocol news' – coverage of official functions and state visits – was perceived as government propaganda. Where independent journalism existed, the media's freedom to critically examine state policies were severely restricted by the governments' indirect editorial control by introducing draconian censorship laws or threatening to stop newsprint supply.

To improve South–South news and information traffic, regional exchange mechanisms, supported by the IPDC, were established in the late 1970s. Though regional news agencies such as Pan African News Agency (PANA), Caribbean News Agency (CANA) and Organisation of Asia-Pacific News Agencies (OANA), encouraged journalists in developing countries to think in terms of regional issues, they failed to make major difference to the global, or even regional newsflow, as a UNESCO study found (Boyd-Barrett and Thussu, 1992).

The Non-aligned News Agencies Pool, an international exchange designed to promote news among Non-aligned countries, was another international contributor to promoting alternative communication, though as a collection of government-sponsored news agencies, it was seen as lacking journalistic credibility. Other smaller organizations such as the Third World Network features service based in Malaysia have been used among Asian newspapers, though its output – known for advocacy rather than conventional journalism – has been extremely modest. Equally small but a far more effective alternative voice has been that of the London-based Gemini News Service, an international news features agency with an explicit development agenda. Established in 1967, Gemini is a non-profit agency, supplying topical news features to more than 100 subscribers in 80 countries around the world. Gemini's ideology, as characterized by its founder editor Derek Ingram is to promote the 'decolonization of news.' One factor which distinguished it from other Western-based news organisations was its emphasis on using local journalists, to reflect local perspectives rather than the outsider's view provided by most of the transnational news agencies. During the NWICO debates, Gemini was almost alone in the West in recognizing the need to balance press freedom with an understanding of the role of the media for nation-building (Bourne, 1995; Thussu, 2000).

Another key player in international alternative media is the Rome-based Inter Press Service (IPS), an international news agency, set up by a journalists' co-operative in 1964. With its focus on covering the issues affecting developing countries, it was a major news initiative in the 1970s and 1980s, especially in Latin America, where its Spanish language service received a good response. However, by the 1990s it had ceased to be a global presence in the spot news category – with its relatively modest output and limited resources it could not compete with transnational news agencies such as AP and Reuters. It is now known more for its features and commentary pieces than on-the-spot reports. By 1999, it was producing a fortnightly package of 10 features, special reports and analyses, distributed in English, and translated into Bahasa Indonesia, Bangla, Hindi, Nepali, Tamil, Thai and Urdu, through e-mail via Internet and the Association for Progressive Communications, whose services span the electronic globe. In addition, it produces *Terra Viva/IPS Daily Journal,* a selection of its wire stories for UN officials and INGOs, and distributes The *G-77 Journal* for the Group of 77 developing countries within the UN system.

With regional branches in Harare, Manila, Amsterdam, Montevideo, Kingston, Washington and New York and 250 journalists covering more than 100 countries, providing services for more than 1000 clients and users, IPS has been called 'the world's largest purveyor of information about the developing nations' (Giffard, 1998: 191). Yet its financial situation has remained precarious. Dependent on funds from Western aid agencies and the UN organizations, IPS has failed to make itself economically and commercially viable and is recognized as an international non-governmental organization by the UN. Consequently, it has become more of a pressure group, putting Southern concerns on the UN agenda rather than a news organization and the NGO approach to journalism is evident in its coverage of global issues (Giffard and Streck, 1998). By concentrating on news features it has retained a niche for itself in a highly competitive global news market. In addition, the training programmes and projects that IPS undertakes have helped many Southern journalists to develop an alternative news agenda. Its operations are directed 'toward improving South–South and South–North communication capacities, and opening up space to those traditionally marginalised or excluded from communication systems' (Harris, 1997: 160).

Such an approach is crucial for the democratization of international communication. An alternative to corporatized global communication is a moral imperative and a necessary democratic requirement. There is a need for a news agenda which covers issues of relevance to the majority world and examines the impact of globalization on the world's poor, as a result of the policies of such multilateral organizations as the World Bank, the International Monetary Fund and the WTO. However, given the encroachment of market-led media in the South, such an alternative seems difficult to evolve. Media agendas in most developing countries are set by an elitist, urban-based professional class with an emphasis on entertainment. These are defined by the growing commercialization and privatization of state-controlled media, increasingly being bought by global conglomerates, as a result of deregulation in broadcasting. Although the original mandate of many broadcasting systems in the South stressed education and information, there is an unmistakable trend towards commercialization.

The Internet and the South

A limited telecommunication infrastructure has seriously undermined access to the Internet in the developing countries. In 1998, nearly 88 per cent of Internet users were in the North, home to less than 15 per cent of the world's population. According to a 1999 survey of the WWW, more than 86 per cent of all Web pages were in English, while the most linked-to Web page on the Internet was Yahoo!, with more than 750 000 links to other sites (www.inktomi.com). Though the Internet as an international medium has grown at an exceptional rate, less than 3 per cent of the world's population – generally male, middle class and fluent in English – is part of this cyberculture, despite the hype associated with the Internet. As a recent UN report pointed out, English is used in almost 80 per cent of websites, although fewer than one in 10 people worldwide speak the language (UNDP, 1999). As Figure 7.1 show, the number of the Internet domain hosts has increased at an exponential rate. That most hosts are commercial websites and there is a preponderance of websites based in industrial nations is indicated by Table 7.8.

Table 7.8 Distribution by top-level domain name by host count, July 1999

	Domain	Hosts
com	Commercial	18 773 097
net	Networks	12 432 542
edu	Educational	5 141 774
jp	Japan	2 072 529
uk	United Kingdom	1 599 497
mil	US Military	1 561 756
us	United States	1 555 882
de	Germany	1 426 928
ca	Canada	1 294 447
au	Australia	907 637
org	Organizations	821 933
gov	Government	683 363
fr	France	653 686
nl	The Netherlands	637 591
fi	Finland	577 029
Total		56 218 330

Source: Internet Software Consortium (http: //www.isc.org/)

The USA has more computers than the rest of the world combined. Bulgaria has more Internet hosts than the whole of sub-Saharan Africa, excluding South Africa (*see* map, p.254). The Indian subcontinent, with 23 per cent of global population, has less than 1 per cent of the world's Internet users. Internet access divides educated from illiterate (60 per cent of users in China are graduates), men from women (three-quarters of users in Brazil are male), rich from poor (a computer costs the average Bangladeshi more than eight years' income, compared with one month's wage for the average US citizen), young from old (the average British user is under 30) and urban from rural (UNDP, 1999). Though North America has dominated Internet use since its privatization, the shift is towards a global market, because the rate of growth in the USA has slowed down. According to a research firm Cyber Dialogue, the US Internet population grew by 13 per cent in 1999, compared to 58 per cent in 1998. The new growth areas are seen to be in Asia, Europe and Latin America (Eggington, 2000).

Internet connectivity is expensive in the South, as the cost of equipment and software makes it inaccessible for a vast majority of people who do not even have a telephone access. In Africa, for example, though the Internet has opened up new forums of information access, the high telephone charges restrict its use (Wresch, 1998). Where Internet cafés exist, they are relatively expensive and thus out of reach for a majority of people. In many countries state-run telephone monopolies act as Internet providers, thus controlling content. They can use the government-controlled gateway to ban access to certain sites and also to monitor e-mail communication. In addition, many countries lack the infrastructure to allow wide-scale data transmission over their phone lines. In some cases, the local phone lines and phone switching

Global Disparity in Internet Use

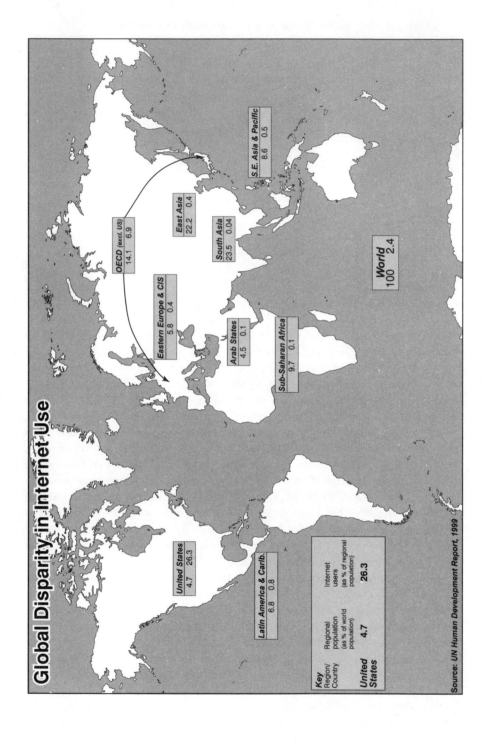

United States
4.7 26.3

Latin America & Carib.
6.8 0.8

OECD (excl. US)
14.1 6.9

Eastern Europe & CIS
5.8 0.4

East Asia
22.2 0.4

South Asia
23.5 0.04

Arab States
4.5 0.1

Sub-Saharan Africa
9.7 0.1

S.E. Asia & Pacific
8.6 0.5

World
100 2.4

Key
Region/
Country

Regional
population
(as % of world
population)

Internet
users
(as % of regional
population)

United
States   4.7   26.3

Source: UN Human Development Report, 1999

networks are insufficient to permit a high level of traffic. In many others there is not enough space on the lines connecting to the Internet. Merely getting a phone line can take many years in countries like India where demand is much higher than supply of telephone network.

In addition, English is the primary language of the Internet, being the language of a majority of web pages and also dominating global electronic mail traffic. Though digital technology has made it easier for non-European languages such as Mandarin, Arabic or Hindi to be made available on the Internet, on-line communication continues to be based on using a Roman alphabet. Those who are not familiar with English are therefore at a disadvantage. New software enables non-Roman alphabets to be displayed but they are still difficult to locate on the WWW, as most search engines are generally optimized to run in English. For non-English users, being nearly invisible to most search engines is a major liability. However, this is set to change as more and more non-Roman search engines start operating on the web.

Cutting communication aid

Reflecting the ideology of privatization, official development assistance from the world's rich countries to the global South has been reduced. The aid allocation in communications was reduced by half between 1992 and 1996 – from $1.4 billion to $0.8 billion, accounting for just 2 per cent of all aid to developing countries. (OECD, 1999) (*see* Figure 7.3). Instead, private companies are financing communication infrastructure and services in selected developing countries. 'In countries where private financing is available, donor countries gladly cede their role to the private sector, in what is generally a profitable and self-sustaining sector of commerce' (OECD, 1999: 237).

Almost 80 per cent of communication aid during the 1987–97 period was provided by just five countries – Japan (42 per cent), France (18 per cent), Germany (18 per cent), Italy (6 per cent) and Canada (5 per cent). Even this limited official aid is given only to certain countries which may be seen as potential markets for communication and media products. Between 1990 and 1997 nearly half of communication aid was given to East Asian nations. Also significant is the geographic distribution of communication aid; for example, Japan was the largest aid giver in Asia and Spain was top donor in Latin America, while France was the second largest donor in Africa (OECD, 1999).

The decline in foreign aid can be contrasted with the unprecedented growth in foreign direct investment (FDI) which has become increasingly relevant as a source of external finance for many developing countries. As the UN's *World Investment Report* shows, it now overshadows inflows from official aid and exceeds lending by international banks. The share of FDI in total capital flows to developing countries doubled from 28 per cent in 1991

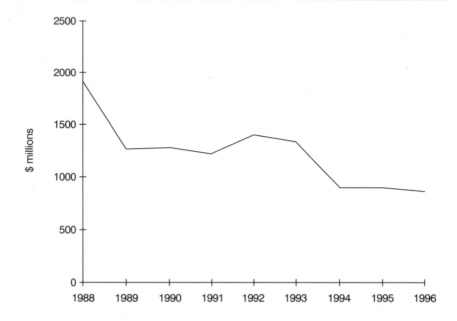

Figure 7.3 Decade of decline in communication aid, 1988–96
Source: OECD

to 56 per cent in 1998. In 1998, for example, the 33 least developed countries in Africa received only $2.2 billion – less than 1.5 per cent of total inflows to all developing countries. The biggest recipients in 1998 were China, with an inflow of $45 billion, and Brazil, attracting $29 billion (UNCTAD, 1999).

If international communication aid has witnessed a decline, the wider availability of new information and communication technologies has ensured the entry of new actors in the US-dominated export of communication products. In 1999, the US Government launched its Internet for Economic Development initiative to spread electronic commerce to developing countries. Creation of 'a pro-competitive policy and regulatory environment where the Internet and e-commerce can flourish' was one of its key goals (US Government, 1999). Within the space of less than a decade India has become the world's second biggest producer of computer software and South Korea has emerged as a key producer of computer chips, while in 1997, China's national telecommunications operator was the world's largest provider of mobile phone services (UNESCO, 1997: 18).

India has the advantages of a computer-literate, English-fluent workforce, well equipped to operate in global electronic commerce. It has become one of the key 'offshore software development centres' where TNCs use India's highly skilled labour to log on to the systems of Western banks, insurance companies and telecom giants to update, repair and write new programmes in what has become a round-the-clock global operation. Indian computer programmers work while US executives sleep – ensuring a seamless and 24-hour work schedule (Mortished, 1999). India is also aiming to bid for a share of the $10 billion space commerce with a reliable and competitive satellite launch vehicle. In 1999, India had a 15 per cent share of selling data from its remote sensing satellites to, among others, the USA, and it had started selling satellite components and sub-systems to such major corporations as Hughes. In 1999, the Indian Space Research Organization (ISRO), helped launch a German and a South Korean satellite (Chengappa, 1999). Nearly half of all Silicon Valley companies were founded by entrepreneurs who were originally from India (Lewis, 2000). However, India's case is more of an exception than a rule. The majority of developing countries lack the human resources and technological infrastructure to benefit from the global electronic economy.

Reducing global distance

There is little doubt that in the Internet Age international communication has become much wider in its scope, going beyond information flows between and among nations. Newspapers, non-governmental organizations, charities, political organizations all have a strong Internet presence, relying on both email and webpages to exchange information. Many governments are creating web-pages, while multilateral organisations like UNDP have dedicated websites to collect funds for development activities, such as netaid.org. The Internet also provides fora such as bulletin boards, newsgroups and electronic journals. It has been argued that the Internet can strengthen cultural identities of diasporic populations through, for example, the on-line publications that help in 'maintaining the cultural and communal ties' for the more than 30 million Chinese living outside China and Taiwan (Zhang and Xiaoming, 1999: 22).

Such developments provide ammunition to those who see information as a strategic resource which can be deployed to create a global village. As one enthusiast comments:

> To communicate may not be enough to keep the nationals of the earth at peace with one another, but it is a start. Free to explore different points of view, on the Internet or on the thousands of television and radio channels that will eventually be available, people will become less susceptible to propaganda from politicians who seek to stir up conflicts. Bonded together by the invisible strands of global communications, humanity may find that peace and prosperity are fostered by the death of distance.
>
> (Cairncross, 1997: 279)

However, much of this new digital connectivity is being used for developing new businesses rather than harnessing it to eradicate mass illiteracy and promote healthcare for the world's under-privileged. Though the cost of imparting basic literacy and spreading awareness of hygiene in rural areas through satellite education is much cheaper, few countries have successfully done this (see Chapter 1).

The Internet through satellite offers new opportunities for education, and, as this technology expands and becomes more affordable, distance learning is likely to become a global industry. Multimedia universities may be the answer to providing education using the Internet. Already the concept of 'University.com' is gaining ground with many universities providing their courses on the net. The world's biggest distance learning institutions such as Anadoly University in Turkey and China TV University System (both with student numbers in excess of 0.5 million), closely followed by Universitas Terbuka in Indonesia and India's Indira Gandhi National Open University, may develop into significant regional players in providing on-line education. However, there is a danger that in a market-driven communication environment, it is possible that these will be undermined by US-based private educational enterprises which may be more interested in 'edutainment', and use the media power of global giants like Microsoft and Disney to project their courses around the world.

Developing countries are also at a disadvantage for not having access to the latest financial data, essential in a globalized electronic economy. Despite the establishment, in 1996, of Special Data Dissemination Standards by the International Monetary Fund, to improve the data collection and publication practice for countries seeking to maintain access to global financial markets, TNCs continue to dominate global data flow whose speed and volume have increased significantly in an era of digital connectivity. Unbiased information about foreign-exchange trading and commodity prices are crucial for developing countries though they are heavily dependent on Western information sources. The dependence is in most spheres of international information – technical, scientific and financial information. The international information technology media sector, for example, is dominated by the US-based International Data Group, which has more than 250 targeted websites in 55 countries, as well as 290 newspapers and magazines and 4 000 book titles reaching 90 million buyers in 80 countries (IDG website). Rogue traders and financial speculators can ruin the economies of developing countries in a system where capital inflow can as quickly turn into capital outflow, as shown during the 1997 financial crisis in east Asia.

In an age when the refrain is 'globalize or perish', the South has to follow the global agenda which privileges privatization and progressively undermines the idea of distributive justice associated with erstwhile socialist and welfare-oriented government policies. Worse, countries in the South have little representation and influence within highly centralized global institutions – the UN Security Council, the G-7, and the World Bank, IMF and WTO troika – despite constant talk of 'global governance'.

In a world where information has become a major tradeable commodity, there is also increasing concern about the capacity of the new technology to dictate the social and political agenda (Postman, 1992; Shenk, 1997). This is another 'revolution' in which the South is lagging behind and letting the West reinvent its hegemony via the 'global knowledge economy', a knowledge which has little ostensible link with wisdom, something which cannot be commodified and sold through mobile satellites. As Mattelart argues:

> The egalitarian representation of a 'global village' that aggregates television viewers around the planet in a common participation in the symbols of modernity is in constant discrepancy with the reality of the standards of living of the immense majority of humankind.
>
> (1996: 304)

International communication – continuity and change

One recurring theme in this study of international communication has been the continued domination of the global information and entertainment industries (both hardware and software), by a few, mainly Western nations and the transnational corporations based in these countries. From Marconi to Microsoft, a continuity can be detected in how mainly Western technology has set the agenda of international communication, whether it was cabling the world, broadcasting to an international audience or creating a virtual globe through the Internet. The rest of the world, by and large, has followed the dominant ideology promoted by major powers through their control of international channels of communication – telegraph, radio, television and the Internet.

The expansion of European capitalism in the nineteenth and the twentieth centuries could not have been possible without the creation of a global communication infrastructure. The post-Second World War US hegemony was built on the use of its 'soft power' to supplement its military supremacy. Much of the Cold War was fought over the airwaves, though in the South it was more often hot, claiming over 20 million lives in conflicts related to superpower rivalry for global domination. In the post-Cold War era, the international media, especially television, have become a conduit for legitimizing the free market ideology, dominated by corporate capitalism. What distinguishes the new form of capitalism from its colonial predecessor is its emphasis on the almost mythical powers of the market and its use of mediated entertainment rather than coercion to propagate this message.

It would appear that a 'global feel-good factor' is being promoted through the myriad of television channels in partnership with the international entertainment industry, which though a fast-growing business, is still in an 'entrepreneurial stage of development'. In 1998, for example, Time Warner, then the world's biggest media conglomerate, had a market capitalization of $52 billion, compared with $180 billion for oil giant Exxon. The total global entertainment market stood at $500 billion, with the USA accounting for half of that market, followed by Europe at about 26 per cent (*The Economist*, 1998).

Although international entertainment has been driven by TNCs, the governments of the countries where these are based play an active part in the promotion of their products. The Los Angeles-based Motion Picture Association, also referred to as 'a little State Department', for example, lobbies for greater access for US film and television programming in international markets. Similarly, TV France International, a trade association of 134 French companies, created in 1994 to promote French television globally, is supported by the Centre National de la Cinématographie (The National Centre for Cinema) and the Ministère des Affaires Etrangères (the Ministry of Foreign Affairs).

With the growing volume of electronic commerce, including entertainment, questions about its regulation will become more pressing. There is a call for greater self-regulation by private sector groupings such as the Global Business Dialogue on Electronic Commerce, a consortium of TNCs, while the UN Commission on International Trade Law has introduced a voluntary Model Law on Electronic Commerce. Will electronic commerce lead to standardization of international currencies? A type of financial globalization was operational in the form of the gold standard in the twentieth century. In a 'borderless' globalized world the demand for a single currency has been expressed. 'Would fewer currencies make more sense?' asked the US journal *Foreign Policy* on the cover of its Fall 1999 issue containing a series of articles about what it called 'a debate over dollarization'. 'A world of 100 floating currencies,' wrote one commentator, is unlikely to be 'compatible with globalisation' (Hausmann, 1999: 78).

It has been argued that an ethical dimension should be added to international communication to make it more equitable (Hamelink, 1983; Mowlana, 1997), while others have emphasized the need to reinvent NWICO to bring issues of information inequality back onto the global agenda (Vincent *et al.*, 1999). Idealists feel that improved communication between and among nations will not only help make the world smaller but also enable a more just and equitable global society (Cairncross, 1997; World Bank, 1999). However, given the global disparity in access to information and communication technologies, how is this to be achieved?

There have been some worthwhile suggestions. UNESCO's World Commission on Culture and Development regards the airwaves and space as part of 'the global commons', a collective asset that belongs to all humankind. Commercial regional or international satellite interests which use the global commons free of charge, it counsels, should pay 'property rights' and thus 'contribute to the financing of a more plural media system.

New revenue could be invested in alternative programming for international distribution' (UNESCO, 1995: 278). To ensure that the communications revolution is truly global, the UNDP has also suggested a 'bit tax' on data sent through the Internet. A tax of one US cent on every 100 lengthy e-mails, according to its estimates, would generate more than $70 billion a year (UNDP, 1999). It has been argued that if proper policies are adopted, globalized liberalism can strengthen protection of 'global public goods' – environment, health, knowledge or peace (Kaul *et al.*, 1999). Yet such promises co-exist with a trend towards the monopolization of media and communication power, reflected in the rise of global media tycoons – Murdoch and Turner, and regional oligarchs such as Berlusconi in Italy, Subhash Chandra in India and Boris Berezovsky in Russia. These unelected power centres can set the parameters of public debate in the media.

As military confrontations between the world's major powers, which defined international interactions for most of the twentieth century, recede, to be replaced by regional and 'ethnic' wars, the focus of global conflict is likely to shift towards the South, the region of 'failed states' with dubious sovereignty (Krasner, 1999). If one were to believe the dominant view in the USA, the global South is also the region from which 'threats' to the Western way of life are likely to emerge, from religious fundamentalism, to proliferation of weapons of mass destruction and international terrorism. According to an authoritative survey of US public opinion, the 'critical threat' to US vital interests in the minds of the American public was international terrorism (Rielly, 1999). The decline in overseas reporting among the main television channels in the USA (Utley, 1997) and Britain (Stone, 2000) and the proliferation of 'docusoaps', replacing serious factual programming, have implications for the level of public understanding of global affairs, especially those concerning the South.

Under such conditions of an apathetic public and a pliant media, the world's major powers can justify military 'intervention' to defend their definitions of 'security', at a time when US domination is celebrated unabashedly, even on the pages of prestigious international journals. 'The benevolent hegemony exercised by the United States is good for a vast portion of the world's population,' proclaimed one commentator (Kagan, 1998: 26). Such supremacy can legitimize the undermining of political, economic and cultural sovereignty. One example of this was NATO's precedent-setting bombing of Yugoslavia in 1999 – the first conflict in which the world's most powerful military alliance intervened in the internal affairs of a sovereign state. The 'Operation Allied Force', the last military campaign of the twentieth century, which set the strategic agenda for the twenty-first century, was presented by US-dominated global media as a 'humanitarian intervention', while the fundamental change in the nature of NATO – from a defence alliance to an offensive peace-enforcing organization – was largely ignored (Lepgold, 1998; Chomsky, 1999; Deutch *et al.*, 1999).

Despite exaggerated claims about the capacity of the free market and new technologies to empower and liberate individuals and create a 'global civil society', capitalism's contradictions are sharper at the beginning of the third millennium than ever before (Amin, 1999). As corporations strengthen their control over the portals of global power while a majority of the world's population is excluded from the benefits of the emerging electronic economy, the potential for social unrest is enormous.

If global peace and prosperity for all have to go beyond merely being platitudes, international communication will have to be harnessed to promote a people-centred capitalism to check the corporate colonization of the planet.

Glossary

Affiliate A broadcast station that airs a network's programmes and commercials, but is not owned by that network.

American Standard Code for Information (ASCII) A binary digital code used in computer and data communications systems.

Analogue A method of storing, processing or transmitting information through a continuous varied signal.

Antenna Device which picks up and delivers satellite signals to a receiver, usually a dish.

ASTRA The trademark and commercial name of Société Européenne des Satellites, which owns and operates the ASTRA Satellite System.

Bandwidth The width (i.e. range of frequencies) of a channel or signal carried between a transmitter and a receiver: the wider the bandwidth, the more information that can be transmitted.

Baud rate A measure of the speed at which data is transmitted, as the number of units of information per second; the speed in which computers can transfer data through a modem using communications software.

Beam The directed electromagnetic rays transmitted from a satellite.

Booster A television or FM broadcast station, that receives, amplifies and retransmits signals on the same channel.

Broadband A channel using a wide bandwidth capable of carrying complex systems. Used to describe the potential of digital technologies to offer consumers integrated access to high-speed voice, data, video and interactive services. Broadband is also used to refer to analogue transmission technologies that provide multiple channels.

Broadcast To transmit a signal from a single point to multiple receivers.

Browser A software programme used to query, search and view information on the Internet.

Byte A group of binary digits that operate as a unit. Usually there are eight bits in a byte.

Cable television A television broadcasting system in which signals are transmitted by cable to subscribers' sets (see also **CATV**).

C-band The range of frequencies from 4 to 6 gigaHertz (billion cycles per second) used by most communications satellites.

Carrier The basic radio signal that transfers the information signal, occupying a single radio frequency (see also **common carrier**).

CATV, Community Antennae Television Television broadcast system in which signals are received on one satellite receiver and retransmitted via cable to subscribers' sets.

Cellular mobile radio telephone system A system of mobile radio-telephone transmission using a number of short-wave radio transmitters covering a defined service area (or cell) and that retransmit signals from one area to another as the user travels about.

Common carrier A provider of communication transmission services to the public, such as telephone and telegraph, on a non-discriminatory basis.

Communications Satellite Corporation (COMSAT) A corporation, chartered by US Congress, as an exclusive provider of international telecommunications satellite channels to the United States. COMSAT also represents the USA in INTELSAT.

Compact disc (CD) A five-inch disc on which a digital audio signal is inscribed so that it can be read especially by a laser beam device in a computer or CD player.

Compression A technique to reduce the amount of data to be transmitted and thus the bandwidth needed to transmit video or audio, increasing the capacity of a satellite transponder. The main way that compression works is by eliminating some of the redundant data in the signal.

Coverage The 'coverage' of a satellite is defined as the number of households receiving at least one channel transmitted by it.

Cyberspace A term introduced by science fiction author William Gibson in 1984. 'Cyberspace' is where human interaction occurs over computer networks, through email, games or simulations.

Cyberwar Information warfare conducted in **Cyberspace**.

DBS band A range of frequencies (11.70–12.40 GHz) intended for direct TV broadcast by satellite.

Decoder Unit that unscrambles a signal protected by encryption, used normally in conjunction with a **smart card**, to allow access to the service.

Digital A system in which information or data from any medium or source is coded in binary form (ones or zeros, corresponding to on/off switches). Digital data has less redundancy (error) in transmission and so can be compressed into a narrower bandwidth than analogue signals (see **compression**).

Digital audio broadcasting (DAB) Radio broadcasting using digital modulation and digital source coding techniques.

Direct broadcast satellite (DBS) Transmits TV signals directly to dishes in viewers' homes. Usually a high-powered satellite that requires only small dishes.

Domain name Name that identifies one or more Internet addresses. The suffix indicates which Top-Level Domain it belongs to. There are only a limited number of such domains, e.g. .com, .org.

Downlink Transmissions from a satellite to a ground station; also, the dish used for reception.

Download (receive) To receive data from another computer. The opposite is **Upload**.

DTH (Direct To Home) The reception of satellite programmes by a satellite dish at the viewer's home (see also **Direct broadcast satellite**).

Earth station The dishes, receivers, transmitters and other equipment needed on the ground to transmit and receive satellite communication signals.

Electronic commerce (e-commerce) The production, advertising, sale and distribution of products via electronic networks, specifically the Internet.

Electronic data interchange (EDI) The exchange of routine business transactions in a computer-processable format.

Electronic funds transfer (EFT) An electronic system that transfers money and records financial transactions, replacing the use of paper.

Electronic mail (e-mail) Messages sent via a computer instantly to one or many persons around the world.

Electronic programme guide (EPG) An interactive on-screen guide to programmes and other services, which can help the viewer to select their choice of programmes.

Facsimile (fax) The electronic transmission of printed material by electronic means over a telephone system. An image is scanned at a transmitting point and reconstructed at a receiving station, where a printed copy can be produced.

Fibre optics Transmission of signals via light pulses travelling down ultra-thin flexible silicon or glass fibres, with very little degradation and providing very high capacity, much greater than that of copper wire.

Footprint The geographic area covered by a satellite, the limit of which is determined by the quality of communication received due to the spacecraft antenna pattern, power of the signal or curvature of the Earth.

Frequency The number of oscillations of electromagnetic waves that pass a given point in a given time period. It is equal to the speed of light divided by wavelengths, and is expressed in Hertz (cycles per second).

G7 Group of seven leading industrial countries: Canada, France, Germany, Italy, Japan, the United Kingdom, the United States.

G77 Group of developing countries set up in 1964 at the end of the first UNCTAD (originally 77, but now more than 130 countries).

Gateway Single source through which users can locate and gain access to a wide variety of computer services. Gateways typically offer a directory of services available through them and provide billing for these services.

Geostationary satellite A satellite that orbits around the Earth at the equator at 36 000 km, thus travelling at the same orbital speed as the Earth's rotation, so that it appears stationary in the sky (see also **Geosynchronous orbit**). This allows satellite dishes to be trained at the same satellite at all times and so can provide 24-hour services.

Geosynchronous orbit The orbit of satellites at a distance of 36 000 km from the Earth so that it is synchronous with the Earth's rotation. Satellite receivers can be trained on the same satellite for 24 hours a day and do not have to move to track its orbit.

High-band The band used for satellite transmission from 11.70 GHz to 12.75 GHz. The **ASTRA** satellite system uses this band to transmit digital services only.

High-definition television (HDTV) An improved television system with around twice the resolution of the existing television standards. It also provides video quality approaching that of 35 mm film, and audio quality equal to that of compact discs.

Home page The main page of a website. Typically, the home page serves as an index or table of contents to other documents stored at the site.

Hybrid satellite A satellite which carries two or more different communications payloads (i.e., **C-band** and **Ku-band**).

Hypermedia 'Hypermedia' implies the facility to navigate across multi-media and hypermedia objects using links.

Hyper-text Electronic text links from one document to another on the Internet.

Hyper-text mark-up language (HTML) HTML is the programming language used to design and present sites on the **World Wide Web (WWW)**, that enables hypertext links to other documents.

Hyper-text transfer protocol (HTTP) The method for moving 'hyper-text' files across the Internet, requiring an HTTP programme at one end and a server at the other.

Information superhighway A term describing a network of integrated telecommunications systems connecting people around the world to information, businesses, governments and each other.

Integrated services digital network (ISDN) Switched network providing end-to-end digital connection for simultaneous transmission of voice and/or data over multiple communication channels using internationally defined standards.

Intellectual property Ownership of ideas, including literary and artistic works (protected by copyright), inventions (protected by patents), signs for distinguishing goods of an enterprise (protected by trademarks) and other elements of industrial property.

Internet Protocol (IP) addresses An identifier for a computer or device on a network, such as the Internet. Within an isolated network, one can assign IP addresses at random as long as each one is unique. However, connecting a private network to the Internet requires using registered IP addresses (called Internet addresses) to avoid duplicates.

Ka-Band The frequency range between 17.7–20.2 and 27.5–30.0 GHz, also known as the 20/30 GHz band, used for HDTV.

Ku-band The frequency range between 10.7–13.25 and 14.0–14.5 GHz, also known as the 11/14 and 12/14 GHz band, used for **DBS TV**.

L-band The frequency range between 0.39–1.55 GHz, also known as the 1.5GHz band, used for **digital audio broadcasting (DAB)**.

LEO Low-Earth orbit of up to 800 km above the Earth. This orbit is used by a constellation of satellites to provide a world-wide mobile phone service.

Multipoint distribution services (MDS) Service with two-way capability to transmit voice, data, and other video information. MDS can offer two-way interactive video, advanced teleconferencing, telemedicine, telecommuting, and high-speed data services.

Mobile satellite service (MSS) Services transmitted via satellites to provide mobile telephone, paging, messaging, facsimile, data, and position location services directly to users.

Modem An abbreviated term for 'modulator-de-modulator'. A modem converts digital signals into analogue signals (and vice versa), enabling computers to send and receive data over the telephone networks.

Modulation The alteration of a carrier wave in relation to the value of the data being transferred. Analogue satellite transmissions use FM modulation.

Multicast To transmit a message to a select group of recipients. An example of multicasting is sending an e-mail message to a mailing list; multicasting refers to sending a message to a select group whereas broadcasting refers to sending a message to everyone connected to a network.

Multimedia The combination of various forms of media (texts, graphics, animation, audio, etc.) to communicate information. The term also refers to information products that include text, audio, and visual content.

Multiplex To combine two or more independent signals into one transmission channel; the combined digital signals transmitted on one satellite **Transponder**.

Narrowband A term applied to telecommunications facilities capable of carrying only voice, facsimile images, slow-scan video images and data transmissions. The term is applied to voice-grade analogue facilities and to digital facilities operating at low speeds.

Narrowcasting Network or programming aimed at a specialized audience; the opposite of a broadcast.

NTSC (National Television Standard Committee) TV transmission standard used in the United States and parts of Asia.

On-line Electronic availability on demand from a computer-based system.

PAL (Phased Alternate Line) Analogue standard for television transmission, mainly used in Europe.

Pay-per-view Programming (usually movies or special events) that a subscriber specially requests to receive for a single fee not available for the subscription fee.

Piracy Unauthorized copying of copyright materials for commercial purposes and unauthorized commercial dealing in copied materials.

Protocol A set of rules or conventions that govern a data communications system and enable devices to intercommunicate.

Public switched telephone network (PSTN) Any **Common carrier** network that provides circuit switching among public users.

Radio frequency A frequency that is higher than the audio frequency but below the infrared frequencies, usually below 20 KHz.

Radiotelegraphy Wireless telegraphy using radiowaves to transmit messages over a distance.

Real time Usually used to describe situations when two or more people are interacting via their keyboards on the computer in real time, versus asynchronous communication, such as e-mail.

Receiver Satellite receiver, part of reception equipment used to tune into a single channel broadcast from a satellite.

Resolution The amount of detail that can be seen in a broadcast image. The resolution of a TV screen is defined by the number of horizontal lines of picture elements that the screen displays and the number of pixels per line.

Satellite A radio relay station that orbits the Earth used to communicate between Earth stations. The satellite receives a signal transmitted by an originating Earth station and retransmits that signal to the destination Earth station(s). Satellites are used to transmit telephone, television, and data signals originated by **common carriers**, broadcasters, and distributors of **CATV** programme material.

Satellite carrier An entity that owns or leases the facilities of a satellite or satellite service to establish and operate a channel of communications for point-to-multipoint distribution of television station signals.

Satellite dish A kind of antenna used to pick up transmissions broadcast from a satellite.

Scrambler A device that electronically alters a programme signal so that it can be seen only by persons, typically paid subscribers, with appropriate decoding devices.

Search Engine A programme that searches documents on the **WWW** for specified keywords and returns a list of the documents where the keywords were found.

Secam *Sequence Coleur à Mémoire*; French broadcasting standard.

Signal A physical, time-dependent energy value used for the purpose of conveying information through a transmission line.

Smart card Card used to enable de-scrambling of encrypted broadcasts when placed in a decoder or receiver with a built-in decoder.

Streaming A technique for transferring data so that it can be processed as a steady and continuous stream. Streaming technologies are becoming increasingly important with the growth of the Internet because most users do not have fast enough access to download large multimedia files quickly. With streaming, the client browser or plug-in can start displaying the data before the entire file has been transmitted.

Surfing Switching a television from channel to channel with a remote control. Also used to describe the process of scanning sites on the Internet.

Transmission Control Protocol (TCP) The suite of communications protocols used to connect hosts on the Internet.

Telecommunications Any transmission, emission or reception of signs, signals, writing, images, sounds or intelligence of any nature by wire, radio, optical or other electromagnetic systems.

Teleconferencing The use of audio, video, or computer equipment brought together through a communications system to permit geographically separated individuals to participate in a meeting or discussion.

Telephony The word used to describe the science of transmitting voice over a telecommunications network.

Teletext Textual and graphic information broadcast in the vertical blanking interval between conventional video frames in television signals.

Telex service A public switched service in which teletypewriter stations are provided with lines to a central office for access to other stations.

Terrestrial broadcasters Broadcasters who transmit through the airwaves from one Earth-bound aerial to another.

Terrestrial transmission Transmission which used transmitters located on the ground, as opposed to satellite and cable. Analogue TV programmes were first transmitted via terrestrial transmission.

Transcoder Device which translates signals from one broadcasting standard to another, e.g. **PAL** to **Secam**.

Transponder Equipment in a satellite which receives a signal via a single uplinked channel from an **Earth station**; amplifies it, converts the frequency and changes the polarization, then rebroadcasts it back to Earth.

Ultra High Frequency (UHF) The part of the radio spectrum from 300 to 3000 megahertz that includes TV channels, as well as many land mobile and satellite services.

Uniform Resource Locator (URL) The standard way to give the address of any resource that is on the Internet and is part of the **World Wide Web (WWW)**.

Uplink The signal from an **Earth station** to a satellite.

Upload To send a text file or software programme via telecommunications to another computer.

Usenet groups Usenet groups are also known as newsgroups, or discussion groups. Users exchange information generally provided in a 'chat room'.

User name A unique name assigned to a user on an Internet service provider's system.

Value-added network (VAN) An enhanced network that is designed expressly to carry data communications. VANs provide special services to their customers, such as access to databases.

Very High Frequency (VHF) The part of the radio spectrum from 30 to 300 megahertz which includes TV channels, the FM broadcast band, and some marine, aviation and land mobile services.

Very small aperture terminal (VSAT) A type of satellite receiving dish, usually 60 cm or less used for high-speed data communication.

Video compression Data reduction and compression of analogue television signals into a digital stream, to allow several channels to be broadcast through a single transponder.

Video-on-demand Films provided to subscribers from a menu of titles. The film starts on the subscriber's request.

Virtual reality A computer simulation usually experienced through head-gear, goggles and sensory gloves that allows the user to experience being present in a computer-generated environment, and to interact with the images being displayed there.

Webcasting Using the Internet, and the **World Wide Web (WWW)** in particular, to broadcast information.

Widescreen TV or TV signal with a wider aspect ratio than the traditional television standard. Widescreen TVs are 16: 9 as opposed to the conventional 4: 3.

World Wide Web (WWW) Created in Switzerland, WWW is a client/server software that enables computers connected to the Internet to access and exchange documents and images using the **HTTP (Hyper-text Transfer Protocol)**.

X-band The frequency range between 7.25–7.75 and 7.9–8.4 GHz, also known as the 7/8GHz band. Typically used for telecommunications.

The definitions in this glossary were adapted from various web-based sources, including International Telecommunication Union, Federal Communication Commission, Hughes, ASTRA, Asiasat, as well as Fortner (1993) and Pavlik (1996).

Appendix I

A chronology of international communication

4000 BC	Sumerian writing on clay tablets.
3000 BC	Early Egyptian hieroglyphics.
2500 BC	Papyrus replaces clay tablets in Egypt.
1500 BC	Phonetic alphabet in use in West Asia.
300 BC	Phoenicians bring Phonetic alphabet to Greece.
100 BC	Roman alphabet developed from Greek model.
AD 100	Papermaking invented in China.
150	Parchment in use, books begin to replace scrolls.
600	Book printing invented in China.
618	China's T'ang Dynasty (618–907) creates a formal handwritten publication, the *ti pao* or 'official newspaper' to disseminate information to the elite.
676	Paper and ink used by Arabs and Persians.
1000	Movable type made of clay in China.
1150	Moors bring paper from China to Europe.
1170	Arabic numerals introduced in Europe.
1453	Gutenberg Bible printed.
1465	First printed music produced.
1476	First print shop in England.
1511	First printing press in the Ottoman Empire.
1535	First press in the Americas set up in Mexico.
1578	First printing press set up in India.
1644	Private bureaux which compose and circulate official news in the printed form known as the *Ch'ing pao*, start in China.
1650	*Einkommende Zeitung* ('incoming news'), the world's first daily publication starts in Leipzig.
1665	Newspapers first published in England.
1704	First newspaper advertisement published in the *Boston News Letter.*
1742	*General Magazine* prints first American magazine advertisement.

1777	First regular newspapers in France.
1780	*Bengal Gazette* founded in India.
1783	*Pennsylvania Evening Post* is America's first daily newspaper.
1785	First issue of *The Times* newspaper in London.
1789	Article XIX of Rights of Man declares 'free communication of thought and opinion'. First Arabic newspaper *Al-Hawadith al-Yawmiyah* (The Daily Events) in Egypt.
1791	First Amendment of the US Constitution provides model for freedom of press. The *Observer*, Britain's oldest surviving Sunday newspaper, established.
1793	Inauguration of the optical telegraph in France.
1821	*Manchester Guardian* founded.
1822	The beginnings of the modern Catholic missionary press in France.
1826	*Le Figaro* founded in France.
1827	Photography invented. *El Mercurio*, Chile's national newspaper, founded.
1828	*Freedom's Journal*, first African-American newspaper in the USA, launched.
1831	*The Sydney Morning Herald* founded. First Turkish newspaper in the Ottoman Empire, the 'Almanac of Events', published.
1833	The first issue of the *New York Sun* – the beginning of the penny press.
1835	Creation of the Havas news agency, the world's first wire service.
1837	Invention of electric telegraph by Samuel Morse.
1838	*The Times of India* founded. First commercial telegraph link in England.
1840	Invention of the adhesive postage stamp and reform of the postal service in England.
1843	Creation of the first modern US advertising agency. *The Economist* founded.
1844	First commercial telegraph – between Washington and Baltimore.
1845	First issue of *Scientific American*.
1848	Creation of *Associated Press*.
1849	Creation of the German news agency Wolff.
1851	France–England underwater cable link. Creation of Reuters.
1852	Havas launches into advertising, then in its infancy.
1854	Telegraph used by military in Crimean War. First overseas Chinese newspaper founded in San Francisco.
1856	British decree regulating the relations between the press and military during the Crimean War.
1858	*The Straits Times* starts as a daily in Singapore.
1860	Telegraph is widely used to distribute news accounts of US Civil War. England and India linked by telegraph.

1861	*New York Times* founded.
1865	Founding of the International Telegraph Union – first telegraph regulations. Creation of the US advertising agency J. Walter Thompson. International Morse code adopted.
1866	First transatlantic cable becomes operational. Typewriter invented.
1869	Creation of the US news agency APA, later UPI.
1870	News agency cartel (Havas/Reuters/Wolff) divides up world market. More than 140 newspaper titles published in Indian languages.
1871	Underwater cables laid down in China and Japanese seas.
1874	Cable network laid down in the South Atlantic.
1875	Creation of the International Bureau of Weights and Measures. Universal Postal Union Founded. *Al-Ahram* established in Cairo.
1876	Alexander Graham Bell patents telephone. *Buenos Aires Herald* founded in Argentina. *Corriere della Sera* founded in Italy.
1878	Invention of the phonograph. First telephone lines in the USA.
1880	*New York Graphic* prints first halftone photographs.
1881	French law passed establishing freedom of the press.
1884	Adoption of Greenwich Mean Time as world standard time.
1885	Berlin Telegraph Conference: first provisions for international telephone service.
1886	Invention of the linotype. Berne International Convention on Copyright.
1888	Founding of the *Financial Times*.
1889	Founding of the *Wall Street Journal*. Launch of Coca Cola in the USA.
1890	French popular daily *Le Petit Journal* reaches a circulation of a million copies. *Asahi Shimbun* (morning sun) founded in Japan.
1891	*Jornal do Brasil* founded.
1893	United International Bureaux for the Protection of Intellectual Property (best known by its French acronym BIRPI) created in Berne. First international press congress in Chicago.
1894	*Rossiiskoe Telegrafnoe Agentstvo* (RTA), first Russian news agency, founded. First comics appear in US newspapers.
1896	Colour printing for comics. Lumière Brothers develop motion picture camera. Britain's first popular newspaper, *Daily Mail*, founded. Adolph Ochs adopts an 'information' style of journalism at the *New York Times*.
1897	The Gramophone Company, predecessor of EMI, founded in London. Marconi patents wireless telegraph.
1898	The Dreyfus Affair in France and the Spanish-American war in Cuba – widely covered by the press.
1899	J. Walter Thompson establishes 'sales bureau' in London. Sun Yat Sen founded *Chung-kuo Jih-pao* (Chinese daily paper).

1901	First wireless transatlantic telegraph transmission – from England to Canada.
1902	First radio transmissions of the human voice.
1905	Radio telegraphy used in Russo-Japanese war. First US public cinema – The Electric Theatre – opens in Pittsburgh.
1906	Berlin Conference on Wireless Telegraphy: creation of the International Radiotelegraph Union. Electromagnetic spectrum divided into bands for different services. Opening of first public cinema in France.
1907	Founding of the French newsreel, *Pathé*.
1909	Creation of the first syndicate for the distribution of comic strips, crossword puzzles and other features.
1911	First marketing firms in the USA. Woodbury Soap launches its 'The skin you love to touch' campaign in the *Ladies Home Journal*, marking the first time sex appeal is used in advertising. First film studio built in Hollywood.
1912	First editions of *Pravda* (Truth). US film companies – Fox and Universal – founded.
1913	First Indian feature length film, *Raja Harishchandra*, released.
1914	Audit Bureau of Circulation formed in the USA, standardizing auditing procedures and tightening up definitions of paid circulation.
1915	First foreign advertising agency established in Shanghai. Creation of the King Feature Syndicate and beginning of the internationalization of comics.
1917	Founding of the American Association of Advertising Agencies. Petrograd Telegraph Agency declared central information organ of Soviet Government. Radio used to announce victory of communist revolution.
1918	Kodak develops portable camera. Establishment in France of a special committee for 'aesthetic propaganda abroad'.
1919	Soviet Russia begins international broadcasting. USA links with Japan via wireless. General Electric creates Radio Corporation of America to take over monopoly of American Marconi Company and create first transnational US communications conglomerate.
1920	First illustrated news magazines published in Germany. KDKA of Pittsburgh is first commercial radio station in the USA. IBM produces first electric typewriter. International Telephone and Telegraph founded. First radio station in Africa set up in Johannesburg. Turkish newsagency Anadolu Ajaansi founded.
1921	The Komintern becomes an instrument of international communication. KDKA transmits the world's first religious broadcast.
1922	First regular radio broadcasts and first radio commercial in New York. First issue of *Reader's Digest*.
1923	*Time*, first 'news magazine,' founded.

1924	Creation of CCIF (International Telephone Consultative Committee) in Paris. Columbia Pictures founded. Disney creates first filmed cartoon.

1924   Creation of CCIF (International Telephone Consultative Committee) in Paris. Columbia Pictures founded. Disney creates first filmed cartoon.

1925   The Telegraph Agency of the Soviet Union (TASS) founded. Creation of CCIT (International Telegraph Consultative Committee) in Paris. Brazil's *O Globo* newspaper founded.

1926   Beginning of sound cinema. NBC begins network broadcasting, linking 25 stations in 21 US cities. First commercial telephone service between the USA and the UK by long-wave radio.

1927   Radiotelegraph Conference in Washington: creation of the CCIR (International Radio Consultative Committee). BBC founded. *One Man's Family,* popular radio soap opera, begins in the USA, lasts until 1959. Establishment of the first two international advertising networks (J. Walter Thompson and McCann Erickson). First radio broadcasts in China. AP begins newsphoto distribution. CBS formed.

1928   First 'all-talking picture' – *Lights of N.Y.* First public display of Disney's *Mickey Mouse* cartoon, with sound.

1929   First regular Soviet radio broadcasts destined for abroad, in German, French and later in English. *Business Week* launched. Cable & Wireless founded, merging all British international communications interests.

1930   First modern supermarket opens in New York.

1931   International religious radio starts with creation of Radio Vatican. India's first talkie motion picture, *Alam Ara,* released. Chinese news agency, Xinhua, founded.

1932   Empire Service of the BBC set up. Telegraph Union changes name to International Telecommunication Union (ITU). Gallup poll established.

1933   Hitler creates the Ministry of Propaganda and Enlightenment of the People under Goebbels. First 'Fireside Chats' by US President Roosevelt utilizes radio medium. Radio Luxembourg, Europe's first major commercial broadcaster, goes on air.

1934   Creation of the Federal Communications Commission in the USA. Regular TV transmission in Soviet Union. First newsagency in Iran, Pars Agency, founded. The documentary *Triumph of the Will* celebrates Nazi power.

1935   Italy begins Arabic broadcasting to the Middle East. France starts shortwave radio transmission for overseas listeners.

1936   First issue of *Life*. First Gallup polls in a political campaign. Inauguration of BBC television studio.

1937   *West African Pilot,* first nationalist newspaper, founded in Nigeria. *Guiding Light,* first radio soap opera, aired in the USA. Disney's first feature-length film, *Snow White and the Seven Dwarfs,* premièred.

1938	The International Convention Concerning the Use of Broadcasting in the Cause of Peace comes into force. The International Advertising Association founded in New York. Radio surpasses magazines as source of advertising revenue in the USA. Arabic Service becomes the first foreign-language section of the BBC Empire Service.
1939	First TV broadcasts in the USA. Paperback books start publishing revolution.
1941	First TV advertisement broadcast – in the USA.
1942	Creation of Voice of America. The USA organizes the War Advertising Council to help voluntary advertising for war effort. *Why We Fight* series of effective documentary propaganda.
1944	Agence France Presse founded. First issue of *Le Monde*.
1945	UNESCO established. France creates commercial international station Radio Monte Carlo.
1946	First large-scale electronic digital computer – Electronic Numerical Integrator And Calculator (ENIAC) founded in the USA. First TV sponsorship for a sporting event in the USA.
1947	Transistor developed. International photo agency, Magnum, founded in the USA. International Organization for Standardization founded.
1948	UN Conference on Freedom of Information. *People's Daily* (*Renmin Ribao*) launched in China. First drive-through McDonald's restaurant – the term 'fast food' coined.
1949	Network TV begins in the USA. *Stop the Music*, first TV quiz show in the USA.
1950	First broadcast by Radio Free Europe. First international credit card, Diner's Club, launched.
1951	NBC's *Today* programme begins, mixing news and features. International Press Institute founded.
1952	Universal Copyright Convention adopted. Sony develops stereo broadcasting in Japan. International Federation of Journalists, the world's largest organization of journalists, founded.
1953	United States Information Agency (USIA) created. Deutsche Welle starts broadcasting. First broadcast by Radio Liberty.
1954	First transistor radio produced in the USA. McCarthy hearings on television. CBS becomes the largest advertising medium in the world. Trans World Radio, US-based global evangelical radio, starts broadcasts from Morocco. Colour TV broadcasting begins in the USA.
1955	'The Marlboro Man' advertisement for Marlboro, the world's best-selling cigarette, launched – it becomes top advertising icon of twentieth century. First Disneyland opens. Independent Television (ITV) starts transmission in Britain.
1956	First transatlantic underwater telephone cable.

1957   The Soviet Union launches the first space satellite – Sputnik ('travelling companion'), sending first radio signals from space.
1958   UN establishes Committee on the Peaceful Uses of Outer Space.
1959   ITU Geneva conference makes first radio-frequency allocations for space communications.
1960   Nixon–Kennedy debates televised. NASA launches ECHO-1, first telecommunications satellite. In-flight movies introduced on airlines.
1962   AT&T launches Telstar-1, first privately owned active communications satellite, linking the USA with Europe. First telephone communication and TV broadcast via satellite – ECHO-1.
1963   ITU organises First World Space Radiocommunication Conference in Geneva. Hughes designs and launches the world's first geosynchronous communications satellite, SYNCOM-II.
1964   Creation of Intelsat (International Telecommunications Satellite Organization). The USSR launches its first communication satellite (Molnya). Inter Press Service founded. First electronic mail – in the USA.
1965   Launching of the first geostationary communications satellite, Early Bird, of the Intelsat system.
1966   Xerox introduces facsimile machines.
1967   The USA and the Soviet Union sign Treaty on Peaceful Uses of Outer Space.
1968   Portable video recorders introduced. Reuters starts the world's first computerized news distribution service.
1969   The Internet born as a US Defense-backed experimental network called APRANET (Advanced Research Projects Agency Network). Brazilian television company Globo established. Intelsat provides global TV coverage of Apollo lunar landing to 500 million people.
1970   International direct dialling between London and New York first introduced.
1971   ITU conference on space communications adopts Regulation 428A to prevent spillover of satellite broadcast signals into countries without their prior consent. Soviet Union organizes Intersputnik, a satellite telecommunications network linking socialist countries. Intel introduces first microprocessor – 'the computer chip'.
1972   Debate in UNESCO and UN General Assembly on an agreement to regulate direct-broadcast satellites. UNESCO adopts declaration of principles for satellite broadcasting, including requirement that for direct satellite broadcasting there be prior agreement between the sending country and the receiving countries.
1973   First steps towards New World Information and Communication Order (NWICO) debate.

1974	First direct broadcasting satellite, ATS 6, launched. Opinion polls show that TV overtakes newspapers as prime source of news for most Americans.
1975	Non-aligned news agencies pool created. European Space Agency formed. Fibre-optic transmission developed. Cable brings multi-channel TV to the USA. Radio France Internationale created. Microsoft founded.
1976	India launches SITE project for use of satellites for education. UNESCO conference in Nairobi endorses call for NWICO. Apple computer launched.
1977	Creation of the International Commission for the study of communications problems (UNESCO) under Sean McBride. Eutelsat (European Telecommunications Satellite Organization) founded.
1978	Videotext developed. Japan launches first Yuri satellite. Intelsat provides coverage of World Cup Football matches to one billion people in 42 countries.
1979	World Administrative Radio Conference (WARC) in Geneva (ITU) revises radio regulations. Inmarsat formed. First consumer advertisements on Chinese television. Sony invents Walkman.
1980	Publication of the McBride Commission report. Ted Turner launches CNN, world's first all-news network.
1981	IBM brings out its first personal computer. The all-music channel MTV goes on air.
1982	The Falklands War: first appearance of the practice of organizing pools of journalists. INSAT (Indian National Satellite) communication satellite launched. Compact Disc (CD) player launched in Japan.
1983	World Communication Year. First Eutelsat satellite launched. Embargo on information by the Pentagon during the US intervention in Grenada. Worldnet, USIA's global public affairs, information, and cultural TV network, launched. USA starts anti-Cuban Radio Marti. Cellular (mobile) telephones available in the USA.
1984	Green Paper by the EC on 'Television Without Frontiers'. US giant Hughes launches Leasat to create a global military communications network. Indonesia launches its first satellite Palapa. Federal Communications Commission grants PanAmSat (Pan American Satellite) rights to launch and exploit a private satellite system. China develops first Chinese-language computer operation system. Canal Plus, first pay TV channel in France, launched. Michael Jackson's *Thriller* album sells more copies than any other to date.
1985	The USA withdraws from UNESCO. PeaceNet – the first alternative national computer network in the USA – established. Arabsat launches its first communication satellite. Brazil

becomes first South American country to launch its own satellite – Brazilsat. CNN International launched. Reuters starts a news picture service and takes control of TV newsagency Visnews. Capital Cities buys American Broadcasting Corporation (ABC), creating the world's largest entertainment company. Reporters Sans Frontières founded in Paris. America Online (AOL) founded.

1986   Uruguay Round of GATT negotiations begin. The UK withdraws from UNESCO. First alternative satellite network Deep Dish TV Satellite Network established in the USA. China's national satellite telecommunications network operational.

1987   EC Green Paper on telecommunications. USSR ends jamming of VOA.

1988   First ASTRA satellite launched by a private European organization. Pan-Arabic newspaper, *Al-Hayat*, launched in London. USSR ends jamming Russian service of Deutsche Welle.

1989   Merger of Time and Warner Bros. Sony buys Columbia pictures. First private satellite launched in the USA. Sky, first satellite TV, launched in Britain. Interfax agency started in Soviet Union to supply news, mainly to foreigners. UNESCO publishes first *World Communication Report*. British researcher Tim Berners-Lee creates World Wide Web.

1990   ASIASAT, first commercial Asian satellite, launched. The USA starts TV Marti. CNN becomes a global news network with Gulf crisis. Microsoft launches Microsoft Windows 3.0.

1991   BBC World television launched as a commercial venture. STAR TV, the first pan-Asian television network, launched. France launches Telecom 2A satellite. Russian edition of *Reader's Digest*.

1992   Turkey's TRT Avrasya channel beams programmes via satellite to Turkic republics in Central Asia. Operation Restore Hope in Somalia backed by media logistics. The browser Mosaic brings the Internet to non-technical computer users. ITU organizes WARC-92 on frequency allocations. Intelsat and NASA in joint space mission. Spain launches Hispasat satellite.

1993   World Radio Network launched on ASTRA in Europe. OIRT, the former union of eastern European broadcasters merges with European Broadcasting Union. First World Telecommunication Standardization Conference in Helsinki (ITU). China's first international optical cable system, linking it with Japan, becomes operational.

1994   CD-ROM becomes a standard feature on personal computers. Turkish-owned satellite Turksat launched. World Trade Organization (WTO) created. APTV, a global video newsgathering agency, launched. Clinton signs International Broadcasting

Act, establishing International Broadcasting Bureau. BBC Worldwide, commercial arm of BBC, created. DirecTV launches first digital DBS service in the USA.

1995   PanAmSat becomes the world's first private company to provide global satellite services with the launch of its third satellite – PAS-4. Trade-Related Aspects of Intellectual Property Rights (TRIPS) agreement, comes into force. Bloomberg television launched. First computer-animated feature film, Toy Story, released.

1996   CNN becomes part of Time Warner, making it the world's biggest media corporation. The USA passes Telecommunications Act. Radio France Internationale takes over Radio Monte Carlo. WIPO enters into a cooperation agreement with WTO to implement TRIPS Agreement. The USA launches Radio Free Asia. Information Technology Agreement signed within WTO to liberalize global trade in IT. The French Canal Satellite becomes Europe's first digital platform. MSNBC, a cable and on-line news service, launched by Microsoft and NBC. Cybermag *Slate* launched. Japan launches Digital Versatile Disc (DVD) video players.

1997   EU revises its directive on 'Television without Frontiers'. European Commission Green Paper on *Convergence of Telecommunications, Media and Information Technology Sectors*. Lockheed Martin Intersputnik, a joint venture of Lockheed Martin and Intersputnik, comes into force. WTO's telecommunication accord. PanAmSat and Hughes Galaxy combine operations.

1998   ITU's World Telecommunication Development Conference launches project on e-commerce for developing countries. RFE/RL launches Radio Free Iraq. AP takes over Worldwide Television News. Internet breaks Monica Lewinsky story. British consortium On-Digital launches world's first terrestrial digital TV service.

1999   World Wide Web used for propaganda during NATO's war in Kosovo. Internet advertising heads toward $3 billion. Global mobile satellite communications provider, Inmarsat, becomes first inter-governmental organization to be transformed into a commercial company. Viacom merges with CBS.

2000   Billions watch millennium celebrations on global TV. AOL merges with Time Warner. EMI and Time Warner music merge to form world's second biggest music company. Internet becomes accessible over mobile phones. Britain's Vodafone merges with Germany's Mannesmann to create world's biggest telecommunications company. GATS negotiations begin.

Appendix II

Useful websites

International organizations

ILO	http: //www.ilo.org/
IMF	http: //www.imf.org/
ITU	http: //www.itu.int/
OECD	http: //www.oecd.org/
UN	http: //www.UN.org/
UNCTAD	http: //www.unctad.org/
UNDP	http: //www.undp.org/
UNESCO	http: //www.UNESCO.org/
WIPO	http: //www.wipo.org/
World Bank	http: //www.worldbank.org/
WTO	http: //www.WTO.org/

Governmental and intergovernmental organizations

Asia-Pacific Broadcasting Union	http: //www.abu.org.my/
Caribbean Broadcasting Union	http: //caribunion.com/
Commonwealth Broadcasting Association	http: //www.oneworld.org/cba/
Department of Commerce (USA)	http: //www.doc.gov/
Department for Culture, Media and Sport (UK)	http: //www.culture.gov.uk/
Department for Trade and Industry	http: //www.dti.gov.uk/
European Broadcasting Union	http: //www.ebu.ch/
European Union	http: //www.europa.eu.int/
Federal Communications Commission	http: //www.fcc.gov/
Indian Space Research Organisation	http: //www.isro.org/

Institut National de l'Audiovisuel   http: //www.ina.fr/
NASA   http: //www.nasa.gov/

Non-governmental and commercial organizations

AC Nielsen   http: //acnielsen.com/
AIDCOM   http: //www.aidcom.com/
AMIC   http: //www.amic.org.sg/
BBC Monitoring Service   http: //www.monitor.bbc.co.uk/
Broadcasters' Audience Research
  Board   http: //www.barb.co.uk/
Free Speech   http: //www.freespeech.org/
Institute for the Advanced Study
  of Infowar   http: //www.psycom.net/iwar/
International Intellectual Property
  Alliance   http: //www.iipa.com/
Internet Society   http: //www.isoc.org/
Internet Software Consortium   http: //www.isc.org/
Inktomi   http: //www.inktomi.com/
Motion Picture Association of America   http: //www.mpaa.org/
OneWorld Online   http: //www.oneworld.org/
Paper Tiger   http: //www.papertiger.org
Project Censored   http: //www.sonoma.edu/
    projectcensored/
Third World Network   http: //www.twnside.org.sg/
TV France International   http: //www.tvfi.com/english/
Undercurrent   http: //www.undercurrent.org/
World Wide Web Consortium   http: //www.w3.org/
Zenith Media   http: //www.zenithmedia.com/

Satellites organizations/companies

Arabsat   http: //www.arabsat.org/
Asiasat   http: //www.asiasat.com.hk/
Astra   http: //www.aia.lu/
Eutelsat   http: //www.eutelsat.org/
Hispasat   http: //www.hispasat.es/
Hughes   http: //www.hughes.com/
Inmarsat   http: //www.inmarsat.telia.com/
Intelsat   http: //www.intelsat.com/
Intersputnik   http: //www.intersputnik.com/
Lockheed Martin   http: //www.lmgt.com/
Loral Space and Communication   http: //www.loral.com/

PanAmSat   http: //www.panamsat.com/

Multimedia corporations

America Online   http: //www.aol.com/
Bertelsmann   http: //www.bertelsmann.com/
Disney   http: //disney.go.com/
News Corporation   http: //www.newscorp.com/
Sony Corporation   http: //www.world.sony.com/
Telecommunication Inc   http: //www.tci.com/
Viacom   http: //www.viacom.com/

Computer and telecommunication companies

AT&T   http: //www.att.com/
Cisco Systems   http: //www.cisco.com/
Dell Computer   http: //www.dell.com/
IBM   http: //www.ibm.com/
Intel   http: //www.intel.com/
MCI WorldCom   http: //www.wcom.com/
Microsoft Corporation   http: //www.microsoft.com/
Network Associates   http: //www.networkassociates.com/
Network Solutions   http: //www.netsol.com/
Oracle   http: //www.oracle.com/
Sun Microsystems   http: //www.sun.com/

News agencies

Agence France Presse   http: //www.afp.com/
APTN   http: //www.aptn.com/
Associated Press   http: //www.ap.org/
Bloomberg   http: //www.bloomberg.com/
Inter Press Service   http: //www.ips.org/
Itar-Tass   http: //www.itar-tass.com/
Reuters   http: //www.reuters.com/
United Press International   http: //www.upi.com/
Xinhua   http: //www.xinhua.org/english/

Radio stations

All India Radio   http: //air.kode.net/

BBC World Service   http: //www.bbc.co.uk/
                              worldservice/

China Radio International   http: //www.cri.com.cn/english/
Deutsche Welle   http: //www.dwelle.de/
Radio France International http: //www.rfi.fr/
Radio Free Europe/Radio Liberty   http: //www.rferl.org/
Voice of America   http: //www.voa.gov/
Voice of Russia   http: //www.vor.ru/
World Radio Network   http: //www.wrn.org/

Television channels

American Broadcasting Corporation   http: //abc.go.com/
ARD (Germany)   http: //www.ard.de/
Asahi Broadcasting Corporation
   (Japan)   http: //www.tv-asahi.co.jp/
Australian Broadcasting Corporation   http: //www.abc.net.au/
BBC World   http: //www.bbcworld.com/
Black Entertainment Television   http: //www.betnetworks.com/
Canadian Broadcasting Corporation   http: //www.cbc.ca/
Canal Plus   http: //www.mon.cplus.fr/
Carlton (UK)   http: //www.carltonplc.co.uk/
Cartoon Network   http: //www.CartoonNetwork.com/
Channel 4 Television (UK) http: //www.channel4.com/
China Central Television   http: //www.cctv.com.cn/english/
Chinese Television Network
   (Hong Kong)   http: //www.ctn.net/
CNBC   http: //www.cnbc.com/
CNN   http: //www.cnn.com/
Columbia Broadcasting System (CBS)   http: //www.cbs.com/
DirecTV   http: //www.directv.com/
Discovery   http: //www.discovery.com/
Doordarshan (India)   http: //www.ddindia.net/
ESPN   http: //espn.go.com/
Fox Network   http: //www.fox.com/
Foxtel (Australia)   http: //www.foxtel.com.au/
France 2   http: //www.france2.fr/
Globo (Brazil)   http: //www.redeglobo.com.br/
Independent Television News (UK)   http: //www.itn.co.uk/
Korean Broadcasting System   http: //www.kbs.co.kr/
Med TV   http: //www.ib.be/med/
Middle East Broadcasting Centre
   (MBC)   http: //sat.rdn.it/eutelsat/
Music Television (MTV)   http: //www.mtv.com/

National Broadcasting Company (NBC)	http: //www.nbc.com/
Nickelodeon	http: //www.nick.com/
Nippon Hoso Kyokai (NHK)	http: //www.nhk.or.jp/
Orbit	http: //orbit.net/
Phoenix Chinese channel	http: //www.phoenixtv.com/
Public Broadcasting Services	http: //www.pbs.com/
Showtime	http: //www.showtimeonline.com/
South African Broadcasting Corporation	http: //www.sabc.co.za/
STAR TV	http: //www.startv.com/
Televisa (Mexico)	http: //www.televisa.com.mx/
Television Corporation of Singapore	http: //www.tcs.com.sg/
ZDF (Germany)	http: //www.zdf.de/
Zee TV (India)	http: //www.zeetelevision.com/

Newspapers and magazines

Advertising Age International	http: //adage.com/international/
Al-Ahram (Egypt)	http: //www.ahram.org.eg/
al Hayat (Saudi Arabia)	http: //www.alhayat.com/
Asiaweek	http: //cnn.com/ASIANOW/ asiaweek/
Buenos Aires Herald (Argentina)	http: //www.buenosairesherald.com/
Business Week	http: //www.businessweck.com/
China Daily	http: //www.chinadaily.com.cn/
Editor & Publisher	http: //www.mediainfo.com/
Filmfare (India)	http: //filmfare.indiatimes.com/
Fortune	http: //www.pathfinder.com/fortune/
Frontline (India)	http: //www.frontlineonline.com/
India Today	http: //www.india-today.com/
International Herald Tribune	http: //www.iht.com/
Le monde-diplomatique	http: //www.monde-diplomatique.fr/en/
Newsweek	http: //www.newsweek.com/
Reader's Digest	http: //www.readersdigest.com/
SatNews magazine	http: //www.satnews.com/
Slate	http: //www.slate.com/
Time	http: //www.pathfinder.com/time/
The Economist	http: //www.economist.com/
The Financial Times	http: //www.ft.com/
The Guardian	http: //www.guardian.co.uk/
The Hindu (India)	http: //www.the-hindu.com/
The New Straits Times (Singapore)	http: //straitstimes.asia1.com.sg/

The New York Times	http: //www.nyt.com/
The Times	http: //www.the-times.co.uk/
The Times of India	http: //www.timesofindia.com/
The Washington Post	http: //www.wp.com/
Variety	http: //www.variety.com/
Via Satellite magazine	http: //www.satellitetoday.com/ viaonline/
Wall Street Journal	http: //www.wsj.com/

Publishers

Amazon.com	http: //www.amazon.com/
Barnes and Noble	http: //shop.barnesandnoble.com/
International Data Group	http: //www.idg.net/
International Thomson	http: //itp.thomson.com/
McGraw-Hill	http: //www.mcgraw-hill.com/
Pearson Group	http: //www.pearson-plc.com/
Random House	http: //www.randomhouse.com/
Reed-Elsevier	http: //www.reed-elsevier.com/
Wolters-Kluwer	http: //www.wolters-kluwer.com/

Internet Search Engines

Alta Vista	http: //www.altavista.com/
Excite	http: //www.excite.com/
Infoseek	http: //www2.infoseek.com/
Lycos	http: //www.lycos.com/
Webcrawler	http: //www.webcrawler.com/
Yahoo!	http: //www.yahoo.com/

Note: Web addresses current at the time of publication.

References

Adorno, T. (1991) *The cultural industry: selected essays on mass culture.* London: Routledge.

Adorno, T. and Horkheimer, M. (1979) *Dialectic of enlightenment.* London: Verso. (originally published in German in 1947).

Aggarwala, N. (1979) What is development news? *Journal of Communication,* **29,** 180–1.

Agrawal, B. (ed.) (1977) *Satellite Instructional Television Experiment, social evaluation: impact on adults.* Two volumes, Bangalore: Indian Space Research Organisation.

Agrawal, B. (1978) *Satellite Instructional Television Experiment: television comes to villages.* Bangalore: Indian Space Research Organisation. [On SITE, see also articles in *Journal of Communication,* 29, 4 in 1979.]

Ahmad, A. (1992) *In theory: classes, nations, literatures.* London: Verso.

Ahmed, R. (1999) Bhangra and Bollywood for British Asians, *The Times of India,* 5 November.

Aksoy, A. and Robins, K. (1992) Hollywood for the 21st century – global competition for critical mass in image markets. *Cambridge Journal of Economics,* **16,** 1, 1–22.

Alexandre, L. (1993) Television Marti: 'open skies' over the South. In Nordenstreng, K. and Schiller, H. (eds), *Beyond national sovereignty.* Norwood, N.J: Ablex Publishing.

Allen, R. (ed.) (1995) *To be continued ... soap opera around the world.* New York: Routledge.

Alterman, J. (1998) *New media new politics?: from satellite television to the Internet in the Arab world.* Washington: The Washington Institute for Near East Policy, Policy Paper 48.

Althusser, L. (1971) *Lenin and philosophy and other essays.* London: New Left Books.

Amin, H. (1996) Egypt and the Arab world in the satellite age. In Jacka, E., Sinclair, J. and Cunningham, S. (eds), *New patterns in global television.* Oxford: Oxford University Press.

Amin, S. (1976) *Accumulation on a world scale: a critique of the theory of underdevelopment.* New York: Monthly Review Press.

Amin, S. (1988) *Eurocentrism.* Translated by R. Moore, New York:

Monthly Review Press. First published in French as *L'eurocentrisme: critique d'un ideologie*. Paris: Anthropos.

Amin, S. (1997) *Capitalism in the age of globalization*. London: Zed Books.

Amin, S. (1999) Not a happy ending, *Al-Ahram Weekly*, 30 December. 1999 – 5 January 2000, Issue No. 462, translated from the French by P. Ghazaleh.

Anderson, B. (1991) *Imagined communities: reflections on the origin and spread of nationalism*. Second edition, London: Verso.

Ang, I. (1985) *Watching Dallas: soap opera and the melodramatic imagination*. London: Metheun.

Ang, I. (1996) *Living room wars: rethinking media audiences for a postmodern world*. London: Routledge.

Appadurai, A. (1990) Disjuncture and difference in the global cultural economy. *Public Culture*, 2, 2, 1–24.

Appadurai, A. (1996) *Modernity at large: cultural dimensions of globalization*. Minneapolis: University of Minnesota Press.

Archibugi, D. and Held, D. (eds) (1995) *Cosmopolitan democracy*. Cambridge: Polity Press.

Armstrong, S. (1999) Money spinner, *Television Business International*, January/February, 49–52.

Ash, T. (1990) *The magic lantern: the revolution of '89 witnessed in Warsaw, Budapest, Berlin and Prague*. New York: Random House.

Atkinson, D. and Raboy, M. (eds) (1997) *Public service broadcasting: the challenges of the 21st century*. Paris: UNESCO.

Bagdikian, B. (1997) *The media monopoly*. Fifth edition, Boston: Beacon Press.

Bailie, M. and Winseck, D. (eds) (1997) *Democratizing communication? Comparative perspectives on information and power*. Cresskill, NJ: Hampton Press.

Baker, S., Ewing, J. and Capell, K. (1999) The race to wire Europe. *Business Week*, 7 June, 20–4.

Ballestero, D. (1999) Hispanic love affair. *Television Business International*, January/February, 31–4.

Banks, J. (1996) *Monopoly television – MTV's quest to control the music*. Boulder, COL: Westview Press.

Baran, P. (1957) *The political economy of growth*. New York: Monthly Review Press.

Barber, B. (1995) *Jihad vs. McWorld*. New York: Times Books.

Barnett, S. (1990) *Games and sets: the changing face of sport on television*. London: British Film Institute.

Barnouw, E. and Krishnaswamy, S. (1980) *Indian film*. Second edition, New York: Oxford University Press.

Barrie, C. (1999) Beeb gears up for Internet. *The Guardian*, 13 October, p. 29.

Barrie, C. and Martinson, J. (1999) Net sets Reuters a new deadline. *The Guardian*, 21 October, p. 27.

Barrier, M. (1999) *Hollywood cartoons: American animation in its golden age*. Oxford: Oxford University Press.

Baudrillard, J. (1994) *The illusion of the end*. Translated by C. Turner, Cambridge: Polity Press. First published in 1992 as *L'illusion de la fin*, Paris: Editions Galilee.

BBC (1999a) *BBC World Service annual report, 1998–99*, London: British Broadcasting Corporation.

BBC (1999b) *BBC Worldwide annual report, 1998–99*, London: British Broadcasting Corporation.

Bell, D. (1973) *The coming of post industrial society: a venture in social forecasting*. New York: Basic Books.

Bellamy, R. (1998) The evolving television sports marketplace. In L. Wenner, (ed.), *MediaSport*. New York: Routledge.

Beniger, J. (1986) *The control revolution*. Cambridge, MA: Harvard University Press.

Bennett, W. and Paletz, D. (1994) *Taken by storm: the media, public opinion and US foreign policy in the Gulf War*. Chicago: University of Chicago Press.

Berfield, S. (1996) Satellite TV: Asia's no pushover. *Asiaweek*, 8 November.

Berners-Lee, T. and Fischetti, M. (1999) *Weaving the web*. London: Orion Business.

Bettig, R. (1996) *Copyrighting culture: the political economy of intellectual property*. Boulder, COL: Westview.

Bhabha, H. (1994) *The location of culture*. London: Routledge.

Bloomberg, M. (1997) *Bloomberg by Bloomberg*. New York: John Wiley.

Blumenthal, H. and Goodenough, O. (1998) *This business of television*. Second edition, New York: Billboard Books.

Boeke, C. and Fernandez, R. (1998) Global satellite survey 1998 – satellite trends and statistics. *Via Satellite*, July.

Bonnell, V. and Freidin, G. (1995) *Televorot* - the role of television coverage in Russia's August 1991 coup. In Condee, N. (ed.) *Soviet hieroglyphics: visual culture in late-twentieth century Russia*. Bloomington: Indiana University Press, and London: British Film Institute.

Borger, J. (1999) General heralds age of cyberwar. *The Guardian*, 5 November, p. 17.

Bourgault, L. (1995) *Mass media in sub-Saharan Africa*. Bloomington: Indiana University Press.

Bourne, R. (1995) *News on a knife-edge*: *Gemini journalism and a global agenda*. London: John Libbey.

Boyd-Barrett, O. (1977) Media imperialism: towards an international framework for the analysis of media systems. In Curran, J., Gurevitch, M. and Woollacott, J. (eds) *Mass communication and society*. London: Edward Arnold.

Boyd-Barrett, O. (1980) *The international news agencies*. London: Constable.

Boyd-Barrett, O. (1998) Media imperialism reformulated. In Thussu, D. (ed.) *Electronic empires*. London: Arnold.

Boyd-Barrett, O. and Rantanen, T. (eds) (1998) *The globalization of news*. London: Sage.

Boyd-Barrett, O. and Thussu, D. (1992) *Contraflow in global news: international and regional news exchange mechanisms*. London: John Libbey, in association with UNESCO.

Brandt Commission (1981) *North-South: a programme for survival*. The Report of the Independent Commission on International Development Issues under the Chairmanship of Willy Brandt, London: Pan Books.

Briggs, A. (1970) *A history of broadcasting in the United Kingdom, vol. 3, The war of words*. Oxford: Oxford University Press.

Brockes, E.(1999) Cash for questions. *The Guardian*, 24 August, p. 4.

Brown, D. (1998) *Regionalisation and market positioning for pan-European pay-TV*, London: Management Report. Financial Times Media and Telecom.

Brown, P. (1998) Asian satellites: the demand is still there. *Via Satellite*, December.

Brown, P. (1999) Demand soars as satellites feed the Internet. *Via Satellite*, November.

Burnett, R. (1996) *The global jukebox: the international music industry*. London: Routledge.

Business Week (1998a) Information technology annual report: doing business in the Internet age. 22 June, 61–89.

Business Week (1998b) The 21st century economy. Special Report, 31 August, 24–84.

Business Week (1999a) Information technology annual report, 21 June, 47–81.

Business Week (1999b) Discovery: beyond bloody gazelles, 21 June, 83, 85.

Business Week (1999c) 1999 Leaders: the Business Week global 1000. 12 July, 43–50.

Business Week (1999d) The Internet age, special section. 4 October, 40–113.

Business Week (2000) Industry outlook 2000 – information. 10 January, 55–63.

Cairncross, F. (1997) *The death of distance: how the communications revolution will change our lives*. London: Orion Business Books.

Calhoun, C. (ed.) (1992) *Habermas and the public sphere*. Cambridge, MA: MIT Press.

Callard, S. (1998) Breaking news. *Cable and Satellite Europe*, October, 67–70.

Callard, S. (1999) Reaching the converted. *Cable and Satellite Europe*, January, 14–16.

Carey, J. (1988) *Communication as culture*. Boston: Unwin Hyman.

Castells, M. (1996) *The information age: economy, society and culture*, vol. 1: *The rise of the network society*. Oxford: Blackwell.

Castells, M. (1997) *The information age: economy, society and culture*, vol. 2: *The power of identity*. Oxford: Blackwell.

Castells, M.(1998) *The information age: economy, society and culture*, vol. 3: *End of millennium*. Oxford: Blackwell.

Catalbas, D. (2000) Broadcasting deregulation in Turkey: uniformity within diversity. In Curran, J. (ed.), *Media organisations in society*. London: Arnold.

Chakraborty, S. (1999) Pak coup warning was posted on the Net. *The Times of India*, 29 October.

Chalaby, J. (1996) Journalism as an Anglo-American invention. *European Journal of Communication*, **11**, 2, 303–26.

Chamorro, E. (1987) *Packaging the Contras: a case of CIA disinformation*. New York: Institute for Media Analysis.

Chanan, M. (1985) The Reuters Factor: myth and realities of communicology: a scenario. In *Making waves: the politics of communications*, Radical Science Collective (eds). London: Free Association Books.

Chandler, R. (1981) *War of ideas: the US propaganda campaign in Vietnam*, Boulder, COL: Westview Press.

Chang, T., Wang, J. and Cen, C. (1998) The social construction of international imagery in the post-Cold War era: a comparative analysis of US and Chinese national TV news. *Journal of Broadcasting and Electronic Media*, 42, 3, 277–96.

Cheah, P. and Robbins, B. (eds) (1998) *Cosmopolitcs: thinking and feeling beyond the nation*. Minneapolis: University of Minnesota Press.

Chengappa, R. (1999) Coming of age. *India Today International*, 7 June, 38–40.

Chengxiang, Z. (1998) TV turns viewers to classics. *China Daily*, 26 January.

Cherry, C. (1978) *World communication: threat or promise?*, New York: John Wiley.

Chevaldonne, F. (1987) Globalization and Orientalism: the case of TV serials. *Media, Culture and Society*, **9**, 137–148.

Chohan, S. (1999) When Holly met Bolly. *The Guardian*, 2 December, p. 13.

Chomsky, N. (1999) *The new military humanism: lessons from Kosovo*. Monroe, ME: Common Courage Press.

Clark, I. (1997) *Globalization and fragmentation: international relations in the twentieth century*. Oxford: Oxford University Press.

Clifton, R. and Maughan, E. (eds) (1999) *The future of brands*. London: Macmillan Business.

Cohen, B. (1963) *The press and foreign policy*. Princeton, NJ: Princeton University Press.

Colino, R. (1985) Intelsat: facing the Challenge of tomorrow. *Journal of International Affairs*, **39**, 1, 129–46.

Collins, R. (1998) *From satellite to single market: new communication technology and European public service television*. London: Routledge.

Corliss, R. (1996) Chinese movie magic. *Time*, 29 January, 46–54.

Corner, J, Schlesinger, P. and Silverstone, R. (eds) (1997) *International media research: a critical survey*. London: Routledge.

Critchlow, J. (1995) *Radio Hole-in-the-Head:Radio Liberty: an insider's story of Cold War broadcasting*. Washington: American University Press.

Crossman, M. (1999) Cyclical growth ahead for satellite manufacturing. *Via Satellite*, June.

Cruise O'Brien, R. (ed.) (1984) *Information, economics and power: the North-South dimension*. London: Hodder and Stoughton.

Crystal, D. (1997) *English as a global language*. Cambridge: Cambridge University Press.

Curran, J. and Seaton, J. (1997) *Power without responsibility: the press and broadcasting in Britain*. fifth edition, London: Routledge.

Curwen, P. (1997) *Restructuring telecommunications: a study of Europe in a global context*. London: Macmillan.

Dahlgren, P. (1995) *Television and the public sphere: citizenship, democracy and the media*. London: Sage.

Das, B. (1998) *The WTO agreements: deficiencies, imbalances and required changes, trade and development issues and the World Trade Organisation*. Penang: Third World Network and London: Zed Books.

Davies, L. (1999) A question of culture. *Television Business International*, January/February, 36–38.

Dayan, D. and Katz, E. (1992) *Media events: the live broadcasting of history*. Cambridge, MA: Harvard University Press.

Deshpande, S. (2000) Dear reader, *The Hindu*, 2 January.

Desmond, R. (1978) *The information process: world news reporting to the twentieth century*. Iowa City: University of Iowa Press.

Deutch, J., Kanter, A. and Scowcroft, B. (1999) Saving NATO's foundation. *Foreign Affairs*, 78, 6, 54–67.

Dicken, P. (1998) *Global shift: transforming the world economy*. Third edition, London: Paul Chapman Publishing (Sage).

Dillon, B. and Ryan E. (1998) Porn to be wild. *Cable and Satellite Europe*, November, 18–22.

Dinnick, R. (1999) Caught in the web of war. *Internet Magazine*, June, 38–41.

Dissanayake, W. (1993) (ed.) *Melodrama and Asian cinema*. Cambridge: Cambridge University Press.

Dizard, W. (1997) *Meganet: how the global communications network will connect everyone on Earth*. Boulder, COL: Westview Press.

Dorfman, A. and Mattelart, A. (1975) *How to read Donald Duck: imperialist Ideology in the Disney comic*. New York: International General Editions.

Dowmunt, T. (ed.) (1993) *Channels of resistance: global television and local empowerment*. London: British Film Institute in association with Channel 4 Television.

Drake, W. (1993) Territoriality and intangibility: transborder data flows and national sovereignty in Nordenstreng, K. and Schiller H. (eds), *Beyond national sovereignty*. Norwood, NJ: Ablex Publishing.

Drake, W. and Nicolaidis, K. (1992) Ideas, interests and institutionalization: 'trade in services' and the Uruguay Round. *International Organization*, 46, 37–100.

Dunn, J. (ed.) (1992) *Democracy: the unfinished journey*. Oxford: Oxford University Press.

Dunnett, P. (1990) *The world television industry: an economic analysis*. London: Routledge.

During, S. (ed.) (1999) *The cultural studies reader*. Second edition, London: Routledge.

Dyson, K. and Humphreys, P. (eds) (1990) *The political economy of communications: international and European dimensions*. London: Routledge.

Echikson, W., Woodruff, D., Larner, M., Robinson, A. (1997) Move over, Hollywood! *Business Week*, 15 December, 24–7.

Eggington, B. (2000) Waging global war. *The Guardian* (Media), 10 January, p. 84.

Einhorn, B. and Roberts, D. (1999) China's web masters. *Business Week*, 2 August, 25–8.

Eisenberg, D. (1999) The Net loves old media. *Time*, 1 November.

Eisenstein, E. (1979) *The printing press as an agent of change*. 2 vols, Cambridge: Cambridge University Press.

Ellinghaus,W. and Forrester, L. (1985) A U.S. effort to provide a global balance: The Maitland Commission Report. *Journal of Communication*, Spring, 14–21.

Elliot, I. (1988) How open is 'openness'? *Survey*, 30, 3, 1–24.

Elmer-Dewitt, P. (1994) Battle for the heart and soul of the Internet. *Time*, 25 July, 50–6.

Elster, J. (ed.) (1997) *Democratic deliberation*. Cambridge: Cambridge University Press.

European Broadcasting Union (1998) *The information society: from scarcity of frequencies to scarcity of content and scarcity of access to the audience?* Report, Geneva: European Broadcasting Union.

European Commission (1994) *Europe and the global information society*. Bangemann Task Force Report to the European Council, Brussels: European Commission.

European Commission (1997a) *Advertising*. The Single Market Review, Subseries III – Impact on Services, vol. 7, Luxembourg: Office for Official Publications of the European Communities.

European Commission (1997b) *Audio-visual services and production*. The Single Market Review, Subseries III – Impact on Services, vol. 8, Luxembourg: Office for Official Publications of the European Communities.

European Commission (1997c) *Green Paper on the convergence of the telecom, media and information technology sectors and the implications for regulation – towards an information society approach*. Document (97) 623 final, 3 December, Brussels: European Commission.

European Commission (1998) *Telecommunications: liberalised services*. The Single Market Review, Subseries III – Impact on Services, vol. 6, Luxembourg: Office for Official Publications of the European Communities.

European Commission (1999) *Principles and guidelines for the Community's audio-visual policy in the digital age*. Document (99) 657, 14 December, Brussels: European Commission.

Ewen, S. (1976) *The captains of consciousness*. New York: McGraw-Hill.

Fannin, R.(1999a) National Geographic crosses more borders. *Advertising Age International*, May, 29.

Fannin, R. (1999b) Internet waves hit Asia shores. *Advertising Age International*, November, 43–53.

Fanon, F. (1970) *A Dying colonialism*. Harmondsworth: Pelican. Originally published in the UK in 1965 under the title *A study in dying colonialism*. London: Monthly Review Press.

Febvre, L. and Martin, H. (1990) *The coming of the book: the impact of printing 1450–1800*. London: Verso. Translated by D. Gerard. Originally published in 1958 as *L 'Apparition du livre*. Paris: Editions Albin Michel.

Federal Communications Commission (1999) *A new FCC for the 21st century*. (http: //www.fcc.gov/21stcentury/)

Ferguson, M. (1992) The mythology about globalisation. *European Journal of Communication*, 7, 1, 69–93.

Fischer, H. and Merrill, J. (eds) (1976) *International and intercultural communication*. Second edition, New York: Hastings House Publishers.

Fiske, J. (1987) *Television culture*. London: Routledge.

Flournoy, D. and Stewart, R. (1997) *CNN: making news in the global market*. Luton: University of Luton Press.

Foley, T. (1999) Mega operators, BIG fish in a very big pond. *Via Satellite*, October.

Forbes (1999) 200 Global billionaires. *Forbes*, 5 July, 153–55.

Fortner, R. (1993) *International communication: history, conflict and control of the global metropolis*. Belmont: Wadsworth Publishing.

Fortune (1999a) The year of the megamerger. 11 January, 24–6.

Fortune (1999b) The Fortune Global 5 Hundred: The World's Largest Corporations. 2 August, F1-F43.

Fortune (1999c) The new China survey. 11 October, 60–2.

Fox, E. (1997) *Latin American broadcasting: from tango to telenovela*. Luton: University of Luton Press.

Franklin, B. (1997) *Newszak and news media*. London: Arnold.

Fredebeul-Krein, M. and Freytag, A. (1999) The case for a more binding

WTO agreement on regulatory principles in telecommunication markets.*Telecommunications Policy*, 23, 625–44.

Frederick, H. (1992) *Global communication and international relations*. Belmont: Wadsworth.

Freire, P. (1974) *Pedagogy of the oppressed*. Translated by M. Ramos, New York: Seabury Press, originally published in 1970.

Frieden, R. (1996) *International telecommunications handbook*. Boston: Artch House Publishing.

Friedland, L. (1992) *Covering the world: International television news services*. New York: Twentieth Century Fund.

Fukuyama, F. (1992) *The end of history and the last man*. London: Hamish Hamilton.

Galperin, H. (1999) Cultural industries in the age of free-trade agreements. *Canadian Journal of Communication*, 24, 49–77.

Galtung, J. (1971) A structural theory of imperialism. *Journal of Peace Research*, 8, 2, 81–117.

Galtung, J. and Ruge, M. (1965) The structure of foreign news. *Journal of Peace Research*, 2, 1, 64–91.

Gamini, G. (1999) Presidential talk-show tops ratings. *The Times*, 27 August, p. 16.

Gandy, O. (1993) *The panoptic sort: a political economy of personal information*. Boulder, COL: Westview.

Garcia Canclini, N. (1995) *Hybrid cultures: strategies for entering and leaving modernity*. Minneapolis: University of Minnesota Press. Original Spanish edition published in 1989 as *Culturas hibridas: estrategias para entrar y salir de la modernidad*. Mexico City: Grijalbo.

Garga, B. (1996) *So many cinemas: the motion picture in India*. Mumbai: Eminence Designs.

Garnham, N. (1990) *Capitalism and communication: global culture and the economics of information*. London: Sage.

GATT (1993) *Final Act embodying the results of the Uruguay Round (General Agreement on Trade in Services – Annex on Telecommunications)*. Geneva: General Agreement on Tariff and Trade Secretariat.

Gershon, R. A. (1990) Global cooperation in an era of deregulation. *Telecommunication Policy*, 14, 3, 249–59.

Gibbons, F. (1999) Tweenies follow in Tinky Winky's footsteps. *The Guardian*, 29 July, p. 9.

Giddens, A. (1990) *The consequences of modernity*. Cambridge: Polity Press.

Giffard, C. A. (1984) Inter Press Service: news from the Third World. *Journal of Communication*, 34, 4, 41–59.

Giffard, C. A. (1998) Alternative news agencies. In Boyd-Barrett, and Rantanen, T. (eds) *The globalization of news*. London: Sage.

Giffard, C. A. and Streck, J. M. (1998) News agency coverage of the UN

Conference on Human Rights. *The Journal of International Communication*, 5 (1 and 2), 149–164.

Gittings, J. (2000) China blocks Internet explosion. *The Guardian*, 27 January, p. 3.

Globo website: http: //www.redeglobo.com.br

Goldberg, D., Prosser, T. and Verhulst, S. (eds) (1998) *Regulating the media: a comparative study*. Oxford: Clarendon Press.

Golding, P. (1998) Worldwide wedge: divisions and contradictions in the global information infrastructure. In Thussu, D. (ed.) *Electronic Empires*. London: Arnold.

Golding, P. and Harris, P. (eds) (1997) *Beyond cultural imperialism: globalisation, communication and the new international order*. London: Sage.

Golding, P. and Murdoch, G. (eds) (1997) *The political economy of the media*. Two vols, Cheltenham: Edward Elgar.

Goonasekera, A. (1997) Cultural markets in the age of globalisation: Asian values and Western content: *Inter Media*, Special Report, 25, 6, 4–43.

Goonasekera, A. and Lee, P. (eds) (1998) *TV without borders: Asia speaks out*. Singapore: Asian Media Information and Communication Centre.

Gould, S. and Grein, A. (1996) Globally integrated marketing communications. *Journal of Marketing Communications*, 2, 3, 141–58.

Gould, S., Lerman, D. and Grein, A. (1999) Agency perceptions and practices on global IMC. *Journal of Advertising Research*, 39, 1, pp. 7–20.

Gouldner, A. (1976) *The dialectic of ideology and technology*. London: Macmillan.

Gramsci, A. (1971) *Selections from the prison notebooks*. Edited and translated by Q. Hoare, and G. Nowell-Smith, G. London: Lawrence and Wishart.

Grover, R. (1999) Disney: out on a limb. *Business Week*, 19 July, 46–8.

Guback, T. (1969) *The international film industry: Western Europe and America since 1945*. Bloomington: Indiana University Press.

Gunder Frank, A. (1969) *Capitalism and underdevelopment in Latin America*. New York: Monthly Review Press.

Gunther, M. (1998) Bertelsmann's new media man. *Fortune*, 23 November, 58–68.

Gupta, N. (1998) *Switching channels: ideologies of television in India*. New Delhi: Oxford University Press.

Ha, L. (1997) Limitations and strengths of Pan-Asian advertising media: a review for international advertisers. *International Journal of Advertising*, 16, 148–63.

Haass, R. (1999) What to do with American primacy. *Foreign Affairs*, 78, 5, 37–49.

Habermas, J. (1989) *The structural transformation of the public sphere: an inquiry into a category of bourgeois society*. Cambridge: Polity. Original German edition published in 1962.

Hachten, W. (1999) *The world news prism: changing media of international communication*. Fifth edition, Ames: Iowa State University Press.

Haddow, I. (1999) MMDS – wireless broadcasting, the African context. *Cable and Satellite Europe*. April, 26–30.

Hafner, K. and Lyons, M. (1996) *Where wizards stay up late: the origins of the Internet*. New York: Simon & Schuster.

Halarnkar, S. (1999) Prime-time war. *India Today International*, 14 June, 20–1.

Halarnkar, S. and Ramani, P. (1999) Digital dawn. *India Today International*. 5 July, 34–9.

Hale, J. (1975) *Radio power: propaganda and international broadcasting*. London: Paul Elek.

Hall, S. (1980) Encoding and decoding in the television discourse. In Hall, S., Hobson, D., Lowe, A. and Willis, P. (eds) *Culture, media, language*. London: Hutchinson.

Hall, S. (1991) The local and the global: globalization and ethnicity: In King, A. (ed.), *Culture, globalization and the world-system: contemporary conditions for the representation of identity*. London: Macmillan.

Hallin, D. (1986) *The uncensored War: the media and Vietnam*. Oxford: Oxford University Press.

Hallin, D. (1994) *We keep America on top of the world: television journalism and the public sphere*. New York: Routledge.

Halloran, J. (1997) International communication research: opportunities and obstacles. In Mohammadi, A. (ed.), *International communication and globalization*. London: Sage.

Hamel, G. and Sampler, J. (1998) The e-corporation – more than just Web-based, it's building a new industrial order. *Fortune*, 7 December, 52–63.

Hamelink, C. (1979) Informatics: Third World call for new order. *Journal of Communication*, **29**, 4, 144.

Hamelink, C. (1983) *Cultural autonomy in global communications*. New York: Longman.

Hamelink, C. (1994) *The politics of world communication: a human rights perspective*. London: Sage.

Hannerz, U. (1997) *Transnational connection*. London: Sage.

Harasim, L. (ed.) (1994) *Global networks: computers and international communication*. Cambridge, MA: MIT Press.

Harley, W. (1984) Memorandum presented by Harley, William G, Communication consultant, United States Department of State, 9 February 1984, reflecting the views of the state department on what the US government is thinking and doing about UNESCO. *Journal of Communication*, **34**, 4, 89.

Harris, P. (1981) News dependence and structural changes. In Richstad, J. and Anderson, M. (eds) *Crisis in international news: policies and prospects*. New York: Columbia University Press.

Harris, P. (1997) Communication and global security: the challenge for the next millennium. In Golding, P. and Harris, P. (eds), *Beyond cultural imperialism*. London: Sage.

Harrison, F. (1999) Malaysian soap shows life of humble leader, in 33 parts. *The Guardian*, 31 August, p. 10.

Harvey, D. (1989) *The condition of postmodernity*. Oxford, Blackwell.

Hausmann, R. (1999) Should there be five currencies or one hundred and five? *Foreign Policy*, Fall, 65–79.

Headrick, D. (1981) *The tools of empire: technology and European imperialism in the nineteenth century*. New York: Oxford University Press.

Headrick, D. (1991) *The invisible weapon: telecommunications and international politics, 1851–1945*. New York: Oxford University Press.

Held, D., McGrew, A., Goldblatt, D., Perraton, J. (1999) *Global transformations: politics, economics and culture*. Cambridge: Polity Press.

Hemel, van A. (ed.) (1996) *Trading culture: GATT, European cultural policies and the transatlantic market*. Amsterdam: Boekman Foundation.

Herman, E. (1999) *The myth of the liberal media: an Edward Herman reader*. New York: Peter Lang Publisher.

Herman, E. and Chomsky, N. (1994) *Manufacturing consent: the political economy of the mass media*. London: Vintage. Originally published in 1988 by Pantheon, New York.

Herman, E. and McChesney, R. (1997) *The global media: the new missionaries of corporate capitalism*. London: Cassell.

Hess, S. (1996) *International news and foreign correspondents*. Washington, DC: Brookings Institution.

Hickman, T. (1995) *What did you do in the war, Auntie?: The BBC at war 1939–45*. London: BBC Books.

Hindes, A. (1999) Par likes MTV's tune – Viacom subsid rides 'Beavis,' 'Blues' and synergy to success. *Variety*, 19–25 July, 7–8.

Hirst, P. and Thompson, G. (1996) *Globalisation in question: the international economy and the possibilities of governance*. Cambridge: Polity Press.

Hitchcock, D. (1988) *US public diplomacy*. Washington, DC: Center for Strategic and International Studies.

Hjarvard, S. (1998) TV news exchange. In Boyd-Barrett, O. and Rantanen, T. (eds), *The Globalization of News*. London: Sage.

Hoekman, E. and Kostecki, G. (1995) *The political economy of the world trading system: from GATT to WTO*. Oxford: Oxford University Press.

Hoge, J. (1994) Media pervasiveness. *Foreign Affairs*, 73, 4, 136–44

Holub, R. (1991) *Jürgen Habermas: vritic in the public sphere*. London: Routledge.

Hong, J. (1993) China's TV programme imports 1958–1988: towards the internationalisation of television? *Gazette*, 52, 1–23.

Hong, J. (1997) The evolution of China's media function during the 1980s: a new model in a new era? In Bailie and Winseck, D. (eds) *Democratizing communication?* Cresskill, NJ: Hampton Press.

Horsman, M. (1997) *Sky high: the inside story of BSkyB*. London: Orion Business Books.

Hoskins, G. and Mirus, R. (1988) Reasons for US dominance of the international trade in television programmes. *Media, Culture and Society*, **10**, 499–515.

Huber, P. (1997) *Law and disorder in cyberspace: abolish the FCC and let common law rule the telecosm*. New York: Oxford University Press.

Huntington, S. (1993) The clash of civilizations. *Foreign Affairs*, **72**, 3, 22–49.

IIPA (1999) *Copyright industries in the U.S. economy: the 1999 report*. International Intellectual Property Alliance, downloaded from www.iipa.com.

ILO (1998) *The world employment report 1998–99*. Geneva: International Labour Organisation.

IMF (1997) *World economic outlook: globalization – challenges and opportunities*. Washington, DC: International Monetary Fund.

Inglis, A. (1990) *Behind the tube: a history of broadcasting technology and business*. London: Focal Press.

Innis, H. (1972) *Empire and communications* (revised edition). Toronto: University of Toronto Press, originally published in 1950 by Oxford University Press.

Intelsat (1999a) Annual report 1998. International Telecommunications Satellite Organisation. Intelsat website.

Intelsat (1999b) Hearing before the Subcommittee on Communications Committee on Commerce, Science and Transportation, United States Senate, 25 March 1999.

Oral Testimony of Conny Kullman, Director General and CEO.

Intelsat (1999c) Address by Mr Conny Kullman, Intelsat Director General and CEO, to Third United Nations Conference on the Exploration and Peaceful Uses of Outer Space, Vienna, Austria, 20 July 1999.

Ito, Y. (1981) The *Johoka Shakai* approach to the study of communication in Japan. In Wilhoit, G. and de Bock, H. (eds), *Mass communication review yearbook*. Vol. 2, London and Beverley Hills: Sage.

ITU (1985) *The missing link*. Report of the Independent Commission for World-wide Telecommunications Development (Maitland Commission), Geneva: International Telecommunication Union.

ITU (1998) *World telecommunication development report 98*. Geneva: International Telecommunication Union.

ITU (1999a) *Trends in telecommunication reform*. Geneva: International Telecommunication Union.

ITU (1999b) *World telecommunication development report*. Fifth edition, Geneva: International Telecommunication Union.

ITU (1999c) *Challenges to the network: Internet for development*. Geneva: International Telecommunication Union.

ITU (1999d) *Yearbook of statistics: telecommunication services: 1988–1997*, Geneva: International Telecommunication Union.

ITU (1999e) *Direction of traffic: trading telecom minutes*. Third edition, Geneva: International Telecommunication Union.

ITU (1999f) *World telecommunication development report: mobile cellular.* Geneva: International Telecommunication Union.

Jain, M. (1997) The God factory. *India Today*, 31 May, 70–3.

Jameson, F. (1991) *Postmodernism, or, the cultural logic of late capitalism.* London: Verso.

Jarvie, I. (1992) *Hollywood's overseas campaign: the North Atlantic movie trade, 1920–1950.* Cambridge: Cambridge University Press.

Jeffrey, J. (1978) The Third World and the Free Enterprise Press. *Policy Review*, Summer, 5, 59–70.

Jensen, K. (ed.) (1998) *News of the world: world cultures look at television news.* London: Routledge.

Jones, J. (ed.) (1999) *The advertising business: operations, creativity, media planning, integrated communications.* Thousand Oaks, CA: Sage.

Joseph, A. and Sharma, K. (eds) (1994) *Whose news? the media and women's issues.* New Delhi: Sage.

Kabbani, R. (1986) *Europe's myths of orient.* London: Pandora Press.

Kagan, R. (1998) The benevolent empire. *Foreign Policy*, Summer, 24–35.

Kahin, B. and Nesson, C. (eds) (1997) *Borders in cyberspace: information policy and the global information infrastructure.* Cambridge, MA: MIT Press.

Kamath, S. (1999) Bringing MTV to Tamil viewers. *The Hindu*, 14 November.

Kapur, G. (1997) Globalisation and culture. *Third Text*, 39, Summer, 21–38.

Kashlev, Y. (1984) *Information imperialism.* Moscow: Novosti Press.

Kasoma, F. (1995) The role of the independent media in Africa's change to democracy. *Media, Culture and Society*, 17, 537–55.

Katz, I. (1999) Final edition, *The Guardian* (Media), 13 December, pp. 2–3.

Katz, E. and Liebes, T. (1990) *The export of meaning: cross-cultural readings of Dallas.* New York: Oxford University Press.

Kaul, G. (1998) *Cinema and the Indian freedom struggle.* New Delhi: Sterling.

Kaul, I., Grunberg, I., Stern, M. (eds) (1999) *Global public goods: international cooperation in the 21st century.* New York: Oxford University Press.

Kazmi, N. (1999) Hindi films make pretty picture in Japan. *The Times of India*, 3 November.

Kazmi, N. (2000) And now the world is Rahman's stage. *The Times of India*, 28 January.

Kennedy, P. (1971) Imperial cable communications and strategy, 1879–1914, *English Historical Review*, 86, 728–52.

Kessler, K. M. (1998) The Latin American satellite market: a prophecy fulfilled. *Via Satellite*, March.

Kettle, M. (1999) NBC finds nuclear waste too hot. *The Guardian*, 15 May, p. 19.

Khare, H. (2000) President cautions against social, economic disparities. *The Hindu*, 26 January.

Knowles, W. and Price, C. (1998) Kids stuff. *Cable and Satellite Europe*, December, 22–9

Kobrin, S. (1998) The MAI and the clash of globalizations. *Foreign Policy*, Fall, 97–109.

Koranteng, J. (1999) Rivals, youth force MBC to alter image. *Advertising Age International*, September, 21–4.

Krasner, S. (1999) *Sovereignty: organized hypocrisy*. Princeton, NJ: Princeton University Press.

Krauss, M. (1992) The world's languages in crisis. *Language*, 68, 1.

Kriplani, M. (1999) McCaw, Malone, Murdoch – Chandra? With the deal for ICO, an Indian media mogul may go global. *Business Week*, 20 December, 25.

LaFeber, W. (1999) *Michael Jordan and the new global capitalism*. New York: W. W. Norton.

Lall, B. (1999) Moguls make moves for Bollywood production. *Screen International*, 8 October, 20.

Lasswell, H. (1927) *Propaganda techniques in the world war*. New York: Alfred Knopf.

Latouche S. (1996) *The Westernization of the world: the significance, scope and limits of the drive toward global uniformity*, translated by R. Morris, Cambridge: Polity Press. Originally published in French in 1989 as *L'occidentalisation du monde: Essai sur la signification, la portée et les limites de l'uniformisation planétaire*, Paris: Editions la Découverte.

Lawrence, S. (1999) Captive audience, *Far Eastern Economic Review*, 8 July, 70, 72.

Lawrenson, J. and Barber, L. (1985) *The price of truth, the story of the Reuters £££ millions*. London: Mainstream Publishing.

Lazarsfeld, P. (1941) Remarks on administrative and critical communications Research. *Studies in Philosophy and Social Sciences*, 9, 2–16.

Leigh, D. (2000) Global disclosure. *The Guardian* (Media), 31 January, pp. 8–9.

Lendvai, P. (1981) *The bureaucracy of truth: how communist governments manage the news*. London: Burnett Books.

Lepgold, J. (1998) NATO's post-Cold War collective action problem. *International Security*, 23, 1, 78–106.

Lerner, D. (1958) *The passing of traditional society: modernizing the Middle East*. New York: Free Press.

Levy, B. and Spiller P. (eds) (1996) *Regulation, institutions and commitment: comparative studies of telecommunication*. Cambridge: Cambridge University Press.

Lewis, M. (2000) *The new new thing: a Silicon Valley story*. London: Hodder & Stoughton.

Lewis, S. (1996) *News and society in the Greek polis.* London: Duckworth.

Li, X. (1991) The Chinese television system and television news. *The China Quarterly,* June, 126, 341–56.

Li, Y. (1999a) Market research booms along with reforms. *China Daily,* 1 June.

Li, Y. (1999b) CCTV movie channel gets large investment. *China Daily,* 24 June.

Lippmann, W. (1922) *Public opinion.* New York: Free Press.

Lisann, M. (1975) *Broadcasting to the Soviet Union: international politics and radio.* New York: Praeger Publishers.

Lloyd, C. (1999) Advertising Media: a changing marketplace. In Jones, J. (ed.), *The advertising business.* Thousand Oaks, CA: Sage.

Lopez, A. (1995) Our welcome guests: *telenovelas* in Latin America. In Allen, R. (ed.), *To be continued ...* New York: Routledge.

Lord, C.(1998) The past and future of public diplomacy. *Orbis,* Winter. 49–72

Lucas, M., and Wallner, M. (1993) Resistance by satellite: the Gulf Crisis project and the deep dish satellite TV network. In Dowmunt, T. (ed.) *Channels of resistance.* London: BFI in association with Channel 4 Television.

Lull, J. (ed.) (1988) *World families watch television.* Beverley Hills, CA: Sage.

Lull, J. (1991) *China turned on: television, reform and resistance.* London: Routledge.

Lull, J. (1995) *Media, communication, culture: a global approach.* Cambridge: Polity Press.

Luther, S. (1988) *The United States and the direct broadcast satellite: the politics of international broadcasting in space.* New York: Oxford University Press.

Lyon, D. (1994) *The electronic eye: the rise of surveillance society.* Minneapolis: University of Minnesota Press.

Lyotard, J. (1984) *The postmodern condition: a report on knowledge.* Translated by G. Bennington and B. Massumi, Manchester: Manchester University Press. Original published in French in 1979.

MacBride Report (1980) *Many voices, one world: communication and society today and tomorrow.* International Commission for the Study of Communication Problems, Paris: UNESCO.

MacGregor, B. (1997) *Live, direct and biased? Making television news in the satellite age.* London: Arnold.

Machet, E. (1999) *A decade of EU broadcasting regulation.* Dusseldorf: The European Institute for the Media.

Machlup, F. (1962) *The production and distribution of knowledge in the United States.* Princeton, NJ: Princeton University Press.

MacLean, D. (1999) Open doors and open questions: interpreting the results of the 1998 ITU Minneapolis Plenipotentiary Conference. *Telecommunications Policy,* **23,** 147–58.

Madden, N. (1999) Cable, satellite media lure influential viewers. *Advertising Age International*, September, 36.

Mader, R. (1993) Globo village: television in Brazil. In Dowmunt, T. (ed.), *Channels of resistance*. London: BFI in association with Channel 4 Television.

Manheim, J. (1994) *Strategic public diplomacy and American foreign policy: the evolution of influence*. New York: Oxford University Press.

Mansell, R. (1993) *The new telecommunications: a political economy of network evolution*. London: Sage.

Mansell, R. and Wehn, U. (eds) (1998) *Knowledge societies: information technology for sustainable development* (Report of the UN Commission on Science and Technology for Development). Oxford: Oxford University Press.

Manuel, P. (1993) *Cassette culture: popular music and technology in North India*. Chicago: Chicago University Press.

Marcuse, H. (1964) *One dimensional man*. Boston: Beacon Press.

Mardesich, J. (1999) How the Internet hits the big music. *Fortune*, 10 May, 40–4.

Marghalani, K., Palmgreen, P. and Boyd, D. (1998) The utilization of direct satellite broadcasting (DBS) in Saudi Arabia. *Journal of Broadcasting and Electronic Media*, **42**, 3, 297–314.

Martin, J. (1976) Effectiveness of international propaganda. In Fischer, H. and Merrill, J. (eds) *International and intercultural communication*. New York: Hastings House Publishers.

Martin-Barbero, J. (1993) *Communication, culture and hegemony: from media to mediations*. Translated by E. Fox. London: Sage.

Masmoudi, M. (1979) The new world information order. *Journal of Communication*, **29**, 2, 172–85.

Matlack, C. (1999) France Telecom: now the hunting begins. *Business Week*, 2 August, 16.

Matlack, C., Rae-Dupree, J. and Armstrong, L. (1999) It's a mad mad Internet space race. *Business Week*, 30 August, 25.

Mattelart, A. (1979) *Multinational corporations and the control of culture*. Atlantic Highlands, NJ: Humanities Press.

Mattelart, A. (1991) *Advertising international: the privatisation of public space*. transl. M. Chanan. London: Routledge. Originally published in 1989 as *L'Internationale publicitaire*, Paris: Editions La Découverte.

Mattelart, A. (1994) *Mapping world communication: war, progress, culture*. Transl. S. Emanuel and J. Cohen. Minneapolis: University of Minnesota Press. Originally published in 1991 as *La Communication-monde, Histoire des idées et des stratégies*, Paris: Editions La Découverte.

Mattelart, A. (1996) *The invention of communication*. Minneapolis: University of Minnesota Press.

Mattelart, A. and Mattelart, M. (1990) *A carnival of images: Brazilian Television fiction*. New York: Bergin and Garvey.

Mattelart, A. and Mattelart, M. (1998) *Theories of communication: a short introduction*. London: Sage.

Mazrui, A. (1997) Islamic and Western values. *Foreign Affairs*, **76**, 5, 118–32.

McAnany, E. and Wilkinson, K. (eds) (1996) *Mass media and free trade*. Austin, TX. University of Texas Press.

McChesney, R. (1993) *Telecommunications, mass media and democracy: the battle for the control of US broadcasting, 1928–1935*. New York: Oxford University Press.

McChesney, R. (1999) *Rich media, poor democracy: communication politics in dubious times*. Champaign, IL: University of Illinois Press.

McGuire, T. (1999) Is this the (alternative) news? *Intermedia*, **27**, 1, 24–6.

McLean, B. (1999) More than just dot-coms, *Fortune*, 6 December, 64–8.

McLuhan, M. (1964) *Understanding media*. London: Methuen.

McNamara, K. (1992) Reaching captive minds with radio. *Orbis*, Winter, 23–40.

McNeal, J. (1992) *Kids as customers*. New York: Lexington Books.

McPhail, T. (1987) *Electronic colonialism: the future of international broadcasting and communication*. London: Sage.

McQuail, D. (1994) *Mass communication theory: an introduction*. Third edition, London: Sage.

McQuail, D. and Siune, K. (eds) (1998) *Media policy: convergence, concentration and commerce*. Euromedia Research Group, London: Sage.

Melkote, S., Shields, P. and Agrawal, B. (eds) (1998) *International satellite broadcasting in South Asia: political, economic and cultural implications*. Lanham, MD: University Press of America.

Mermin, J. (1999) *Debating war and peace: media coverage of US intervention in the post-Vietnam era*. Princeton, NJ: Princeton University Press.

Mickelson, S. (1983) *America's other voice: the story of Radio Free Europe and Radio Liberty*. New York: Praeger.

Mickiewicz, E. (1997) *Changing channels: television and the struggle for power in Russia*. New York: Oxford University Press.

Milliot J. (1999) Sales, losses soar at online bookstores. *Publisher's Weekly*, 28 June.

Mills, M. (1997) A space age coup with a Cold War rival – Lockheed's satellite deal with Intersputnik once unthinkable. *The Washington Post*, 5 June, p. D01.

Mitra, A. (1993) *Television and popular culture in India: a study of the Mahabharat*. New Delhi: Sage.

Mitsui, T. and Hosokawa, S. (eds) (1998) *Karaoke around the world: global technology, local singing*. London: Routledge.

Mohammadi, A. and Sreberny-Mohammadi, A. (1994) *Small media, big revolution: communication, culture and the Iranian revolution*. Minneapolis: University of Minnesota Press.

Mooij, M. (1998) *Global marketing and advertising: understanding cultural paradoxes*. London: Sage.

Moran, A. (1998) *Copycat TV: globalisation, program formats and cultural identity*. Luton: University of Luton Press.

Mortished, C. (1999) Bangalore's program for success. *The Times*, 24 March, p. 29.

Mosco, V. (1996) *The political economy of communication: rethinking and renewal*. London: Sage.

Mowlana, H. (1996) *Global communication in transition*. London: Sage.

Mowlana, H. (1997) *Global information and world communication: new frontiers in international relations*. Second edition, London: Sage.

Mowlana, H., Gerbner, G. and Schiller, H. (eds) (1992) *Triumph of the image: the media's war in the Persian Gulf*. Boulder, COL: Westview Press.

Munk, N. (1999) Barnes and Noble title fight. *Fortune*, 21 June, 58–67.

Murdoch, G. and Golding, P. (1977) Capitalism, communication and class relations. In Curran, J. *et al.* (eds) *Mass communication and society*. London: Edward Arnold.

Naficy, H. (1993) *The making of exile cultures: Iranian television in the United States*. Minneapolis: University of Minnesota Press.

Naughton, J. (1999) *A brief history of the future*. London: Weidenfeld and Nicolson.

Nederveen Pieterse, J. (1995) Globalisation as hybridization. In Featherstone, M., Lash, S. and Robertson, R. (eds) *Global modernities*. London: Sage.

Nederveen Pieterse, J. (1996) Globalization and culture: three paradigms. *Economic and Political Weekly*, **31**, 23, 1389–93.

Nee, E. (1999) Microsoft gets ready to play a new game. *Fortune*, 26 April, 59–61.

Negroponte, N. (1995) *Being digital*. New York: Alfred A. Knopf.

Negus, K. (1992) *Producing pop: culture and conflict in the popular music industry*. London: Edward Arnold.

Nelson, M. (1997) *War of the black heavens: the battle of western broadcasting in the Cold War*. Syracuse: Syracuse University Press.

Neuman, W. (1991) *The future of the mass audience*. Cambridge: Cambridge University Press.

News Corporation (1999) *Annual report 1998–1999*.

Ninan, S. (1999) Murdoch's match, *The Hindu*, 3 October.

Nincovich, F. (1981) *The diplomacy of ideas: US foreign policy and cultural relations, 1938–1950*. Cambridge: Cambridge University Press.

Noam, E. (1993) Media Americanization, national culture, and forces of integration. In Noam, E. and Milonzi, J. (eds), *The international market in films and television programmes*. Norwood, NJ: Ablex Publishing.

Nordenstreng, K. (ed.) (1986) *New international information and communication order source book*. Prague: International Organisation of Journalists.

Nordenstreng, K. and Schiller, H. (eds) (1993) *Beyond national sovereignty: international communications in the 1990s.* Norwood, NJ: Ablex Publishing.

Nordenstreng, K. and Varis, T. (1974) *Television traffic – a one-way street? A survey and analysis of the international flow of television programme material.* Reports and Papers on Mass Communication, no. 70, Paris: UNESCO.

Nowell-Smith, G. and Ricci, S. (eds) (1998) *Hollywood and Europe: economics, culture, national identity, 1946–95.* London: British Film Institute.

Nye, J. (1990) Soft power, *Foreign Policy,* 80, 153–71.

Nye, J. and Owens, W. (1996) America's information edge. *Foreign Affairs,* March/April, 20–36.

Oberst, G. (1999) Regulatory review: European spectrum policy. *Via Satellite,* February.

O'Donnell, H. (1999) *Good times, bad times: soap operas and society in Western Europe.* London: Leicester University Press.

OECD (1985) *Declaration on transborder data flows.* (Press/A(85) 30), 11 April, Paris: Organisation for Economic Cooperation and Development.

OECD (1992) *Telecommunications and broadcasting: convergence or collision?* Paris: Organisation for Economic Co-operation and Development.

OECD (1993) *Services: statistics on international transactions, 1970–1991.* Statistics Directorate, Paris: Organisation for Economic Cooperation and Development.

OECD (1996) *The knowledge-based economy.* Paris: Organisation for Economic Cooperation and Development.

OECD (1998) *Open markets matter: the benefits of trade and investment liberalization.* Paris: Organisation for Economic Cooperation and Development.

OECD (1999) *Communication outlook 1999.* Paris: Organisation for Economic Cooperation and Development.

Ohmae, K. (1995) *The end of the nation state: the rise and fall of regional economies.* London: HarperCollins.

Okrent, D. (2000) Happily ever after. *Time,* 24 January, 43–7.

Oledzki, J. (1981) Polish perspectives on the new information order. *Journal of International Affairs,* 35, 2, 155–64.

Oliveira, O. (1993) Brazilian soaps outshine Hollywood: is cultural imperialism fading out? In Nordenstreng, K. and Schiller, H. (eds), *Beyond national sovereignty.* Norwood, NJ: Ablex Publishing.

Oslin, G. (1992) *The story of telecommunications.* Macon, GA: Mercer University Press.

Palmer, B. (1998) The wired warrior. *Fortune,* 21 December, 132–33.

Pandit, S. (1996) *From making to music: the history of Thorn EMI.* London: Hodder & Stoughton.

Panikkar, K. (ed.) (1999) *The concerned Indian's guide to communalism.* New Delhi: Viking.

Papathanassopoulos, S. (1999) The political economy of international news channels: more supply than demand. *Intermedia*, 27, 1, 17–23.

Parker, R. (1995) *Mixed signals: the prospects for global television news.* New York: Twentieth Century Fund.

Parkes, C. (1999) Inside the Magic Kingdom. *Financial Times*, 4 June, p. 6.

Partos, G. (1993) *The world that came from the cold.* London: BBC World Service/Royal Institute of International Affairs.

Paterson, C. (1998) Global battlefields. In Boyd-Barrett, O. and Rantanen, T. (eds), *The globalization of news.* London: Sage.

Pavlik, J. (1996) *New media technology – cultural and commercial perspectives*, Boston: Allyn and Bacon.

Pecora, N. (1998) *The business of children's entertainment.* New York: Guilford Press.

Peet, J. (2000) Shopping around the world, a survey of e-commerce. *The Economist*, 26 February, 42 pages.

Pendakur, M. and Subramanyam, R. (1996) Indian cinema beyond national borders. In Jacka, *et al.* (eds). *New patterns in global television.* Oxford: Oxford University Press.

Pfaltzgraff, R. and Shultz, R. (eds) (1997) *War in the information age.* Washington, DC: Brassey's.

Phillipson, R. (1992) *Linguistic imperialism.* Oxford: Oxford University Press.

Philo, G. (ed.) (1995) *The Glasgow media group reader.* Vol. 2, London: Routledge,

Philo, G., Hilsum, L., Beattie, L. and Holliman, R. (1999) The media and the Rwanda crisis: effects on audiences and public policy. In Philo, G. (ed.) *Message received: Glasgow media group research 1993–1998.* London: Longman.

Phoenix website: http: //www.phoenixtv.com.

Port, O. and Resch, I. (1999) They're listening to your calls. *Business Week*, 31 May, 58–60.

Poster, M. (1995) *The second media age.* Cambridge: Polity Press.

Postman, N. (1985) *Amusing ourselves to death: public discourse in the age of show business.* London: Methuen.

Postman, N. (1992) *Technopoly: the surrender of culture to technology.* New York: Alfred A. Knopf.

Prasad, M. (1998) *Ideology of the Hindi film: a historical construction.* New Delhi: Oxford University Press.

Preston, W., Herman, E. and Schiller, H. (1989) *Hope and folly: the United States and UNESCO, 1945–1985.* Minneapolis: University of Minnesota Press.

Price, M. (1995) *Television, the public sphere and national identity.* Oxford: Oxford University Press.

Price, M. (1999) Satellite broadcasting as trade routes in the sky. *Public Culture*, 11, 2, 69–85.

Pye, L. (ed.) (1963) *Communications and political development*. Princeton, NJ: Princeton University Press.

Raghavan, C. (1990) *Recolonisation: GATT, the Uruguay Round and the Third World*. London: Zed Books and Penang: Third World Network.

Rajadhyaksha, A. and Willemen, P. (1994) *Encyclopaedia of Indian cinema*. New Delhi: Oxford University Press and London: British Film Institute.

Rangnekar, S. (1999) The fact of Zee matter. *The Economic Times*, 26 September.

Rantanen, T. (1997) The globalisation of electronic news in the 19th century. *Media, Culture and Society*, 19, 4, 605–20.

Rawnsley, G. (1996) *Radio diplomacy and propaganda: the BBC and VOA in international politics, 1956–64*. Basingstoke: Macmillan,

Read, D. (1992) *The power of news: the history of Reuters, 1849–1989*. Oxford: Oxford University Press.

Real, M. (1996) *Exploring media culture: a guide*. Thousand Oaks, CA: Sage.

Reeves, B. and Nass, C. (1996) *The media equation: how people treat computers, television, and new media like real people and places*. Cambridge: Cambridge University Press.

Renaud, J. (1986) A conceptual framework for the examination of transborder data flows. *The Information Society*, 4, 3, 146–9.

Reuters (1999) *Annual report*. London: Reuters Holdings PLC.

Richardson, K. and Meinhof, U. (1999) *Worlds in common: television discourse and a changing Europe*. London: Routledge.

Richardson, M. (1999) Freer airwaves in Indonesia give big push to democracy. *International Herald Tribune*, 5 June, p. 7.

Rielly, J. (1999) Americans and the world: a survey at century's end. *Foreign Policy*, Spring, 97–114.

Riggs, K., Eastman, S. and Golobic, T. (1993) Manufactured conflict in the 1992 Olympics: the discourse of television and politics. *Critical studies in mass communication*. 10, 253–72.

Righter, R. (1978) *Whose News? politics, the Press and the Third World*. London: Burnett Books.

Ritzer, G. (1993) *The McDonaldization of society*. Thousand Oaks, CA: Sage.

Ritzer, G. (1999) *Enchanting a disenchanted world: Revolutionising the means of consumption*. Thousands Oaks, CA: Pine Forge Press.

Roach, C. (1987) The US Position on the new world information and communication order. *Journal of Communication*, 37, 4, 36–51.

Robertson, R. (1992) *Globalization: social theory and global culture*. London: Sage.

Robins, K. (1995) The new spaces of global media. In Johnston, R., Taylor, P. and Watts, M. (eds), *Geographies of global change*. Oxford: Blackwell.

Robinson, A. (1989) *Satyajit Ray: the inner eye*. London: André Deutsch.

Robinson, E. (1998) The Pentagon finally learns how to shop. *Fortune*, 21 December, 124–30.

Rogers, E. (1962) *The diffusion of innovations.* Glencoe, IL: Free Press.

Rogers, E. (1976) Communication and development: the passing of a dominant paradigm. *Communication Research,* **3**, 2, 213–40.

Rogers, E. and Antola, L. (1985) *Telenovelas*: a Latin American success story. *Journal of Communication,* **35**, 4, 24–35.

Roncagliolo, R. (1995) Trade integration and communication networks in Latin America. *Canadian Journal of Communication,* **20**, 3, 335–42.

Rose, F. (1998) There's no business like show business. *Fortune,* 22 June, 42–54.

Rosenblum, M. (1979) *Coups and earthquakes: reporting the world for America.* New York: Harper and Row.

Rosenblum, M. (1993) *Who stole the news? Why we can't keep up with what happens in the world and what we can do about it.* New York: John Wiley.

Rothkopf, D. (1997) In praise of cultural imperialism? *Foreign Policy,* Summer, 38–53.

Rothkopf, D. (1999) The disinformation age. *Foreign Policy,* Spring, 82–96.

Roxburgh, A. (1987) *Pravda: inside the Soviet news machine.* London: Victor Gollancz.

Ryan, E. (1999) More than a game. *Cable and Satellite Europe,* February, 26–8.

Ryan, N. (1997) Television nation. *Wired,* March, 42–8 and 88–93.

Ryan, N. (1999) Hatemongers make their voices heard. *The Guardian* (online supplement), 26 August, pp. 2–3.

Said, E. (1978) *Orientalism,* London: Routledge and Kegan Paul.

Said, E. (1993) *Culture and imperialism.* London: Chatto and Windus,

Said, E. (1997) *Covering Islam: how the media and the experts determine how we see the rest of the world.* Second edition, New York: Vintage. First edition published in 1981, London: Routledge and Kegan Paul.

Samarajiva, R. (1985) Tainted origins of development communication. *Communicator,* April–July, 5–9.

Sassen, S. (1996) *Losing control? Sovereignty in an age of globalization.* New York: Columbia University Press.

Satchidanandan, K. (1999) Globalisation and culture. *Indian Literature,* **190**, XLIII, 2, March-April, 8–11.

SatNews (1999a) Loral Skynet wins bid for Brazilian satellite slot. March.

SatNews (1999b) Loral leases transponder payload of APSTAR IIR Asia-Pacific Satellite. August.

SatNews (1999c) Satellite market growing at 15% annually according to new study. 2 November.

SatNews (1999d) INTELSAT members decide to privatize. 8 November.

Schiller, H. (1969) *Mass communications and American empire.* New York: Augustus M. Kelley. Second revised and updated edition published by Westview Press in 1992.

Schiller. H. (1976) *Communication and cultural domination*. New York: International Arts and Sciences Press.

Schiller H. (1996) *Information inequality: the deepening social crisis in America*. New York: Routledge.

Schiller, H. (1998) Striving for communication dominance: a half-century review. In Thussu, D. (ed.), *Electronic empires*. London: Arnold.

Schiller, D. (1999) *Digital capitalism: networking the global market system*. Cambridge, MA: MIT Press.

Schneider, C. and Wallis, B. (eds) (1988) *Global television*. New York: Wedge Press and Cambridge, MA: The MIT Press.

Schramm, W. (1964) *Mass media and national development: the role of information in the developing countries*. Stanford, CA: Stanford University Press.

Schramm, W. (1988) *The story of human communication: cave painting to microchip*. New York: Harper and Row.

Schreiber, D. (1998) News world. *Cable and Satellite Europe*, November, pp. 16–17.

Schreiber, D. (1999) Losing its religion? *Cable and Satellite Europe*, January, 18–22.

Schudson, M. (1995) *The power of news*. Cambridge, MA: Harvard University Press

Screen Digest (1995) African television leaps to satellite age. December, 273–6.

Screen Digest (1999) Children's television: a globalised market. May, 105–7.

Seib, P. (1997) *Headline diplomacy: how news coverage affects foreign policy*. Westport, CT: Praeger.

Serwer, A. (1999) Tech is king, now meet the prince. *Fortune*, 6 December, 50–63.

Shahryar, F. (1999) Krishna back in Gita Rahasya. *The Asian Age*, 17 July, 6.

Shapiro, A. (1999) The Internet. *Foreign Policy*, Summer, 11–27.

Shaw, M. (1996) *Civil society and media in global crises*. London: Pinter.

Shenk, D. (1997) *Data smog: surviving the information glut*. New York: HarperCollins.

Shohat, E. and Stam R. (1994) *Unthinking Eurocentrism: multiculturalism and the media*. New York: Routledge.

Siklos, R. (1999) 'They have it all now,' but can Redstone and Karmazin make the colossus work? *Business Week*, 20 September, 72–4.

Sinclair, J. (1996) Mexico, Brazil, and the Latin world. In Jacka, E. *et al.* (eds), *New patterns in global television*. Oxford: Oxford University Press.

Sinclair, J. (1997) The business of international broadcasting: cultural bridges and barriers. *Asian Journal of Communication*, 7, 1, 137–55.

Sinclair, J., Jacka, E. and Cunningham, S. (eds) (1996) *New patterns in global television: peripheral vision*. Oxford: Oxford University Press.

Singh, G. (1999) Love in Tokyo, evening in Paris, money in Mumbai. *The Economic Times*, 28 December, p. 1.

Singh, K. and Gross, B. (1981) 'MacBride': The report and the response. *Journal of Communication*, **31**, 4, 104–17.

Singhal, A. and Udorjpim, K. (1997) Cultural shareability, archetypes and television soaps. *Gazette*, **59**, 3, 177–88.

Slater, J. and Amaha, E. (1999) King of the crisis. *Far Eastern Economic Review*, 6 May, 10–14.

Smith, A. (1979) *The newspaper: an international history*. London: Thames and Hudson.

Smith, A. (1980) *The geopolitics of information: how Western culture dominates the world*. London: Faber and Faber.

Smith, A. (ed.) (1998) *Television: an international history*. Second edition, Oxford: Oxford University Press.

Smith, R. (1997) *Broadcasting law and fundamental rights*. Oxford: Oxford University Press.

Snoddy, R. (1999) A new player on the block. *The Times*, 12 September, p. 41.

Somavia, J. (1976) The transnational power structure and international information. *Development Dialogue*, 2, pp. 15–28.

Sony (1999) *Annual report, 1998–99*. Tokyo: Sony Corporation.

Sorensen, T. (1968) *The word war – the story of American propaganda*. New York: Harper and Row.

Sosin, G. (1999) *Sparks of liberty – an insider's memoir of Radio Liberty*. University Park, PA: Penn State University Press.

South Commission (1990) *The challenge to South: the report of the South Commission*. Geneva: The South Centre.

Sparks, C. (1998) Is there a global public sphere? In Thussu, D. (ed.) *Electronic empires*. London: Arnold.

Splichal, S. (1994) *Media beyond socialism: theory and practice of East Central Europe*. Boulder, COL: Westview Press.

Sreberny-Mohammadi, A. (1991) The global and the local in international communication. In Curran, J. and Gurevitch, M. (eds) *Mass media and society*. London: Edward Arnold.

Sreberny-Mohammadi, A. (1994) *Women, media and development in a global context*. Paris: UNESCO.

Sreberny-Mohammadi, A. (1997) The many cultural faces of imperialism. In Golding, P. and Harris, P. (eds), *Beyond cultural imperialism*. London: Sage.

Stevenson, R. (1988) *Communication, development and the Third World: the global politics of information*. London: Longman. Reprinted by the University Press of America in 1993.

Stevenson, R. (1992) Defining international communication as a field. *Journalism Quarterly*, **69**, 543–53.

Stone, J. (2000) *Losing perspective*. (Report of the Third World and Environment Broadcasting Project). London: International Broadcasting Trust.

Strobel, W. (1997) *Late-breaking foreign policy: the news media's influence on peace operations.* Washington, DC: United States Institute of Peace Press.

Sung, L. (1992) WARC-92: Setting the agenda for the future. *Telecommunications Policy*, 16, 8, 624–34.

Sutherland, F. (1999a) Local heroes. *Cable and Satellite Europe*, February, 30-4.

Sutherland, F. (1999b) Three of a kind. *Cable and Satellite Europe*, May, 58–60.

Swami, P. (1999) Recording media trends, *Frontline*, 25 Sept.–8 Oct.

Tan, Z. (1999) Regulating China's Internet: convergence toward a coherent regulatory regime. *Telecommunication Policy*, 23, 261–76.

Tarjanne, P. (1999) Preparing for the next revolution in telecommunications: implementing the WTO Agreement. *Telecommunication Policy*, 23, 51–63.

Tawney, R. (1937) *Religion and the rise of capitalism.* London: Penguin Books. First edition published in 1926.

Taylor, P. (1992) *War and the media: propaganda and persuasion in the Gulf War.* Manchester: Manchester University Press.

Taylor, P. (1995) *Munitions of the mind: a history of propaganda from the ancient world to the present era.* Second edition, Manchester: Manchester University Press.

Taylor, P. (1997) *Global communications, international affairs and the media since 1945.* London: Routledge.

Taylor, P. (1999a) How the Internet will reshape worldwide business activity, *Financial Times*, Financial Times Survey: Information Technology, 7 April.

Taylor, P. (1999b) Software exports at record level. *Financial Times*, Financial Times Survey India: Information Technology, 1 December.

Taylor, S. (1999) Books across the border: publishing in Latin America. *Publisher's Weekly*, 13 September.

Teather, D. (2000) Options row sours £12bn marriage. *The Guardian*, 25 January.

Tehranian, M. (1999) *Global communication and world politics: domination, development and discourse.* London: Lynne Reiner.

The Economist (1998) Wheel of fortune: a survey of technology and entertainment. 21 November, 22 pages.

The Times of India (1999) *Ramayan, Mahabharat* will always shine on TV. 14 October.

Thompson, J. (1995) *The media and modernity: a social theory of the media.* Cambridge: Polity Press.

Thussu, D. (ed.) (1998a) *Electronic empires: global media and local resistance.* London: Arnold.

Thussu, D. (1998b) Localising the global – Zee TV in India. In Thussu, D. (ed.) *Electronic empires.* London: Arnold.

Thussu, D. (2000) Development news versus globalised infotainment. In Kavoori, A. and Malek, A. (eds), *The global dynamics of news: studies in international news coverage and news agenda*. Stamford: Ablex Publishing.

Time (1988) New silence, new disquiet with glasnost and no jamming, what about those radios? 19 December, p. 19.

Tobin, A. (1999a) Playboy plans to localise across the globe. *Cable and Satellite Europe*, February, 8.

Tobin, A. (1999b) In the doc. *Cable and Satellite Europe*, February, 14–18.

Tobin, A. (1999c) New Zee lands. *Cable and Satellite Europe*, May, 73–4.

Toffler, A. (1980) *The third wave*. London: Collins.

Tomlinson, J. (1991) *Cultural imperialism: a critical introduction*. London: Pinter.

Tomlinson, J. (1999) *Globalization and culture*. Cambridge: Polity Press.

Tracey, M. (1998) *The decline and fall of public service broadcasting*. Oxford: Oxford University Press.

Tsering, L. (1999) Controversial *Xena* episode will be back with changes. *The Asian Age*, 24 August, 18.

Tuch, H. (1990) *Communicating with the world: US public diplomacy overseas*. New York: St Martin's Press.

Tufte, T. (2000) *Living with the rubbish queen: telenovelas, culture and modernity in Brazil*. Luton: University of Luton Press.

Tunstall, J. (1977) *The media are American: Anglo-American media in the world*. London: Constable.

Tunstall, J. and Palmer, M. (1991) *Media moguls*. London: Routledge.

Tunstall, J. (1992) Europe as world news leader. *Journal of Communication*, 42, 84–99.

UN (1961) UNGA Resolution 1721D(XVI), New York.

UN (1995) *Our global neighbourhood: the report of the commission on global governance*. Oxford: Oxford University Press.

UN (1998) *The UN and business: a global partnership*. New York: United Nations Department of Public Information – DPI/1820/Rev.1, June.

UNCTAD (1998) *Trade and development report 1998*. Geneva: United Nations Conference on Trade and Development.

UNCTAD (1999) *World investment report 1999: foreign direct investment and the challenge of development*. Geneva: United Nations Conference on Trade and Development.

UNCTC (1990) *Transnational corporations, services and the Uruguay Round*. United Nations Centre on Transnational Corporations, New York: UN Publications.

UNDP (1999) *Human development report*. United Nations Development Programme, Oxford and New York: Oxford University Press.

UNESCO (1980) The new world information and communication order. Resolutions 4/19 in Records of the General Conference Twenty-First Session, Belgrade, 23 September to 28 October, Paris: United Nations Economic, Social and Cultural Organisation.

UNESCO (1982) *Culture industries: a challenge for the future of culture.* Paris: United Nations Economic, Social and Cultural Organisation.

UNESCO (1995) *Our creative diversity: report of the World Commission on Culture and Development.* Paris: United Nations Economic, Social and Cultural Organisation.

UNESCO (1997) *World communication report: the media and the challenge of the new technologies.* Paris: United Nations Educational, Scientific and Cultural Organisation.

UNESCO (1998a) *Statistical yearbook.* Paris: United Nations Educational, Scientific and Cultural Organisation.

UNESCO (1998b) *World culture report 1998: culture, creativity and markets.* Paris: United Nations Educational, Scientific and Cultural Organisation.

Urban, G. (1997) *My war within the Cold War.* New Haven, CT: Yale University Press.

US Government (1993) *Globalization of the mass media.* Washington, DC: US Department of Commerce.

US Government (1995) *Global information infrastructure: agenda for cooperation.* Information Task Force, February, Washington, DC: US Government Printing Office.

US Government (1997) *A framework for global electronic commerce.* Washington, DC: The White House, 1 July.

US Government (1999) *Towards digital equality, U.S. Government Working Group on electronic commerce.* 2nd Annual Report, Washington. www.ecommerce.gov.

Utley, G. (1997) The shrinking of foreign news: from broadcast to narrowcast. *Foreign Affairs,* **76**, 2, pp. 2–10.

Varan, D. (1999) The dynamics of dependency: a Polynesian encounter with television. *Critical Studies in Mass Communication.* **16**, 97–225.

Varis, T. (1985) *International flow of television programmes.* Reports and Papers on Mass Communication, no. 100, Paris: UNESCO.

Variety (1999) Domestic box office. *Variety,* 22 November.

Varma, P. (1998) *The great Indian middle class.* New Delhi: Viking.

Vasey, R. (1997) *The world according to Hollywood.* Madison, WI: University of Wisconsin Press.

Venturelli, S. (1998) *Liberalizing the European media: politics, regulation and the public sphere.* Oxford: Oxford University Press.

Vidal, J. (2000) The world@war, *The Guardian* (Society), 19 January, pp. 4–5.

Vidyasagar, N. (1999) From cradle to computer. *The Times of India,* 1 December.

Vincent, R., Nordenstreng, K. and Traber, M. (eds) (1999) *Towards equity in global communication: MacBride Update.* Cresskill, NJ: Hampton Press.

Vistica, G. (1999) Cyberwar and sabotage – President Clinton has OK'd a top-secret plan to destabilize Milosevic – and go after his money. *Newsweek International*, 31 May.

Vittachi, A. (1998) The right to communicate. In Thussu, D. (ed.), *Electronic empires*, London: Arnold.

Vogel, H. (1998) *Entertainment industry economics: a guide for financial analysis*. Fourth edition, Cambridge: Cambridge University Press.

Volkmer, I. (1999) *News in the global sphere: a study of CNN and its impact on global communications*. Luton: University of Luton Press.

Vulser, N. (1999) French bliss. *Cable and Satellite Europe*, May, 70–3.

Walker, A. (1992) *A Skyful of freedom: 60 years of the BBC World Service*. London: Broadside Books.

Walker, S. (1998) The localisation of Hollywood. *Television Business International*, October, 30–46.

Wallace, C. (2000) Vodacious. *Time*, 14 February, p. 72.

Wallerstein, I. (1974, 1980) *The Modern World-System*. 2 volumes, New York: Academic Press.

Wasko, J. (1994) *Hollywood in the information age: beyond the silver screen*. Cambridge: Polity Press.

Waters, M. (1995) *Globalization*. London: Routledge.

Waters, R. (2000) A new media world. *Financial Times*, 11 January, p. 22.

Watson, J. (1999) Ball watching. *Television Business International*, September, 48–52.

Webster, F. (1995) *Theories of the information society*. London: Routledge.

Wells, A. (1972) *Picture tube imperialism? The impact of US television on Latin America*. New York: Orbis.

Wells, A. (ed.) (1996) *World broadcasting: a comparative view*. Norwood, NJ: Ablex Publishing.

Wells, C. (1987) *The UN, UNESCO and the politics of knowledge*. London: Macmillan.

Whittell, G. (2000) Hollywood targets Russia's Mir. *The Times*, 18 February, p. 19.

Williams, M. (1999) Global ambitions: potential partnerships would expand reach of French pay TV giant across 75% of Europe. *Variety*, 28 June–11 July, 32 and 64.

Windrich, E. (1992) *The Cold War guerrilla: Jonas Savimbi, the US media and the Angolan war*. New York: Greenwood Press.

Winseck, D. (1997) The shifting contexts of international communication: possibilities for a New World Information and Communication Order, in Bailie, M. and Winseck, D. (eds), *Democratizing communication?* Cresskill, NJ: Hampton Press.

Winston, B. (1998) *Media technology and society: a history from the telegraph to the Internet*. London: Routledge.

Wolf, M. (1999) *Entertainment economy: how mega-media forces are transforming our lives*. New York: Times Books.

Woll, J. (1989) Fruits of glasnost: a sampling from the Soviet press. *Dissent*, Winter, 25–38.

Wood, J. (1992) *History of international broadcasting*. London: Peter Peregrinus.

Woodman, C. (1999) Arabian dishes. *Cable and Satellite Europe*, February, 36–8.

Wooldridge, A. (1999) Telecommunications: the world in your pocket. *The Economist Survey*, 9 October, 44 pages.

World Bank (1998) *Knowledge for development, world development report 1998–1999*. Washington, DC: World Bank Publications.

World Bank (1999) *Entering the 21st century: the changing development landscape. world development report 1999–2000*. Washington, DC: World Bank Publications.

Wresch, W. (1998) Information access in Africa: problems with every channel. *The Information Society*, 14, 295–300.

Wright, E. (1998) Sell global, market local. *Television Business International*, June, pp. 32–6.

WTO (1997) *Fourth Protocol to the General Agreement on Trade in services* (Global Telecoms Agreement). S/L/20, Geneva: World Trade Organization.

WTO (1998) *Annual report 1998*. Geneva: World Trade Organization.

Zee TV website (1999) http//www.zeetelevision.com

Zhang, K. and Xiaoming, H. (1999) The Internet and the ethnic press: a study of electronic Chinese publications. *The Information Society*, 15, 21–30.

Zhang, X. (1993) The market versus the state: the Chinese press since Tianamen. *Journal of International Affairs*, 47, 195–221.

Zhao, B. (1999) Mouthpiece or money-spinner? The double life of Chinese television in the late 1990s. *International Journal of Cultural Studies*, 2, 3, 291–305.

Zhao, Y. (1998) *Media, market and democracy in China: between the party line and the bottom line*. Urbana: University of Illinois Press.

Author Index

Subject Index

Page numbers in *italics* refer to figures and those in **bold** refer to tables